NEW LIVES, NEW LANDSCAPES
REVISITED

For over 100 years the *Proceedings of the British Academy* series has provided a unique record of British scholarship in the humanities and social sciences. These themed volumes drive scholarship forward and are landmarks in their field. For more information about the series, please visit www.thebritishacademy.ac.uk/proceedings

PROCEEDINGS OF THE BRITISH ACADEMY · 256

NEW LIVES, *NEW LANDSCAPES* REVISITED

RURAL MODERNITY IN BRITAIN

Edited by
LINDA M. ROSS, KATRINA NAVICKAS,
MATTHEW KELLY, AND BEN ANDERSON

Published for THE BRITISH ACADEMY
by OXFORD UNIVERSITY PRESS

Oxford University Press, Great Clarendon Street, Oxford OX2 6DP

© The British Academy 2023

Database right The British Academy (maker)

First edition published in 2023

British Library Cataloguing in Publication Data
Data available

Library of Congress Cataloging in Publication Data
Data available

Typeset by Newgen Publishing UK
Printed in Great Britain by TJ Books Ltd, Padstow, Cornwall

ISBN 978-0-19-726745-5
ISSN 0068-1202

Contents

List of Figures

Every effort has been made to trace the copyright holders of any of the images contained herein and we apologise in advance for any unintentional omissions, which we would be pleased to correct in any subsequent edition of this volume.

Notes on Contributors

Ben Anderson is Senior Lecturer in Environmental History at Keele University. His work revolves around the interaction between people and their environments in the modern era, with a particular focus on outdoors leisure, embodied environmentalism, and post-industrial heritage in Europe. His recent research includes finding co-creative ways to express the memories and meanings of carbon infrastructure, and histories of commons and trespass in the early 20th century.

Kristin Bluemel is Professor of English and Wayne D. McMurray Endowed Chair in the Humanities at Monmouth University. In 2022 she served as Leverhulme Visiting Professor at Newcastle University. In addition to publishing on modernist and intermodernist writers and artists, she has edited *Rural Modernity in Britain: A Critical Intervention*, with Michael McCluskey (Edinburgh University Press, 2018), and *Intermodernism: Literary Culture in Mid-Twentieth-Century Britain* (Edinburgh University Press, 2009). Her work in progress is *Enchanted Wood: Women Artists, Rural Britain, and the Twentieth-Century Wood Engraving Revival* (Minnesota University Press, forthcoming).

Jeremy Burchardt is a rural historian based in the Department of History, University of Reading. His research interests focus on three intertwined themes: the affective significance of the countryside in modern Britain; perceptions and experiences of rural childhood; and leisure in the 19th- and 20th-century countryside. Drawing mainly on diaries, his forthcoming book on the experience of rural landscape in England c.1880–1960 explores the personal meanings of landscape in this period, emphasising how landscape helped many people make sense of their lives and of the changes in the world around them during this turbulent period.

Moa Carlsson is an architect, historian, and Lecturer at the Edinburgh School of Architecture and Landscape Architecture (ESALA). Focusing on histories of landscape, urban planning and computing, her research and teaching explore past and present relationships between lived environments and their abstractions, with a specific focus on Great Britain after 1945. She was awarded her PhD (2019) and SMArchS (2013) in Design and Computation from MIT, and her MA in Architecture (2008) from Lund University, Sweden. She is an Associate Fellow of the Royal Historical Society and a fellow of the Canadian Centre for Architecture (CCA) Digital Now: Architecture and Intersectionality research project.

Ysanne Holt is Professor Emerita in Art History at the University of Northumbria, Newcastle. She has long-standing interests in landscapes and in imaginings and experience of the UK rural north, especially its islands and border regions as registered across forms of creative practice through the 20th century to today. Recent publications include 'Place on the border and the LYC Museum and Art Gallery', in Tim Edensor, Ares Kalandides and Uma Kothari (eds), *The Routledge Handbook on Place* (Routledge, 2020) and *Visual Culture in the Northern UK Archipelago: Imagining Islands*, co-edited with David Martin Jones and Owain Jones (Routledge, 2018). She is currently completing a monograph on interrelations between artists and the material resources of the Anglo-Scottish borders.

Matthew Kelly is Professor of Modern History at Northumbria University. He focuses on the history of Britain and Ireland in the modern period, with an emphasis on the development of environmental politics since the middle of the 19th century, particularly with respect to protected areas. Recent work includes *Quartz and Feldspar. Dartmoor: A British Landscape in Modern Times* (Jonathan Cape, 2015) and *The Women Who Saved the English Countryside* (Yale University Press, 2022).

Katrina Navickas is Professor of History at the University of Hertfordshire. She is author of *Protest and the Politics of Space and Place, 1789–1848* (Manchester University Press, 2016) and numerous articles on the history of social movements in England. She is currently working on a history of public space, 1750–2000.

Tim O'Riordan is Professor Emeritus of Environmental Sciences at the University of East Anglia and Fellow of the British Academy. He is the author of numerous books and articles, including the pioneering *Environmentalism* (Pion, 1976), and has held senior academic positions at Oxford and Cambridge. He has served on a number of influential public boards, including the UK Sustainable Development Commission (2000–2009), the ASDA Social Responsibility Board (2004–2007), and the Soil Association Council (2004–2011), and was Advisory Co-Chair for the Working Group on Sustainable Development, European Association of Environment and Sustainable Development (2007–2009).

Paul Readman is Professor of Modern British History at King's College London. Much of his work has focused on the interconnection of land, landscape, and British national identities, a subject he explored in *Land and Nation in England* (2008) and *Storied Ground* (2018). Since 2013, he has led a major AHRC-funded project on historical pageants in Britain, details of which are available on the *Redress of the Past* project website. He is co-investigator on the AHRC-funded network *Changing Landscapes, Changing Lives*. Readman's current book project explores the inter-relationship between landscape and history-writing in Britain, from c. 1750 to the present.

Gareth Roddy is a historian of modern Britain and Ireland. His research focuses on the cultural history of landscape, borders, peripheries, heritage, and the history of travel writing and tourism. Gareth joined Northumbria University as a Leverhulme Early Career Fellow in 2020, after completing his PhD at the University of Sheffield in 2019. His current project examines the conflicts that erupted during the expansion of the British state and the creation of heritage landscapes in the 19th and 20th centuries. He has also published on English regional identities, and on the western peripheries of Britain and Ireland.

Linda M. Ross is a historian focusing on the fusion of technological, social, and cultural histories. She is currently Research Fellow in the Department of Criminology, Politics and Sociology at Kingston University, working on the Nuclear Spaces: Communities, Materialities and Locations of Nuclear Cultural Heritage (NuSPACES) project. This role builds on prior research undertaken during her AHRC-funded PhD study with the University of the Highlands and Islands and Historic Environment Scotland, where she examined the social and cultural impact of the Dounreay Experimental Research Establishment on the far north of Scotland.

Karen Sayer is Professor of Social and Cultural History at Leeds Trinity University, UK. Current Chair of the British Agricultural History Society, she has authored many publications on rural and agricultural history, including *Women of the Fields* (Manchester University Press, 1995), *The Country Cottage: A Cultural History* (Manchester University Press, 2000), and, with Paul Brassley and Jeremy Burchardt, is a contributing editor to *Transforming the Countryside: The Electrification of Rural Britain* (Routledge, 2017). She is currently a co-lead principal investigator on the National Collaborative Award, 'Thinking forward through the past: Linking science, social science and the humanities to inform the sustainable reduction of endemic disease in British livestock farming', a collaborative inter-disciplinary project funded by the Wellcome Trust, 2018–22, https://field-wt.co.uk/.

Ian Waites is a retired lecturer in the history of art and design. His research interests centre on the sense of place and community within post-1945 modernist landscapes, being specifically interested in the relationship between post-war planning and the principles of 18th-century picturesque theory, and the use of the 'Radburn Idea' in the design of 1960s and 1970s council estates. His most recent publication (with Professor Carenza Lewis) is 'New light on an old problem: Child-related archæological finds and the impact of the "Radburn" council estate plan' (*Journal of Contemporary Archaeology*, 2019).

1

Introduction

LINDA M. ROSS, KATRINA NAVICKAS, MATTHEW KELLY,
AND BEN ANDERSON

THIS BOOK IS about the compact between government, state, and citizen in rural life
and rural landscapes in the middle decades of the 20th century. A new rights-based
political agenda, intensified by the Second World War, radically transformed the
British public's expectations of government, rendering it responsible for delivering
a wide range of public goods and services. A dirigiste state nationalised industries and imposed planning regimes in order to deliver clean water and electricity,
radio and television, housing and transport, and spaces for leisure to Britain's entire
population. Such changes are usually associated with urban modernity, but, as the
chapters in this book demonstrate, these expectations equally applied to the same
rural places in which the new infrastructure was often located. Every time someone
plugged in an electrical appliance, ran a bath in their indoor bathroom, or travelled
to work on a train or in a car along a new motorway, they made use of national
networks largely constructed in the countryside. Reservoirs, power stations, television and radio-transmitter masts, and electricity and telephone pylons, as well as
local authority housing and new or improved roads, had a transformative effect on
rural landscapes. So did state-subsidised agricultural intensification, wider public
access to the countryside, and environmentally protective measures, including landscape designations such as National Park, Area of Outstanding Natural Beauty, and
Site of Special Scientific Interest. The accumulative effect of these new landscapes
was a distinct, but little understood, rural modernity.

Inspiration

The beginnings of academic collaborations are often hazy, but in this case, there
is no uncertainty. In December 2017, Katrina Navickas started to tweet her
rural sightings of electricity pylons and 20th-century infrastructure. She quickly
attracted the attention of a group of enthusiasts, and for a time the Twitter account

@ruralmodernism was a minor social media cult, with posts picturing modern rural infrastructure rapidly accumulating a host of likes. Matthew Kelly, Ben Anderson, and Linda M. Ross, all of whom had written histories of modernity in rural places, were quick to respond to Navickas's enthusiasm. That their shared fascination with modernism's aesthetic impact on the countryside might lead to collaborative research was enticing. Such is the subject's wider appeal, it proved easy to put together a stellar line-up of speakers as part of a successful application to the British Academy for conference funding.

Navickas's initiative reflected a wider wave of interest in the cultural, aesthetic, and ecological dimensions of rural modernity that surely reflected generational experiences. For those born in the latter decades of the 20th century, the rural modern explored in this volume was their countryside. Although much loved, this countryside was not necessarily sentimentalised. In popular culture, pastoral ideals were challenged in the theatre by Jez Butterworth's Blakean dystopia *Jerusalem* (2010, revived 2022) and by gentler yet subversive television comedy dramas like *Detectorists* (2014–2017, 2022) and *This Country* (2017–2020). Renewed concern about the environmental impact of agricultural intensification shaped the reception of books like George Monbiot's *Feral: Searching for Enchantment on the Frontiers of Rewilding* (2013), which helped popularise 'rewilding' and challenge the old shibboleth that upland grazing regimes produced desirable landscapes. The 'new nature writing', reflecting a broader trend in literary non-fiction that centred subjective or embodied experiences, often captured the tension between the positive feelings induced by being in rural or 'wild' places and the consciousness of ecological depletion. Robert Macfarlane helped establish a modern nature writing canon and was among the first to popularise Paul J. Crutzen's idea that human and more-than-human nature inhabits a new epoch known as the Anthropocene, a proposition that became increasingly accepted, irrespective of its formal geological status.[1]

Modernism, particularly in mid-century architecture and design, had already caught the fascination of urbanists. The Manchester Modernist Society was founded in 2009 and spread through 'chapters' in other post-industrial cities. Their academic colleagues at the Manchester School of Architecture fostered interest in the aesthetics of post-war design and the built environment, including power stations.[2] A 'new urban history' has flourished around the transformations enacted in British, European, and North American cities in post-war reconstruction, planning, and architecture.[3] According to this literature, the purpose of rebuilding cities and building completely new towns was modernisation. Paternalist planners, architects,

[1] Innes M. Keighren and Joanne Norcup (eds), *Landscapes of Detectorists* (Axminster, Uniform Books, 2020); Robert Macfarlane, *The Wild Places* (London, Granta Books, 2008); Paul J. Krutzen, 'Geology of mankind: The Anthropocene', *Nature*, 415 (2002), 23.
[2] *The Modernist* magazine (2011–present); Manchester School of Architecture, Landscapes of Post-War Infrastructure project, www.msa.ac.uk/postwarinfrastructure/.
[3] For a historiographical review, see James Greenhalgh, 'The new urban social history? Recent theses on urban development and governance in post-war Britain', *Urban History*, 47 (2020), 535–545.

and government policies drove this top-down process, predicated on social democratic ideals. Achieving modernity would birth a new society, bringing about a utopian future. That, at least, was their hope.[4] Together with more popular books on the history of council housing, this interest reflects a wider reappreciation of the vision and values of the post-war welfare state. The aesthetics of, say, the Festival of Britain 1951 are valorised less for their design and more for what they represent about a democratic socialist ideal that has now been lost.[5]

The 'New Lives, New Landscapes' conference was held at Northumbria University in August 2019. Some of the papers delivered at the conference have been developed for this collection, together with specially commissioned contributions based on new research. The conference title referred to Nan Fairbrother's *New Lives, New Landscapes* (1970), which had emerged as a key reference point. Fairbrother (1912–1971), a grocer's daughter from Coventry, authored several books on nature themes before being invited to contribute to the Institute of Landscape Architects' annual conference in 1968. *New Lives, New Landscapes* was the published output of her research, and won the WHS Literary Prize in 1971. The book has been highly influential in landscape and environmental writing ever since, although there have been few studies of Fairbrother herself.[6] The appeal of Fairbrother's text is manifold. It is exceptionally lucid, brilliantly illustrated, and forthright in its opinions, qualities expected of a book published by the Architectural Press. Histories of mid-century modernity often highlight the Architectural Press' most notorious publication, *Outrage* by Ian Nairn (1955), which offered a broadside denunciation of the 'subtopian' degradations of post-war (sub)urban development, from bungalows to litter.[7] For the rural setting, by contrast, Fairbrother's polemic was constructive rather than destructive, making not just the case for change but also the case for the present. In this respect, Fairbrother helped to date Nairn, throwing into sharp relief how much common cause he made with Clough Williams-Ellis's equally pugnacious interwar classic, *England and the Octopus* (1929).

Fairbrother was not marked out from this company by her disregard for the concerns of Williams-Ellis and Nairn, since their concept of good design and, in Nairn's case, effective planning by trained professionals, is central to her argument in *New Lives, New Landscapes*. Instead, Fairbrother wrote at a time when the full impact of post-war infrastructural developments had become legible. Whereas Nairn

[4] Otto Saumarez Smith, *Boom Cities: Boom Cities: Architect-Planners and the Politics of Radical Urban Renewal in 1960s Britain* (Oxford, Oxford University Press, 2019).
[5] John Boughton, *Municipal Dreams: The Rise and Fall of Council Housing* (London, Verso, 2018); John Grindrod, *Concretopia: A Journey Around the Rebuilding of Postwar Britain* (London, Old Street Publishing, 2013); Ian Waites, *Middlefield: A Postwar Council Estate in Time* (Axminster, Uniform Books, 2017).
[6] Jane Brown, 'Fairbrother, Nancy Mary [Nan] (1912–1971)', *Oxford Dictionary of National Biography*, 2011, https://doi.org/10.1093/ref:odnb/67032.
[7] Rosemary Shirley, *Rural Modernity, Everyday Life and Visual Culture* (London, Routledge, 2015), pp. 24–26.

was fixated by aerodromes and other wartime detritus, street clutter and the baleful effects of uniformity in design that he satirised as 'Municipal Rustic', Fairbrother was principally concerned with the transformative scale of the new rural modernity, as much social as it was infrastructural. Some of this infrastructural development reflected private enterprise enabled by the state, but much was explicitly statist and social democratic, reflecting the determination of successive governments to deliver a string of universal public goods, particularly near-unlimited supplies of electricity, gas, and clean water. In this respect, Fairbrother's principal antecedent was the work of the landscape architect Sylvia Crowe. In *Tomorrow's Landscape* (1956), Crowe argued that if Britain was to maintain the quality of its landscapes, it had to respond to the impact of modern developments on landscape scale. She wrote:

> Power stations, hydro-electric schemes, huge mineral workings, factories, gasometers and vast areas of conifer forests are all on a scale totally divorced from that of our geologically varied and intimately humanized landscape. We have to accept these new colossi, but in doing so we are faced with the alternatives of either linking them by siting and design with the existing scale or of creating around them a new landscape related to their own scale.[8]

Writing a decade or so later, Fairbrother reiterated Crowe's argument about scale, illustrating her case with examples of where the rescaling effects of landscaping had been successful, implicitly challenging Crowe's claim that rescaling might have a dehumanising effect. Rather than the people being subdued by the rescaling, they happily adapted, evolving 'new lives' in conjunction with these 'new landscapes', central to which was the greater mobility that gave their greater prosperity much of its value. As such, Fairbrother's vision of the successful integration of lives and landscapes was predicated on effective planning and a social democratic fundamental: effective action by the state enabled personal freedoms. And something of the appeal of Fairbrother's text is the sympathy evinced for the unregulated, spontaneous desire for the rural by the new car-borne 'industrial democracy'. The exercise of these freedoms needed to be facilitated rather than restrained and, deploying a technique that was largely observational, she documented the preferences and impulses of the democratic 'we' as a privileged insider, challenging old hierarchies and sources of authority.[9] The motorist content to picnic close to the road if there was a pleasant view seemed emblematic.

For all that Fairbrother reified the new freedoms, the anarchic free-for-all they enabled could prove harmful. With the picnicker by the side of the road came litter, disturbance to livestock, and trespass (often innocently done), generating micro-disturbances that reflected larger macro challenges. 'We … enjoy unreservedly' landscapes 'the twentieth century has not reached', she wrote, but the 'old agricultural landscape quite simply cannot accommodate our new industrial

[8] Sylvia Crowe, *Tomorrow's Landscape* (London, Architectural Press, 1956), p. 15.
[9] Nan Fairbrother, *New Lives, New Landscapes* (London, Architectural Press, 1970), p. 142.

society, and the longer we take to accept this the more thoroughly we shall destroy what we have in the interval'.[10] Much was made at the time of the high visitor numbers drawn to landscapes designated for access and natural beauty, especially the National Parks, and Fairbrother argued that the new 'industrial democracy' created pressures – numerical and behavioural – that far exceeded the class-based expectations of the originators of the National Park system.[11] This claim was part of a larger argument about how modern agriculture, shaped by mechanical and chemical technologies, did not just drive rural depopulation by lowering the demand for farm labour. Grubbing up hedgerows, enlarging fields, and ploughing and planting to field margins also confined the people to ever-narrowing peripheries. The new visual openness, exposing a 'raw new landscape of amalgamation', constituted a new form of enclosure, rendering public access ever-more interstitial.[12]

A further paradox. Fairbrother's text highlighted the visual and ecological continuities between the new downland agricultural landscapes, the conifer plantations of industrial forestry, and the upland sheepruns of the National Parks and elsewhere. Ever sharp for her purposes, she described the latter as boasting 'an austerity and absoluteness, a stimulating violence which is blurred and softened by trees', whereas the cherished lowland landscapes lost to agricultural modernity were the 'mellowed' landscapes of enclosure. To claim that these lost lowland landscapes were not natural now seems unremarkable, but most startling was Fairbrother's implication that the modernisation of downland monocultures meant they now more closely resembled the 'sheep-mown mountains', the upland 'desert' long celebrated by poets and seekers after the sublime.[13]

Fairbrother's iconoclastic account of the uplands seems prophetic, anticipating contemporary arguments for rewilding, for she imagined the decline of upland grazing regimes leading to natural regeneration. She discerned an 'incipient new pattern' of agricultural intensification where it paid and abandoned farmland reverting to woodland where it did not. These observations, broadly environmental in their framing, co-habited with aesthetic commitments that found a formal beauty in ecologically diminished landscape continuities. Denuded of natural and human-made cover, the Earth itself became more legible, its structures and contours restored to the human eye: 'stripping the ground of all vegetation but level crops', she wrote, 'can reveal unexpectedly subtle land-forms'. Landscape on this scale could only be experienced at 60 miles per hour. The flora and fauna that had once waylaid the visitor no longer had value, the picturesque winding lane was an irritant, but travelling by car we 'actually *feel* the curve and moulding of the ground as we move over it, and in place of the intimate surface detail of the foot-pace countryside we are conscious of the underlying structure of the earth itself'.[14] This extraordinary account of

---

[10] Fairbrother, *New Lives*, p. 5.
[11] Fairbrother, *New Lives*, p. 140.
[12] Fairbrother, *New Lives*, p. 233.
[13] Fairbrother, *New Lives*, p. 127.
[14] Fairbrother, *New Lives*, p. 245. Emphasis in original.

embodiment, of the four-wheeled cyborgs taking to roads whose backdrop had been designed according to a minimalist Scandinavian aesthetic, might seem distant from the roadside picnickers and their hampers but it aligned with Fairbrother's alarmingly techno-triumphalist description of junky crops 'prosperous as never before, thriving and exuberantly healthy: thousands of golden acres of cereals, lavish prairies of untrodden grass grown lush and green with nitrogen'.[15]

Perhaps Fairbrother had allowed herself to get a bit carried away, but her farmers were a peculiarly amoral, technocratic bunch. Not quite the men in lab coats envisioned by the futurists, but here nonetheless were farmers reified as an ultra-efficient, professional caste whose aesthetic and ecological preferences were determined by narrowly productivist purposes. No more could, nor should, be expected of them. The farmers were but one component of a cast of technocrats, whose expertise, if suitably empowered by statute, could successfully manage the balanced use of new landscapes, meeting the needs of the new industrial democracy. And this possibility lay at the heart of Fairbrother's optimism. Just as the 'raw new landscape of amalgamation' would mellow over time, so too the landscape architects would design new landscapes that could integrate aesthetically the power stations, the reservoirs, and the gas towers, and those authorities responsible for enhancing amenity – local government, the Countryside Commission – would respond to the new agricultural settlement with the car parks, picnic grounds and footpaths that enable rather than blunt the exercise of new freedoms.

Fairbrother's polemic contained unresolved tensions, particularly with respect to the value that should be attached to the landscapes produced by past social, political and economic configurations. In seeking guidance for a planned, modern rural landscape, she stated that the past should 'show us the direction we are travelling in' before ten pages later declaring that 'the past cannot help us'.[16] Rather than resolve this contradiction, she bypassed it by claiming that the countryside was already the product of total planning: 'simple country', she argued, 'is a highly artificial creation of the Enclosure Commissioners ... the new pattern obliterated the old'.[17] Radical tradition had of course long taught the progressively minded to disapprove of parliamentary enclosure, but whether or not Fairbrother's sleight of hand was sufficient to neutralise the cultural authority freighting popular conceptions of the rural past, her broad claim was clear enough: the past licences us to write our new lives onto our old landscapes.

New Lives, New Landscapes has suffered the fate of all prophecies. In becoming a period piece, its futurism now reads as an upbeat social commentary on the near past, too sure of its achievements, rather than a portent of the future. Fairbrother's 'industrial democracy', for example, was perhaps narrower than it first appears,

[15] Fairbrother, *New Lives*, pp. 243–244.
[16] Fairbrother, *New Lives*, pp. 7, 17–18.
[17] Fairbrother, *New Lives*, p. 31.

reflecting a particular post-war class configuration that could not survive the dein-dustrialisation of the next two decades. She also wrote prior to the UK's accession to the European Community, and all this meant for the subsidised revival of marginal agriculture. In Britain, if not always elsewhere in Europe, farm consolidation rather than land abandonment has been the story since then, agricultural intensification co-existing with the preservation of what Fairbrother considered agricultural inefficiencies, ensuring little marginal farmland was made available for social or ecological purposes. Without well-considered design, Fairbrother feared it would take only 'another generation' before the 'disastrous' transformation of landscape would 'spread to every mile of our highly-populated island'. She did not live to see the rise of market liberalism and the determination of the Thatcher governments to 'roll back the frontiers of the state', weakening exactly those public sector bodies, repositories of expertise and a socially just planning ethos, she set such store by.[18] Nor did she anticipate how these developments would be mirrored by investment in notions of 'rural heritage' based on a stable and uncontested version of the past that eschewed its transformation for socially progressive reasons. In the two decades after the publication of *New Lives, New Landscapes*, what Peter Mandler has called a 'heritage panic' fixed an iconographic countryside heritage, visible above all in the stately home and accessible to an urban working class able to use cars and motorways to see it.[19]

Many social democrats shared Fairbrother's conviction that effective planning was central to the successful integration of new lives into new landscapes, but few grounded their accounts so thoroughly in the quotidian desires of people. Fairbrother's idealist conviction that rural modernity need not be a story of loss but instead a story of social integration has made *New Lives, New Landscapes* an irresistible *pont dé depart* for an historical project not a little enamoured of the rural modern and the statist optimism of mid-20th-century Britain.

Infrastructure

Modernity is considered by the scholars in this book by taking Fairbrother's account of landscape change in the British countryside as their starting point. We do not seek to provide a definitive definition of modernity: there is already a growing literature on how individuals and communities expressed and experienced the impact of change in different ways and at different points in the 20th century. Modernity could be understood through culture, through gender and family relations, through

---

[18] Fairbrother, *New Lives*, p. 5.
[19] Peter Mandler, 'The heritage panic of the 1970s and 1980s in Great Britain', in Peter Itzen and Christian Müller (eds), *The Invention of Industrial Pasts: Heritage, Political Culture, and Economic Debates in Great Britain and Germany, 1850–2010 = Beiträge zur England-Forschung* 69 (Augsburg, Wissner, 2013), pp. 58–69.

war and the state, and so on. We are interested in the modernity of national and nationalising infrastructure in Britain. This volume examines how the modernity of the post-war decades was not just an urban experiment, but wrought a fundamental transformation of Britain's rural places. At the same time, we underline how, despite the nationalising and integrative aims of mass infrastructure, there were significant national and regional differences in landscape change. If post-industrial landscapes in southern England became fixed according to preservationist dicta, conventional thinking welcomed change to the aesthetically sub-optimal industrial landscapes in the north, and this notwithstanding the appeal of northern uplands, and their formalisation as sites of leisure, as National Parks, during the middle decades of the 20th century.[20] Scottish and Welsh landscapes offered different imperatives for experimentation, and parallel narratives of local and national government intervention in an age of nationalisation. Pressure group politics ensured the preservation of landscapes for amenity or for nature and also disrupted technocratic judgments about the siting of energy and communications infrastructure.[21] The introduction of an 'amenity clause' to legislation concerning first hydro-power stations, then the 1957 Electricity Act, and later the Countryside Acts of 1967–1968, mandated utility companies to consider the amenity needs of inhabitants and the preservation of 'natural beauty' when siting their infrastructure. Protection of the natural environment was initially a secondary concern, notably separated from that.[22]

Our work builds on earlier studies that highlighted the material and economic aspects of change. David Matless's now classic study, *Landscape and Englishness*, identified the popular and preservationist anxieties in the 1920s and 1930s with the effects of blurring town and countryside, not least in spreading suburbia.[23] As we will show, a lingering desire for ordering, the need to distinctly delineate and separate urban from rural, continued well into the post-war era. The wide-ranging work of John Sheail provides a grounding in the impact of different aspects of technology and infrastructure on the environment, including sewerage, pest-control, forestry and electrification.[24] Paul Brassley, Karen Sayer, and Jeremy Burchardt's study of electrification in rural Britain in the 1930s demonstrates the material, economic, and social benefits it brought to the British countryside, though the positive aspects of the new National Grid were counter-balanced by increasing pressure on farmers and agricultural workers to adapt rapidly to urban norms.[25]

---

[20] Patrick Wright, *On Living in an Old Country* (London, Verso, 1985).

[21] See chapters 3 and 4 of Matthew Kelly, *The Women Who Saved the English Countryside* (London: Yale University Press, 2022).

[22] John Sheail, 'The "amenity" clause: An insight into half a century of environmental protection in the United Kingdom', *Transactions of the Institute of British Geographers*, 17:2 (1992), 152–165.

[23] David Matless, *Landscape and Englishness* (London, Reaktion Books, 1998).

[24] For example, John Sheail, *An Environmental History of Twentieth-Century Britain* (London, Palgrave, 2002); see also John Agar and Jacob Ward, *Histories of Technology, the Environment and Modern Britain* (London, UCL Press, 2018).

[25] Paul Brassley, Jeremy Burchardt and Karen Sayer (eds), *Transforming the Countryside: The Electrification of Rural Britain* (London, Routledge, 2016).

Recent interpretations of rural modernity have also understood its multiple dimensions through aesthetic and literary depictions. Rosemary Shirley has examined visual culture, with an emphasis on how the study of everyday life and its perceptions rescues rural change from something to be witnessed from afar to a process experienced from within.[26] Kristin Bluemel and Michael McCluskey's exploration of rural modernity traces its origins in the 1920s and 1930s. Their volume centres artistic and literary responses to change between the world wars, focusing on the emergence of film and new theatre about rural Britain, and artists' depictions of modernity through wood engravings and Cubism.[27]

We take up where these existing studies of rural modernity leave off, examining the even larger changes in the period after 1939. The Second World War was a catalyst, accelerating the pace and scale of change, involving statist projects, though not always with social democratic intentions.[28] A telling example was the establishment of munitions factories and other wartime plants in West Cumberland that presaged the establishment of the Windscale Nuclear Power Station at Sellafield. The requisition of land by the War Office and later the Ministry of Defence for military training and the siting of new military technologies transformed the control and uses of significant proportions of open countryside well into the Cold War era. From the pre-war soundmirrors at RAF Dungeness to the 1970s 'golf ball' radome satellites of RAF Menwith Hill in Yorkshire, military infrastructure brought an ultra-modern aesthetic to rural landscapes. RAF bases became major airports or nuclear testing sites. Linda Ross's chapter about the Dounreay atomic establishment in the north of Scotland shows how scientific experimentation necessitated the acquisition and transformation of new landscapes, often in regions considered remote. A high-tech infrastructure was imposed on a largely agricultural economy. These interventions were regarded as the necessary perquisite for halting depopulation and enabling economic revival but were not always solely based on the expansion of energy infrastructure for efficiency's sake. Whereas the development of the National Grid was driven by increased demand from domestic and industrial consumers, the context for Dounreay and other atomic experiments was geo-political.

While literary scholars have placed modernism in the early decades of the 20th century, and studies of aesthetics and architecture tend to associate it with the middle decades, our focus on infrastructure requires more fluid temporalities. Water preceded electricity, which preceded nuclear. One form of infrastructural

[26] Shirley, *Rural Modernity*, p. 9.
[27] Kristin Bluemel and Michael McCluskey (eds), *Rural Modernity in Britain: A Critical Intervention* (Edinburgh, Edinburgh University Press, 2018).
[28] See Marianna Dudley, *An Environmental History of the UK Defence Estate: 1945 to the Present* (London, Continuum, 2012); Gary Willis, '"An arena of glorious work": The protection of the rural landscape against the demands of Britain's Second World War effort', *Rural History*, 29:2 (2018), 259–280.

demand on the rural began in the 19th century with urban corporations claiming land for ecosystems services (controversies over the construction of reservoirs in upland landscapes have been examined by several authors).[29] In this volume, Kristin Bluemel's study of literatures of modernity offers further reflections on this earlier period of dams and reservoirs. Bluemel takes Francis Brett Young's *The House under the Water* (1932) as just one example of a rural and regional writer who contributed to cultural understandings of the disorienting experiences of modernity in the countryside. But after 1939, these pressures broaden appreciably, as nationalised industries and the military intensified need. At the same time, new statist bodies with conflicting purposes made the rural a site of significant political contestation, including the National Parks Commission, the Nature Conservancy, and different government ministries responsible for Defence, Environment, Housing and Local Government, Agriculture, Forestry and Fisheries. Technological change, new consumer demands, and military expansion often required a smaller number of larger sites: long-range field artillery meant larger military training ranges, regional water planning meant larger reservoirs, electricity demand saw the Central Electricity Generating Board commission the construction of dozens of the coal-, oil-, and nuclear-fired power stations, and higher planting quotas made the Forestry Commission ever land-hungry.

To argue, for example, that the great plantation–reservoir–forestry village complex at Kielder in Northumberland, now marketed as lake and forest, is the quintessential landscape of rural modernity is to overlook what is arguably the most significant landscape manifestation of rural modernity, namely, the landscapes of the 'second agricultural revolution'. Karen Sayer's chapter offers a vital corrective to what could be an otherwise one-sided or indeed urban view of rural modernity. The intensification of farming in the post-war era sought to eliminate rural poverty and avoid the food shortages of the 1930s by expanding the efficiency and profitability of food production. Post-war agricultural subsidies were a 'cheap food' policy, as much concerned with changing how farmers farmed as they were with propping up the rural economy. The 1947 Agricultural Act promoted specialisation and the use of chemical fertilisers and pesticides on a mass scale, applying scientific and technological research to a conception of the farm as a site of modern industry. Sayer explores how the modernisation of farming for food production was promoted in techno-optimist accounts like Garth Christian's conservationist *Tomorrow's Countryside* (1966) and the myriad publications of the Ministry of Agriculture, Forestry and Fisheries. Recalling arguments made by Fairbrother, Sayer shows how the 1968 Countryside Act was an attempt to reconcile this emphasis on agricultural efficiency in food production with the leisure and amenity concerns of the countryside preservation bodies.

---

[29] Harriet Ritvo, *The Dawn of Green: Manchester, Thirlmere and Modern Environmentalism* (Chicago, University of Chicago Press, 2009); Matthew Kelly, *Quartz and Feldspar. Dartmoor: A British Landscape in Modern Times* (London, Jonathan Cape, 2015).

The aesthetic impact of energy and utility requirements is the other key aspect of the rural modernity represented in this volume. Serious attempts were made to naturalise new structures within the landscape through careful site design, visual planning and landscaping. Landscape architecture in the mid-20th century formed a nexus where planning, design, and art met. Outwith Fairbrother and Crowe's publications, the broader influence of the Architectural Press is tangible in the ways in which such landscapes were perceived and designed. Government and corporate demands for cost efficiency had positive as well as negative impacts, often resulting in clean lines and minimal ornamentation, producing a new picturesque. Ian Waites's chapter argues that the picturesque underwent a sustained revival as part of various intersecting post-war debates about architecture, planning, modernity, and the landscape. By situating power stations in flatland sites in the East Midlands, the Central Electricity Generating Board instigated what Waites identifies as 'a publicly-funded post-war social democratic remodelling of the countryside on a scale not seen since the days of Capability Brown and Humphry Repton'. Colour, shape, and placing were at the forefront of design. The landscape of power station cooling towers was specifically conceived to be viewed from afar, in particular from the window of passing cars. Fairbrother once again. Rural modernism nevertheless demanded new technology and new ways of seeing. Moa Carlsson's chapter analyses the innovative methods used by landscape architects and planners to measure, draw, and categorise the changing landscape. Their ways of seeing were based on an ideal of rationality and objectivity, using geometry and mathematics and new technologies to model lines of sight for planning the locations of power station cooling towers. Many of the familiar names associated with rural modernism, from Clough Williams-Ellis and Sir Patrick Abercrombie to Sylvia Crowe, were influenced by these technocratic forms of landscape design. As Carlsson shows, the use of isovist analysis and computer programming corresponded with a broader shift to systematic and scientific planning in the post-war period.

Form and function were at the basis of rural modernist design, though as Katrina Navickas's study of the industrial areas of the southern Pennines establishes, the pushback from preservationist lobbying sometimes led to compromises with the vernacular. Modern infrastructure was eventually accepted as part of the landscape, though the recent introduction of updated technology and renewable energy structures, from wind turbines to solar power installations, has revived debates about the value and form of landscape amenity. Landscape change was not as neat as planners and technocrats strove to ensure, many landscapes resisting easy categorisation as urban or rural, and not all valued landscapes could be classified according to the amenity clause's definition of 'natural beauty'. Examining how people engaged with landscapes around Bolton in Lancashire, Jeremy Burchardt reveals contemporary conceptions and experiences of 'in-between landscapes'. And as Gareth Roddy's chapter on conflicts over excavation and preservation near to Hadrian's Wall, and Sayer's consideration of agricultural progress show, landscapes of modernity were, at base, what anthropologist Tim Ingold termed 'taskscapes', worked and shaped by their inhabitants as much as by outside architects and engineers.[30] Roddy demonstrates how these conflicts could effect-ively reverse Fairbrother's priorities, as modern, planned efforts to ensure the preservation of the Roman wall met with fierce local resistance. Quarrying was crucial for local industrial employment, income, and services, but to see the land like a quarryman was to make the historical as well as the material case for the continued expansion of the industry. Ysanne Holt meanwhile demonstrates that embedding artists in sites of commercial forestry in Cumbria and Northumberland enabled engagement with the landscape changes brought by forestry, and pitted regional identities against the centralising direction of the post-war British state, so part and parcel of the post-war transformation of the rural. Fairbrother, writing in the late 1960s, might be forgiven for assuming the practical disappearance of the past, but this volume demonstrates that what emerged in subsequent decades was as much an integration of the 'old setting' into the new modernity of the rural, as it was the caricature of 'museumisation' so hated by often-elitist critics. These chapters therefore also contribute to the effort to recover histories of rural agency in response to the literature's predominant focus on the activities of preservationists and the development of rural tourism.[31]

A sense of heritage as a dynamic and evolving historical phenomenon provides another major theme of the volume, including evidence of slowly chan-ging 'official' mindsets about what might constitute heritage. This was the case regarding Second World War infrastructure, a set of landscape features neither embraced as a legitimate 'heritage', nor included in paeans of planned modernity such as Fairbrother's, but representing an important element of landscapes across Britain nonetheless. These sites often underlay, physically, the infrastructure of rural modernism: motorways ran along runways, power stations – or at least their construction workers – occupied barracks, and experts drew on armed forces training. Notwithstanding how much post-war civilian infrastructure was built on physical and intellectual foundations laid down by mid-century militarisation, enthusiasts for the post-war built environment have not established its status as part of the heritage of the war, despite the centrality of this heritage to British national identity. As Ross's examination of Dounreay attests, and the chapter by Ben Anderson and Matthew Kelly examines in some detail, it is not enough to explain the reluctance to celebrate militarised landscapes as a product of their relative youth, since other – equally 'functional' – sites have moved to heritage more rapidly. Rather, as Readman points out, military structures have long been understood to disturb landscapes often praised for their tranquility and peace – their inability to be contextualised according to established heritage narratives made them vulnerable.

---

[30] Tim Ingold, 'The temporality of the landscape', *World Archaeology*, 25:2 (1993), 152–174.
[31] Ben Anderson, 'Alpine agency: Locals, mountaineers and tourism in the eastern Alps, c. 1890–1914', *Rural History*, 27:1 (2016), 61–78.

If military sites posed an awkward question for countryside heritage in the late 20th century, in the 21st, the infrastructure of the carbon economy's 'great acceleration' is rapidly occupying a similar role. Many of the infrastructure sites constructed in the 20th century, not least power stations, are being decommissioned or fast becoming redundant as a consequence industrial decline and environmental regulations, enabling the government to wean Britain off the carbon economy. As carbon culture's vast infrastructure becomes obsolete, as the first generation of nuclear sites move to decommissioning, and as the polarising presence of the pylon is re-imagined as heritage for a post-carbon future, this volume asks what might now happen to the infrastructure of this rural modernity, and the new lives that it created. The story, to be sure, is not simple. The heritage value of sites such as Dounreay, Chatterley Whitfield colliery in Staffordshire, or Fawley power station in Hampshire, is neither established at the moment of closure nor erased with demolition. Instead, what is happening to these sites is more effectively understood as 'ruination', a concept coined by scholars of deindustrialisation to describe industrial closure as a long and difficult process rather than moment of rupture. Viewed in this way, the dynamic and multi-layered character of this emerging heritage becomes clearer. In her chapter, Linda M. Ross places the contested narratives of Dounreay in dialogue with the attempt by officials to develop a 'heritage strategy' equal to the task of managing radioactive waste into an unknowable future. Matthew Kelly and Ben Anderson's chapter, meanwhile, examines how decisions made in the immediate post-war era, and the progress those decisions once represented, now delimit and define the future of sites such as Chatterley Whitfield and Fawley beyond the apparent finality of closure and demolition.[32]

At the same time, and less pressingly, the rise of the digital economy is gradually undermining older communication infrastructure, particularly television and radio transmission masts. Sprouting up in their place is a new rural modernity of mobile phone masts, windfarms and solar panels – natural gas extraction (fracking) installations are still in prospect – with consequent political and public debate about their efficiency and place within the landscape recalling the debates of the 1950s and 1960s. Equally, as the recent 'State of Nature' reports make clear, much contemporary environmental concern is focused on how modern agriculture degrades the natural environment, throwing into sharp relief Fairbrother's positive account of the 'Scandinavian' minimalism of modernist agricultural landscapes. At Dounreay and at Fawley, we witness the reaction of local populations to the completion of an industrial lifecycle; the latter is something which many projects conceived in the post-war period are now facing, while a new rural modernity of windfarms, solar panels and natural gas extraction rapidly develops. Like Fairbrother in 1970, we are therefore at an important juncture of 'looking backwards while moving forward'.[33]

---

[32] Alice Mah, *Industrial Ruination, Community and Place: Landscapes and Legacies of Urban Decline* (London, University of Toronto Press, 2012). See Steven High and David W. Lewis, *Corporate Wasteland: The Landscape and Memory of Deindustrialisation* (London, Cornell University Press, 2007); Steven High, Lachlan MacKinnon and Andrew Perchard (eds), *The Deindustrialized World: Confronting Ruination in Postindustrial Places* (Vancouver, University of British Columbia Press, 2017).

[33] Fairbrother, *New Lives*, p. 8.

Fairbrother and the post-war modernisers could not predict the impact that the demolition and decommissioning of sites would have on communities which were created or sustained by the technocracy. Nor, to shift the optic, did they consider the toxic environmental legacy of modern infrastructure, the material consequences of which will far outlast the buildings themselves. The 'new landscapes' of Fairbrother's dreams did not obliterate the old, but soon became a part of it. Only now are we beginning to consider how the heritage of the great acceleration might be narrated, or how the stories of its many 'new lives' might be told.

2

In-between Landscapes

JEREMY BURCHARDT

THE TYPOLOGICAL CONTRAST between urban and rural settlements was one of the foundations of the discipline of sociology as it developed in the early 20th century. This drew on Tönnies's celebrated distinction between loose 'gesellschaft' societies, often equated with cities, and tight knit, face-to-face 'gemeinschaft' communities, typically construed as rural. The Chicago school of rural sociology, in which Louis Wirth played a central role, developed this typology further, arguing that there was a continuum between close rural communities and the anonymous, atomised social relations taken to be characteristic of 'modern' urban settlements. There was an affinity between these ideas and Durkheim's concern with *anomie*, the isolated condition of personal, social, and ideological rootlessness he identified as a feature of modernity. Although academic sociology largely eschewed Marxism, these ideas also bore a relationship to the analysis of alienation that Marx argued in his early writing was inherent in the capitalist mode of production. Hence by the mid-20th century a strong contrast between urban and rural was well established in academic, and especially sociological, discourse.

It was this contrast at which Ray Pahl took aim in his celebrated 1966 article, 'The rural-urban continuum'. Pahl argued that the concept of a single continuum was unsustainable. Sociological studies had revealed the existence of 'urban villages', typically densely settled working-class areas, where close 'gemeinschaft' community bonds prevailed, and conversely of ex-urban dormitory settlements inhabited by mainly middle-class commuters, whose social relations bore a stronger correspondence to a 'gesellschaft' model. Hence there were people who were in the city but not of it, and of the city but not in it. Class and lifecycle were, Pahl argued, far more decisive in shaping experience than whether someone lived in the town or the country. On the basis of a review of the global sociological literature, he suggested that more attention should also be paid to cross-cutting tensions between the local and the national in both urban and rural settings. He concluded that scholars should abandon the concept of a rural–urban continuum,

Proceedings of the British Academy, **256**, 15–36, © The British Academy 2023.

recommending that settlement patterns should be understood instead as a multiva-
lent series of superimposed meshes.[1]

Pahl's critique proved highly influential and enduring. Its initial impact was
strongest among sociologists and rural geographers. Howard Newby, the leading
rural sociologist of the 1970s, took it forward through works such as his 1977
study of British farmworkers, *The Deferential Worker*, in which he argued that
the deferential behaviour of farmworkers was a product of a particular configuration of class relationships rather than reflecting inherent features of rural communities. In this and other works, Newby excoriated the 'community studies'
approach that had dominated British rural sociology in the 1950s and 1960s, on the
grounds that its microcosmic, single-settlement methodology obscured the national
and transnational forces, notably in relation to class and the intensification of capitalist relations of production, that his research and that of other contemporary
sociologists suggested shaped life experience far more profoundly than factors
operating at a local level.[2] 'Rural' and 'urban' as analytical terms fell into disrepute
among sociologists and geographers, to such an extent that by 1990 Keith Hoggart
could publish a paper in the *Journal of Rural Studies* with the provocative but more
than half-serious title 'Let's do away with the rural'.[3]

Parallel developments, motivated by a similar discontent with the apparent
arbitrariness of the urban–rural distinction and a desire to identify more universal
forces and processes operating across all spatial settings and scales, were at work in
literary and historical studies. Pahl's impact was eventually felt here too but more
influential was Raymond Williams's *The Country and the City* (1973). Williams
showed that the persistent town–country contrasts in English literature from the
16th century onwards registered but simultaneously disguised the real social forces
at work, and argued that the role of the critical scholar was to expose these by
close reading and critical analysis. He concluded that 'capitalism, as a mode of
production, is the basic process of most of what we know as the history of country
and city'.[4] Since the publication of *The Country and the City*, literary critics and
historians have construed 'town' and 'country' almost entirely through the prism
of ideology and cultural construction. Although Williams tended to avoid such
ahistorical terms himself, the trope of the 'rural idyll' became (and remains) very
popular among scholars. Among the most influential contributions to this extensive
literature were Martin Wiener's *English Culture and the Decline of the Industrial
Spirit* (1981) and Angus Calder's *The Myth of the Blitz* (1991), both arguing
that mystified representations of the rural as distinct from and antithetical to the
modern and the urban had distorted and retarded English social, political, and even

[1] Ray Pahl, 'The rural-urban continuum', *Sociologia ruralis*, 6:3 (1966), 299–329.
[2] Howard Newby, *The Deferential Worker: A Study of Farmworkers in East Anglia* (London, Allen
Lane, 1977).
[3] Keith Hoggart, 'Let's do away with rural', *Journal of Rural Studies*, 6:3 (1990), 245–257.
[4] Raymond Williams, *The Country and the City* (Oxford, Oxford University Press, 1975), p. 302.

economic development.[5] Michael Bunce's *The Countryside Ideal* (1994) explored these representations in greater depth and vigorous scholarly efforts to deconstruct the town–country contrast have continued since then, exemplified by studies such as Peter Borsay's 'Nature, the past and the English town: a counter-cultural history' (2017), which argued that far from being antithetical to them, a historicised and commodified version of the rural was in fact one of the characteristic products of urban modernity.[6]

Yet despite the Sisyphean labours of multitudes of scholars over more than half a century, binary distinctions between town and country remain stubbornly embedded at the level of public policy and discourse. In the UK, planning legislation continues to be framed with reference to protecting rural land from urban development. The decisive legislative change was the passing of the Town and Country Planning Act of 1947; after many iterations, a successor (the Town and Country Planning Act, 1990) remains on the statute book. 'Rural proofing' to ensure that the impact of policy on rural areas has been considered before it is implemented has become an established part of the UK policy process. The Countryside Alliance may have toned down some of its anti-urban rhetoric since its heyday in the early 2000s but remains an active force in UK rural politics. Much of the 'new nature writing', epitomised by best-selling authors such as Helen Macdonald, Isabel Hardman, and Amy Liptrot, is concerned with various forms of retreat to the countryside to escape from oppressive features of urban modernity, while the COVID-19 pandemic has reinvigorated counter-urbanisation, with rural house prices rising twice as fast as those in urban areas since 2019.[7]

To the perplexity and vexation of many scholars, then, the relationship between urban and rural, or what is regarded as such, remains a vibrant, often politically controversial, issue with powerful cultural resonances. This chapter seeks to contribute to our understanding of the strange survival of rural England through the 20th and into the 21st century by attending to an intermediate type of landscape that, it is argued, became increasingly significant during this period, referred to here as 'in-between' landscapes. These were accessible, 'rural-like' spaces within, on the fringe of, or just outside, urban areas. They were usually, but not always, 'green spaces' – not always because the cultural coordinates of the countryside cannot simply be reduced to 'nature', at least in an English context. Similarly, they overlapped with but differed in ways that will become apparent from the 'edgelands' about which Marion Shoard, Michael Roberts, Paul Farley, and others have

---

[5] Martin Wiener, *English Culture and the Decline of the Industrial Spirit* (Cambridge, Cambridge University Press, 1981); Angus Calder, *The Myth of the Blitz* (London, Cape, 1991).

[6] Michael Bunce, *The Countryside Ideal* (London, Routledge, 1994); Peter Borsay, 'Nature, the past and the English town: A counter-cultural history', *Urban History*, 44:1 (2017), 27–43.

[7] Robert Booth, 'Rural house prices in England and Wales rise twice as fast as in cities', *The Guardian*, 20 June 2021, www.theguardian.com/society/2021/jun/20/rural-house-prices-in-england-and-wales-rise-twice-as-fast-as-in-cities [accessed 15 August 2021].

written eloquently.[8] Attending to in-between landscapes contributes to scholarly questioning of the adequacy of the rural–urban divide as a conceptual framework (or continuum): they can be understood as another of the 'superimposed meshes' that Pahl argued together constituted the system of urban–rural spatial relationships. At the same time, however, research on in-between landscapes can help us understand the persistence of sharply polarised conceptions in popular ('lay') discourse. As Halfacree, Jones, and others have pertinently argued, to dismiss those who espouse such discourse as unwitting dupes of 'the rural idyll' is facile because it fails to recognise that the contrast between urban and rural gains discursive purchase in part because aspects of it resonate with popular experience.[9]

In-between landscapes could take a wide variety of forms. Probably the most important were green spaces of various kinds: gardens, allotments, parks, churchyards and cemeteries; urban commons; water meadows and flood plains; river and canal banks; wooded slopes and ravines too steep for building; awkward strips and corners of land trapped between roads, railways, or other infrastructure, or temporarily reprieved from development due to disputes over ownership or planning permission. Urban green spaces like these could be, and often were, construed as refuges for nature within a predominantly unnatural urban environment, or as surviving fragments of the previous, now otherwise built-over, rural landscape. In this sense, there was something inherently limited or incomplete about them. They functioned partly as a suggestion or reminder of nature on its own terms, of a still-unconquered countryside somewhere beyond the city limits. Other urban spaces, not conventionally regarded as green spaces, could do so too: spots, perhaps along roads or footpaths, that afforded views out to distant countryside; 'ruralised' roads planted with trees, perhaps especially flowering trees and shrubs such as cherries and rhododendrons; and what were perceived to be 'rural' enclaves, typified by groups of buildings visibly much older than those encompassing them.

In-between landscapes were in one sense highly modern, in that they were characteristic, indeed well-nigh universal, elements in 20th-century urban and peri-urban landscapes. Their ubiquity was inherent in the processes of urban development: in its messiness and haphazardness, whereby the theoretical perfection of market forces in allocating land as a factor of production was always in practice stumbling and unfinished; in the irrepressible persistence of the non-human, whether in the guise of geology, relief, watercourses, birds and insects, wild mammals stealthily reclaiming the city at night, or plants cracking even the most forbidding concrete; or in the willed retention or recreation of natural and other rural-like elements,

[8] Richard Mabey, *The Unofficial Countryside* (London, Collins, 1973); Marion Shoard, 'Edgelands of promise', *Landscapes*, 1:2 (2000), 74–93; Michael Roberts and Paul Farley, *Edgelands: Journeys into England's True Wilderness* (London, Vintage Digital, 2011); Rob Cowen, *Common Ground* (London, Cornerstone Digital, 2015).

[9] Keith Halfacree, 'Talking about rurality: Social representations of the rural as expressed by residents of six English parishes', *Journal of Rural Studies*, 11:1 (1995), 1–20; Owain Jones, 'Lay discourses of the rural: Developments and implications for rural studies', *Journal of Rural Studies*, 11:1 (1995), 35–49.

either as a result of private actions (planting garden flowers or trees, for example) or public decisions (such as land purchases and designations by local authorities, or through the planning system).

Yet at the same time, in-between landscapes were resistant to modernity in their marginality and 'left-behindness'. These were places that turned their backs on the conventional tropes of modernity: no surging crowds, roaring traffic or dazzling lights, skyscrapers or plate-glass windows, cinemas or sports stadiums, streamlined trains or super-fast cars, electricity cables or communications masts. They were relics of the past rather than harbingers of the future. They demurred from the city's brazen commercialism. True, some green spaces could be quite valuable economic assets – directly in the case of private gardens, indirectly in the case of parks, which could substantially raise house prices in their immediate vicinity. But this economic value, paradoxically, depended on the apparent *absence* of commercial purpose of the uses to which the land was put – walking, playing games, the pleasures of gardening and being amongst trees, shrubs, and flowers. Most other in-between landscapes were genuinely without commercial value – places that had escaped from, even defied, the economic logic of the market. They existed, or survived, because no entrepreneur had been able to extract a profit from them.

In their marginality and left-behindness, in-between landscapes shared much with edgelands. But there was a critical difference. In the main, the literature on edgelands celebrates their untidy neglected dereliction as an antidote to the 'pure' countryside beyond, of which scholars have often been suspicious because of its idealising pastoral connotations. Hence edgelands functioned as a third pole to town and country, partaking of both but with their own distinctive ambience and redu-cible to neither. In-between landscapes were quite different. Some were regarded as preferable to others, and what counted as 'better' corresponded quite closely to what was figured as 'more rural' in lay discourse. Hence, unlike edgelands, in-between landscapes were hierarchical and directional: when a 'better' space became avail-able, previously used spaces were often quickly abandoned. A better space might become available as a result of moving house (perhaps the most common reason), because a person's circumstances changed (they bought a bicycle, for example, or as a result of their children growing older) or, less commonly perhaps, because of a material change in the neighbourhood in which someone lived (a new park being opened or trees planted). Conversely, all three of these factors could shift in the opposite direction, forcing people temporarily or permanently to move down the hierarchy and accept 'worse' spaces. Few neighbourhoods or situations were so circumscribed that no in-between place of any kind at all was available. To take an extreme and very short-term example, the Bristol bookshop worker Fred Catley took comfort from the bright green leaves of a tree just in leaf seen through a window while he sat in a dentist's chair to have a tooth extracted in April 1939.[10] A more typical in-between landscape experience, however, was the happiness

[10] Bristol Record Office, F. J. Catley diary, 41419/38, 18 April 1939.

and contentment he felt for a few minutes 'looking at the greening hawthorns on Brandon Hill [park], in the midday sunshine' during his lunch hour on 22 March the previous year.[11]

One of the reasons that in-between landscapes have largely evaded scholarly attention is that they were low-key and quotidian. Few of them were ever noted in a guidebook or represented in a painting. Moreover, they were highly personal: one person's in-between landscapes might be quite different from another's. Just as in-between landscapes typically arose as unintended by-products of modern urban development, so they were characteristically encountered in the interstices of everyday life: a tree-lined lane en route between home and shops, perhaps, or a glimpse of distant countryside from an office-block window. Being so transient and ephemeral, in-between landscapes easily slip through the historian's net. Catching a trace of them requires a micro-historical approach, drawing on ego-documents like diaries. To give substance to the claims made above, the remainder of this chapter therefore considers how in-between landscapes functioned in three modern British lives: Dr John Johnston, a GP with a large, mainly working-class practice in Bolton; Katherine Spear Smith, a young artist and ornithologist who shuttled between Hampshire and London; and William Hallam, a fitter at the vast Great Western Railway works in Swindon. All three lives spanned the last years of the 19th century and extended into or through the interwar period. I have chosen to focus on these three individuals because in-between landscapes played a significant role in each of their lives, in contrasting ways and because exceptionally rich diary and ancillary evidence is available for each of them. Where appropriate and available, however, I will supplement this material with evidence drawn from other lives.

Dr John Johnston

John Johnston grew up in the small country town of Annan in Dumfriesshire. His staunchly Presbyterian parents were devoted to him and gave him every possible encouragement, including the benefit of an excellent education at Annan Academy. Johnston went on to study medicine at the University of Edinburgh. In search of professional advancement, he came south to Birmingham, where he worked at the children's hospital, after which he was able to obtain a medical practice in Bolton. He worked hard and achieved both professional success and financial security. At least as important to him, however, were his ethical and ideological commitments and the friendship networks that expressed and sustained these. In his youth, Johnston suffered something akin to the proverbial Victorian 'crisis of faith', rejecting the powerful but narrow Presbyterianism in which he had been brought up. Subsequently, he came under the influence of Walt Whitman, becoming a lynchpin of the small group of Bolton Whitmanites, known from their regular meeting place

---

[11] Bristol Record Office, F. J. Catley diary, 22 March 1938.

as the 'Eagle Street College'. At the same time, Johnston was moving to the left politically, becoming active in the Bolton Independent Labour Party, a development that he feared would alienate his middle-class patients. However, his talents, energy, and dedication to his patients ensured that he remained a popular and respected doctor in Bolton, at Queen Mary's military hospital in Whalley, where he served during the First World War, and at Townleys Hospital back in Bolton again thereafter. He died in 1927.

Both in Bolton and in other places where he was temporarily resident, in-between landscapes played an indispensable role in Johnston's life. Figure 2.1 shows some of those that were most significant to him in his early years in Bolton.

For most of this period, Johnston lived at 54 Manchester Road, adjacent to the Lancashire and Yorkshire Railway station in a densely built-up part of the town. His practice extended across a large part of Bolton and its outlying settlements. It was a mixed practice of working- and middle-class patients, and Johnston used the receipts from his middle-class patients to subsidise working-class patients too poor to pay. Many of these lived in the mining township of Darcy Lever just over a mile to the south-east. Raikes Wood, between Darcy Lever and Manchester Road, was Johnston's preferred in-between landscape at this time: it was the 'nearest accessible spot where I can enjoy the society of my favourites the trees', although several other nearby places could serve, at least to an extent, as a substitute when

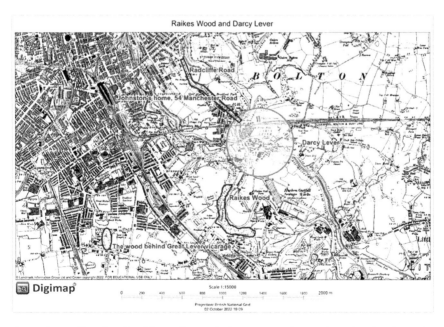

Figure 2.1 Raikes Wood and Darcy Lever. © Crown Copyright and Landmark Information Group Limited (2022). All rights reserved (1911)

Figure 2.2 'Annandale' and 'Sunnybrae'. © Crown Copyright and Landmark Information Group Limited (2022). All rights reserved (1909)

necessary, among them Radcliffe Road, on the route between Johnston's home and Darcy Lever, and a small wood adjacent to Great Lever vicarage about a mile to the south-west.[12]

Figure 2.2 shows another of Johnston's in-between places, a wood in the Sharples area (close to Ivy Bank Lane) to the north of Bolton. He had patients up here too. As his practice expanded, his income rose and he was able to afford to move out of central Bolton, first to 'Annandale' and then to 'Sunnybrae', in open country near Lostock Junction. Each, unlike 54 Manchester Road, had a large garden and successively took on the functions that previous in-between places had once fulfilled.

As this indicates, Johnston had a flexible, even opportunistic attitude to his in-between landscapes. This applied both over short and long timescales. Over a short timescale, he would take whatever was available. Even if he did not have time to sit in Raikes Wood or one of the other small areas of woodland within reach of 54 Manchester Road, he could enjoy Radcliffe Road as he cycled along it on the way to or from Darcy Lever. Sometimes he would find a quiet spot to sit after visiting a patient, usually a patch of woodland, as on Friday, 20 May 1892, when he

---

[12] Bolton Archives History Centre, John Johnston diary, ZJO/1/9, note opposite entry for 22 May 1890.

wrote the following entry in his diary under some trees at Sharples after attending 'Mr B.' in Ivy Bank Lane:

> I am sitting on the projecting root of a big tree whose newly opened green fans are widespread to the sun. All around are other big trees – some of them as yet almost leafless (probably oaks and ashes) – swaying to and fro in the high wind which *soughs* through them with a sound like the sound of the sea in a storm – the cindered roadway covered with the interlaced shadows moving to and fro – birds singing – larks soaring and carolling – grand clouds sailing along the blue sky – in the distance seen through trees the green hills bathed in the sunlight – everything at peace – no sound but that of the wind through the trees and the birds singing – a beautiful scene which impressed itself upon me very deeply.[13]

It was probably also because he had been visiting a patient in Great Lever that he chose, on Monday, 26 May 1890, to spend a quiet hour sitting in the wood behind the vicarage there, rather than make his way to what at this time was his usual resort of Raikes Wood.[14] Similarly, when he was away from home, whether on holiday, visiting friends or relatives, or for work purposes, Johnston made use of whatever in-between landscape he could find. At Bournemouth in May 1902 he sat alone for an hour 'on the heather and gorse tangled grass' in the shade of a small pine tree on the cliff top.[15] Easter 1909 found him at the bustling Lancashire seaside town of St Anne's but in the same way he sought out a secluded private spot, hidden among the sandhills to the south of the town, with only the sea, sky, grass, and larks for company.[16]

Years later, when he was working at Queen Mary's Hospital in Whalley, he was in some respects in an even less propitious environment – it was a huge, bustling establishment, he had little time for leisure, and the immediate surroundings were not appealing. Nevertheless, when he had time to do so, he would walk out beyond the railway and road, across a malodorous stream, to fields and hedgerows where he could enjoy the blossoming hawthorn in spring, and the river, which reminded him of the River Annan.[17] When there was insufficient time for a walk, he would sometimes sit on a deck chair outside his hut, looking at the patch of grass in front of him. This was one of his most circumscribed in-between spaces but his diary indicates that, in subdued form, it served similar purposes for him:

> I am sitting on my deck chair on the buttercup-starred grass outside my hut taking in the sunshine and the warmth and beauty of this sequestered nook. All around me are the tall grasses waving in the gentle breeze and among them the upturned cups of gold varnished glittering in the sunshine while encompassing me are the wooden walls of the huts made of overlapping boards with here and there the windows of our rooms.[18]

---

[13] Bolton Archives History Centre, John Johnston diary, ZJO/1/20, 20 May 1892. Emphasis in original.
[14] Bolton Archives History Centre, John Johnston diary, ZJO/1/9, 26 May 1890.
[15] Bolton Archives History Centre, John Johnston diary, ZJO/1/31, 24 May 1902.
[16] Bolton Archives History Centre, John Johnston diary, ZJO/1/34, 10 April 1909.
[17] Bolton Archives History Centre, John Johnston diary, ZJO/1/40, 5 June 1916.
[18] Bolton Archives History Centre, John Johnston diary, ZJO/1/40, 16 June 1916.

But these in-between spaces were very far from equal and where circumstances allowed Johnston much preferred some to others. Among the qualities he looked for were seclusion and solitude; what he perceived as beauty, especially rich colours; trees and flowers; wildness and profuse growth; and the non-human world actively manifest around him, for example through birdsong, leaves and branches swaying in the wind, insects buzzing, clouds hurrying across the sky, or the sound of running water. All of these were qualities that contributed to what he regarded as 'rural'. Hence he referred to Raikes Wood as 'my little rural retreat' just as later he was to describe his house and garden near Lostock Junction as 'our little countrified home'.[19] The more fully an in-between place corresponded to the full package of what constituted the rural for Johnston, the greater his preference for it. Radcliffe Road, for example, had some of these qualities: plenty of trees; cherry blossom in the spring; flowering shrubs in a rich variety of colours; birdsong and ample evidence of nature's profusion:

> Radcliffe Road gets lovelier every day – the recent rain has brought out the leaves of every tree, hedge and shrub with the exception of the oak and the ash. ... In the gardens of the houses on the right side of the road the lustrous green trees and shrubs are particularly pretty today – there being several cherry trees in full blossom, white and red rhododendrons bursting in to bloom and a lilac bush laden with unopened flowers and the combination of colours is very charming. But this will be excelled before long for shortly the hawthorn, red and white and the yellow laburnum will be out and add their superb colouring to the show. As I drove along in my phaeton my ears were greeted with the sweet songs of birds hid among those shrubs and the trees which meet overhead a little further on – a robin singing, a blackbird fluting, a thrush piping, sparrows chirruping, other little birds trilling, and a glorious lark carolling in the sky.[20]

Johnston responded with gladness and enthusiasm to these attributes, at least when his mood conduced to this, but for all this, there were vital rural qualities that Radcliffe Road lacked, notably quietness, solitude, seclusion, and peace. This was why he so much preferred Raikes Wood during the period he lived at 54 Manchester Road:

> This [has] been a week of glorious sunshine which I have enjoyed in various ways during my scanty leisure for enjoyment of it. One of these is to wander off alone to Raikes Clough which is within easy distance of my house and having searched out a secluded nook where I can sit entirely unobserved by the few passers by to sit down with a favourite book ... there to absorb the delights of the place surrounded by the gracefully swaying green robed trees and the sweet warbling of the birds thrushes blackbirds robins starlings etc. Here I have spent many a pleasant hour and many more do I hope to spend.[21]

[19] Bolton Archives History Centre, John Johnston diary, Bolton AHC, ZJO/1/22 and ZJO/1/32, 7 June 1892 and 8 December 1902.
[20] Bolton Archives History Centre, John Johnston diary, ZJO 1/20, 26 May 1892.
[21] Bolton Archives History Centre, John Johnston diary, ZJO 1/9, 20 May 1890.

But although Raikes Wood was much further along Johnston's spectrum of rurality than Radcliffe Road, and was a place of vital, life-restoring significance to him at this time, it remained simply the best regularly available to him while he lived in central Bolton. Incompatible sights and sounds often obtruded into his reflections – in the following passage, 'rural' and 'urban' qualities jostle for ascendance, with the latter repeatedly disrupting Johnston's efforts to achieve the 'rural serenity' he sought in places like Raikes Wood:

> I have finished my work till 6pm and have come out here for a quiet hour to hear the birds sing and to enjoy the delights of eternal [?] nature wh[ich] even on this small scale are so dear to me. And what do I see and hear? The day has been a really splendid one and the sun is now shining in all his glory his rays filtering through the thickly leaved trees illuminating the recesses of the little wood and lighting up the foliage and grass in a beautiful way. … Across the brook – alas that it is so discoloured! – are three hawthorn trees thickly covered with blossom – a most charming sight. … Over all is a clear blue sky besmirched here and there with the filthy smoke from some hideous big chimnies [*sic*] in the distance. A corncrake is 'crake crake craking' in the meadow.[22]

Even when the machinery stopped, it was not entirely out of mind:

> One of the most supremely beautiful days of this summer – warm benignant sunshine, soft balmy airs, blue sky dappled with masses of white cloudlets – for this is the operatives general holiday and all the manufactories are stopped and their chimnies have ceased to belch forth their usual all polluting smoke. Bolton looks at its very best and life in it today is tolerable and in a sense enjoyable.

> Here I sit again on my old sylvan throne – a fallen tree trunk – and overlook the peaceful valley and absorb the quiet beauty of this little bit of primitive nature.[23]

Hence it is not surprising that despite the critical role Raikes Wood played for years in his inner life, and the deeply felt experiences he had had there, Johnston dropped it without ceremony when a 'better rural' became available to him, in the form of the garden of his new house in the suburbs at 'Annandale':

> I have got through my morning's work and am now 4pm sitting in the front garden beneath the shade of a wide spreading and very graceful weeping ash tree which rustles its newly opened leaves and sways its branches over my head. The sun is shining brightly and warmly out of an almost cloudless sky of blue.[24]

Yet even this proved too urban and when his circumstances allowed Johnston moved further out into the countryside proper, to a house near Lostock Junction that he named 'Sunnybrae', in an open, breezy location, with a prospect of a wide sweep of hills and valley, plenty of birds in the garden, and a farmhouse and fields nearby.[25] Henceforth it was the garden and rural surroundings of Sunnybrae that

[22] Bolton Archives History Centre, John Johnston diary, ZJO 1/22, 7 June 1892.
[23] Bolton Archives History Centre, John Johnston diary, ZJO/1/22, 20 August 1892.
[24] Bolton Archives History Centre, John Johnston diary, ZJO/1/30, 30 May 1899.
[25] Bolton Archives History Centre, John Johnston diary, ZJO/1/31, 8 April 1902.

fulfilled the functions once occupied by Raikes Wood, except when Johnston was
away from home, when, as before, he sought out the best 'rural' conveniently
accessible to him.

Why did in-between places, and the rural landscapes they approximated to,
matter so much to Johnston? What functions did they fulfil in his life? Partly,
of course, he was seeking refuge from the disamenities of industrial Bolton: its
ugliness, pollution, noise, and 'unnaturalness'.[26] These attributes of Bolton were
accentuated in his mind by their contrast with Annan, an elegant red sandstone
country town in constant interchange with its rural hinterland which in fact,
in the form of the River Annan and the meadows that fringed it, passed right
through the town. In seeking out places with rural attributes, Johnston was also
seeking to keep in touch with Annan and to reconnect with the securities of his
happy childhood.

In-between places served another, less obvious and at times more acutely necessary role in Johnston's life, however. They provided relief from the demanding,
and at times distressing, nature of his work. The two influences resonated with
each other: Bolton with its grime and pollution was the scene of his professional
labours, while his rural refuges were quiet, clean places to which he turned for rest
from them: '[a]fter a week of toil in the hot noisy + dirty town what a relief it is to
get the Sunday off – what a joy to spend it at Sunnybrae!'[27] Often, however, it was
more the work than the town that Johnston sought relief from, as on the evening he
walked out to Raikes Wood and sat there for an hour after a 'tedious and difficult'
midwifery case from 11am to 1.30pm that morning which 'fairly took it out of
me'.[28] The urgency of Johnston's need, at times, for a rural refuge seems to be the
explanation for his resort to otherwise inferior in-between spaces such as the wood
behind Great Lever vicarage and at Sharples. These woods were smaller and less
detached from their urban surroundings than Raikes Wood but were closer to where
some of his patients lived. Certainly the note he wrote in his diary while sitting in
the wood at Sharples on 20 May 1892 followed immediately from a consultation
at the nearby Ivy Bank Lane house of the dying 'Mr B.', by which Johnston was
greatly affected.

Katherine Spear Smith

The same pattern of a hierarchy of in-between places, with the most rural being
preferred when available and less rural spaces being discarded unceremoniously
when 'better' (more rural) options became available, is apparent in the life of
Katherine Spear Smith, daughter of the academic administrator Walter Smith and

[26] Bolton Archives History Centre, John Johnston diary, ZJO/1/31, 29 August 1902.
[27] Bolton Archives History Centre, John Johnston diary, ZJO/1/31, 7 September 1902.
[28] Bolton Archives History Centre, John Johnston diary, ZJO 1/22, 21 August 1892.

his wife Kate. Like Johnston, Smith was initially constrained in her ability to access the countryside. For him, this arose largely as a result of professional necessity. Her situation was different, in that she did not work. But she was economically dependent on her parents and, even had she wanted to, could not have afforded to live apart from them. When her diaries begin in the early 20th century, she was in her late teens and the Smiths were living in Kensington. She did not have many opportunities to go out but made the most of their garden, observing the blackbirds that nested there closely and taking careful notes on their habits.[29] In 1903 she joined the Selborne Society, one of the principal institutional expressions of late Victorian popular natural history:

> Just before we went to Weston, I joined the 'Selborne Society', & became a member; so now I am a 'Selbornian'; & it is my duty as such, to protect wild birds & flowers etc: & to promote the study of Natural History! I have a little magazine sent me every month, called 'Nature Notes'.[30]

Shortly thereafter, she and her brother Alic went to stay with relatives in Weston-super-Mare for Easter. However, doubtless with Katherine's Selbornian responsibilities in mind, they took every opportunity to get out of the town and explore the woods on its northern fringe: 'Alic & I used to go into the Woods every day, except one; we enjoyed them so much; the trees are coming out, & in one part of the wood, it is covered with wood anemones & bluebells; it is so lovely.'[31]

Henceforth, holidays were to provide some of Smith's best opportunities for encountering nature and exploring the countryside. Initially, the family favoured the Hampshire seaside town of Lee-on-Solent, not on the face of it the most promising location for Katherine, but she was quick to find an in-between landscape in the form of the common, where she walked almost every day, enjoying the gorse and birds such as chiffchaffs and goldcrests. The essence of in-between landscapes is making the most of small-scale, limited or flawed manifestations of the rural and Smith was adept at this: '[f]ound a beautifull [sic] moss on the Common, with lovely golden brown, and red flowers, like little stars; it looked like an old medieval pattern'.[32]

One of the limitations of in-between landscapes is that because of their small scale and proximity to areas of active urban development, they were (and are) more vulnerable to change that drastically affects their character than large tracts of countryside further from urban centres. Smith was badly affected by this when the family came down to Lee again on 29 March 1905 and she found that '[t]he beautiful Common here is being turned into a Golf Ground! I am very sorry'.[33] After a walk on the common on 20 April she noted in her diary that 'they have so altered

[29] Hampshire Record Office, Katherine Spear Smith, Nature Notebooks, 19M99/2/1, 1903.
[30] Hampshire Record Office, Katherine Spear Smith, Diaries, 19M99/1/1, April 1903.
[31] Hampshire Record Office, Katherine Spear Smith, Diaries, 19M99/1/1, April 1903.
[32] Hampshire Record Office, Katherine Spear Smith, Nature Notebooks, 19M99/2/1, April 1904.
[33] Hampshire Record Office, Katherine Spear Smith, Nature Notebooks, 19M99/2/3a, 1905.

the Common for Golf, that I hardly care to go there, so much gorse is cut down, and worse still some trees; they have quite spoiled the spot where we sketched last spring, and where it was so beautiful'.[34] Perhaps if Katherine had never known the common in its previous guise, she might have been able to make use of it even in its diminished form as a golf course. But in-between landscapes are fragile in an affective as well as material sense. They are make-dos that 'work' as much because of what they suggest as what they are. Often the suggestion of countryside or wild nature depends on one or two elements and if these are impaired or destroyed, the landscape can lose its affective value. For Katherine, the bright-flowered gorse on Lee Common played an essential role in this respect and even though by early July she noted that the grass was growing on the golf links again, she concluded ruefully that 'it can never be the same again to me'.[35]

However, Katherine's parents and her brother Alic were devoted to her and went to great lengths to accommodate her growing desire to live in a more rural setting. In December 1906 the Smiths moved out to Rickmansworth, in London's northern 'metroland' suburbs, with a good railway link to allow Walter and Alic to commute in to central London every day, but with a 'very pretty' view over Rickmansworth Park. Better still was the countryside nearby: 'The country round (*real* country) is really very beautiful, valleys and rivers, and hills clothed in woods, splendid trees everywhere, and fields and lanes. ... Also I must add, this is a splendid place for birds.'[36] Even from Rickmansworth, however, to reach this countryside was something of an expedition, so she had to make do with the large garden much of the time, hanging coconuts for the tits, putting out a bird box that she hoped the nuthatches would use and watching the blackbirds. She also walked in the park, making the best of its trees and wildlife. She observed animal tracks in the snow in March 1909,[37] for example, and relished the rich autumn colours:

> Today was a glorious autumn day, sun shining, and warm and mild. Went for a walk in the Park. The trees are exquisite now in their autumn colours, better than they have been for several years; and they are earlier turned. The chestnuts are a deep yellow, and the elms pale gold (sometimes a little spoilt by going yellow in patches, while the rest is green), the wild cherries a lovely red, and the hawthorns are most wonderfully shaded with all colours from yellow to red and purple.
>
> Down by the pond are two lovely tall specimens of the Wild Service Tree (Pyrus Torminalis); they have turned a most lovely orange-russet colour flushed with crimson. I hope to study these service trees throughout the year.[38]

[34] Hampshire Record Office, Katherine Spear Smith, Nature Notebooks, 19M99/2/3a, 20 April 1905.

[35] Hampshire Record Office, Katherine Spear Smith, Nature Notebooks, 19M99/2/3a, 9 July 1905.

[36] Hampshire Record Office, Katherine Spear Smith, Diary, 19M99/1/21, July and August 1906. Emphasis in original.

[37] Hampshire Record Office, Katherine Spear Smith, Nature Notebooks, 19M99/2/7, January to March 1909.

[38] Hampshire Record Office, Katherine Spear Smith, Diary, 19M99/1/3a, 17 October 1911.

She was able to take a further step along the spectrum of rurality in July 1911, when her father bought a house for the family at Titchfield in Hampshire. The house had a 'lovely garden of an acre, surrounded by a high red-brick wall' with many fruit trees that were attractive to birds. There was a field the other side of the road, and beyond that a copse and extensive marshes. Both the house and its location had been chosen with Katherine in mind. Initially the house was intended just for the holidays, although the intention was that the Smiths would move there permanently once Walter retired.[39] But with this 'better rural' now available to her, Katherine increasingly spent her time at Titchfield, to the point that when her parents formally relinquished their London home in 1919 (they had shifted back from Rickmansworth to Kensington now that Katherine had Titchfield), it can have made little difference to her.

William Hallam

Johnston and Spear Smith were able to adopt progressively more satisfactory in-between landscapes over time, in his case as a result of professional success, and in hers due to her parents' ability and willingness to respond to her strengthening self-identity as a 'lover of nature'. However, circumstances could shift in the other direction too, forcing people to turn to 'less good' in-between landscapes. Adjusting to this could be a difficult and protracted process. The experiences of William Hallam illustrate this well. Born in the small Berkshire estate village of East Lockinge in 1868, Hallam seems to have had an unusually happy childhood. His father John was Lord Wantage's stud groom, a responsible position of some standing in the community. The Lockinge estate was the subject of a remarkable paternalist experiment instigated by Wantage, a man of staunch High Church Tory convictions. During the late 19th-century agricultural depression, he took many tenant farms in hand rather than allowing the land to go out of cultivation. This helped to maintain agricultural employment on the estate. Wantage also developed extensive craft workshops which again helped to keep employment and wages on the estate at higher levels than would otherwise have been the case. Workers on the estate lived in good quality housing, by the standards of the time, with well-developed social infrastructure including a reading room, club, pub (serving non-alcoholic beverages) as well as an Anglican church and school. While some may have chafed under the tight control Wantage exercised, the Hallam family identified wholeheartedly with Wantage and his paternalist ideals.

Having grown up on the estate and securely ensconced within its social hierarchy, Hallam felt entirely at home in Lockinge and the landscape around it. As a youth and young man, he used to go on long walks across the Berkshire Downs, which extended for miles south, east, and west of the village. A typical example was

[39] Hampshire Record Office, Katherine Spear Smith, Nature Notebooks, 19M99/2/9, 1911.

a 17-mile tramp with his friends George and Lex Whittle to the Uffington White Horse, Wayland's Smithy, and the Blowing Stone, notable local landmarks.[40] He began keeping a diary systematically in August 1886 and initially there are many enthusiastic accounts, full of landscape, historical, archaeological, and natural history detail, of long walks over the downs. However, despite Wantage's patronage of the family and his efforts to maintain employment on the estate, there was no work for Hallam in Lockinge and he was forced, much against his will, to seek employment at Swindon's Great Western Railway Works, the best part of a day's walk to the west.

Hallam started at the Works, then one of the largest industrial undertakings in the world, on 26 May 1891, living initially at 125 Stafford Street and later a few streets away at 60 Kent Road, close to the town centre. He loathed the Works – it was cold and draughty in winter, often too hot in summer, the work itself was both tedious and dangerous (indeed he suffered several serious injuries), he found himself frequently forced to undertake night work, which he particularly disliked, and he detested the factory hooter which woke everyone in the town at what he considered an unjustifiably early hour. Although the pay was not bad by working-class standards, the work was insecure and the shadow of unemployment hung over Hallam throughout the half-century he worked there. His feelings about Swindon as a town were less intensely hostile but for decades his comments about it were nevertheless almost unremittingly negative. He decried some expensive ornamental gates put up by the Council, for example, and thought that the town's one notable sight, the long subway under the railway lines, was bad for the town's morals. In July 1919 he was disgusted that a 'mob of riff-raffs' had burnt down the new flagpole at the Town Hall, and then broken windows in Regent and Bridges Streets, so much so that he inferred the reason the flag on the Institute was flying at half-mast was 'on account of the behaviour in the Town' (but in fact it was because the General Manager of the Great Western Railway had died).[41] Indeed his alienation from Swindon was such that for decades he continued to refer to Lockinge as 'home'.

In view of his enjoyment of rural walks and the cold, antagonistic eye with which he looked on the town, it is not surprising that after moving to Swindon, Hallam began to go on long walks to reach the countryside beyond its built-up area. Among the destinations mentioned in his diary are those marked in Figure 2.3 (walk destinations between 1891 and 1896 marked with a red balloon).

However, much of his walks were taken up with low-quality 'urban fringe' countryside; and even when he did get out into 'real' countryside, it was not the wide open downs that he had on his doorstep at Lockinge. In contrast to the long, enthusiastic descriptions of his walks over the downs from Lockinge, Hallam had little to say about his walks from Swindon in his diary and the few observations he

---

[40] Berkshire Record Office, Hallam Diary, D/EX 1415/1, 26 April 1886.
[41] Berkshire Record Office, Hallam Diary, D/EX 1415/25, 22 and 23 July 1919.

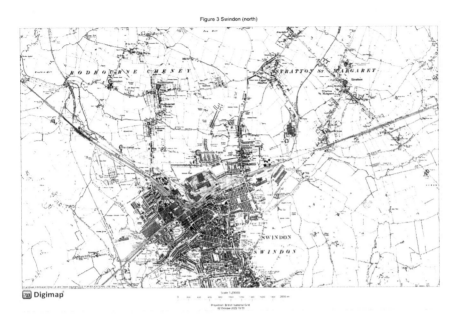

Figure 2.3 Swindon (north). © Crown Copyright and Landmark Information Group Limited (2022). All rights reserved (1925)

does make are often pejorative. 'Jolly hot again and my feet ache' was his summary of a walk round Gorse Hill (scarcely out of Swindon's urban penumbra) on 21 June 1891, while going along the canal a few weeks later on a long walk round Bassett Down, '[t]he blessed flies nearly eat one up'.[42] A walk to Chisledon (to the south of Swindon – not shown on this map) on 4 October elicited the downbeat comment that there were '100 acres of wheat uncut at Burderop', while a 10-mile walk to the same place next year with his friend Austin was 'very muddy'.[43] While these unimpressed tones to some extent reflect Hallam's alienation from Swindon, it also seems clear that neither the town's edgelands nor the flat countryside immediately beyond appealed as strongly as the downs around Lockinge he had walked over so extensively in his youth. Even Bassett Down, the nearest downland to Swindon, was far enough away that although Hallam could just about set foot on the hill, he then had to turn round and go home again.

Marriage and children meant Hallam's diaries stopped for two years. When his diaries resume in 1896, it is evident that there has been a major change – long walks out to the countryside are now conspicuous by their absence. Sometimes Hallam

---

[42] Berkshire Record Office, Hallam Diary, D/EX 1415/2, 21 June and 25 July 1891.
[43] Berkshire Record Office, Hallam Diary, D/EX 1415/2, 4 October 1891 and 6 November 1892.

went on short walks with the children (sometimes accompanied by his wife Sophie) within the town itself but he was rarely able to muster much enthusiasm for these. But during this period when he could hardly get out into the countryside, the garden of 60 Kent Road, where they now lived, offered elements of compensation, as on 20 April 1900, '[a] lovely day again', when he noted in his diary that 'My plum tree is a mass of blossom'.[44] So also did views out to the distant, and now largely inaccessible, countryside, although the anticipated views did not always materialise:

> Hudson and his daughter came up to tea and supper. It was wonderfully clear in the early evening so much so that Hudson said he thought we must be able to see Malvern Hills and he and I went specially along by the Hospital to see but we could not. He has seen them 3 or 4 times in 30 years.[45]

Gradually it became possible to get out into the fields immediately proximate to the town again. Some of the destinations the Hallams reached on these occasions are shown in Figure 2.4, marked with blue circles. Almost invariably these lay on the south side of Swindon, more accessible than the countryside to the north of the town from Kent Road. Westlecot was a favourite destination once the children were able to walk but even this was initially quite an undertaking: 'We started, all of us, to go for a long walk after dinner but when we got to Westlecote [*sic*] it was so hot we were tired and came back across the Common Field.'[46] As the children grew older, longer walks became possible, as far as Wroughton Fields to the south-west of Swindon. Gradually Hallam's comments on the Swindon countryside become more positive, although he still held himself apart from the town itself. On 10 June 1906, for example, the Hallams went for 'a delightful nature study ramble, the children said', across Wroughton Fields.[47] By the 1920s, a stroll over Westlecot Fields could elicit an unreservedly appreciative comment: '[b]eautiful out in the count[r]y and met hardly a soul'.[48]

In principle, Hallam could of course have continued the long walks he used to undertake out to the countryside beyond Swindon's immediate hinterland, to places like Coate, Chisledon or Bassett Down. However, after his wedding he rarely went on walks without Sophie, and after the births of Marjorie (1896), Dorothy (1897) and Muriel (1900), the children accompanied them too. Although once the children were in their teens, they could certainly have gone on long walks with their father, Sophie was less of a walker so even in the later 1910s and the 1920s Hallam rarely ventured further than places such as the old mill stream, Black Horse fields and Wroughton fields. Indeed, by the late 1920s Hallam's range was contracting again. This was partly because he had become a grandfather and some of his walks were now in company not only with Sophie but also Dorothy, her husband and their baby

---

[44] Berkshire Record Office, Hallam Diary, D/EX 1415/3, 20 April 1900.
[45] Berkshire Record Office, Hallam Diary, D/EX 1415/5, 29 June 1902.
[46] Berkshire Record Office, Hallam Diary, D/EX 1415/5, 16 August 1902.
[47] Berkshire Record Office, Hallam Diary, D/EX 1415/10, 10 June 1906.
[48] Berkshire Record Office, Hallam Diary, D/EX 1415/32, 13 May 1928.

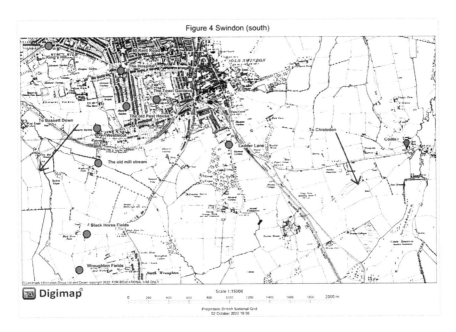

Zoe, as on 13 May 1928 when they all went for a walk across Westlecot Fields. By this time he and Sophie were also growing older – he was 60 in 1928 – and as the years went by, they increasingly resorted to in-between landscapes within Swindon itself as their (especially Sophie's) ability to access the 'real' countryside contracted. Their garden became more and more important again – Hallam particularly appreciated the blossom on their loganberry trees.[49] The Town Gardens (Swindon's principal park) were the other in-between landscape within Swindon's urban envelope that he and Sophie came increasingly to cherish, enjoying especially the rich display of flowers during the summer.[50]

Yet there is a sense that William, and perhaps in some degree Sophie too, missed the aspects of the 'real' countryside that their garden and the Town Gardens did not provide. In his old age, just as he had when the children were too young for rural walks, he sought out in-between landscapes that offered traces or indications of the countryside. Finding old buildings that harked back to a rural past within what had become urban Swindon gave him particular pleasure, as on 28 September 1924 when he successfully located the site of the old Pest House at the back of

---

[49] Berkshire Record Office, Hallam Diary, D/EX 1415/32, 30 May 1928.
[50] Berkshire Record Office, Hallam Diary, D/EX 1415/30, 7 June 1925; D/EX 1415/54, 3 July 1945; D/EX 1415/60, 6 August 1949; D/EX 1415/63, 23 September 1951.

Goddard Avenue (where his daughter Marjorie lived). Similarly on 17 May 1939 he was much interested to look at South Brook Farm: '[t]his house must be I judge 250 years old of stone and stone tiled. 2 or 3 families live in it now for no land attaches to it now in fact it isn't a farm for all the land is built over'.[51]

Some of the most powerful of these traces of the countryside were aural rather than visual – the call of wild birds. Hallam was gladdened one night to hear '2 owls hooting to one another somewhere over Kings Hill way'. But it was the cuckoo's call that meant most to him. He had taken pleasure in it for years but as his ability to access the countryside contracted, the cuckoo's call counted for more, although it did as much to stir up as assuage his ruralist yearnings: 'I heard the cuckoo this morning when I was getting up. I was so pleased the first time Ive [*sic*] heard him this year. A most glorious day today. It makes me long to be living in an old cottage in the country.'[52] The cuckoo's call became even more important to William and Sophie after her severe illness in early 1936, which left her wheelchair-bound. Now they were entirely unable to reach the countryside on their own account, although occasionally Marjorie's husband Bob would take one of them for a drive in his car. During these last years of Sophie's life, William often took her down the rustic Ladder Lane in spring and early summer, hoping to hear the cuckoo.[53]

Although these old-age accounts of in-between landscapes certainly lack the exhilaration of his grand youthful walks over the downs, and the element of yearning for connection with a rural life and landscape from which he has been severed cannot be ignored, a note of contentment also sounds clearly. It had taken many years but Hallam had eventually adjusted to Swindon. The town's in-between landscapes including his own garden, the Town Gardens, traces of the rural past such as South Brook Farm, and auditory links such as the hooting of owls and the call of the cuckoo had played a vital part in this protracted, decades-long process of coming to terms with his 'new' home town. His fluctuating relationship with in-between landscapes shows that circumstances (such as moving to a town, marriage, the birth of children and grandchildren, the onset of disability for oneself or a spouse, and growing old) can force people to move down as well as up the hierarchy of in-between landscapes. Forced moves down the hierarchy, such as when Hallam had to relocate from Lockinge to Swindon, could evidently sometimes be difficult to accept, and were liable to be reversed if (and as soon as) circumstances allowed. Nevertheless, Hallam's experiences also show that where there was no alternative and 'inferior' in-between landscapes had to be accepted, adjustment was sometimes possible, even if this process might take many years and perhaps never be complete.[54]

---

[51] Berkshire Record Office, Hallam Diary, D/EX 1415/45, 17 May 1939.
[52] Berkshire Record Office, Hallam Diary, D/EX 1415/25, 26 May 1917.
[53] Berkshire Record Office, Hallam Diary, D/EX 1415/45, 30 May 1939; D/EX 1415/48, 7 June 1942.
[54] The difficulties all three of the diarists considered here had in adapting to imposed changes in their affective landscapes reinforces Kristin Bluemel's claim in Chapter 3 of this book that the rural 'nostalgia'

Conclusion

Pahl was surely right to reject the concept of an urban–rural continuum as a typology of communities. But although the distinction between urban and rural may have limited utility as a tool of sociological analysis, this has little bearing on its relevance to understanding the affective experience of landscape, which responded more strongly to aspects such as quietness, vegetative cover, wildlife and traces of the past than to the sociological attributes of the communities inhabiting a particular landscape. As the examples given above indicate, what they regarded as rural mattered greatly to many urban people. Put in that way, this is familiar ground – few historians would question the popularity of the countryside as a leisure amenity in the 20th century and the 'outdoor movement' has been studied in depth by scholars such as Taylor, Howkins, Walker, and Edwards.[55] So, too, have efforts to restrict building and infrastructure development in cherished rural landscapes like the Lake District or Cotswolds, even if most recent studies have construed planner-preservationists as self-appointed elitists rather than imperfect spokespeople of a voiceless multitude.[56] By contrast, historians have given less thought to what urban people in whose lives the countryside played a significant affective role did when it was inaccessible, or insufficiently accessible, to them. This is where in-between landscapes came into their own. People for whom the countryside was affectively significant sought out the best in-between landscapes their circumstances allowed them to access; 'best' in this context largely corresponded to what in popular discourse would be construed as 'most rural', although there were certainly differences between people in which elements of the discursive mix that constituted 'countryside' were most significant.[57] For Hallam, for example, historical continuity was important, so somewhere like South Brook Farm retained a rural flavour he cherished, whereas for Johnston, evidence of nature vigorously alive and in motion was more important. 'Less rural' in-between landscapes could

---

of interwar middlebrow novels like Francis Brett Young's *The House under the Water* was a pertinent response to, rather than an evasion of, a characteristic experience of modernity.

[55] Harvey Taylor, *A Claim on the Countryside: A History of the British Outdoor Movement* (Edinburgh, Edinburgh University Press, 1997); Helen J. Walker, 'The outdoor movement in England and Wales, 1900–1939' (unpublished PhD thesis, University of Sussex, 1987); Alun Howkins, *The Death of Rural England: A Social History of the Countryside since 1900* (London and New York, Routledge, 2003); Sian Edwards, *Youth Movements, Citizenship and the English Countryside: Creating Good Citizens, 1930–1960* (London, Palgrave Macmillan, 2017).

[56] Catherine Brace, ' "A pleasure ground for the noisy herds"? Incompatible encounters with the Cotswolds and England, 1900–1950', *Rural History*, 11:1 (2000), 75–94; David Matless, *Landscape and Englishness: Second Expanded Edition* (London, Reaktion Books, 2016). Francesca Church discerns a more democratic 'amenity of approach' in the work of the Council for the Preservation of Rural England: Francesca Church, 'Amenity as educator: Geographies of education, citizenship, and the CPRE in 1930s England', *Geographical Journal*, 185:3 (2019), 258–267.

[57] The sources of these differences, which it is argued were primarily psychological rather than discursive, are explored in Jeremy Burchardt, *Lifescapes: The Experience of Landscape in Britain, 1870–1960* (Cambridge, Cambridge University Press, 2023).

be abandoned quickly and without ceremony when a 'better' rural became available, as when Johnston relinquished Raikes Wood once he was able to move out to 'Annandale' with its large garden and more rural location, or when the Smiths sold their suburban Rickmansworth residence after buying a house in Titchfield, among the fields, woods, and marshes of south Hampshire. In this respect, in-between landscapes functioned quite differently from the edgelands with which they sometimes coincided spatially. Despite their lower profile, however, they may well have played a valued role in more people's lives: as Macfarlane implies, it is unclear how far beyond a small minority of landscape sophisticates the edgelands taste for waste grounds, rubbish dumps and sewage treatment works has ever extended.[58]

In-between landscapes took a wide variety of forms: not only gardens, parks, commons, and other urban green spaces, but less obviously old buildings (or their sites) whose erstwhile rural settings had been swallowed up by urban development, places from which a good view of distant countryside could be obtained and auditory traces or suggestions of the countryside such as the hooting of owls or the call of the cuckoo. Such in-between spaces were pervasive and characteristic features of 20th-century British towns and cities. Seen from one perspective, this further undermines any notion of a sharp distinction between urban and rural: elements of the rural continued to be a major component of the modern urban landscape. From another perspective, however, recognising the existence and significance of in-between landscapes suggests that at least as figured in people's minds (in ways that may have been quite personal and variable, more perhaps than they were socially patterned or discursively constructed), there was very much a rural–urban continuum of affective landscapes. Whichever way we choose to look at it, what was regarded as 'rural' continued to play a vital role in structuring the lived experience of many urban dwellers in 20th-century Britain.

[58] Robert Macfarlane, 'Edgelands by Paul Farley and Michael Symmons Roberts: Review', *The Guardian*, 19 February 2011, www.theguardian.com/books/2011/feb/19/edgelands-farley-symmons-roberts-review#comments [accessed 27 February 2022].

3

Rural Modernity in Britain:
Landscape, Literature, Nostalgia

KRISTIN BLUEMEL

We want the creative faculty to imagine what we know ... we want the poetry of life.[1]
To be truly rural is also to be doomed.[2]

IMAGINATION AND CREATIVITY, the stuff of literature, novels, stories, and poems, provide a framework and foundation for Nan Fairbrother's *New Lives, New Landscapes*.
She begins her appeal for planned landscapes with an invocation of Shelley's
lament about his newly industrial world: 'There is no want of knowledge ... but we
want the creative faculty to imagine what we know: we want the generous impulse
to act that which we imagine: we want the poetry of life.'[3] Fairbrother comments,
'Yet our only hope is exactly that—to *imagine* what we know and to plan creatively
for the future.'[4] Imagination and creativity turn her 'bitter' observation that 'most
of the landscape we still enjoy unreservedly is where the twentieth century has
not yet reached' into the materials of radical hope;[5] without flinching from the real
depredations of her industrial, post-atomic present, she envisions a beautiful, useful
landscape for the Britain of the future. Fairbrother's landscape is an ever-changing
'living entity', an 'interaction of a society and the habitat it lives in'.[6] It not only
promises to provide societies with renewal and revival, but in dialectical fashion,

[1] Percy Bysshe Shelley, quoted in Nan Fairbrother, *New Lives, New Landscapes: Planning for the 21st
Century* (New York, Alfred A. Knopf, 1970), p. 6.
[2] Fairbrother, *New Lives*, p. 42.
[3] Quoted in Fairbrother, *New Lives*, p. 6.
[4] Fairbrother, *New Lives*, p. 6.
[5] Fairbrother, *New Lives*, p. 5.
[6] Fairbrother, *New Lives*, p. 4.

Proceedings of the British Academy, **256**, 37–60, © The British Academy 2023.

invites those same societies to recreate and revive their landscapes. About the past, Fairbrother is less sanguine. She writes:

> [The] past cannot help us. There are no traditions for industrial landscape, nor for mechanised farming, nor pylons in the countryside, nor urban housing in rural areas, nor mass motorised leisure, nor for any of our other new land-uses.
>
> The choice then is not between old and new but between good landscape and bad.[7]

Surveying the derelict, 'bad' landscapes of her society, Fairbrother overlooks an influential tradition, the British rural tradition in literature, which flourished during an earlier post-war period of development and despair. Rural writers of the 1920s and 1930s, many of whom inadvertently contributed to the interwar 'cult of the countryside', bemoaned as they documented the blights upon landscape that Fairbrother assigns to a post-Second World War generation.[8] Seeking to preserve landscape, architecture, community, and social feeling in the face of aggressive urban development of rural lands, their fictions extended into the 1930s ideas popularised in a previous decade by Clough Williams-Ellis's *England and the Octopus* (1928).[9] As we shall see, many of the rural writers examined in this chapter protested destruction and ugliness resulting from what Williams-Ellis called 'this planless scramble'; a few, also like Williams-Ellis, found reason to hope that future decades might bring 'a new beauty from a new and intelligent synthesis of needs and factors'.[10]

---

[7] Fairbrother, *New Lives*, p. 7.

[8] For historical treatments of interwar print culture's impact on the nation's 'image' of English countryside (and countryside as Englishness) see Jeremy Burchardt, *Paradise Lost: Rural Idyll and Social Change in England since 1800* (London, I. B. Tauris & Co., 2002); Malcolm Chase, 'This is no claptrap: This is our heritage', in Christopher Shaw and Malcolm Chase (eds), *The Imagined Past: History and Nostalgia* (Manchester, Manchester University Press, 1989), pp. 128–146; Alun Howkins, 'New countrymen and women', in Alun Howkins, *The Death of Rural England: A Social History of the Countryside since 1900* (New York, Routledge, 2003), pp. 95–111; and Alun Howkins, 'Death and rebirth? English rural society, 1920–1940', in Paul Brassley, Jeremy Burchardt, and Lynne Thompson (eds), *The English Countryside between the Wars: Regeneration or Decline?* (Woodbridge, Boydell Press, 2006), pp. 10–25; John Lowerson, 'Battles for the countryside', in Frank Gloversmith (ed.), *Class, Culture and Social Change: A New View of the 1930s* (Atlantic Highlands, NJ, Humanities Press, 1980), pp. 258–280; David Matless, *Landscape and Englishness* (London, Reaktion Books, 2016 [1998]); and Marion Shaw, 'Cold comfort times: Women rural writers in the interwar period', in Paul Brassley, Jeremy Burchardt, and Lynne Thompson (eds), *The English Countryside between the Wars: Regeneration or Decline?* (Woodbridge, Boydell Press, 2006), pp. 73–86. For more broadly social historical accounts of rural England, see Howard Newby, *Country Life: A Social History of Rural England* (London, Weidenfeld & Nicolson, 1987) and Trevor Wild, *Village England: A Social History of the Countryside* (London, I. B. Tauris, 2004). See Judith S. Page and Elise L. Smith, *Women, Literature, and the Arts of the Countryside in Early Twentieth-Century England* (Cambridge, Cambridge University Press, 2021) for an important monograph on the efforts of women gardeners, writers, and artists to revitalise rather than preserve or regret rural homesteads changed by the crises of modernity.

[9] Clough Williams-Ellis, *England and the Octopus* (London, Geoffry Bles, 1928), commissioned by the Campaign to Protect Rural England (CPRE). See also his edited volume, *Britain and the Beast* (London, Dent, 1937), whose contributors, including G. M. Trevelyan, Patrick Abercrombie, and R. G. Stapeldon, and popular rural writers H. J. Massingham, Sheila Kaye-Smith, and A. G. Street, represented the most influential voices in interwar preservationist discourse.

[10] Williams-Ellis, *England and the Octopus*, pp. 12, 118. See Matless, *Landscape and Englishness*, for a late 20th-century account that finds in Williams-Ellis's writings and the allied work of the early CPRE a commitment to 'preservation and progress, tradition and modernity', p. 31; Nigel Harrison and Iain Robertson, 'Beyond Portmeirion: The architecture, planning, and protests of Clough Williams-Ellis',

This chapter finds hope and wisdom in this literary past, claiming special creative insight and imaginative stature for those rural writers who confronted industrial landscape, mechanised farming, pylons in the countryside, urban housing in rural areas, and mass motorised leisure during the interwar years when Fairbrother was a youth in the West Riding of Yorkshire.[11] In particular, it argues that rural 'middlebrow' literature, represented here by works of Richard Llewellyn, Mary Webb, Stella Gibbons, A. G. Street, Adrian Bell, H. E. Bates, Flora Thompson, and Francis Brett Young, constitutes a uniquely imaginative and creative response to rural modernity in Britain.[12]

In the 1920s and 1930s one could find bestselling books about the countryside that reinforced the idea of a vulnerable and vanishing country England, while other bestsellers represented country England as dynamic and resilient. This chapter focuses on the latter, although for the sake of contrast it begins with an examination of Richard Llewellyn's *How Green Was My Valley* (1939), one of the most potent and most nostalgic of the interwar narratives on rural life and the only one examined here to have been written by an urban author.[13] Llewellyn's bestselling novel, set in a mining town in southern Wales, deserves the subtitle 'Old Lives, Old Landscapes' as it remorselessly forces its hero Huw Morgan to contemplate the extinction of a well-loved, traditional way of rural life on the grounds of an exterminated landscape. Telling the story of seemingly inevitable and irreversible destruction,

in Kristin Bluemel and Michael McCluskey (eds), *Rural Modernity in Britain: A Critical Intervention* (Edinburgh, Edinburgh University Press, 2018), pp. 187–206, for recovery of Williams-Ellis as deserving of recovery for the totality of his interests, architecture chief among them; and John Sheail, *Rural Conservation in Inter-War Britain* (Oxford, Clarendon Press, 1981), for an examination of the social and economic changes that inspired public figures like Patrick Abercrombie and G. M. Trevelyan and voluntary organisations like the CPRE to lead a national rural preservationist movement during the interwar years.

[11] See Samuel Hynes *The Auden Generation: Literature and Politics in England in the 1930s* (Princeton, Princeton University Press, 1976 [1972]) and Valentine Cunningham, *British Writers of the Thirties* (Oxford, Oxford University Press, 1988) for classic accounts of these themes in the works of the youthful Pylon Poets, who acquired their group name from Stephen Spender's 1933 poem, 'The Pylons'. See Matless, *Landscape and Englishness*, Part II, for discussion of a very different group of 1930s ruralist writers who engaged with concerns of land and soil in order to advance regressive myths of 'organic' Englishness.

[12] For one of the first calls to define middlebrow as a cultural category see John Baxendale and Christopher Pawlings, *Narrating the Thirties: A Decade in the Making: 1930 to the Present* (New York, St. Martin's Press, 1996), pp. 48–56. See also Erica Brown and Mary Grover (eds), *Middlebrow Literary Cultures: The Battle of the Brows, 1920–1960* (New York, Palgrave Macmillan, 2012); Kate Macdonald (ed.), *The Masculine Middlebrow, 1880–1950: What Mr. Miniver Read* (New York, Palgrave Macmillan, 2011); Kristin Bluemel, 'Beyond Englishness: The regional and rural novel in the 1930s', in Benjamin Kohlmann and Matthew Taunton (eds), *A History of 1930s British Literature* (Cambridge, Cambridge University Press, 2019), pp. 17–30; and Kristin Bluemel, 'The regional and the rural', in James Smith (ed.), *The Cambridge Companion to British Literature of the 1930s* (Cambridge, Cambridge University Press, 2019), pp. 160–174.

[13] See Chris Hopkins, *English Fiction in the 1930s: Language, Genre, History* (London, Continuum, 2006), pp. 71–72, for a brief biography of Llewellyn, who was born in Hendon, London, and whose real name was Vivien Lloyd.

Huw begins with memories of an idyllic childhood, one in which the smell of his
mother's leek soup is both perpetually, mystically present, and absolutely positive,
conveying 'everything in it that was good'.[14] These comforting kitchen smells are
available through an essential connection between home and garden, through the
'herbs fresh from the untroubled ground' that convey the 'peaceful smell of home
and happy people'.[15] Only when we're 100 pages into the novel do we realise that
Huw, his ancestral home, and his entire village are about to be buried under a vast
pile of black slag. There is no more trenchant image of rural modernity as rural despair than Llewellyn's modern, changing, moving landscape, a dynamic but deathly
'interaction of a society and the habitat it lives in':

> But the slag heap moves, pressing on, down and down, over and all round this house
> which was my father's and my mother's and now is mine. Soon, perhaps in an hour, the
> house will be buried, and the slag heap will stretch from the top of the mountain right
> down to the river in the Valley. Poor river, how beautiful you were, how gay your song,
> how clear your green waters, how you enjoyed your play among the sleepy rocks.[16]

All life in the valley is represented by the 'poor river', once singing and green, now
silent and black. Modern change, in Morgan's fantastic tragedy, means total death
of rural community and tradition, both of which are buried alive in the mechanised
waste of rapacious industrial capitalism. It is the literary equivalent of Fairbrother's
undated photograph of 'Coal-tip on a South Wales hillside'.[17] Fairbrother, like
Llewellyn before her, insists that only those 'fortunates' who have never had to live
with spoil-heaps find them 'exciting'.[18] For those who must live with or, in Huw's
case, under them, it is the 'scenery of violence'.[19]

   A paradox of rural modernity and mass print culture manifests in the materials
of Fairbrother's black and white photo and Llewellyn's black and white type. Their
different visual and verbal forms adopt similar representational rhetorics, protesting
industry's capitalist efficiencies and wasteful technologies through vivid scenes of
rural devastation. Yet it is only through the efficiencies of industrial printing and
cutting-edge technologies of mass production and distribution that these images
and their protests circulated among vast numbers of British readers.[20] Social
historians of interwar Britain observe a similar kind of paradox at work in images
of populous southern rural landscapes, which during the interwar years came to be
seen as playspaces for masses of newly leisured white-collar commuters rather than
workspaces for farmers and agricultural labourers.[21] According to John Lowerson,

[14] Richard Llewellyn, *How Green Was My Valley* (New York, Simon & Schuster, 1997), p. 4.
[15] Llewellyn, *How Green*, p. 5.
[16] Llewellyn, *How Green*, p. 101.
[17] Fairbrother, *New Lives*, p. 97.
[18] Fairbrother, *New Lives*, p. 96.
[19] Fairbrother, *New Lives*, p. 97.
[20] On social effects of interwar publishing innovations, see Chase, 'This is no claptrap', p. 129.
[21] See Howkins, 'New countrymen and women', pp. 95–111, for a good summary chapter on this
development.

'Paradoxically, for many people [the countryside] was the "real" England and the urge to locate oneself within it was strengthened in the 1930s as never before by a powerful current of "countryside" literature'.[22] This countryside literature was not uniform in 'direction, structure or quality',[23] and included everything from rural fantasies like J. R. R. Tolkien's *The Hobbit*, children's books like *Winnie-the-Pooh*, to estate agents' seductive brochures, magazines like *Country Life* and *The Field*, Shell posters, illustrated guide books, and poetry volumes like W. H. Auden's *Look, Stranger!* In all its diversity, this body of literature provided visual and verbal pictures of country England that came to represent the precious, fading rural landscape that these very same images promised to preserve. Both symptom and cause of the cult of the countryside, countryside literature, in Lowerson's words, 'distorted urban vision in such a way as to spread the process of spoliation it had emerged to resist'.[24]

How Green Was My Valley is just one of dozens of middlebrow novels and memoirs that contributed to the paradoxical and distorted relationship city and country people developed with their interwar landscapes. To the extent that Llewellyn's novel urges its readers to rebel against aggressive industrial destruction of rural landscapes, it is an active, positive, critical book. Yet unlike the other interwar books examined in this chapter, and unlike Fairbrother's post-war manifesto, it sets up a false and utterly rigid dichotomy between old and new lives, old and new landscapes. The grief, regret, and nostalgia that saturate *How Green Was My Valley* and that represented for many readers the proper feelings for countryside literature reverberate in the titles or subtitles of late 20th- or early 21st-century histories of rural Britain. Too careless a glance at dramatic titles like *Paradise Lost: Rural Idyll and Social Change since 1800*, *The Death of Rural England*, and *The English Countryside between the Wars: Regeneration or Decline?* can discourage readers from close study of the diverse forms, motivations, aesthetics, and impacts of the literature of rural modernity. We need to seek records of rural people's inspiration from and understanding of rural life *as modern* life; we need to register representations of the rural as the place of *modern* possibility, even the place of progressive industry, nurturing new lives in the new landscapes of interwar Britain.

Literary criticism, book history, rural modernity

The interwar cult of the countryside grew up alongside Britain's dominant art movement of the period, metropolitan modernism, although its proponents rarely

---

[22] Lowerson, 'Battles', p. 260.
[23] Lowerson, 'Battles', p. 260.
[24] Lowerson, 'Battles', p. 261.

engaged directly with modernism's creators.[25] Modernism, conventionally defined, means literature of urban sophisticates, an avant-garde literature of experiment, of European influence, of cosmopolitan sympathies.[26] Any scholar of modernism can rattle off names of modernist artists who vacationed in the Sussex downs or wrote about the Cornish coast or Chiltern Hills, but few could identify modernist writers other than D. H. Lawrence and Thomas Hardy who emerged from and identified with rural communities. Studies of England of the 1930s as a shrinking island or island of romantic moderns have associated Virginia Woolf, T. S. Eliot, and other urbanites with what could be seen as rural modernist art in interwar Britain.[27] This rural modern*ism* is an expression of city vision, of essentially urban ways of seeing. It is for the most part the visitor's or off-comers' representation of rural Britain, one indebted to the structures of perception found in and defined by classical pastoral.[28] Fairbrother associates these same structures with England's non-metropolitan rural literary tradition – that established by 'the Izaak Waltons and Gilbert Whites and Mr. Jorrockes and their modern equivalents'.[29] These are the comfortable, well-shod men and women who had time to stroll about the country rather than work its land.

While Fairbrother implicitly bands together all writers of rural literature, no matter their place, politics, class, or cultural effects, this chapter makes distinctions between the writers of pastoral modernism, leisured rural literature, and the literature of working rural life. It focuses mainly on the latter group of writers, those rural working people who created a literature about rural landscapes in order to represent and investigate their experiences of the modern world. The concept of rural modernity, as opposed to rural modernism or a generic rural tradition, encourages us to find a literature by and for rural workers, those people invested in 'country reality' rather than country ideality, as well as their better-off neighbours and urban visitors.

Modernist or middlebrow, urban, suburban, or rural, British rural literature of any cultural category exists because influential London editors, printers, publishers,

[25] See Kristin Bluemel and Michael McCluskey, 'Introduction: Rural modernity in Britain', in Kristin Bluemel and Michael McCluskey (eds), *Rural Modernity in Britain: A Critical Intervention* (Edinburgh, Edinburgh University Press, 2018), pp. 1–16, for an interpretation of rural literature and culture's relation to the history of modernism and modernity.

[26] See Douglas Mao and Rebecca Walkowitz, 'Introduction: Modernisms bad and new', in Douglas Mao and Rebecca Walkowitz (eds), *Bad Modernisms* (Durham, NC, Duke University Press, 2006), pp. 1–17, for explanation of the ways the New Modernist Studies have reshaped canonical definitions of modernism. The Space Between: Literature and Culture, 1914–1945, a scholarly society that publishes an interdisciplinary journal with the same name, has also exerted a powerful revisionary force upon canonical modernist studies. See https://spacebetweensociety.org

[27] See Jed Esty, *A Shrinking Island: Modernism and National Culture in England* (Princeton, Princeton University Press, 2004) and Alexandra Harris, *Romantic Moderns: English Writers, Artists, and the Imagination from Virginia Woolf to John Piper* (London: Thames & Hudson, 2010). Sam Wiseman's *The Reimagining of Place in English Modernism* (Liverpool, Liverpool University Press, 2015) testifies to the continuing influence of Esty's study.

[28] Bluemel and McCluskey, 'Introduction', pp. 3–8.

[29] Fairbrother, *New Lives*, p. 42.

and booksellers made and circulated books by and about rural places. To re-examine British literature in terms of rural modernity is to grapple with tensions between rural contents and urban production. It is also to grapple with a subtle, slippery terminology (modern, modernism, and modernity), whose confusions are multiplied by the different meanings these words accrue as they cross disciplinary fields. In literary studies, for example, scholars of canonical or 'old' modernism (Yeats, Eliot, Pound, Joyce, Woolf, and so on), would have regarded the popular interwar rural writers as creators of a debased, commercial literature, of potential interest to scholars of 20th-century Britain only to the extent that they offered lessons on a book trade in British heritage.

Recently, the once polarised categories of modernist and middlebrow, urban and rural, national and regional, have come together in literary critical conversations. Neal Alexander and James Moran's edited collection *Regional Modernism* broke new ground with its critique of the conventional notion that modernism is, in the classic view of Malcolm Bradbury and James McFarlane, 'the art of cities'.[30] Also recently, the rural regional novel, an important art form for anyone contemplating the new landscapes of industrialised rural Britain, was revived as a subject for serious literary study in Dominic Head's *Modernity and the English Rural Novel*.[31] Considering novelists from H. E. Bates, Adrian Bell, and Constance Holme to George Orwell, Leo Walmsley, and Henry Williamson, Head sees rural novels' interrogation of 'the apparent disconnection [between the rural tradition and modernisation] as, in itself, a *response* to modernity rather than a refusal to engage with it'.[32] Central to Head's reclamation of rural regional novels is his view that nostalgia can be a critical, not conservative, mode.[33] Head's analysis extends the work of feminist scholar Marion Shaw, who argues that women middlebrow rural writers were unfairly diminished by critics who despised sentiment and nostalgia, regarding these feelings as signs of feminine weakness.[34] Shaw concludes that the

---

[30] Quoted in Neal Alexander and James Moran (eds), *Regional Modernisms* (Edinburgh: Edinburgh University Press, 2013), p. 1. On regional literature, see W. J. Keith, *Regions of the Imagination: The Development of British Rural Fiction* (Toronto, University of Toronto Press, 1988); K. D. M. Snell (ed.), *The Regional Novel in Britain and Ireland, 1880–1990* (Cambridge, Cambridge University Press, 1998); Steven Matthews, 'English regional fiction and national culture', in Patrick Parrinder and Andrzej Gasiorek (eds), *The Reinvention of the British and Irish Novel, 1880–1940* (New York, Oxford University Press, 2011), pp. 506–521; and the classic by Phyllis Bentley, *The English Regional Novel* (London, George Allen & Unwin, 1941).

[31] Dominic Head, *Modernity and the English Rural Novel* (Cambridge, Cambridge University Press, 2017). See key studies on the rural tradition by Glen Cavaliero, *The Rural Tradition in the English Rural Novel 1900–1939* (Totowa, Rowman & Littlefield, 1977) and W. J. Keith, *The Rural Tradition: A Study of the Non-Fiction Prose Writers of the English Countryside* (Toronto, University of Toronto Press, 1974) which appeared during the first wave of widespread environmental awareness and activism. The first decades of the 21st century constitute a second environmental wave, with a concomitant growth of academic attention in all fields on cultural sources, implications, and futures of the Anthropocene.

[32] Head, *Modernity*, p. 1.

[33] Head, *Modernity*, p. 13.

[34] Shaw, 'Cold comfort', p. 78.

fact 'that interwar women's rural novel[s] are cast in a non-modernist form … has much to do with their middle-brow status and readership'.[35] The gendered middle-brow cultural landscape that Shaw outlines and Head fills in is the backdrop against which this chapter works out its materialist methodology. Fairbrother's terms and values invite middlebrow rural writing into our discussions of rural modernity, but it will take new literary critical terms, values, and methods to keep it there, at the forefront of our thinking about rural modernity.

Waterways: Mary Webb and Stella Gibbons

Mary Webb's *Precious Bane* (1924) is the women's rural middlebrow novel that critics most love to hate.[36] Set in Shropshire during the Napoleonic wars, it dramatises rural ambition, retribution, and transfiguring love in sentences whose 'primitive' diction, 'earthy' cadences, and romantic natural imagery earned Webb the endorsement of Prime Minister Stanley Baldwin shortly after her death in 1927.[37] Baldwin's praise catapulted the book to spectacular bestsellerdom, which the award the previous year of the Femina Vie Heureuse Prize had failed to do.[38] Typical of the prose that struck her fans as authentic and her critics as mendacious is this description of the Sarn family's fields in late summer:

> It was a great delight to me, apart from the thought of all this, to look at the standing corn and see it like a great mere under the wind. Times it was still, without a ripple; times it went in little waves, and you could almost think the big bosses of wild onion flowers under the far hedges were lilies heaving gently on the tide.[39]

The speaker is Prue Sarn, good, true, slender, and strong, yet set outside the connections of community and courtship by a 'hare-shotten' lip that also earns her the reputation of being a witch. Prue is 'modern', unwomanly, in her field work but even more so in her pursuit of knowledge. She buys lessons in reading and writing from Wizard Beguildy with every furrow she ploughs for him. This wizard is the

---

[35] Shaw, 'Cold comfort', p. 86.

[36] Mary Webb, *Precious Bane* (Notre Dame, IN, University of Notre Dame Press, 1980).

[37] See Stanford University Libraries, *Mary Webb: Neglected Genius*, https://library.stanford.edu/spc/exhibitspublications/past-exhibits/mary-webb-neglected-genius. Philip Williamson points out that Baldwin's praise for the novels of Francis Brett Young had a similar effect on his sales in the 1930s. Yet as Baldwin made 'abundantly clear', his favourite authors were not English ruralists but Sir Walter Scott and Charles Dickens. See Philip Williamson, *Stanley Baldwin: Conservative Leadership and National Values* (Cambridge, Cambridge University Press, 1999), pp. 244, 251.

[38] In the decade after Baldwin's endorsement, *Precious Bane* sold more than three quarters of a million copies. The English-language Femina Vie Heureuse Prize was awarded annually by a committee of eminent French women writers who chose a work from a list of three that in the opinion of a subcommittee of English women writers had not received 'sufficient recognition'. See Faye Hammill, *Women, Celebrity, and Literary Culture between the Wars* (Austin, University of Texas Press, 2007), pp. 173–175 at 174.

[39] Webb, *Precious*, pp. 212–213.

father of Jancis, a young woman whose rose lips and blond curls earn the love of Prue's brother, Gideon, who is also the story's sin-eater, having pawned his soul for the gift of his father's farm. The fairy tale logic of the novel, with its 'Gold-over' landscape of cowslip, drives the tragic plot to its melodramatic conclusion. Beguildy forbids Gideon his daughter, and when defied by the young couple, sets fire to the Sarn corn ricks and thus the 'golden' harvest that Gideon values above all else. Jancis is renounced by Gideon for her father's crime, and she and her mother disappear in tears and shame from the region. Returning just over nine months later, 'golden Jancis' drowns herself and her and Gideon's newborn son in Sarn Mere, to be followed months later by Gideon himself. Sarn Mere is the vehicle of Prue's corn metaphor, as well as the novel's site of moral justice that dominates the rural landscape that Prue describes as 'the most beautiful thing I'd ever seen'.[40]

Highbrow readers resisted the metaphors and manipulations of Webb's novel, which at its end nearly drowns Prue in the witch's dunking chair before her true love, the weaver Kester Woodseaves, rescues her and turns Sarn Mere into the site of her antagonist's humiliation. The most influential of these resistant highbrow (or higherbrow) readers was Stella Gibbons, a London journalist whose delicious satire of 'loam and lovechild' fictions, *Cold Comfort Farm* (1932), won the Femina Vie Heureuse Prize in 1933.[41] Gibbons's orphaned heroine, Flora Poste, goes to the countryside armed only with her 'higher common sense', quickly tidying up her eccentric Starkadder relatives, parodies of the Sarns. *Cold Comfort Farm* is more comic than *Precious Bane* but its metaphors are no less heavy-handed; at the end of the novel, Flora sends one of her cousins off the farm for a career as a leading man in Hollywood talkies, and another one to Paris in 'the smartest flying kit of black leather'.[42] Flora herself is whisked off in an aeroplane by a modern-day Kester Woodseaves in a self-conscious mirroring of Prue Sarn's romantic elevation by her lover at the end of *Precious Bane*. To discover rural modernity in *Cold Comfort Farm* one just follows its heroine and her machines out of 'deepest Sussex'.

Webb's debts to 20th-century modernity are more subtle than Gibbons's, evident primarily in the material traces of the novel's relations of production and consumption. Written by a woman who was born and raised in Shropshire and whose fierce attachments to the region kept her there for most of her life, *Precious Bane* has earned its place in literary history because Webb negotiated publication through London editors, printers, reviewers, and booksellers. Without London, no Starkadders, but also no Sarns. Rural modernity is evident in *Precious Bane*'s rural themes, characters, setting, and language once they are seen as the effects of

---

[40] Webb, *Precious*, pp. 212–214.
[41] Stella Gibbons, *Cold Comfort Farm* (New York, Penguin Books, 2006). Gladys Mary Coles, *The Flower of Light: A Biography of Mary Webb* (London, Gerald Duckworth & Co., 1978), p. 326, confirms from correspondence with Stella Gibbons that the latter intended to parody the whole genre of rural novel, not specifically *Precious Bane* or Mary Webb's work.
[42] Gibbons, *Cold Comfort*, p. 220.

modern industrial relations: of contemporary literary networks, print technologies, new systems of mass marketing, distribution, publicity, and sales.

Landways: Adrian Bell, A. G. Street, Flora Thompson, and H. E. Bates

More so even than Webb's romantic, nostalgic novels, popular interwar farming memoirs and novels used rural landscapes to measure the aesthetic and emotional costs and gains of rural people's engagements with modernity. Adrian Bell's three-part fictionalised memoir of farming in Suffolk, *Corduroy* (1930), *The Cherry Tree* (1931), and *Silver Ley* (1932) and A. G. Street's fictionalised autobiography of farming in Wiltshire, *Farmer's Glory* (1932), are perhaps the most widely cited texts in this subgenre, admired by scholars for their historical accuracy, cultural authenticity, and putative freedom from sentiment and nostalgia.[43] Yet these texts about rural landscapes freely admit sentiment and nostalgia into their narratives and encourage their modern readers to do so also. For example, Bell's young narrator and fictionalised alter ego, newly promoted from farming apprentice in *Corduroy* to farm owner in *Silver Ley*, visits the neighbouring farmer's daughter for tea. The girl, Emily Jarvis, is consigned to the duty of caring for her aged, deaf father, who in the judgement of the narrator, is 'far from realising … that he had given birth to someone of a different calibre from a would-be farmer's wife'.[44] Emily also judges our narrator, regarding his flight from London and literature into the Suffolk countryside as a 'pity'.[45] Her regret over his lost access to 'the concerts, the art-galleries, the plays' provokes him to reply with anti-modernist conviction:

> 'One can have too much art. One gets so that one longs to see something that isn't spun out of somebody's brain; a field of mangolds, or dawn that an artist daren't paint because it would be called sentimental. Art is in a curious state,' I added—this was a matter on which I felt strongly, and probably wrongly—'when a man isn't allowed to paint a sunset because it is too beautiful'.[46]

---

[43] According to Cavaliero, *Rural Tradition*, p. 105, Street wrote his first novel at the urging of Wiltshire novelist and biographer Edith Oliver who thought he could complement Bell's *Corduroy* with an account of a farmer's life written from 'the inside out'. This is the same Edith Oliver who, in an early book review of Flora Thompson's *Lark Rise* published in *Country Life*, praised the book as 'a little masterpiece of description'. Quoted in Gillian Lindsay, *Flora Thompson: The Story of the Lark Rise Writer* (Headley Down, John Owen Smith, 2007 [1990]), p. 167. Head, *Modernity*, pp. 69, 70, describes Bell as 'the most accomplished of the farmer-novelists' whose trilogy 'comprises "a literary farmscape", rather than a landscape'.

[44] Adrian Bell, *Corduroy, Silver Ley, The Cherry Tree* (London, The Bodley Head, 1936, repr. 1942), p. 37.

[45] Bell, *Silver*, p. 39.

[46] Bell, *Silver*, p. 40.

The style of this writing earned Bell critical praise for his 'honest statement', 'complete authenticity', and 'quiet austerity of language', distancing him from the coy performances of more conventional country writers.[47] In other words, Bell is deemed a good rural writer because his actual and represented flights from the city into Suffolk farming endorse the very modernist aesthetic codes of austerity, simplicity, and irony that his narrator in *Silver Ley* disclaims.

Bell himself might encourage us to question critics' distinctions between rural novels like Webb's and more hard-nosed, tearless memoirs like his own. Surely *Farmer's Glory*, representative of the latter category of good rural books, invites its readers to feel regret over disappearing landscapes of the romanticised past recalled in this passage from its 'Spacious Days' section:

> Sedgebury Wallop is a Wiltshire village on the banks of the river Avon. It is almost untouched by modern improvements, and, save for one eyesore in the shape of a garage, it presents to the passing motorist the same picturesque serenity as to the passenger in the stage coach of years ago.[48]

Almost two hundred pages later, after our author-narrator has described his years farming in northwestern Manitoba, his return home under the influence of First World War patriotism, and his post-war purchase of his father's farm, we find the same kind of nostalgia generated in response to a rural landscape that has abandoned stagecoach landscapes of picturesque serenity through adoption of new farming and transportation technologies:

> Apart from the effects of the depression which was more and more rapidly creeping over the countryside, the actual farming itself lacked romance and charm at this date as compared with pre-war days. Agriculture was becoming mechanized. The horse was disappearing from the landscape, and giving place to the hideous tractor. I did not purchase one of these implements until our old portable steam-engine came to the point in its long and dignified career.[49]

Critics excuse such expressions of Street's desire for countryside romance and charm, affirming his importance as a rural writer of 'unassuming' prose, 'faithful to its subject and full of shrewd comment on rural psychology',[50] while rural and regional writers such as Webb and Sheila Kaye-Smith are often chastised for their implicitly feminine sentimentality. At the level of theme and tone, one is left wondering how much different is Street's resistance to Depression-era tractors and, say, Prue Sarn's dismay over 'these new-fangled days, when strange inventions crowd upon us, when I hear tell there is even a machine coming into use in some parts of the country for reaping and mowing'.[51]

---

[47] Cavaliero, *Rural Tradition*, pp. 109–110.
[48] A. G. Street, *Farmer's Glory* (London, Faber & Faber, 1947 (1956 edn)), p. 58.
[49] Street, *Farmer's Glory*, p. 223.
[50] Cavaliero, *Rural Tradition*, p. 105.
[51] Webb, *Precious*, p. 17.

Like Street's and Bell's memoirs, Flora Thompson's fictionalised memoir of her impoverished childhood in the late 19th-century Oxfordshire hamlet of Juniper Hill offers readers memorable images and resonant symbols of the experience of rural modernity, while like Webb's novel it recreates both individual and collective rural history through a girl's perspective.[52] The heroine of *Lark Rise to Candleford* is Laura Timmins, who we meet as a dreamy, bookish child, destined to be a white-collar clerk working in the Candleford Green post office, rather than the typical farm wife.

If the *Lark Rise* trilogy conveys more warmth and earns more readers than other interwar rural novels and memoirs, it is in part because it ties its images of the landscapes of the recent rural past, vividly remembered but no longer available, to rural childhood. This narrowed childhood vision is communicated through the vocabulary and judgement of that child all grown up and far from home. As a result of this double vision, the novel's rendering of rural modernity is realistic, but also nostalgic, a style emerging from dual structures of feeling evident from *Lark Rise*'s first sentences:[53]

> The hamlet stood on a gentle rise in the flat, wheat-growing north-east corner of Oxfordshire. We will call it Lark Rise because of the great number of skylarks which made the surrounding fields their springboard and nested on the bare earth between the rows of green corn.

> All around, from every quarter, the stiff, clayey soil of the arable fields crept up; bare, brown, and windswept for eight months out of the twelve. Spring brought a flush of green wheat and there were violets under the hedges and pussy-willows out beside the brook at the bottom of the 'Hundred Acres'; but only for a few weeks in later summer had the landscape real beauty. Then the ripened cornfields rippled up to the doorsteps of the cottages and the hamlet because an island in a sea of dark gold.[54]

Certainly the imagery of a 'sea of dark gold' enriching the visual lives of the hamlet residents is nostalgic and idealising. However, Thompson's insistence on the nearly year-round sight of bare brown fields cuts short readers' inclinations to assume the landscape's few annual weeks of 'real beauty' can amply sustain the minds and spirits, let alone the pockets of the Lark Rise labourers and their families. What does sustain them is unceasing work, mutual aid, and a rich oral culture that 'sprang

[52] Flora Thompson, *Lark Rise to Candleford*, intro. H. J. Massingham (London, The Reprint Society, 1945). Oxford University Press first published the separate parts of the trilogy as *Lark Rise* (1939), *Over to Candleford* (1941), and *Candleford Green* (1943).
[53] The influence of Raymond Williams on this reading of *Lark Rise* and on this chapter's understanding of relations between literature and rural modernity more generally will be obvious to those familiar with *The Long Revolution* (London, Chatto & Windus, 1961), *The Country and the City* (Oxford, Oxford University Press, 1973), and *Marxism and Literature* (Oxford, Oxford University Press, 1977). See Richard Mabey, *Dreams of the Good Life: The Life of Flora Thompson and the Creation of* Lark Rise to Candleford (London, Allen Lane, 2014), pp. xvii–xix and pp. 140–150, on the narrative's 'double viewpoints'.
[54] Thompson, *Lark Rise*, p. 15.

direct from the soil'.[55] Acknowledging that 'All times are times of transition',[56] Thompson's narrator avoids the kind of nostalgia that make critics uncomfortable. She may insist that the poor people of her remembered rural Victorian childhood 'were happier' than people of the interwar and wartime radio days who received her books,[57] but she never represents song and skylarks as sufficient to the basic needs of her characters. She tells us in tones free of blame or regret that when Laura and her brother Edmund later read about children 'whose lives were very different from their own, children who had nurseries with rocking-horses and went to parties and for sea-side holidays ... they wondered why they had alighted at birth upon such an unpromising spot as Lark Rise'.[58]

Like *Lark Rise to Candleford*, H. E. Bates's *The Fallow Land* (1932) measures the costs and benefits of an ambivalently valued modernity through woman's work on the land.[59] However, in contrast to Thompson's nostalgic and realistic rural landscapes, Bates delivers only realistic rural landscapes of his native Northamptonshire. His heroine, Deborah Loveday, is a 25-year-old 'town-bred' orphan whose life is transformed when she meets the young farmer Jess Mortimer at the Staveson Fair. Working as a servant to the ugly, bed-ridden, neurotic Mrs Arbuthnot, whose days are filled with whiskey and poetry writing, Deborah finds herself in a matter of months married to Jess and the land that he hates.

> She began to understand the relation of things at the farm very early. She realized that there was and had always been a struggle. She became aware of the existence of the land. The land was something more than the earth; the earth was something vague, primitive, poetic; the land was a composite force of actual, living, everyday things, fields and beasts, seed-time and harvest, ploughing and harrowing, wind and weather; bitterness and struggle; the land was an opponent, a master.[60]

With this and similar passages, Bates might be accused of a grim, heroic, land romanticism, but in his insistence on the difference rural labour makes to ways of rural seeing, and in his imaginative venture into the fields as worker, his novel speaks directly to Thompson's, constructing an alternate, more brutal, comment on the experience of rural modernity.[61]

When Deborah firsts visits the Mortimer farm, she sees the land as landscape, with the eyes of a painter or naturalist, or with the eyes of Bates's narrator who describes the autumnal 'bright colours of trees and hedges, the colours of leaves and hips and haws and spindle-berries fading in the falling light'. 'Admiring the

---

[55] Thompson, *Lark Rise*, p. 52.

[56] Thompson, *Lark Rise*, p. 63.

[57] Thompson, *Lark Rise*, p. 58.

[58] Thompson, *Lark Rise*, p. 40.

[59] Herbert Ernest Bates, *The Fallow Land* (London, Jonathan Cape, 1936).

[60] Bates, *Fallow*, pp. 57–58.

[61] Deborah is 25, born in 1862, so the year Bates's story begins is 1887, aligning his novel with the period covered by *Lark Rise* and *Over to Candleford*. *Candleford Green* begins in 1891, when Laura, like Flora, leaves her hamlet home for town work at the age of 14-and-a-half.

colours', she sees and speaks in the town girl's pastoral similes: 'It's just like a bit of poetry.'[62] Years later, after Jess abandons her and their two sons and she is farmer rather than farmer's wife, she must see the fields as the narrator does in the first paragraph of the novel, without colour, and with a fallow promise that can only be fulfilled through unstinting human labour:

> Half-way across the field the land dipped suddenly away, dropping four or five feet. In winter the rains streamed down the slope, washing out the stones and silting the earth across the hollow in a smooth yellowish drift, and in summer the sun baked the drift to a white crust impressed with the iron-hard footprints of horses and men, and the slope dried out into a belt of white stones and pebbles, the soil thin and shallow.[63]

This is the description of the field that gives the novel its title and guiding metaphor. Fields are left fallow to gather strength, to prevent or repair damages of overfarming by restoring nutrients to the soil. A hope for a better future is implied by fallow fields, as they are signs of intentional human management of agricultural lands with potential for greater productivity. But the Mortimers' fallow field is doomed, described in an anti-pastoral palate of arid yellow, white, and iron. It fails to satisfy human needs for landscape and land, defying the narrator's poetic vision and the farmer's plans for easy ploughing.

  While far from the grinding poverty of Lark Rise's women, Deborah, like them, works ceaselessly. Her hope for a modern rural future, one with more wealth, more land, and more leisure, resides in her children. Her oldest son, David, responsible and loving and destined to inherit the farm, is killed in the trenches of the First World War. The other son, Benjamin, returns healthy and whole from war service, but in thrall to the new machines that have defined his relationship to foreign landscapes. Demobilised in 1919, he eagerly attends a local Agricultural Show where he leads his mother from one gleaming machine to another, 'dragging her from an electric milking-machine to see an electric water-pump and from that to an oil-engine and finally to a tractor working noisily in a cloud of petrol fumes'.[64] Deborah walks in a daze, 'marvelling'.[65] Listening to her son's promises of efficiencies and savings, she agrees to buy a binder that arrives by harvest time. She watches with pride 'as it rattled round and round the golden square of wheat'.[66] Recalling Thompson's 'sea of dark gold', the machine works across a richly coloured patchwork, for a moment turning Deborah's land back into pastoral landscape.[67] When Benjamin's tractor

---

[62] Bates, *Fallow*, p. 49.

[63] Bates, *Fallow*, p. 9.

[64] Bates, *Fallow*, p. 213.

[65] Bates, *Fallow*, p. 213.

[66] Bates, *Fallow*, p. 215.

[67] See William Empson, *Some Versions of Pastoral: A Study of the Pastoral Form in Literature* (London, Chatto & Windus, 1935) for a modernist theorisation of pastoral. See Nick Hubble, 'Transformative pastoral: Lewis Grassic Gibbon's *A Scot's Quair*', in Kristin Bluemel and Michael McCluskey (eds), *Rural Modernity in Britain: A Critical Intervention* (Edinburgh, Edinburgh University Press, 2018), pp. 149–164, for an exemplary reading of a key text of rural modernity as revolutionary pastoral.

later causes Deborah to slip on a 'greasy furrow' and fall in agony to the ground, it is not the symbol of modernity that fails Deborah, the land, or landscape but rather human character. Bates seems to be arguing that the machine cannot save humanity from its traditional foibles of sloth, impulsivity, temper, sexual bias, passion, and drunkenness. It is Benjamin who destroys the reader's desires for narrative reward in terms of revived land or landscape, rural nostalgia or rural romance, as he sells off his portion of the farm to buy a doomed motor-bus partnership, and then disappears into the world of Thompson's radio listeners.

New lives, new landscapes: Francis Brett Young's
The House under the Water

Critics who sort writers into good and bad regionalists, more or less embarrassing ruralists, or more or less authentic countryside writers, tend do so according to schemes of literary value that align with differently valued kinds of nostalgia.[68] Such critics fail to register how all of these nostalgic rural texts, whether about Webb's Prue Sarn with her 'hare-shotten lip' or Street's remembered self with his flat feet, mediate readers' engagements with rural modernity through their material forms and institutional processes. From a book history angle, virtually all English books of the mid-20th century, no matter what their author's origin, regional identity, or proximity to avant-garde practice, were products of city publishers. In a material sense, then, virtually all literature of 20th-century England, and much of 20th-century Britain, is metropolitan literature, the literature of urban modernity. From the same book-historical standpoint, all these London books can be sorted into hierarchies not merely by their contents – the grandeur or 'charm' of their landscapes, the artifice or authenticity of character dialects, the more or less modernist their style – but also by the commercial and social relations implied by the name of a publisher on a title page. Oxford University Press's imprint granted Thompson stature through proximity to academic prestige while Faber and Faber's culturally elevated Street's rural literature through proximity to modernist poet and Faber and Faber editor T. S. Eliot. We should not be surprised that Thompson and Street are today typically regarded as more serious writers, cited in more 'modernist' studies of literature, than authors like Webb or even Bell who were published by more popular or middlebrow houses like Constable, Jonathan Cape, or John Lane, The Bodley Head.

---

[68] Svetlana Boym, in *The Future of Nostalgia* (New York, Basic Books, 2001), similarly sorts nostalgia into two primary types, the 'good' or 'reflective' and the 'bad' or 'restorative' nostalgia. By way of contrast, Matless, *Landscape and Englishness*, p. 35, does not use nostalgia per se as a term of value, questioning the scholarly habit of lumping 'all cultural expressions of ruralism together as representing a simple, nostalgic and conservative longing for a "rural idyll" '.

But no matter how closely allied with academic or popular publishing firms, all the writers considered in this chapter were not rural naïfs but professionals who sold their rural writing to editors who valued it as culture and commodity. To say they worked outside of urban or modernist literary culture is itself a ruralist fantasy.[69] Flora Thompson's biographer, Gillian Lindsay, comments that when Thompson's first published essay appeared in *The Ladies Companion* in 1911, she was 'thirty-five, a self-taught writer and a largely self-educated woman. She was later to be seen as ... someone whose achievements began with *Lark Rise*, but she was consciously developing her literary skills all her life'.[70] Lindsay rightly emphasises the importance of Thompson's editor at Oxford University Press, Geoffrey Cumberlege, to the success of her *Lark Rise* trilogy. Once under Cumberlege's kindly auspices, she never lacked for wise editorial advice, real friendship, or a sure path to publication.[71] The young, untutored H. E. Bates did indeed write his first published novel in the office of a Northamptonshire leather warehouse. But upon his receipt of an acceptance letter from Edward Garnett addressed to 'Miss H. E. Bates', congratulating her on 'her delineation of female characters in a novel called *The Two Sisters*', he was by default working at the centre of London's literary culture.[72] A few weeks after publication of *The Two Sisters* in April 1926, he was invited by Garnett to see the matinée of Sean O'Casey's play *Juno and the Paycock* and then go together by train to Surrey, to spend the weekend in the Garnett's country house, The Cearne. Bates, then 21, was 'nervous and delighted':

> The Cearne was for me already a legend ... Hudson and W. H. Davies and Edward Thomas had walked the lovely commons and woodlands about it; Conrad and Galsworthy and Crane had often met there; the Russian classics ... had all been translated there; D. H. Lawrence had worked in the garden there and thrown plates at Frieda in the kitchen; *Lady into Fox* had been written in the summerhouse among the apple trees.[73]

---

[69] See, for example, the entry for H. E. Bates in the *Oxford Dictionary of National Biography*, Robert Lusty, rev. Claire L. Taylor, 'Bates, Herbert Ernest', *ODNB*, https://doi-org.libproxy.ncl.ac.uk/10.1093/ref:odnb/30796 [accessed 6 Feburary 2022], which claims that H. E. Bates was 'always outside literary circles and untouched by modernism'.

[70] Lindsay, *Flora Thompson*, p. 87.

[71] Lindsay, *Flora Thompson*, p. 163.

[72] Herbert Ernest Bates, *Edward Garnett* (London, Max Parish, 1950), p. 9. This is the same Edward Garnett who believed that Mary Webb's *Precious Bane* would eventually become a bestseller despite disappointing initial sales in 1924, and the same Edward Garnett who supported Francis Brett Young at the outset of his career. Garnett was right to back Bates, Webb, and Young, proving himself an important contributor along with Jonathan Cape to the literature of rural modernity. See Coles, *Flower of Light*, p. 278, and Jessica Brett Young, *Francis Brett Young: A Biography* (London, Heinemann, 1962), pp. 52, 83, 84, 86, 91.

[73] Bates, *Edward Garnett*, p. 21. To say that H. E. Bates was 'always outside literary circles and untouched by modernism' is to underestimate the importance of the London institutional contexts that made him a household name. See Lusty, 'Bates, Herbert Ernest'.

Ever afterwards Bates would earn contracts, publication, and royalties even though his 1930s books about rural life did not earn back their advances.[74] Francis Brett Young is another writer examined in this chapter whose remote homes on the island of Capri and then in the Lake District could not disguise his secure position at the centre of modern literary culture.[75] As early as 1917, when, wounded and ill from military service in the German East African Campaign, he went to Dublin to recover, he was tended by Dr Oliver Gogarty, youthful companion to James Joyce, and met Maud Gonne and A. E. (George Russell). He was already friendly with Poet Laureate Robert Bridges, having published *Robert Bridges: A Critical Study* in 1913, and would come to name as friends Compton Mackenzie, Hugh Walpole, Edward Marsh, J. C. Squire, and Charles Morgan.[76]

Without reference to literary and especially London publishing contexts, critical judgements of British rural writing tend to sway on the vexed questions of taste, including taste for sentimentality, idealisation, and nostalgia. We can see Street gaining historical credibility by mention in Howkins, while Thompson's stature as an 'authentic' rural writer is earned through citation by social historians Wild, Burchardt, and Newby.[77] Literary and art critics Judith W. Page and Elise L. Smith describe her as 'optimistic about the resilience of nature in an increasingly industrialized countryside' but also 'clear-eyed and unsentimental' while Harris respectfully describes the point of *Lark Rise* as 'its density of observation' which implicitly compensates for its nostalgic 'outline of a lost Eden and lost childhood'. Keith in the late 20th century felt compelled to defend Thompson's 'legitimate' position as a 'refreshingly *un*-sentimental' writer of a 'minor classic'.[78] More than a decade later, in a second study devoted to rural literature, Keith attempts to rehabilitate Webb for literary critics who are 'ill at ease with her fiction', describing her as 'one of the most original, possibly idiosyncratic, of regional writers' active during the 'golden age' of regionalism.[79] His contemporary Cavaliero's appreciative treatment of Mary Webb occasionally teeters on the edge of dismissal when

---

[74] It is a perverse irony of commercial fate that Jonathan Cape lost Bates as soon as he became an undisputedly bestselling author with publication of *The Greatest People in the World* (1942), a collection of short stories about the Royal Air Force pilots written under the pseudonym Flying Officer X. Bates adopted as his new publisher Michael Joseph, another London firm and publisher of Richard Llewellyn.

[75] In *Francis Brett Young*, pp. 49–50, Jessica Brett Young recalls that her husband urged his literary agent, J. B. Pinker, to shop around the manuscript of his first novel, *Undergrowth*, to 'one of the newer men (Secker, or Sedgwick, or Daniel and Oliver)'. Martin Secker eventually accepted the book after 13 others had refused it. She comments: 'He [Francis] was in good company: on Secker's list were D. H. Lawrence's *Sons and Lovers*, Compton Mackenzie's *Sinister Street*, and Hugh Walpole's *Fortitude*' (p. 50). Brett Young would never again struggle to get his fiction into print.

[76] Cavaliero, *Rural Tradition*, p. 82. See F. E. Brett Young, *Robert Bridges: A Critical Study* (London, Secker, 1913), co-authored by Francis and Eric Brett Young.

[77] For example, Wild, *Village England*, p. 81, Burchardt, *Paradise Lost*, p. 67, and Newby, *Country Life*, pp. 79–80, while Street's historical credibility is signalled by mention in Howkins, *Death*, p. 39.

[78] Page and Smith, *Women*, p. 85; Harris, *Romantic*, p. 187; and Keith, *Rural Tradition*, p. 255. Emphasis in original.

[79] Keith, *Regions*, pp. 129, 176.

he registers discomfort with her 'sensitivity' and a 'sensibility ... too soft to be convincing'.[80] Shaw, while defending Webb's 'heightened romantic descriptions of landscape', acknowledges that Webb's novels 'trade in nostalgia'.[81] Head grants Street, Webb, and Thompson attention, but hedges his bets on Webb's relative literary value by defending against historians' classification of her as a 'minor writer' while affirming the basis for this diminishing judgement, namely her popularising of 'the idea of the English countryside as a refuge from modernity'.[82]

This brief survey suggests that several decades' worth of literary critical analysis and historical judgements about the value of rural and regional writing may raise or lower an individual writer's reputation or the reputation of a literary genre based on criteria that are structured by the proximate, dominant, but unstated and unexamined values of prestige modernism. Rather than focusing on degrees of sentiment or nostalgia, production of conservative or progressive politics, critics and historians are better served by the question: To what extent does a given literary text or genre *itself* theorise the experience of rural modernity – of a modernity not borrowed from metropolitan centres but actively lived in and lived out as the contemporary real of rural places – through representations of landscapes that, whether developed or preserved at any particular moment, are always dynamic, changing, and at the centre of their own social, economic, and natural networks? Seeking interwar narratives that teach us about rural modernity regardless of affinity with or distance from modernist values liberates us to study books about rural Britain in representational, formal, and book historical dimensions. It sets up terms that encourage examination of a novel by Francis Brett Young, *The House under the Water* (1932), that has earned passing treatment by scholars even as it exemplifies the best practices of rural and regional writers who responded and contributed to British readers' understanding of the disorienting experiences of rural modernity.[83]

Brett Young's thinking, mediated through forms and materials that destined his book for middlebrow markets and readers, achieves what few modernist books could aspire to: mass consumption by a popular audience whose devoted and immersive reading of *The House under the Water* brought them into sympathy with realistic contemporary rural landscapes felt to be part of the modern world. Brett Young's representations of English and Welsh landscapes drive the narrative's grand drama of modernity – the development in the late 19th century of the Elan Valley Reservoirs along the River Elan (River Garon in the novel) to

---

[80] Cavaliero, *Rural Tradition*, pp. 141, 142.

[81] Shaw, 'Cold comfort', p. 80.

[82] Burchardt, *Paradise Lost*, quoted in Head, *Modernity*, pp. 5–6. See Coles, *Flower of Light*, for description of Webb's increasingly erratic and off-putting behaviors that damaged her relations with her publishers, particularly Cape, who took on Webb and *Precious Bane* in 1923 hoping for a bestseller. Webb may have generated within English mid-century literary and book cultures a personal legend powerful and negative enough to influence even her posthumous critical reputation.

[83] Francis Brett Young, *The House under the Water* (London, Heinemann, 1932).

supply Birmingham (North Bromwich) with clean drinking water – as well as its intimate human dramas of family and community life.

Brett Young's extraordinary literary career began with his co-authorship with his brother of the novel *Undergrowth* in 1913, his invaliding out of the Royal Army Medical Corps in 1917, his publication of over 30 novels and books of short stories, autobiography, travel, criticism and epic poetry through the 'modernist' decades, and his death in Capetown, South Africa, in 1954.[84] *The House under the Water* is one of the most famous of his Mercian novels, all of which play out against the rural landscapes of the Welsh Marches and West Midlands. Brett Young's ability to create drama out of his characters' perceptions and interactions with rural place is evident in novel after novel; here for example is his description in *House under the Water* of his young adult heroine, Phil's, return to her home Nant Escob located deep in a mountain valley of Forest Fawr after four years spent finishing her education in an Italian convent:

> As the train approached Pont Escob the rain which had kept them company all day stopped suddenly, and the leonine shape of Forest Fawr rose out of the plain. It was huge and meek and incredibly soft, like some great kind monster. The sun broke out on the tops and the mountain smiled as though it welcomed her, and Phil, too, smiled eagerly.[85]

In this passage of what Gibbons would regard as ruralist purple prose, Brett Young's tamed forest modifies many other images in the book of the forest as enraged, antagonistic, intent on deception, drownings, and murder. And in each instance, whether kindly or ferocious, the landscape is not mere backdrop but symbol and interpretation of the human emotion experienced in its foreground. Compare, for example, the above scene of late adolescent return to Phil's 'dreamlike … moment of arrival' at the impressionable age of 13:

> She didn't feel, as Tregaron [her father] had felt, that she had been there before, or that she was taking possession. It was the other way round: the place took possession of her. Completely and instantly. At the sight of the house and the great ash standing before it she knew that no other place in which she had ever been mattered at all. She belonged to Nant Escob; from that moment she would always belong to it.[86]

This is a representation of place attachment captured through literary manipulation of particular details that recreate a distinctive rural locality for readers urban, sub-urban, or rural. In a plot that leads characters from Worcestershire fields to Welsh hills, South Africa's gold mines, Italy's heat, Coventry's streets, and back to the valley of Nant Escob, the fulfilment of Phil's 691-page quest for love is predicted by her youthful shared attachment to the mountainous place that the neighbouring farmer Evan Vaughan also loves. The mountain's smile in the scene above brings

---

[84] Cavaliero, *Rural Tradition*, pp. 81–92.
[85] Brett Young, *House*, p. 268.
[86] Brett Young, *House*, p. 97.

back Vaughan's words to her: '"*I always knew that I should come back and end my days here.*" Now, more than ever, Phil understood what he felt. She had come home. She hoped she would never again go away.'[87] Poor Phil is destined to go away again, the tempestuous, careless Tregaron intent as always on asserting himself through defiance of the wishes of neighbours and traditions of ancestors. He sells his lands to the North Bromwich Corporation which has been authorised through an Act of Parliament to dam up the River Garon near its source in order to 'slake the thirst of North Bromwich and the Black Country's millions'.[88] As the engineer Charles Lingen explains to Phil from a vantage point high above the river:

> Seventy-five million gallons a day, and another thirty of compensation water! We can see the whole plan from here. ... 'Do you see that farm there—Cwm Gwilt? You probably know it.'
>
> She nodded. 'Of course. Ivor Morgan is one of our tenants.'
>
> 'Well, the first dam will run just below it: a hundred and thirty feet above the river-bed. Then another one, slightly lower, blocks the mouth of the Afon Llwyd; and the third, which is bigger than either of the others, will lie right across the jaws of Dol Escob, above Trenant. Can't you see that God made this valley for that and for nothing else?'[89]

This vision of rural modernity, of a sophisticated system of dams and aqueducts built in the mountains in order to satisfy the growing population of England's third largest city, fills Lingen with enthusiasm and Tregaron with riches, as the latter serves to gain 250,000 pounds sterling from sale of the lands that his family has held for 800 years. Phil, in contrast, is devastated:

---

[87] Brett Young, *House*, p. 168.

[88] Brett Young, *House*, p. 472. Brett Young does not represent the vitality or diversity of Welsh reaction to English planning and damming of the Elan Valley. In this he followed Thomas Barclay, *The Future Water Supply of Birmingham*, 3rd edn, rev. and enl. (Birmingham, Cornish Brothers; London, Simpkin, Marshall, 1898), web, www.icevirtuallibrary.com [accessed 6 February 2022], whose biases are immediately evident from this fulsome dedication: 'To Edward Lawley Parker, Esq., J.P., Alderman and sometime Mayor of the City of Birmingham, during whose Mayoralty the Birmingham Corporation Water Bill was Promoted by the City Council, who rendered conspicuous Service during the Parliamentary Campaign, which resulted in the Bill being carried into Law, and upon the Death of Sir Thomas Martineau, was unanimously chosen to occupy the highly onerous and honorable Position of Chairman of the Water Committee.' Brett Young anticipated 21st-century accounts of the history of the dam which paper over any local or national efforts to defy the engineers. See, for example, the soothing narrative of the dams' construction told at https://www.elanvalley.org.uk/discover/reservoirs-dams/birminghams-water [accessed 6 February 2022]. Sheail, *Rural Conservation*, pp. 39–40, does not mention preservationist activity around the Elan or any other Welsh dams, but does record the words of the Scottish Secretary of State who in 1941 'referred to "the vehemence, and indeed violent controversy" which had surrounded the question of hydro-electric power in the Highlands'. Some 50–60 years after King Edward VII and Queen Alexandra opened the Elan dams in 1904, resistance to the flooding of the village of Capel Celyn in north-west Wales as part of the Tryweryn scheme to provide Liverpool with water became a focal point for Welsh nationalism. See Ed Atkins, 'Building a dam, constructing a nation: The "drowning" of Capel Celyn', *Journal of Historical Sociology*, 31:4 (2018), 455–468.

[89] Brett Young, *House*, pp. 472–473.

The company of the doomed valley haunted her; for even at its loveliest (and, indeed, it had never been lovelier) it seemed aware of the impeding destruction and increasingly eager, as are nations shuddering under the blows of war, to assume in the article of death an exaggerated show of permanence. That sublime and pitiful illusion sustained her in a tenor of life too high-pitched to be real, when, leaving the house ... she wandered away to the company of her mute fellow-victims, the river, the meadows rosy with sorrel, the patient woods. Brooding over them there in the thunder of Cabn Mawrion – so soon to be stilled! – she contrived to discover a certain melancholy ecstasy in the happiness of their fate compared to her own.[90]

The romance, the sentimentality, the nostalgia of this scene are undeniable. Rather than providing evidence of Brett Young's failure to employ the dispassionate, highbrow vocabulary of abstracting experimental modernists, these qualities are evidence of a cultural production that aims through the mediating cycles of urban publishing – in this case through the editorial, production, and distribution activities of William Heinemann, Ltd. – to attract a middlebrow readership interested in buying a specific kind of literary experience. Brett Young's sentences combine a fearless embrace of vocabulary from lowbrow melodrama ('doomed valley', 'haunted' heroine, 'lovelier' and 'loveliest' landscape) with a sophisticated ironic narrative stance that asks us to regard Phil's sublime suffering as 'pitiful illusion', an expression of an unreal 'tenor of life', as 'contrived' emotion. This is a modern, though not modernist, narrative form. It is delivered and mediated by dual romance plots determined by Phil's love of rural place and Phil's love of men who inhabit that place: her half-brother Rob, the engineer Lingen, the farmer Vaughan. Phil and the reader are rewarded with happy endings to both plots, but neither resolution is worked out in predictably pastoral or preservationist terms.

Key to the vision of rural modernity communicated by *The House under the Water* is the character of Phil's brother Rob. Having been cruelly banished by his father from the Welsh family farm he manages so well, Rob is rewarded by Coventry's modern urban economy for his interest in new technologies. He invents patents improving the safety bicycle that is all the rage and then finds a business partner who supports his inventions with factory production. Bicycles lead to motor cars and both bring Rob satisfaction, social affirmation, wealth, all sanctified by love and marriage to his youthful love interest, Janet Delahaye. Rob and Janet take in the displaced Phil before she finds her way back to Glan Elan, Dol Escob, and Nant Escob, the latter now covered by nearly 120 feet 'of the purest water in England'.[91] Phil, by age 30, anticipates trauma upon trauma, grief upon grief, when approaching a first sighting of her drowned house. Instead, she finds 'two shining lakes' lying over her home that bring her torn heart a sense of peace and redemption.[92] The new landscape suggests to Phil that despite the cost of 'unimaginable massacre' of unknowing animal life and loss of thousands of acres of arable and grazing land,

---

[90] Brett Young, *House*, p. 489.
[91] Brett Young, *House*, p. 474.
[92] Brett Young, *House*, p. 680.

'the spirit of Forest Fawr, resurgent, inviolable, had perfected, out of man's dis-figurement, a new loveliness surpassing any that conscious man could achieve'.[93] This is indeed an image of 'a new earth, if not a new heaven',[94] an insistence on the possibility of revival in the face of engineered death. Brett Young's story is more documentary than fable, finding sources of hope in the dialectical possibility of rural landscape and human development even as it denies any naïve faith in pastoral retreat. In contrast to Llewellyn's nostalgic fictional Welsh elegy, *The House under the Water* urges readers to reject the idea that rural places are 'mute fellow-victims' of modernity, but rather will originate, respond to, and survive social and economic changes, with their own sources of defiance and resilience.

The forms of Brett Young's books, from their sentences to their beautiful navy blue covers and simple gilt colophon of three pears, signal to devoted readers a promise of immersion in particulars of regional rural landscapes. These readers wanted to realise, among other things, feelings of nostalgia and sensibilities as soft as those attributed to heroine Phil. Brett Young reminds us that the 'hard' and difficult prose of modernism is not the only or best way to represent the hard and difficult experience of modernity. Like Webb, Bell, Street, Bates, and Thompson, Brett Young chose to represent landscapes which shaped and were shaped by rural people's struggles and innovations in the face of modern changes.

Rural nostalgia

The concept of rural modernity assumes that rural people create, consume, and respond to diverse forces and ideas of modernity: of industrialism, modernisation, standardisation, mass culture and media, including the media of popular books about rural Britain. Such creativity is best represented by the popular literature of rural regional writers, who pursued literary careers through publication of middle-brow texts read by ordinary, non-academic, non-elite readers. Contributing to a rural literary tradition conventionally separated from modernism by aesthetic form, aim, and endorsement, the popular literature of rural modernity emerged from the pens and typewriters of people who identified themselves with rural homes and communities, encountering, inventing, and circulating modernity in forms and media that differed from those adopted by their contemporaries, the culturally pres-tigious metropolitan modernists.

Literary scholars interested in British experiences of modernity have scorned these writers in part because they fear their rural nostalgia and its suspect origin in the 'incurably sentimental mind' with which Brett Young self-consciously graces his heroine Phil Tregaron.[95] Malcolm Chase and Christopher Shaw would argue

---

[93] Brett Young, *House*, p. 680.
[94] Brett Young, *House*, p. 680.
[95] Brett Young, *House*, p. 324.

we are right to be wary of nostalgia. They begin *The Imagined Past: History and Nostalgia* with the epigraph, 'Of all the ways of using history, nostalgia is the most general, looks the most innocent, and is perhaps the most dangerous'.[96] Chase and Shaw emphasise that modern nostalgia does not retain its traditional meaning of homesickness because 'the home we miss is no longer a geographically defined place but rather a state of mind'.[97] Similarly, literary critic Linda M. Austin traces the 'metamorphosis of nostalgia from an occasional disease (of displaced soldiers during wartime) to a cultural aesthetic—a way of producing and consuming the past'.[98] In her parenthetical allusion to displaced soldiers, Austin reminds us that nostalgia was first seen as an illness *of place* that beset people who could be cured by movement to another place. Nostalgia was a debilitating homesickness or place-sickness.

   Austin's gaze upon an English nostalgic aesthetic of rural representation, her construction of nostalgia as, in part, a problem of place, and her challenge to those who think of nostalgia as a specially debased form of modern consumption and repetition, places her at the theoretical centre of this chapter's reclamation project. Also central is the work of cultural geographer Alastair Bonnett, whose *Geography of Nostalgia: Global and Local Perspectives on Modernity and Loss* is concerned with the politics, rather than aesthetics, of nostalgia.[99] Together, Bonnett and Austin make the case that nostalgia's origins as an illness of displacement throw into question its contemporary status as a debased effect of modern feeling or of modernity more generally. There is substantial opposition to this approach. Boym, for example, writes that nostalgia is 'coeval with modernity', Peter Fritzsche claims 'nostalgia stalks modernity as an unwelcome double', and Bruno Latour imagines 'the modern time of progress and the anti-modern time of "tradition"' as 'twins who fail to recognise one another'.[100] In contrast, Bonnett insists that study of place, not merely time past, present, and future, still matters for our understanding of nostalgia and its politics. Surveying social theorists and historians from Boym, Fritzsche, and Bruno Latour, to Karl Marx, Nadia Atia and Jeremy Davies, H. G. Wells, Lowenthal, Doreen Massey, Chase and Shaw, Bonnett does not try as others have to '*rescue* nostalgia for progressive politics'.[101] Rather, he presents 'nostalgia as a disruptive and unsettling force; something that has the power to

---

[96] Malcolm Chase and Christopher Shaw, 'The dimensions of nostalgia', in Christopher Shaw and Malcolm Chase (eds), *The Imagined Past: History and Nostalgia* (New York, Manchester University Press, 1989), pp. 1–17 at 1.

[97] Chase and Shaw, 'Dimensions', p. 1.

[98] Linda M. Austin, *Nostalgia in Transition, 1780–1917* (Charlottesville, University of Virginia Press, 2007), p. 2.

[99] Alastair Bonnett, *The Geography of Nostalgia: Global and Local Perspectives on Modernity and Loss* (New York, Routledge, 2016).

[100] All quoted in Bonnett, *Geography*, p. 4.

[101] Bonnett, *Geography*, p. 1. Emphasis in original.

question standard political labels and distinctions between "progressive" and "reactionary", radical and conservative, left and right'.[102]

If Bonnett is correct and nostalgia is necessary, ubiquitous, and global and that 'nearly everyone [is] in some kind of nostalgic relation to the world',[103] it is not only scholars of rural modernity who need to examine nostalgia and the forms, subjects, and genres of art that are presumed to 'naturally' evoke it. We all do. Rather than suggesting as Fairbrother does that 'to be truly rural is also to be doomed',[104] such revaluation of nostalgia and its relations to rural landscapes and rural literature may produce a new kind of theoretical confidence in the claims of rural people to full participation in British modernity.

---

[102] Bonnett, *Geography*, p. 1.
[103] Bonnett, *Geography*, p. 1.
[104] Fairbrother, *New Lives*, p. 42.

4

Seeing like a Quarryman: Landscape, Quarrying, and Competing Visions of Rural England along Hadrian's Wall, 1930–1960

GARETH RODDY*

Introduction

IN 1930, NEWS began to spread that an engineer from Darlington called John F. Wake planned to commence quarrying operations in the vicinity of Hadrian's Wall. Wake had leased the mineral rights for five miles of land near Melkridge, a village in southwest Northumberland. Using the name Roman Stones Ltd., Wake intended to extract whinstone, a basaltic rock that made excellent material for road building, and under existing ancient monuments legislation his quarry was permitted to extend to up to 10 feet from Hadrian's Wall.[1] Wake's quarry proved controversial because it was to be located between the curtain wall and the Vallum, in the middle of the old Roman frontier system.[2] His proposal also drew widespread attention to the nearby Cawfields and Walltown quarries, which were situated on the line of Hadrian's Wall. These quarries became the focus of passionate debates about landscape, employment, community, and the national interest between 1930 and 1960.

Cawfields Quarry opened in the 1890s and Walltown Quarry, which was also known as Greenhead Quarry due to its proximity to Greenhead village, opened in

* I am grateful to Professor Paul Readman and Dr Jeremy Burchardt for inviting me to present at the third Changing Landscapes, Changing Lives symposium in October 2021; to the generous audiences of the Environmental Humanities Research Group and the Institute of Humanities Research seminar at Northumbria University in 2022; and to Professor Matthew Kelly for his insightful comments on several drafts. The archival research for this paper was supported by a Leverhulme Trust Early Career Fellowship.
[1] Stephen Leach and Alan Whitworth, *Saving the Wall: The Conservation of Hadrian's Wall 1746–1987* (Stroud, Amberley, 2011), pp. 18–20.
[2] The Vallum is an earthwork that runs parallel to the curtain wall, situated to the south.

Figure 4.1 Cawfields Quarry and the Whin Sill escarpment, pictured in 'Road from the Great Whin Sill', *Mine & Quarry Engineering* (January 1937). Courtesy of the Scottish Mining Museum

1876. They belonged to a series of quarries situated along the Whin Sill, a horseshoe-shaped layer of dolerite stretching from Durham along the Eden Valley, the North Pennines escarpment, and the South Tyne Valley to Alnwick and the Farne Islands (see Figure 4.1).[3] This tabular sheet of igneous rock formed when magma rose from deep within the earth 295 million years ago, before cooling and solidifying between layers of limestone, sandstone, and shale. Over millions of years the softer layers of rock eroded, producing the Whin Sill escarpment on which the Romans strategically positioned their frontier wall from AD 122. But this landscape is not merely a once-Roman frontier; it was (and remains) a quarried landscape, too, and these histories have always been intertwined. According to the British Geological Survey, around 500 dolerite, limestone, and sandstone quarries are known to have existed within 10km of Hadrian's Wall, seven of which bear inscriptions made by quarrymen from the Roman period.[4]

We can trace some of the major contours of medieval and modern British history by following quarried stone and repurposed Roman stone, which provided building materials for 7th-century abbeys at Monkwearmouth-Jarrow and Hexham (15 miles east of Haltwhistle) as Christianity spread across the Anglo-Saxon kingdoms. After the Norman Conquest, the 12th-century 'boom' in the construction of stone buildings can be seen in Newcastle and Carlisle cathedrals, Lanercost Priory (7.5 miles west of Greenhead village), and the castles at Thirlwall (half a mile north of Greenhead), Newcastle, and Carlisle. After the Jacobite rising

---

[3] This landscape description is adapted from A. R. Chown, Inquiry Report, 21 November 1960, p. 2, The National Archives, Kew (hereafter TNA), WORK 14/2662.
[4] Kathleen Emily Ann O'Donnell, 'Quarries of Hadrian's Wall: Materials and logistics of a large-scape Imperial building project' (unpublished PhD thesis, University of Edinburgh, 2020), p. 18.

(1745–1746), this landscape once again became the site of a major infrastructural project – the Military Road – which used parts of Hadrian's Wall as its foundation. In the late 18th and early 19th centuries, the spike in the demand for quarried limestone (used as a soil improver), was connected to the need for greater yields in response to land enclosure and the Napoleonic Wars.[5]

In the 19th and 20th centuries, the transformations of the British economy and society had their foundations in quarried stone. Commercial quarries increased their output of stone, aggregates, and mortar in response to the growth of urban centres and a rapidly expanding transport network of railway lines, roads, viaducts, and harbours. The products of the quarrying industry also supported the steel, iron, and chemical industries, expanding until the middle decades of the 20th century, when mechanisation boosted output as the number of workers and firms declined.[6] Whinstone from the quarries at Cawfields and Walltown provided material for highways including part of the M6 motorway near Penrith (opened in 1958), as well as for building stone, railway ballast, aerodrome runways, slabs and kerbstones, and paving setts (see Figure 4.2). Walltown stone was also used to build the RAF Depot near Harker Bridge (1941), the Ministry of Supply's Missile Test Centre at Spadeadam (from 1956), and the Atomic Energy Authority's nuclear site at Sellafield. Cawfields and Walltown quarries played an important role in the creation of new landscapes that constituted a distinctive rural modernity.

However, our current understanding of the quarrying debates (1930–1960) is shaped by a perspective from which Hadrian's Wall is the defining feature of the landscape. From this perspective, the 19th- and 20th-century history of the area is a success story of protection, preservation, and the development of a systematic approach to rural conservation in Britain.[7] This history has its roots in the mid-19th century, when antiquarians such as John Collingwood Bruce and John Clayton conducted pioneering work to protect, excavate, reconstruct, and disseminate knowledge of the wall. Their work was bolstered by the increasing involvement of the state in the ownership and protection of ancient monuments from the late 19th century. When local working people are acknowledged as part of this history, it is for their role as labourers supporting excavations at nearby sites such as Corbridge Roman Town (1906–1914).[8]

By the 1920s, parts of the wall were scheduled as an ancient monument and legislative protection was eventually extended to the surrounding landscape in the central rural sections in the years following the Ancient Monuments Act (1931) and

---

[5] O'Donnell, 'Quarries of Hadrian's Wall', pp. 58–82.

[6] Thomas Bennett Spires, 'An historical geography of the British quarrying industry, c.1850–1950' (unpublished PhD thesis, Manchester Metropolitan University, 2002), pp. 10–11, 167–168, 172–182.

[7] John Sheail, *Rural Conservation in Inter-War Britain* (Oxford, Clarendon Press, 1981), pp. 53–57, 60–62.

[8] 'Extraordinary Exploration: The Edwardian Discovery of Coria', exhibition of photographs at Corbridge Roman Town (English Heritage), opened 7 April 2022.

Figure 4.2 A sett maker at work, pictured in 'Road from the Great Whin Sill', *Mine & Quarry Engineering* (January 1937). Courtesy of the Scottish Mining Museum

the first Roman Wall and Vallum Preservation Scheme (published in 1938).[9] The development of the landscape-as-heritage continued in the post-war period, when the Countryside Commission published the Dartington Amenity Research Trust report (1976) and the Hadrian's Wall Consultative Committee's strategy document (1984), which called for more coherent management of the monument as a whole.[10]

---

[9] Christopher J. Young, 'Hadrian's Wall: Conservation and archaeology through two centuries', in Roger J. A. Wilson (ed.), *Romanitas: Essays on Roman Archaeology in Honour of Sheppard Frere on the Occasion of his Ninetieth Birthday* (Oxford, Oxbow, 2006), pp. 203–210; Alison Ewin, *Hadrian's Wall: A Social and Cultural History* (Lancaster, 2000); Leach and Whitworth, *Saving the Wall*; Richard Hingley, *Hadrian's Wall: A Life* (Oxford, Oxford University Press, 2012), pp. 177–200.

[10] Dartington Amenity Research Trust, *Hadrian's Wall: A Strategy for Conservation and Visitor Services* (Cheltenham, Countryside Commission, 1976); Hadrian's Wall Consultative Committee, *Strategy*

In 1987, the management of Hadrian's Wall entered a new phase when the curtain wall and associated forts, milecastles, the Vallum, and a surrounding buffer zone became a UNESCO World Heritage Site (WHS), which since 2005 comprises one part of the Frontiers of the Roman Empire WHS alongside the Antonine Wall and the German Limes.[11]

The prevailing historical narrative of the quarrying debates emphasises the important role played by antiquarians, archaeologists, and historians such as F. G. Simpson, G. M. Trevelyan, T. Parker Brewis, Ian Richmond, Eric Birley, R. G. Collingwood, and groups such as the Newcastle Society of Antiquaries, who alerted the general public to the quarrying 'threat' in articles and letters published in newspapers such as *The Times*.[12] The efforts to restrict quarrying and save the wall also relied on the work of government officials such as George Lansbury and W. G. A. Ormsby-Gore,[13] F. J. E. Raby and Eric de Normann,[14] and Charles Peers and P. K. Baillie Reynolds.[15] Together, these individuals and groups raised public awareness of Hadrian's Wall and its historical importance, successfully redirected and restricted the quarries, negotiated compensation payments for the sterilisation of land, and ultimately ensured the preservation of the wall and its surroundings in the atmospheric and aesthetically treasured central rural sections.[16]

The existing scholarship has improved our understanding of the campaign to save Hadrian's Wall, but as a history of landscape transformation it is incomplete because it echoes the planner-preservationist assumptions epitomised by the Scott Report (1942) and Nan Fairbrother's *New Lives, New Landscapes* (1970), which

---

for Hadrian's Wall (Newcastle upon Tyne, Countryside Commission, 1984). Conflicting priorities of different sites along the wall are discussed in Robin Birley, *Vindolanda: A Roman Frontier Fort on Hadrian's Wall* (Stroud, Amberley, 2009).

[11] For the management of Hadrian's Wall since its inscription as a World Heritage Site, see Peter G. Stone and David Brough (eds), *Managing, Using, and Interpreting Hadrian's Wall as World Heritage* (London, Springer, 2014); Sophie Turley, 'Hadrian's Wall (UK): Managing the visitor experience at the Roman frontier', in Myra Shackley (ed.), *Visitor Management: Case Studies from World Heritage Sites* (Oxford, Butterworth-Heinemann, 2000), pp. 100–120; Gary Warnaby, Dominic Medway, and David Bennison, 'Notions of materiality and linearity: The challenges of marketing the Hadrian's Wall place "product"', *Environment and Planning A*, 42 (2010), 1365–1382; an interview with Rob Collins, 'Roman walls, frontiers and public archaeology', in K. Gleave, H. Williams, and P. Clarke (eds), *Public Archaeologies of Frontiers and Borderlands* (Oxford, Archaeopress, 2020), pp. 37–54.

[12] A table summarising the contents of these letters is included in Lindsay Allason-Jones and Frances McIntosh, 'The wall, a plan and the Ancient Monuments Acts', *Museum Notes* (2011), 267–276 at 272–273.

[13] First Commissioner of Works, 1929–1931 and 1931–1936, respectively.

[14] Assistant Secretary at the Office of Works, 1927–1948 and 1943–1954, respectively.

[15] Chief Inspector of Ancient Monuments, 1913–1933 and 1954–1961, respectively.

[16] John Charlton, 'Saving the wall: Quarries and conservation', *Archaeologia Aeliana*, 5:33 (2004), 5–8; Allason-Jones and McIntosh, 'The wall, a plan and the Ancient Monuments Acts'; Ewin, *Hadrian's Wall*, pp. 42–44; Matthew Symonds, *Hadrian's Wall: Creating Division* (London, Bloomsbury Academic, 2020), pp. 151–154; Hingley, *Hadrian's Wall*, pp. 255–261; Leach and Whitworth, *Saving the Wall*, pp. 18–60; Jim Crow, *Housesteads: A Fort and Garrison on Hadrian's Wall* (Stroud, Amberley, 2004), pp. 137–140.

considered non-agricultural industry 'an unsightly intrusion' in the countryside and detrimental to the wellbeing of rural communities.[17] What is missing is a detailed account of the arguments made in favour of the quarrying industry in Haltwhistle, Greenhead, and the surrounding area. It has been suggested that evidence of local opinion is scant, providing only a 'rare glimpse' of attitudes that must be speculated about or assumed.[18] However, this chapter shifts the focus away from prominent antiquarians, archaeologists, preservationists, and national press coverage, and instead recovers the voices of the local landowners and quarry managers, trade union representatives, quarry workers, their families and neighbours, and their allies in the Haltwhistle Rural District Council (RDC).[19]

Their voices are best understood using Tim Ingold's concept of the 'taskscape', which describes the environment as experienced through dwelling and working, in contrast to an aesthetic appreciation of landscape as 'scenery viewed from afar'.[20] Approaching the quarrying debates in this way reveals an alternative idea of rural England based on an understanding of land inseparable from its use, in which the rural and the industrial overlapped. From this perspective industries such as quarrying sustained the rural community, and the preservation of Hadrian's Wall brought change and destruction. Building on recent work in art history that explores quarries as sites of rural modernity,[21] this chapter deepens our understanding of the quarrying debates by recasting a success story of preservation as a conflict between incompatible visions of the English countryside, Roman history, and the national interest.[22] It does so by foregrounding the voices of those who resisted the creation of a new, planned rural landscape that prioritised 'farming and … amenity, including recreation', and found no place for industries such as quarrying along Hadrian's Wall.[23] Furthermore, recovering local voices broadens our knowledge of

[17] *Report of the Land Commission on Land Utilisation in Rural Areas*, Cmnd 6378 (1942); Nan Fairbrother, *New Lives, New Landscapes* (London, Architectural Press, 1970), quotation at p. 313.
[18] Leach and Whitworth, *Saving the Wall*, pp. 68–69. This comment is made with reference to John Parker, *Cawfields Quarry and Railway* (Washington, TUPS Books, 2008).
[19] Leona J. Skelton takes a similar approach in her history of regeneration and environmentalism along the River Tyne. Leona J. Skelton, *Tyne after Tyne: An Environmental History of a River's Battle for Protection, 1529–2015* (Winwick, The White Horse Press, 2017), chapter 8.
[20] Quotation from Katrina Navickas, 'Luddism, incendiarism and the defence of rural taskscapes in 1812', *Northern History*, 48:1 (2011), 59–73 at 72. Also see Katrina Navickas, 'Conflicts of power, landscape and amenity in debates over the British Super Grid in the 1950s', *Rural History*, 30:1 (2019), 87–103 at 95. The taskscape is outlined in Tim Ingold, 'The temporality of landscape', *World Archaeology*, 25:2 (1993), 152–174, and Tim Ingold, *The Perception of the Environment: Essays on Livelihood, Dwelling and Skill* (London, Routledge, 2000), p. 198.
[21] Samuel Shaw, 'Weighing down the landscape: The quarry as a site of rural modernity', in Kristin Bluemel and Michael McCluskey (eds), *Rural Modernity in Britain: A Critical Intervention* (Edinburgh, Edinburgh University Press, 2018), pp. 69–83.
[22] The taskscape has been criticised for emphasising the harmony and coherence of the landscape. See Doreen Massey, 'Landscape as provocation: Reflections on moving mountains', *Journal of Material Culture*, 11 (2006), 33–48 at 41–43. This article emphasises the conflicts that emerge when different rhythms of the landscape come into contact.
[23] Fairbrother, *New Lives*, p. 222.

embodied experiences in the landscape, and this research offers important insights to historians of the environment, heritage preservation, and the expanding remit of the state in matters of landscape planning in Britain and internationally.[24]

This chapter focuses on four flashpoints in the quarrying debates, when two ways of seeing the landscape collided. First, it examines the conflict in the 1930s, when Wake announced his plans for the quarry near Melkridge, and competing claims were made about whether creating local jobs or preserving an ancient monument of national historical significance was in the best interests of 'the people'. Second, after economic depression stifled the demand for stone, the next conflict flared from around 1938, when the urgency of rearmament and the Second World War empowered the arguments against restricting Cawfields and Walltown quarries, which now claimed to represent the 'national interest'. Third, the chapter considers two failed attempts to extend the life of Walltown Quarry, in 1954 and finally in 1960, when a public inquiry was held in the village of Haltwhistle amid the decline of heavy industry and depopulation in the South Tyne Valley. The testimonies given at the inquiry, though they failed to secure an extension for the quarry, articulated the rural-industrial taskscape and associated the quarrying industry with the life of the community and the preservation of rural England.

Quarrying, employment, and the protection of ancient monuments, 1930–1934

In the months after Wake's quarrying proposals became public knowledge, a deluge of passionate letters appeared in the press.[25] In April 1930, a letter in *The Times* from the Society of Antiquaries of Newcastle upon Tyne declared that group's opposition to Wake's quarry, and their stance was endorsed by the president of the Society of Antiquaries of London. The chairman of the National Trust's executive committee recommended that parliament intervene in the matter, and this drew public support from the Council for the Preservation of Rural England.[26] In the interwar period, the rate of ribbon development, growth in motorcar use, and destruction of the English countryside alarmed preservationist groups, as conservation became a matter of

---

[24] Paul Betts and Corey Ross (eds), *Heritage in the Modern World: Historical Preservation in Global Perspective* (Oxford, Oxford University Press, 2015). For the turn to exploring embodied experiences of the 'Hadrian's Wall' landscape, see Robert Witcher, Divya P. Tolia-Kelly, and Richard Hingley, 'Archaeologies of landscape: Excavating the materialities of Hadrian's Wall', *Journal of Material Culture*, 15:1 (2010), 105–128 at 119–122; Robert Witcher, 'Fabulous tales of the common people, part 2: Encountering Hadrian's Wall', *Public Archaeology*, 9:4 (2011), 211–238; Claire Nesbitt and Divya Tolia-Kelly, 'Hadrian's Wall embodied archaeologies of the linear monument', *Journal of Social Archaeology*, 9 (2009), 368–390. These works build on Christopher Tilley, *The Materiality of Stone: Explorations in Landscape Phenomenology* (Oxford, Berg, 2004).

[25] Several examples have been collected in an album of newspaper cuttings at Northumberland Archives, Woodhorn (hereafter NA), SANT/PRI/8/15.

[26] Allason-Jones and McIntosh, 'The wall, a plan and the Ancient Monuments Acts', 272–273.

urgency for 'rural elegists' such as G. M. Trevelyan.[27] The agitation intensified in relation to Hadrian's Wall, which was revered by classically educated statesmen, scholars, and artists as a grand physical vestige of Britain's classical inheritance – a material manifestation of the Roman foundation on which modern British civilisation had been built – and the reimagined classical past became central to the state's ideas about civic duty and national reconstruction after the First World War.[28] In this instance, at the heart of the issue was the inadequacy of the Ancient Monuments Act (1913), which protected a scheduled monument's adjoining land for the purposes of fencing, covering, and otherwise protecting and accessing it. Crucially, the existing legislation did not protect the wider surrounding landscape.[29] In a letter to *The Times*, Trevelyan highlighted the inadequate legislative protection for Hadrian's Wall, and the call for stronger ancient monuments legislation was endorsed in letters from the president of the British Academy, a group of historians, and the Women's Institute, and the geographer Vaughan Cornish suggested that the affected area be made a National Park.[30] In the current literature, the details of these responses are well known, and opinions at odds with those described above are deemed 'exceptional'.[31] However, this section reveals that such 'exceptional' voices were in fact numerous.

The most comprehensive case for the new quarry was made by Wake himself, who provided detailed descriptions of his preparations in his correspondence with the Office of Works in 1930. Wake provided a collection of reports and papers that set his quarry into the wider context of national road maintenance and growing motor transport use. He estimated that there were 2–2.5 million vehicles on British roads and the number 'is rapidly increasing'. Accordingly, expenditure on roads in Britain had risen from £17,242,454 in 1918–1919 to approximately £60 million by 1929–1930, and Wake argued that stone of the highest quality was essential for building safe roads and keeping maintenance costs low.[32] To bolster his case, Wake sent a copy of a report made by Dr Knight, chief engineering assistant to the Metropolitan Borough of Deptford, which confirmed that the whinstone at the proposed quarry site was of the very highest quality, in contradiction to claims made in the press 'practically stating that all whinstone is alike'.[33]

---

[27] For a detailed discussion of Trevelyan, whose family estate was at Wallington Hall, Northumberland, see David Cannadine, *G. M. Trevelyan: A Life in History* (London, Fontana, 1993), pp. 141–179.

[28] Ana Carden-Coyne, *Reconstructing the Body: Classicism, Modernism, and the First World War* (Oxford, Oxford University Press, 2009), especially chapter 1.

[29] In June 1930, the Law Officers of the Crown advised the Office of Works to this effect. 'Opinion of the Law Officers of the Crown', 16 June 1930, TNA WORK 14/1257.

[30] Allason-Jones and McIntosh, 'The wall, a plan and the Ancient Monuments Acts', pp. 272–273. Vaughan Cornish also set out the case for National Parks in *National Parks and the Heritage of Scenery* (London, Sifton, Praed & Co., 1930) and *The Preservation of our Scenery* (Cambridge, Cambridge University Press, 1937).

[31] Leach and Whitworth, *Saving the Wall*, p. 20.

[32] 'Notes on road finance and output of road materials with probable future requirements' (1930), TNA WORK 14/1258.

[33] Letter, John F. Wake to Office of Works, 1 September 1930, TNA WORK 14/1258.

Furthermore, while the proposed quarry site drew public attention because of its position between the wall and the Vallum, it comprised just one part of Wake's scheme. After the stone was quarried it would be treated at the Blackett sidings in Melkridge, while concrete flags, sills, curbs, and pipes as well as tar and bitumen materials for road making and roofing would be produced at a third site near Scotswood Bridge. Wake had also secured a site at Redheugh, Gateshead, for shipping purposes.[34] Setting out the full extent of his preparations enabled Wake to argue that his scheme would bring direct employment 'over these various districts', and 'indirectly other men will find employment and a good deal of work will be created' in the steel, iron, and engineering trades.[35] At the same time, should his scheme be stopped, Wake warned that 'a considerable amount of permanent work for men will be lost', his investment wasted, and the opportunity squandered to provide a business 'of interest to the whole community'.[36] Wake's case was widely reported in the local and regional press. In April 1930, an article in *Blyth News* quoted Wake at length, and claimed that 'work will be found for 500 men if the scheme is permitted'.[37] In the *Haltwhistle Echo* (hereafter *Echo*), Captain Frederick Charles Wake found a broader audience for his father's claim that the quarrying scheme would be 'of benefit to the whole community', and added that 'it is quite erroneous to talk of "vandalism" ' because '[w]e shall not interfere with Roman remains'.[38]

Wake's description of his enterprise as a creator of new jobs met with the preservationist counter-argument that quarrying was a destructive force in the landscape. In a statement to the Office of Works on 21 February 1930, Parker Brewis argued that the surroundings of Hadrian's Wall should 'be held immune from industrial enterprises', and that quarrying at Cawfields had destroyed part of the wall 'and the spirit of the place is lost'.[39] As these two ways of seeing the landscape collided, competing claims emerged about what would be in the interests of the people. For Wake and his supporters, the contention that the new quarry would benefit the 'whole community' referred to the Haltwhistle district, where direct and indirect employment would be created in communities dependent on extractive heavy industries such as quarrying and coal mining. From their perspective, the quarrying industry was not a destructive force, but part of a process of land and work that produced the spirit of the place. This was a worked landscape; a taskscape of quarries and coal mines, as well as gasworks, mills, lime kilns, and brickworks. Wake's quarry,

---

[34] Letter, John F. Wake to Office of Works, 25 April 1930, TNA WORK 14/1257.

[35] Letter, John F. Wake to Office of Works, 25 April 1930, TNA WORK 14/1257.

[36] Letter, John F. Wake to Office of Works, 20 February 1930, TNA WORK 14/1257.

[37] 'Quarrying promoter denies any danger', *Blyth News*, 17 April 1930, p. 6. Wake's own claim was that employment would be found for 200 men in the district.

[38] *Haltwhistle Echo*, 18 April 1930, NA SANT PRI/8/15.

[39] Minute sheet, statement from Parker Brewis, 21 February 1930, TNA WORK 14/1257. Parker Brewis also described a meeting in which there was 'a strong feeling that our local press is soulless', given their support for Wake's scheme: Letter, Parker Brewis to Charles Peers, 3 April 1930, TNA WORK 14/1257.

therefore, was not simply a question of employment and raw materials but a matter of community.

In the interwar period, the rural-industrial communities of the Haltwhistle district were threatened by the precarious state of heavy industry, and in November 1928 more than 600 men and lads employed at the local South Tyne Colliery were served their notices, with arrangements made to work on a day-to-day basis.[40] By contrast, in July 1930 a report by the Cawfields branch secretary of the Amalgamated National Union of Quarrymen and Settmakers indicated that 'there are plenty of orders for crushed stone' and setts, and in June 1931 it was reported that the quarry was 'working overtime' to supply their orders.[41] With demand high and trade seemingly booming at Cawfields Quarry at the same time that the local collieries threatened to close, the prospect of a new quarry opening nearby was very appealing.

In contrast, the preservationist argument bemoaned the 'disfigurement' of the English countryside and articulated a compelling claim to the national interest.[42] The Bishop of Durham said in a sermon that quarrying near the wall would bring 'disfigurement' that 'would involve a national loss of a most serious kind, and inflict a lamentable wound on the reputation of the English people'.[43] Similarly, the chairman of the National Trust's executive committee, John Bailey, acknowledged that employment for 'a certain number of men' could not be dismissed out of hand, but questioned 'whether their work is of a nature to injure and not to benefit the country'.[44] Even with local or regional employment at stake, it was widely supposed that this issue was trumped by the need to protect Hadrian's Wall, which was part of the national historical inheritance.

Nevertheless, the importance of local employment was acknowledged by the Labour government's First Commissioner of Works, George Lansbury.[45] Lansbury visited Hadrian's Wall in April 1930 to investigate the situation, and he sought compromise wherever possible. On the one hand, the Labour government was under pressure from the preservationist lobby to oppose Wake's quarry, Lansbury was the cabinet minister responsible for historic monuments, and in 1929 he worked alongside the Minister of Agriculture Noel Buxton and Prime Minister Ramsay

---

[40] 'South Tyne colliery to close down', *Newcastle Journal*, 17 November 1928, p. 16; 'South Tyne colliery', *Newcastle Journal*, 1 December 1928, p. 9.

[41] 'Branch reports. Cawfields', *Settmakers' and Stoneworkers' Journal*, 1 July 1930, p. 5; 'Branch reports. Cawfields', *Settmakers' and Stoneworkers' Journal*, 1 June 1931, p. 5.

[42] The idea of 'disfigurement' was applied by preservationists to a wide range of changes taking place in the countryside. For example, see Paul Readman, 'Landscape preservation, "advertising disfigurement", and English national identity, c.1890–1914', *Rural History*, 12:1 (2001), 61–83.

[43] *Blyth News*, 12 May 1930, p. 5.

[44] *The Times*, 12 April 1930, p. 13.

[45] For the development of the Labour Party's interest in the countryside, see Clare V. J. Griffiths, *Labour and the Countryside: The Politics of Inter-War Britain, 1918–1939* (Oxford, Oxford University Press, 2007).

MacDonald to establish the National Parks Committee.[46] On the other hand, Lansbury's political instincts were of the left. He came from a working-class background and experienced unemployment earlier in life when his family emigrated to Australia in 1884, where he eventually found work as a stone breaker. After returning to Britain, he was appointed to the Poor Law Commission (1905–1909) and was elected as a Labour MP for the first time in 1910. Between 1912 and 1922 Lansbury was editor-proprietor of the Labour-supporting *Daily Herald*, and in 1929 he sat on the committee appointed to find a solution to the growing unemployment problem.[47]

During his visit to Hadrian's Wall Lansbury spoke with Wake, who reiterated his argument that 'a lot of poor people want jobs, and we can give them jobs'.[48] Wake also enjoyed the support of the local landowners Sir Hugh and Lady Blackett, who would benefit financially from the further exploitation of the mineral wealth of their land. Moreover, Sir Hugh was reticent about the idea of making Hadrian's Wall a protected and preserved monument for the enjoyment of the public, because he worried that increased footfall across his land might interfere with his sporting rights.[49]

Lansbury also spoke with a group of people who, according to the *Echo*, 'urged the local employment side of the quarry question'.[50] These people included William Straker, the secretary of the Northumberland Miners' Association; R. J. Taylor, the chairman of the Haltwhistle local Labour Party; and 'a deputation of quarrymen'.[51] We do not know the exact phrasing of their petitions to the minister on this particular day, but shortly afterwards the Haltwhistle Labour Party passed a resolution on the subject and forwarded it to Lansbury. 'We urge the Government', it declared, 'to give immediate consent for quarrying to be commenced in view of the need for employment, believing as we do that the principal portions of the Wall can be preserved without danger by quarrying operations'.[52] Back at the wall, the *Echo* reported that, hearing the arguments in favour of 'local employment', Lansbury replied with a twinkle in his eye: '[y]ou are in favour of a capitalistic monopoly exploiting and destroying the countryside?'[53] It was becoming clear that the

[46] John Mair and John Delafons, 'The policy origins of Britain's National Parks: The Addison Committee 1929–31', *Planning Perspectives*, 16:3 (2001), 293–309 at 295–297. Lansbury set out his vision for rural England, and mentioned his involvement in the National Parks Committee, in *My England* (London, Selwyn & Blount, 1934), pp. 59–60.
[47] John Shepherd, 'Lansbury, George', *Oxford Dictionary of National Biography*, https://doi.org/10.1093/ref:odnb/34407 [accessed 31 May 2022].
[48] 'Move to safeguard Hadrian's Wall. Mr. Lansbury's inspection the outcome. A hint of agreement', *Yorkshire Post and Leeds Intelligencer*, 24 April 1930, p. 8.
[49] These concerns were discussed in a memo detailing Clifton Brown's conversation with Lady Blackett, 9 March 1933, TNA WORK 14/1260. Raby also mentioned this in a letter to D. L. Paton at the Valuation Office, 6 April 1933, TNA WORK 14/1262.
[50] *Haltwhistle Echo*, 25 April 1930, NA SANT/PRI/8/15.
[51] Wake confirmed that Lansbury met a 'deputation of quarrymen', who attested to the superior quality of the whinstone in the area: letter, John F. Wake to Office of Works, 1 September 1930, TNA WORK 14/1258.
[52] Quoted in Letter, George Lansbury to Ramsay MacDonald, 9 May 1930, TNA WORK 14/1257.
[53] *Haltwhistle Echo*, 25 April 1930, NA SANT/PRI/8/15.

quarrying debates had produced an unusual coalition that crossed class divisions, including landowners, quarry owners, quarry workers, union representatives, and the local Labour Party.

Despite Lansbury's quip, he was quoted in the *Evening World* with a sincere message of compromise. Combining the preservationist language of amenity with 'the workmen's point of view', Lansbury thought it possible to find an agreement that would 'please not only those who wish to preserve historical amenities, but also those who are anxious to get on with the job of providing work'.[54] Lansbury acknowledged that he was 'charged with a certain degree of responsibility in regard to the relief of Unemployment' in a note to his secretary,[55] and shortly after his visit to Hadrian's Wall he wrote to Prime Minister Ramsay MacDonald proposing that Wake be allowed to quarry in a restricted area, which would provide jobs in a district 'badly hit by trade depression' while reducing the amount of compensation payable by the state for the sterilisation of the remaining land.[56] With the added promise of further legislative protection for the remainder of the wall, Lansbury thought that 'even the archaeologists might feel that their claims had been reasonably met'.[57]

In the press, however, the spirit of compromise typically yielded to more extreme views on both sides, which pitted the relative worth of ancient monuments against the value of bread and butter in the present. In December 1930, an article in the *Leeds Mercury* condemned Lansbury for 'staving off and delaying the provision of employment by a large new quarrying enterprise because it happened to be in the vicinity of the Roman Wall'. Adopting the language of development and progress, the article insisted 'it is the forward-looking men who keep this England going' and concluded emphatically that 'we prefer men to monuments'.[58] Similarly, in 1933 the *Settmakers' and Stoneworkers' Journal* took the unambiguous position that '[i]f ancient things or geographical features are to interfere with men and women earning a living they must go to the wall, and rightly so'.[59] The public debate over Wake's proposed quarry led directly to the 1931 Ancient Monuments Act, which gave the First Commissioner of Works the power to produce preservation schemes and pay compensation to landowners and mineral rights holders to protect the settings of ancient monuments from damage. Accordingly, work began on the Roman Wall and Vallum Preservation Scheme, and the Office of Works reached a compromise with Wake on the nature and extent of his quarrying operations, which were, in principle, allowed to proceed.

---

[54] 'State officials view north's Roman wall', *Evening World*, 23 April 1930, TNA WORK 14/1257.
[55] George Lansbury, note to secretary, 28 May 1930, TNA WORK 14/1257.
[56] The 'sterilisation' of a landscape prevents its mineral resources from being extracted.
[57] Letter, George Lansbury to Ramsay MacDonald, 9 May 1930, TNA WORK 14/1257.
[58] 'Why not export old houses?', *Leeds Mercury*, 13 December 1930, p. 6.
[59] 'Rant about quarrying operations', *Settmakers' and Stoneworkers' Journal*, 1 October 1933, pp. 1–2. The journal was published by the Amalgamated National Union of Quarryworkers & Settmakers.

However, in 1931 the immediacy of the conflict faded when struggling heavy industries were hit by economic crisis during the Great Depression, Haltwhistle and the surrounding area suffered excessive unemployment, and Wake was unable to finance his new quarry. Work ceased at Cawfields in August 1931 when the Newcastle Granite and Whinstone Company went into voluntary liquidation, and although the quarry reopened in 1932 under the management of the Alston Limestone Company, orders for roadstone fluctuated and workers were suspended during periods of low demand.[60] In 1931 the South Tyne Colliery (which employed over 500 men) closed, followed by the Plenmeller Colliery (over 300 men) in 1932, and the Housing Committee of Haltwhistle RDC was preoccupied by matters relating to poor living conditions and overcrowding.[61] The extent of the hardship is indicated by statistical evidence collected in the *Ministry of Labour Reports of Investigations into the Industrial Conditions in Certain Depressed Areas* (1934). The report for the West Cumberland and Haltwhistle area, compiled by J. C. C. Davidson, demonstrates that economic depression and industrial decline affected rural, as well as urban, communities.[62] The unemployment rate for insured men in Haltwhistle stood at 57.3 per cent in April 1934, which accounted for 779 men, 60 per cent of whom had been claiming for more than 12 months (the national figure for those claiming for over 12 months was 26 per cent). The figures for Haltwhistle are remarkably high, but they represented a significant improvement on the figures for November 1931, when 1,101 men were on the Branch Office unemployment register.[63] The report also cited Cumberland County Medical Officer Dr Fraser, who raised concerns about the effects of prolonged unemployment in the region, including elevated levels of rickets and eye conditions among malnourished children, higher than average infant and maternal death rates, and a rise in cases of pulmonary and non-pulmonary tuberculosis.[64]

In the report's prefatory letter to the Minister of Labour, Davidson demonstrated some understanding of the taskscape when he noted that the inhabitants were 'most deeply attached' to the land. Davidson drew on his own observations and

---

[60] For an account of the fluctuating fortunes of Cawfields Quarry at this time, see 'Editorial', *Settmakers' and Stoneworkers' Journal*, 1 August 1931, p. 1; 'Cawfields', *Settmakers' and Stoneworkers' Journal*, 1 September 1932, p. 5; 'Cawfields', *Settmakers' and Stoneworkers' Journal*, 1 December 1932, p. 5; 'Cawfields', *Settmakers' and Stoneworkers' Journal*, 1 September 1933, p. 5.

[61] Haltwhistle RDC. Housing Committee meeting minutes, 1938–9, NA LHA/A/2/9.

[62] In 1921, 336,485 people in rural areas were employed in coal mining and quarrying. Alun Howkins, *The Death of Rural England: A Social History of the Countryside since 1900* (London, Routledge, 2003), p. 98.

[63] John Colin Campbell Davidson, *Ministry of Labour Reports of Investigations into the Industrial Conditions of Certain Depressed Areas. 1 – West Cumberland and Haltwhistle* (London, HMSO, 1934), pp. 10–12, 24–26.

[64] Davidson, *Ministry of Labour Reports*, pp. 32–33. The Ministry of Health, however, questioned whether elevated levels of disease and infant mortality were caused by prolonged unemployment: 'Notes of the Ministry of Health on report of an investigation into the industrial conditions in Cumberland and Haltwhistle', August 1934, TNA HLG 30/49.

on the Manchester University Investigators' *Industrial Survey of Cumberland and Furness* (1933), whose remarks also applied to the Cumberland and Haltwhistle area. The *Industrial Survey* explained that the worker in Cumberland and Furness feels 'strongly attached to his own hills and valleys' and 'his home place'. As a result, the policy of 'transference' tended to fail because workers could not contemplate leaving their place of dwelling for the purpose of work; the two were coexistent. This observation is borne out by the statistics for Haltwhistle, which show that between July 1932 and May 1934 only 16 men – mostly 'colliery or quarry workers' – were transferred to employment in other districts. Instead of transference, Davidson recommended developing and re-establishing small industries in Haltwhistle itself, the possibility of which was 'directly resting upon the raw materials of the area'. The reserves of stone and coal meant that Haltwhistle was 'not strictly "derelict" but it is so severely depressed as to come near to inclusion in that category'.[65]

From the outbreak of the quarrying debates in 1930 the preservation of Hadrian's Wall and the surrounding landscape was a contested issue. The calls for quarrying restrictions were far from unanimous, and the acknowledgement of the landscape as a working environment was evident at the local level, by central state actors such as Lansbury and Davidson, and in the press. The experiences of hardship in the 1930s, and the inseparable union of place and work, shaped subsequent attempts to extend the life of the Cawfields and Walltown quarries.

Quarrying in the national interest, 1938–1945

From around 1938 the quarrying debates were transformed by the expansion of Britain's 'warfare state'.[66] The demand for stone from Cawfields and Walltown rose sharply in connection with the state's growing expenditure on the Royal Air Force during rearmament and the Second World War. By 1939 aircraft structure weight production was 15 times higher than in 1935, and in 1940 British aircraft production was unequalled.[67] The quarries provided stone materials for the construction of metalled RAF aerodrome runways; essential infrastructure for training fighter pilots and bomber crews, and for the Hurricanes and Spitfires that were crucial to national defence during the Battle of Britain. As their output increased, the quarries expanded and the Office of Works faced growing calls to impose more stringent restrictions than those contained in the Roman Wall and Vallum Preservation

---

[65] Davidson, *Ministry of Labour Reports*, pp. 5–6, 12, 23, 30, 60–61. In recognising the need for industrial development in rural areas, Davidson anticipates Stanley Raymond Dennison, 'Minority report', in *Report of the Land Commission on Land Utilisation in Rural Areas*, Cmnd 6378 (1942), pp. 100–123.

[66] David Edgerton, *Warfare State: Britain, 1920–1970* (Cambridge, Cambridge University Press, 2006), chapters 1 and 2.

[67] Edgerton, *Warfare State*, p. 74.

Scheme (1938).[68] In response, supporters of the quarrying industry claimed that the work of the quarries was no longer simply a matter of regional employment but was also in the 'national interest'. The language of the national interest was wielded effectively by the preservationist cause in the early 1930s, but by 1938 this was fiercely contested terrain as the local Haltwhistle community, empowered by the changing wartime circumstances, claimed this language for its own.

Mr E. Marshall, managing director of the Northumberland Whinstone Company, explained the new importance of his industry in letters to the Office of Works. 'We have a very large contract for the supply of material to Messrs. John Laing & Son, Ltd.', he wrote in 1938, 'who are erecting the RAF Depot at Harker Bridge, near Carlisle'. The ongoing negotiations about further quarrying restrictions prevented Marshall from fulfilling his orders, leaving the company liable to claims made by customers for non-delivery of material, loss of goodwill and, ultimately, loss of profit. John Laing & Son had already informed Marshall that unless he could guarantee to maintain their demand of 200 tons daily 'they intend to take steps to obtain supplies elsewhere'.[69] Similarly, at a union meeting of Greenhead and Cawfields quarrymen in November 1943, northern district organiser Charles Lowthian warned that there would be 'serious consequences' if quarrying were stopped because '[t]his whinstone is urgently needed for a variety of war purposes'.[70] At an interdepartmental meeting that month, F. G. Turner from the Ministry of War Transport made it clear to John Dower (Ministry of Town and Country Planning) and F. J. E. Raby that 'stone-production for defence-works must not suffer – in particular, where Air Ministry contracts were concerned'.[71]

During the Second World War the language of local and national interest became fused. In a meeting on 9 September 1943, Haltwhistle RDC resolved to protest against the suggestion of quarrying restrictions by what it considered 'outside minority interests not concerned in the local welfare'. The RDC expressed alarm at the proposed restrictions, which would cause 'great unemployment of the local population dependent for their livelihood upon the quarry industry' and would be 'contrary to the National interest in the successful prosecution of the war effort'.[72] The notion that protecting Hadrian's Wall was the cause of 'minority interests' was echoed by the manager of Walltown Quarry, C. E. Carss, who explained that to win 'a war for our very existence ... we must have aerodromes', and to restrict the production of the vital stone would be to 'appease the whim of

---

[68] The Roman Wall and Vallum Preservation Scheme (1938) was developed in 1931, published in 1938, and eventually confirmed in 1943. Given their slow rate of work in the 1930s, the existing quarries at Cawfields and Greenhead were permitted to continue working under this Preservation Scheme.

[69] Letters, E. Marshall to Ministry of Works, 18 and 19 May 1938, TNA WORK 14/1124.

[70] 'Protest at quarries closed to save Wall', *Newcastle Journal*, 15 November 1943, p. 4.

[71] John Charlton, 'Note of a meeting at Ministry of War Transport, Devonshire House', 16 April 1943, TNA WORK 14/1459.

[72] Haltwhistle RDC, Council meeting minutes, 9 September 1943, NA LHA/A/1/9. Capitalisation of 'National' is original.

a very small section of the community'.[73] Elsewhere, Carss – paraphrased in the *Newcastle Journal* – pointed to the fact that '[m]illions of people in this country had never seen the Wall and never would, and they would not have much interest in it, but they were all interested in finishing the war'.[74] The Walltown Quarry workers themselves also expressed anger at what they saw as the ability of 'a few persons who are able to bring pressure to bear on *our* Government to have their whims and wishes gratified', against the wishes 'of at least 99% of the population of the locality'.[75]

Support for the quarries became increasingly assertive, emphasising the industry's crucial role in the war effort and pointing to its protected legal status under Ernest Bevin's Essential Work Orders. The chairman of Haltwhistle RCD, John G. Yeats, used language more commonly found in ancient monuments legislation when he remarked that the quarries 'are *scheduled* under the Essential Works Orders, and make a valuable contribution to the war effort'.[76] The significance of this contribution was the subject of a letter written to the *Newcastle Journal* by an anonymous road haulier from Haltwhistle. The letter praised the quarry workers, who 'have striven to produce in record time the essential road material for the building of several RAF stations'. For their part, the road hauliers had worked 'under many crippling conditions' and 'strained every nerve to keep their vehicles in a fit condition to cope with work of such national importance'.[77] In another anonymous letter, the wife of a quarry worker took the argument even further, asking whether those seeking to protect 'a few stones of Roman times' realised that the quarry 'is helping the war effort to bring peace to us all – quarry workers and antiquaries?'[78]

Furthermore, the war strengthened arguments in favour of employment that rested on a sense of moral responsibility. As the *Newcastle Evening Chronicle* explained, further restrictions would not only mean that 'more than 100 quarrymen would soon be unemployed'. It also meant that 'another 100 fighting with the Forces would not have jobs waiting for them' when they came home.[79] This concern was also raised by W. Abbott (secretary) and J. Lattimer (chairman) of the British Legion's Greenhead branch, who implored the Ministry of Works to give the matter 'a little more thought'. They were alarmed by the preservation orders and

---

[73] 'Correspondence', *Contractors Record and Municipal Engineering*, 6 October 1943, TNA WORK 14/1284.

[74] 'Roman Wall protest may close quarries', *Newcastle Journal*, 6 September 1943, p. 4.

[75] Letter, Geo. W. Heslop (Union Branch Secretary, Greenhead), to Colonel Clifton Brown, 20 May 1945, TNA WORK 14/2103. Emphasis in original.

[76] Emphasis in the original. ' "Save the Wall" plan attacked', *Newcastle Journal*, 29 November 1943, p. 4; also 'Roman wall: Case for continued quarrying', *Northern Echo*, 29 November 1943, TNA WORK 14/1284.

[77] 'Hauliers' protest', *Newcastle Journal*, 3 January 1944, p. 2.

[78] 'Letters to the editor. Roman wall damage', *Newcastle Journal*, 2 September 1943, p. 2.

[79] 'Closing of quarries protest', *Newcastle Evening Chronicle*, 15 November 1943, p. 5.

feared that 'real hardship' and 'distress' would be brought on 'the ex-servicemen now employed at each of these quarries' and 'the sons of these men now fighting'.[80] As the Haltwhistle road haulier put it:

> Surely the efforts of all concerned deserve a little better thanks than to find themselves deprived of their means of livelihood. ... Incidentally, there are boys in the Forces who look to the quarries and the hauliers for the means of sustenance [sic] when they return to civil life. These, above all, need our thought and care for their future.[81]

In this sense, the contribution of the quarry workers during the war – whether at Cawfields, Walltown or in the armed forces – shaped expectations of what a just post-war settlement should look like. Borrowing the words of Winston Churchill in his Mansion House speech on 9 November 1943, Yeats argued that quarrying restrictions ran counter to the government's post-war planning aim of 'Food, work, and homes for all'.[82]

Nonetheless, the arguments made in favour of the quarries did not exclusively look to the future. The pro-quarrying perspective was routinely accused of being anti-historical, condoning irreparable damage that was tantamount to vandalism.[83] There is a danger that this perception endures in existing scholarship, often implicitly, within a narrative of landscape transformation that prioritises the preservation of historic monuments. While some of the passionate rhetoric in newspaper letters did at times express disdain for the past,[84] it is important to recognise that arguments made in favour of the quarries were also deeply historical, even if this historical perspective did not concur with the prevailing classical scholarship of the day.

At a superficial level, the war prompted straightforward comparisons between the Roman legions of the 1st and 2nd century AD and the Italians of the 1940s. As the anonymous 'quarryman's wife' explained:

> After all, the Romans who to-day are the Italians, are fighting us. Not only are they out to destroy ancient monuments, but our homes and all we hold dear. I say, if the destruction of this one monument will help win the war, let it be destroyed by all means. ... I wonder if the Italians would hold up a war job in Italy for the sake of a British monument which happened to be standing there? I don't think so.[85]

[80] 'Wall quarries', *Newcastle Journal*, 30 November 1943, p. 2.
[81] 'Hauliers' protest', *Newcastle Journal*, 3 January 1944, p. 2.
[82] For Yeats, see '"Save the Wall" plan attacked', *Newcastle Journal*, 29 November 1943, p. 4. For a description of Churchill's speech, see 'A minister of reconstruction in Great Britain', *Nature*, 152, 20 November 1943, p. 594. The phrase was also used in the Labour Party's election manifesto, *Let Us Face the Future* (London, 1945), p. 3.
[83] For a contemporary example, see 'Letters to the editor. Wall "intolerance"', *Newcastle Journal*, 9 September 1943, p. 2.
[84] A. J. Redhead, of Newcastle, claimed that relics such as the wall were 'of little, if any, value' and 'should be scrapped'. 'Letters to the editor. Wall controversy', *Newcastle Journal*, 7 September 1943, p. 2.
[85] 'Letters to the editor. Roman Wall damage', *Newcastle Journal*, 2 September 1943, p. 2.

However, there were also distinctive historical understandings of the landscape that emerged from dwelling and working in the area. This perspective emerges in a letter from a resident of Newcastle signed M. B.:

> In view of the great shortage of building material for houses for the living, may I suggest the whole of the ancient tyrants' wall be used for this purpose? ... Our forebears had the sense to do this, as can be seen in the farmhouses and other buildings in the neighbourhood of the Wall.[86]

In this period such a view was considered by many as unthinking, and utterly disrespectful of the history of the landscape and the 'civilising influence' of Rome.[87] Repurposing stones from Hadrian's Wall was often described as 'unwarrantable vandalism',[88] and indicated 'narrow-minded intolerance'.[89] However, M. B.'s letter in fact displays an alternative historical understanding of Hadrian's Wall, focusing instead on its post-Roman history and on a landscape that continued to change over time. In recent decades Hadrian's Wall scholarship has turned its attention to the relatively neglected post-Roman period, recognising the wall as a composite monument that exists as part of a changing and living landscape.[90]

M. B.'s letter demonstrates an understanding of a deeper history, which is far longer than the history of the Romans in Britain, and it is one that emphasises working, using, and repurposing. This *longue durée* history of the landscape was in marked contrast to the views of many contemporary archaeologists, who were known to discard post-Roman and even post-Hadrianic evidence in order to excavate, and in a sense construct, Hadrian's Wall as an exclusively Roman structure at 'a single moment in time'.[91] From M. B.'s distinctive yet equally historical perspective, attempts to preserve what had always been a dynamic and living landscape was in fact to change it by freezing it in time.

Furthermore, M. B.'s letter anticipates more recent scholarship of the Roman Empire in Britain in second way. The use of the term 'ancient tyrants' to describe Hadrian and his successors suggests that M. B. identified with the subjects of Roman imperialism rather than with those who implemented it. This was a view shared by several other letter writers, who described the wall as a 'relic of Roman barbarism', and as 'standing evidence of Roman aggression and British slavery'.[92]

---

[86] 'Letters to the editor. Wall controversy', *Newcastle Journal*, 7 September 1943, p. 2.

[87] See the letter from Doris Swan, Haltwhistle, in 'Divided views on value of relic', *Newcastle Journal*, 13 September 1943, p. 2.

[88] 'Hadrian's Wall. Cottage which was built of stones from it', *Hartlepool Northern Daily Mail*, 19 April 1930, p. 3.

[89] 'Letters to the editor. Wall "intolerance"', *Newcastle Journal*, 9 September 1943, p. 2.

[90] This is a welcome development, although the Roman history of Hadrian's Wall is still prioritised within the history of the landscape. See Richard Hingley, 'Living landscape: Reading Hadrian's Wall', *Landscapes*, 12:2 (2011), 41–62; Robert Woodside and James Crow, *Hadrian's Wall: An Historic Landscape* (Cirencester, National Trust, 2000).

[91] Witcher *et al.*, 'Archaeologies of landscape', pp. 111–112.

[92] For example, see the letter from 'Conclavist', in 'Letters to the editor. "Wall" battle', *Newcastle Journal*, 15 September 1943, p. 2.

Such a perspective on Roman Britain is one that scholars such as David Mattingly have turned to in recent years, reimagining Britain as an 'imperial possession'. This is a history that acknowledges 'defeat, subjugation', 'exploitation', and 'resistance', eschewing historical narratives written at the height of British imperial power that avoided 'the nasty business of empire' while glorifying Roman imperialism as 'a civilising force for good'.[93]

The arguments put forward by quarry managers and workers, their families, road hauliers, anonymous members of the public, and by representatives of Haltwhistle RDC, the British Legion, and the Ministry of War Transport demonstrate that voices speaking in favour of the quarrying industry were loud, expressive, and occupied formidable strategic ground when local and national interests seemed to coincide during the Second World War. This was a cause for concern for government officials at the Ministry of Works, who saw a battle for public opinion that was being lost at a regional and local level. At an inter-departmental meeting between the Ministry of Information and the Ministry of Works in December 1943, it was decided that local reporters should be issued with an information sheet on the history of the Preservation Scheme and be encouraged to consult the Ministry of Works senior regional officer before going to print on the quarrying issue. In addition, copies of the local newspapers would be collected so that the situation could be closely monitored.[94]

Nevertheless, even at the point at which the argument in favour of the quarries seemed strongest, a distinct note of apprehension could also be heard. In September 1943, a meeting of the Haltwhistle Parish Council ended on a sombre note when, after discussing the number of jobs that would be lost in the event of further restrictions, Councillor Laidlaw 'said he did not think anything they said would make any difference, and the discussion closed'.[95] Writing to the *Newcastle Journal* the following month, Douglas Smith (Managing Director of Smith & Walton Paint Works, Haltwhistle), warned that '[s]ome people's memories are all too short', and recalled the 'years of depression' and 'acute distress' when the Haltwhistle district was 'classified as a Special Area'.[96] The workmen of Walltown Quarry appealed to the Ministry of Works for 'common justice', explaining that 'it is not so many years ago since the unemployment figures were astronomical in this district',[97] and A. F. Graham (honorary secretary of Haltwhistle Tradesmen's Association) warned that, if the quarries closed and depression returned 'the only fully employed people will be the cashiers at the Employment Exchange'.[98] Even George Hicks,

[93] David Mattingly, *An Imperial Possession: Britain in the Roman Empire, 54 BC–AD 409* (London, Penguin, 2007), pp. xi–xiii, 4–18.
[94] Minute sheet, inter-departmental meeting between Ministry of Information and Ministry of Works, 9 December 1943, TNA WORK 14/1284.
[95] *Newcastle Journal*, 8 September 1943, p. 3.
[96] 'Quarry – wall controversy', *Newcastle Journal*, 19 November 1943, p. 2.
[97] Letter, Geo. W. Heslop (Union Branch Secretary, Greenhead), to Secretary of the Ministry of Works, received 28 June 1945 (confirmed in a reply by A. Miller), TNA WORK 14/2103.
[98] 'Letters to the editor. Town's need of wall quarries', *Newcastle Journal*, 24 November 1943, p. 2.

Parliamentary Secretary for the Ministry of Works, could not allay the concerns of local tradespeople, quarry owners, councillors, residents, and quarry workers when he held a meeting in Haltwhistle in January 1944. The *Echo* recorded his speech: 'I promise you this, I will not neglect the consideration of the work people. ... If we can find alternative employment we shall. It is paramount in our minds and you shall not be injured by the preservation of this Wall.'[99] Notwithstanding the reassuring words, memories of the 1930s loomed large at the meeting. Graham said that 'two dreadful words, "Special Area" were imprinted on the minds of [the] people', who remembered when 900 men 'were thrown out of employment'. Mrs Douglas Brown, from Bardon Mill, said that 'human life and people's welfare mattered first', and Eldon Lightfoot (representing the RDC) warned that the people 'were likely to suffer if the quarries were closed down'.[100]

As the Second World War ended, the quarrying industry lost its claim over the national interest. Wake's lease was purchased by the state, his quarry never realised, and in 1945 the Roman Wall and Vallum Preservation (Amendment) Scheme was published, imposing the restrictions of the 1938 scheme over a much larger area. In 1947, a compensation payment of £50,000 was made to the Northumberland Whinstone Company for compliance with the restrictions in the amended scheme, which Raby estimated allowed for at least another five years of quarrying at Walltown. At Cawfields, a 'second lift' was implemented whereby the remaining Whin Sill was left alone and a second quarry face was dug out of the quarry floor. In theory, this provided years of work at the quarry and the site would subsequently become a lake, which Raby deemed 'a cheap and easy way of restoring the amenity' of the area once the quarry was worked out.[101] In an echo of Lansbury's spirit of compromise, Raby was happy to put up with 'the nuisance' of the quarry for a few more years if it meant alleviating 'a certain amount of human suffering'.[102] In reality, however, the additional cost of continually pumping out water from the new quarry floor proved too much, and the quarry closed in 1952.

Preserving rural England, 1954–1955 and 1960

Traditionally, quarrying was an intermittent rural industry. Quarries closed, reopened, contracted, and expanded according to the fluctuating demand for stone, and this experience fuelled the hope that the restrictions at Walltown Quarry might

---

[99] 'Roman wall quarries not to close', *Haltwhistle Echo*, 21 January 1944, TNA WORK 14/1284. For a draft of Hicks's speech, see 'Hadrian's Wall. Notes for visit to Haltwhistle, Sat. 15.1.44.', TNA WORK 14/2662.

[100] 'Haltwhistle round table conference on Roman wall controversy. Assurances on quarry work question', TNA WORK 14/1284. No newspaper name or date noted.

[101] Letter, F. J. E. Raby to Eric de Normann, 18 September 1944, TNA WORK 14/1459.

[102] Letter, F. J. E. Raby to John Dower (Ministry of Town and Country Planning), 13 April 1944, TNA WORK 14/1459.

be reversible.[103] The first application to extend Walltown Quarry was submitted to Northumberland County Council in 1954 and was rejected the following year. The second application was submitted in February 1960 and was rejected after a public inquiry held in Haltwhistle in October. During the attempts to reverse quarrying restrictions, local voices recorded in the *Echo* and in the public inquiry testimonies articulated the rural-industrial taskscape by equating the quarrying industry with the life of the community and the preservation of rural England.

On 15 October 1954, a headline on the front page of the *Echo* read: 'New Life for Greenhead Quarry?' In addition to securing long-term employment for the quarrymen, the motivation for extending the life of the quarry was to make room for the growing number of unemployed miners amid the decline of Haltwhistle's heavy industries in the post-war period. The accompanying article explained that, after a recent inspection of the site, the North East Industrial Development Association and Haltwhistle RDC claimed that 'quarry operations could be extended without any serious detriment to the objects of the preservation scheme'.[104] With their support, and the support of Rupert Speir (MP for Hexham) and Colonel Joicey (the landowner), the Northumberland Whinstone Company made an application for the extension to the County Planning Officer, J. B. Ross.[105]

Ross was sympathetic to the application, and his correspondence with the Ministry of Works sheds light on the overlapping planning powers of local government and the central state along Hadrian's Wall. Ross explained that 'stepping up quarrying operations' would 'alleviate the unemployment especially amongst the older type of miner who would not normally move to new mining employment elsewhere'.[106] The prospect of jobs for around 100 men 'in an area threatened with future unemployment' was something that 'must be considered attractive',[107] and Ross felt 'sure … that my Committee would never use their planning powers to effect, or assist in effecting, the closing down of the quarry'.[108]

However, the Ministry of Works had its own planning powers over the Walltown Quarry area via the Roman Wall and Vallum Preservation (Amendment) Scheme, and Ross acknowledged that the two authorities must 'arrive at a common line of action'.[109] Their correspondence suggests that this was lacking. Ross worked

---

[103] Shaw, 'Weighing down the landscape', pp. 78, 83n32.

[104] 'New life for Greenhead Quarry?', *Haltwhistle Echo*, 15 October 1954, p. 1, NA 4261/44.

[105] The Town and Country Planning Act 1947 required that planning permission be obtained for the development of land. The Act transferred planning authority powers from rural and urban district councils to the county councils and borough councils.

[106] Letter, J. B. Ross to Inspectorate of Ancient Monuments (Ministry of Works), 25 February 1954, TNA WORK 14/2662.

[107] Letter, J. B. Ross to Inspectorate of Ancient Monuments (Ministry of Works), 22 March 1954, TNA WORK 14/2662.

[108] Letter, J. B. Ross to Chief Inspector of Ancient Monuments (Ministry of Works), 5 October 1955, TNA WORK 14/2662.

[109] G. R. Armstrong, 'Note of a meeting'. The meeting took place on 22 February 1955. TNA WORK 14/2662.

'[o]n the assumption that some extension of the existing quarry is justified on economic and local employment grounds', and asked the Chief Inspector of Ancient
Monuments P. K. Baillie Reynolds 'which would be the least detrimental way to
carry out the extension?'[110] In contrast, a minute from August 1955 records Baillie
Reynolds' opinion that to subordinate 'a monument of world-wide significance' to
'the financial interests of a local quarry company' or the 'convenience of a small
number of Haltwhistle work-people' would be 'to take a very parochial view'.[111]
By the mid-1950s the quarrying industry's wartime claim to the national interest
had long expired, and it was once again compared unfavourably with the national
significance and international prestige of Hadrian's Wall.

Meanwhile in the *Quarry Managers' Journal*, the manager of Walltown Quarry,
C. E. Carss, made the bold claim that, far from being detrimental, the quarry would
help 'improve the view' from the wall by removing a hill and affording views 'right
across the fells to Bellingham'.[112] Rupert Speir petitioned the Ministry of Works,
pointing out that the 'show places' of Hadrian's Wall such as Housesteads 'are fully
protected already' and at least four miles away from the quarry. At Walltown 'there is
no actual Wall in existence', he claimed, 'but only the site where the Wall once ran'.[113]
Such a view was typical of local residents and the pro-quarrying lobby in general, who
considered each site along the wall in isolation, differentiating between what they saw
as the well-preserved and therefore important sections, and the buried or destroyed
and therefore insignificant ones.[114] For the preservationists, in contrast, the extraordinary significance of the Roman frontier system was its long and continuous nature.
As Baillie Reynolds put it, '[o]ne feature of prime importance in such a monument as
the Wall is its continuity', and the Ministry was determined to 'preserve as much as
possible of the continuous line of Wall which still exists'.[115] These two ways of seeing
the landscape around the quarries were fundamentally different and they were not
reconciled during the quarrying debates.

With the county planning authority and the Ministry of Works at odds over
the extension application, G. R. Armstrong arranged for a 'strong team' from the
Ministry to attend the decisive County Planning Committee meeting on 22 December
1955, with the aim of convincing 'the "Philistines" that our view is the right one'.[116]

[110] Letter, J. B. Ross to Chief Inspector of Ancient Monuments, 5 October 1955, TNA WORK 14/2662.
[111] P. K. Baillie Reynolds (Chief Inspector of Monuments), 4 August 1955, minute on importance of the
Roman Wall, TNA WORK 14/2662.
[112] 'Walltown Quarry restrictions appeal', *Quarry Managers' Journal*, November 1954, TNA WORK
14/2662.
[113] Letter, Rupert Speir to J. R. Bevins, 25 July 1955, TNA WORK 14/2662.
[114] In 1960, Rural District and County Councillor Douglas Smith said that local residents were proud
of certain sections of the wall such as Housesteads, but not sections such as Greenhead. A. R. Chown,
Inquiry Report, 21 November 1960, p. 10, TNA WORK 14/2662.
[115] P. K. Baillie Reynolds (Chief Inspector of Monuments), minute on importance of the Roman Wall,
4 August 1955, TNA WORK 14/2662.
[116] Quotation from Letter, G. R. Armstrong to P. K. Baillie Reynolds, 7 October 1955, TNA WORK 14/
2662. Meeting arrangements were discussed in Letter, G. R. Armstrong to Alan P. Humby (Regional
Director, Ministry of Works), 10 December 1955, TNA WORK 14/2662.

After a 'short informal discussion' with Ross, the Ministry team – which included Baillie Reynolds – spoke to the committee, who had also received 'some arch-aeological considerations' from Professor Ian Richmond 'a day or two' before-hand. It seems that the Ministry delegation exerted some influence, because after 'very little further consideration' the committee 'agreed unanimously to reject the application'.[117]

After planning consent for the extension of Walltown Quarry was refused, the site became part of Northumberland National Park in 1956, and the economic situation in Haltwhistle deteriorated. The National Coal Board announced in advance that nearby Moorwood Colliery would close in June 1960, putting 140 miners out of work and increasing the unemployment rate to twice the national average.[118] This was the fifth colliery in the area to close in recent years, and doubts were raised over the future of Bardon Mill, the last remaining coal mine in the district. The outlook was grim, and in the *Echo* comparisons were once again made with 1931. The columnist 'Westgate' recalled how there was 'not a job to be found in the countryside', and '[m]en, women and children knew the pangs of hunger and extreme poverty. Please God, we shall not see that again'.[119]

On 21 January 1960, a meeting was held in Haltwhistle to discuss extending Walltown Quarry as a means of alleviating some of the unemployment caused by the closure of Moorwood Colliery. The meeting was attended by around 40 people, representing local interests as well as various organs of the central state. The Northumberland Whinstone Company expressed willingness to negotiate on the repayment of compensation received as part of the Roman Wall and Vallum Preservation (Amendment) Scheme, committing to employ an extra 60–70 men if the restrictions were relaxed. Joicey revived his offer (first tabled to the Ministry of Works in 1958) to repay compensation and give the section of Hadrian's Wall in his Blenkinsopp estate 'as a deed of gift to the nation' on the condition that Walltown Quarry be permitted to expand.[120] Councillor George Dent appeared on Tyne Tees Television that week and, while acknowledging the importance of ancient monuments, declared that 'the bread and butter of my fellow men and women is definitely of more importance'.[121]

---

[117] K. Newis, Report of visit to Greenhead Quarry (21 December 1955) and of informal meeting with Ross before attending the Planning Committee meeting (both 22 December 1955), document dated 30 December 1955, TNA WORK 14/2662. The Ministry later rejected the suggestion that it had influenced the Council's decision at this meeting.

[118] These figures vary, and the *Haltwhistle Echo* claimed 205 were employed at Moorwood. The figure cited here, 140, was the Ministry of Works' estimate. K. Newis, Minute on Roman Wall, 9 June 1960, TNA WORK 14/2662.

[119] 'Haltwhistle musings, by Westgate', *Haltwhistle Echo*, 1 January 1960, p. 3, NA 4261/44.

[120] *Haltwhistle Echo*, 29 January 1960, pp. 1–2, NA 4261/44. For the original offer, see Letter, J. M. Clark & Sons (on behalf of Joicey) to D. J. Cockell (Ministry of Works), 20 May 1958, TNA WORK 14/2662. The Ministry refused to bargain in this manner.

[121] 'Haltwhistle musings, by Westgate', *Haltwhistle Echo*, 29 January 1960, p. 3.

During the final attempt to extend the life of the quarry a clearer articulation of the taskscape emerged. For rural district councillors, local business owners and residents, the quarry was more than a matter of employment; it was closely connected to the life of the community, and metaphors of life and death pervaded their language, again recorded in the *Echo*. Councillor George Dent said 'this is the very life of Haltwhistle that we are talking about',[122] chairman John Clark warned that 'Haltwhistle will "die on its feet" unless sufficient work for men is provided in the district',[123] and 'Westgate' lamented that a 'long established' industry in the district was being 'strangled by the Ministry of Works', and drew a comparison with the neighbouring districts in 'the lovely vale of North Tyne' that were also 'slowly being strangled and depopulated'.[124]

Despite economic decline, there was brighter news regarding light industry. Haltwhistle was a listed area under the Local Employment Act (1960), which empowered the Board of Trade to respond to 'impending unemployment' by providing industrial premises and issuing loans or grants.[125] In October 1960 the *Echo* celebrated Cascelloid Ltd.'s plan to open a new factory at Plenmeller, to produce polythene squeeze-cans and bottles. This was the first new industry to open in Haltwhistle in three decades, and by November the factory employed 39 residents, the majority of whom were women. The works manager, R. A. Greenwood, spoke highly of the welcome extended to him by '[t]he local people, including tradespeople and hotel keepers', as the community responded enthusiastically to the good news.[126] In December, another new industry was announced after Perry Industrial Developments purchased the Greystonedale Works in Haltwhistle, and planned to employ an initial labour force of around 25 to produce sub-assemblies for caravans.[127] Nevertheless, despite two new factories alongside the existing Hadrian Paints and Kilfrost (which manufactured de-icing and anti-icing aviation fluids), Westgate warned that Haltwhistle's population had declined by 1,500 over the previous 30 years, and concluded that 'we need a certain amount of heavy industry if we are to thrive as a community'.[128]

The final application to extend Walltown Quarry was submitted in February 1960, and while it was opposed by the Ministry of Works, the National Parks Commission, and the Ramblers' Association, no objections were raised by the Ministry of Agriculture, the National Coal Board, or Haltwhistle RDC.[129] The matter

---

[122] 'Wall quarrying scheme. Council to back application for extension', *Haltwhistle Echo*, 15 January 1960, p. 1, NA 4261/44.

[123] 'Only more jobs can save town', *Newcastle Journal*, 9 July 1960, p. 7.

[124] 'Haltwhistle musings, by Westgate', *Haltwhistle Echo*, 1 January 1960, p. 3, NA 4261/44.

[125] 'Government aid bill to cover mining areas', *The Times*, 10 February 1960, TNA WORK 14/2662.

[126] 'Pilot production starts at new Plenmeller factory', *Haltwhistle Echo*, 14 October 1960, p. 1; for R. A. Greenwood, see *Haltwhistle Echo*, 11 November 1960, p. 1.

[127] 'Another new industry: Factory will employ 25 to start', *Haltwhistle Echo*, 16 December 1960, p. 1, NA 4261/44.

[128] 'Haltwhistle musings, by Westgate', *Haltwhistle Echo*, 11 November 1960, p. 1.

[129] Letter, J. B. Ross to the Secretary of the Ministry of Housing and Local Government, 4 July 1960, TNA HLG 89/855.

came to a head at the public inquiry held in Haltwhistle on 11 October, conducted by Inspector A. R. Chown from the Ministry of Housing and Local Government. The application requested permission to extend the workings 440 yards eastwards from 'number two' quarry face, or alternatively work a trench from 'number one' quarry face eastwards for 800 yards. This, it was believed, would allow for 75–100 men to be employed for 30 years, in addition to the existing labour force of 84 plus 20 transport workers. If a limited concession were granted, then the quarry hoped to employ the existing workforce for 30 years.[130]

Shortly before the inquiry the Ministry of Works was accused of rebuilding parts of Hadrian's Wall near Haltwhistle as a means of strengthening its case, which it denied.[131] News of the inquiry spread, and the quarrying debates found an international audience in the pages of the *Vancouver Sun*.[132] Chown's report and the local press coverage give a detailed impression of the inquiry. The preservationist perspective – that the wall was a Hadrianic structure frozen at a single moment in time – was articulated by Professor Ian Richmond, who spoke of 'the unchanging Wall' in contrast to the 'ephemeral' nature of employment, and the Ministry of Works argued that unemployment was 'transient' when compared with the wall.[133] For local residents, the inquiry provided a forum to confirm their support for the application and articulate their understanding of the taskscape.

The life of the community remained the focus of the statements given by local and regional voices at the inquiry. Representing Haltwhistle RDC, the solicitor Peter Boydell acknowledged the new light industries in the village but warned that this did not provide a long-term solution for manual workers. A quarter of the population had left Haltwhistle since 1921, he explained, and 87 people had left since Moorwood Colliery closed in July.[134] A trade union organiser, Andrew Cunningham, said that even the rumour of job losses caused families to leave the district.[135] Douglas Smith explained that the decline of heavy industry was so detrimental to the whole community because when men left the district to find work their wives and daughters accompanied them, which drained the labour force for Haltwhistle's light industries, too.[136] Unemployment figures from contracting heavy industries simply did not convey the full extent of the damage being wrought on the local community. As Boydell put it, if an established industry such as the quarry were permitted to expand, it 'would hold the community together'.[137] Inspector

---

[130] 'Walltown quarry "war"', *Haltwhistle Echo*, 14 October 1960, pp. 1–2, NA 4261/44.

[131] 'The battle of Hadrian's Wall', *The People*, 9 October 1960, TNA WORK 14/2662.

[132] 'Up against the wall', *Vancouver Sun*, Tuesday 18 October 1960, TNA WORK 14/2662.

[133] For Richmond, see A. R. Chown, Inquiry Report, 21 November 1960, p. 8, TNA WORK 14/2662; For the Ministry, see 'Outline of ministry case at public inquiry', with some handwritten notes added by R. Gilyand-Beer including the quotation cited here, TNA WORK 14/2662.

[134] A. R. Chown, Inquiry Report, 21 November 1960, p. 5, TNA WORK 14/2662.

[135] Proof of Evidence given at the Local Public Inquiry, TNA WORK 14/2662.

[136] Chown's paraphrase. A. R. Chown, Inquiry Report, 21 November 1960, p. 10, TNA WORK 14/2662.

[137] Chown's paraphrase. A. R. Chown, Inquiry Report, 21 November 1960, p. 5, TNA WORK 14/2662.

Chown, however, saw the depopulation of Haltwhistle as inevitable 'whatever steps are taken to try to arrest it'.[138]

Emphasising the historical and national significance of the quarry, director and manager of the Northumberland Whinstone Company, Gerald Ernest Marshall, explained that the quarry itself had existed for 150 years, and it had been leased by his company for 80. He noted that the main customers for the stone 'are highway authorities and civil engineering contractors', and the Atomic Energy Authority 'specified stone from this quarry for special purposes' at Sellafield nuclear site. British Oxygen-Wimpey had also ordered 'large quantities' of stone for the Ministry of Supply's Missile Test Centre at Spadeadam.[139]

Finally, the most comprehensive articulation of the taskscape was made by Mr J. C. Jeffers, a resident of Greenhead who spoke on behalf of the village and parish council. Jeffers explained that the quarry employed over half the men in the village, and it would be 'a major disaster if it ceased working' because '[o]ur homes are at Greenhead, some own their houses and take great pride in them and in their gardens'. At the prospect of losing the quarry, Jeffers said:

> What could we do? There is no work locally, with the Pits closing and the distance we are away from any other place of employment and all we know is Quarry work really because we have worked there most of our lives, it would be difficult to learn new things and after this open air life we feel that we could not work in a factory even if there were one. Travel to work, wherever work of this nature may be, would involve long distances and make very long days. Unless of course we moved away from the place. Surely this is unthinkable. ... Of course there are people who would gladly close all the villages and concentrate people in larger communities – such a shocking idea, the villages are the flower of the country and I feel sure that the men who form the Society to preserve the Roman Wall will also be the men who wish to preserve Rural England.[140]

In his statement Jeffers expressed a devotion to place that captures the meaning of the taskscape. For Jeffers and many like him, quarries, collieries, and other industries were inseparable from the rural landscapes that gave rise to them and the rural-industrial communities they supported. Walter Bell's painting *Derbyshire Quarry* (1937) illustrates Jeffers's description of the quarrying taskscape, in which industrial structures, quarry workers, and vehicles blend naturally into the surrounding rural scene and the smoke rising from the buildings is a benign 'pale chalky brown' rather than an incongruous 'choking black'.[141] Jeffers' was a different vision of rural England in which the rural and industrial overlapped, and in the mid-20th century it fell victim to the planner-preservationist approach to development, which

---

[138] A. R. Chown, Inquiry Report, 21 November 1960, pp. 11–12, TNA WORK 14/2662.
[139] Proof of Evidence given at the Local Public Inquiry, TNA WORK 14/2662.
[140] 'Greenhead parish', document 6: proof of evidence given by Mr Jeffers, TNA HLG 89/855.
[141] Shaw, 'Weighing down the landscape', p. 77.

attempted to bring order to the landscape by separating places deemed industrial and urban from those considered rural.[142]

After the 1960 inquiry, Chown recommended that the application to extend the boundaries of Walltown Quarry be rejected on the grounds that it would damage the Roman remains and the scenic beauty of the National Park.[143] Work continued at Walltown for several years as deeper quarries were excavated, before the quarry closed in 1976. During their lifespans, the Cawfields and Walltown quarries extracted materials for building stone, paving setts, slabs and kerbstones, railway ballast, aerodrome runways, highways, Spadeadam Missile Test Centre, and Sellafield nuclear site. In this sense, the quarries helped build many of the 'large-scale public structures' of rural modernity,[144] only to find that the new dream of the English countryside had no place for a rural industry deemed irreconcilable with the landscape of Hadrian's Wall.

Conclusion

The quarrying debates took place in a period when the state extended its control, ownership, and management of the environment, and increasingly set the boundaries of appropriate landscape use. This took various forms, including the protection of ancient monuments, town and country planning, the designation of National Parks, and nature conservation.[145] The location of Walltown, Cawfields, and Wake's proposed quarry along Hadrian's Wall made the quarrying debates especially urgent, as the quarries became conspicuous symbols of disorder that brought destruction to the celebrated ancient monument and the surrounding landscape. The Second World War briefly empowered rural industry in the Haltwhistle district, but it also acted as a catalyst for the development of an interventionist state that imposed landscape planning regimes prioritising preservation, amenity, and leisure at the expense of the quarries. The state was not a single homogeneous agent, though, and conflict between its bureaucratic arms was evident when the Ministry of Works met resistance from the Ministry of War Transport during the Second World War, and later from Northumberland County Planning Officer J. B. Ross in 1954.

Today, Walltown and Cawfields are leisure sites with facilities for visitors such as parking, picnic areas, toilets, and a new visitor centre at Walltown Country

---

[142] David Matless, *Landscape and Englishness* (London, Reaktion, 1998), pp. 25–61. For a contemporary example, see Ian Nairn, 'Outrage', *Architectural Review*, 117:702 (June 1955). Nairn argued that the role of planning was to 'maintain and intensify the difference between places'.

[143] A. R. Chown, Inquiry Report, 21 November 1960, p. 12, TNA WORK 14/2662.

[144] Fairbrother, *New Lives*, pp. 217–219.

[145] This has been recently termed the 'nature state': Matthew Kelly, 'Conventional thinking and the fragile birth of the nature state in post-war Britain', in Wilko Graf von Hardenberg, Matthew Kelly, Claudia Leal, and Emily Wakild (eds), *The Nature State: Rethinking the History of Conservation* (London, Routledge, 2017), pp. 114–135.

Figure 4.3 Cawfields Quarry in 2022. © Gareth Roddy

Park (see Figure 4.3). Heritage interpretation boards inform visitors about the milecastles and turrets of Hadrian's Wall, the flora of Walltown grassland reserve, and offer stargazing tips at Cawfields Dark Sky Discovery Site. The industrial history of the area is acknowledged on a Hadrian's Wall WHS heritage board at Cawfields, where the Cawfields and Walltown quarries are described as destructive forces in the landscape.[146] Local opinion has shifted since the mid-20th century, and in 2009 residents near Hexham opposed plans to reactivate the dormant planning permission for Cocklaw Quarry (14 miles east of Cawfields) on the grounds that it would damage the setting of Hadrian's Wall.[147] However, the history of the quarrying debates demonstrates that the creation of new heritage landscapes in the central section of Hadrian's Wall was a deeply contested process between 1930 and 1960, when two fundamentally different ways of seeing the landscape collided.

---

[146] Frontiers of the Roman Empire: Hadrian's Wall, World Heritage Site Heritage Interpretation Board, Cawfields. The opening paragraph begins: 'At Cawfields and nearby Walltown, quarries have destroyed Hadrian's Wall by removing the scarp face of the Whin Sill.'
[147] 'Site near Wall to be "scarred" by quarry. Plan approved despite fierce opposition', *The Journal* (Newcastle), 17 February 2009.

These conflicting ways of seeing are embodied in two present-day footpaths that approach the site of the old Cawfields Quarry from different directions: Hadrian's Wall National Trail and Haltwhistle Burn footpath. The National Trail runs east–west alongside the line of the wall (though it diverts from it at certain points), and to experience the landscape in this way is to adopt a line of sight from which Cawfields and Walltown quarries are encountered as abrupt disruptions in the landscape, as vast holes that interrupt the continuity of Hadrian's Wall as a long, coherent, linear monument. The east–west trajectory of this perspective is one that was shared by the planner-preservationists in the mid-20th century, illustrated by John Dower's vision for a Roman Wall National Park (see Figure 4.4).[148] In contrast, Haltwhistle Burn footpath approaches Cawfields from the village of Haltwhistle to the south. The footpath runs along the lower section of what was once a narrow-gauge railway line, which connected the South Tyne Colliery and the Cawfields Quarry with the Newcastle and Carlisle Railway from 1905 until the late 1930s. Passing chimneys, old quarries, and lime kilns along a route that was once a commute for quarry workers, the site of Cawfields Quarry emerges as a natural extension of a rural-industrial taskscape. When examining the period of the quarrying debates (1930–1960), it is only by centring local and regional voices that this second way of seeing emerges, so we can fully understand the layered nature of the landscape and its contested history.

There were, of course, many local and regional voices that spoke loudly in favour of preservation, such as the Societies of Antiquaries in Carlisle and Newcastle, and residents of Haltwhistle such as Doris Swan, who bemoaned the 'disdain for the past' she read in letters to the *Newcastle Journal*.[149] In 1960, a Durham resident wrote to the Ministry to complain about the *Newcastle Journal*'s coverage of the inquiry, which he found biased in favour of 'union officials'.[150] Equally, there were archaeologists, antiquarians, and preservationists who recognised the deep connection between this landscape and local employment. For instance, the archaeologist R. P. Wright wrote that, notwithstanding the national significance of the wall, it was also 'a national duty, and a task not beyond national resource, to find employment for the workers to whose livelihood the destruction of the Wall is incidental'.[151]

Nevertheless, when we shift our scale of focus to the regional and the local, the history of the landscape's transformation takes a different trajectory. We gain a fuller and more complex understanding of the multitude of voices and values in the landscape, which is economic and dynamic as well as aesthetic and historic.[152]

---

[148] John Dower, *National Parks in England and Wales* (London, 1945), Map I, p. 11.

[149] 'Divided views on value of relic', *Newcastle Journal*, 13 September 1943, p. 2

[150] Letter, John Abrey[?] (Western Lodge Cottage, Whitesmocks, Durham City) to Ministry of Works, 14 February 1961, TNA WORK 14/2662.

[151] Richard Pearson Wright, 'Roman Britain in 1943: I. Sites explored: II. Inscriptions', *The Journal of Roman Studies*, 34:1–2 (1944), 76–91 at 78.

[152] David Matless, *In the Nature of Landscape: Cultural Geography on the Norfolk Broads* (Chichester, Wiley-Blackwell, 2014), pp. 6–7; David Matless, 'Describing landscape: Regional sites', *Performance Research*, 15:4 (2010), 74–78; Mike Pearson, *'In Comes I': Performance, Memory and Landscape* (Exeter, University of Exeter Press, 2006), pp. 15, 17.

MAP I

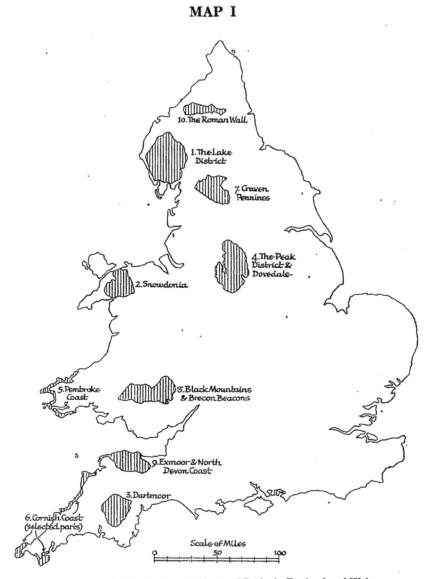

10. The Roman Wall

1. The Lake District

7. Craven Pennines

4. The Peak District & Dovedale

2. Snowdonia

5. Pembroke Coast

8. Black Mountains & Brecon Beacons

9. Exmoor & North Devon Coast

3. Dartmoor

6. Cornish Coast (selected parts)

Scale of Miles
0   50   100

Areas suggested for the first 10 National Parks in England and Wales.

Figure 4.4 Map of areas suggested for the first 10 National Parks in England and Wales, from John Dower, *National Parks in England and Wales*, Cmnd 6628 (May 1945), p. 11. Document from ProQuest's House of Commons Parliamentary Papers, displayed with permission of ProQuest LLC, https://parlipapers.proquest.com/parlipapers/docview/t70. d75.1987-083671

We begin to understand how preservation orders, scheduling ancient monuments, and the restriction of industry are agents of great change in the landscape. We appreciate that the campaigns to save the quarries were not ahistorical but instead revealed alternative understandings of the landscape and its history. In other words, we begin to see like the quarrymen. From this perspective, extending the life of the quarries was a way of saving the communities of rural England, and of preserving continuity in what had always been a worked, quarried, and living landscape.[153] In the period 1930–1960, those who spoke in favour of the quarries were often accused of vandalism, and the underlying assumption that the quarries were essentially destructive agents of change lingers in historical scholarship.[154] However, when we consider the landscape of the quarries and the surrounding villages as a taskscape, we begin to understand the quarries and other rural industries as continuities – rather than disruptions – in the landscape.[155] When local and regional voices are recovered, the quarrying debates reveal a social history of landscape transformation and heritage creation that is complex and sometimes uncomfortable, which involved conservation and preservation as well as conflict, compromise, and loss.

[153] The quarried landscape predates Hadrian's Wall, and the landscape continued to be quarried after the wall ceased to function as the northwest frontier of the Roman Empire. See O'Donnell, 'Quarries of Hadrian's Wall', pp. 58–82.

[154] John Sheail, for instance, describes the countryside around the wall as 'threatened by change' in *Rural Conservation*, p. 53.

[155] Memories, anecdotes, and photographs of Haltwhistle and the local industries at this time have been compiled in two publications by John Parker, who worked at Cawfields Quarry: John Parker, *Haltwhistle and Beyond* (Newcastle upon Tyne, TUPS Books, 2001); Parker, *Cawfields Quarry*.

5

Building Amenity in Areas
of Non-outstanding Natural Beauty
in the Southern Pennines

KATRINA NAVICKAS

In *New Lives, New Landscapes*, Nan Fairbrother considered the impact of energy and communications infrastructure on upland landscapes, including sites for defence, high-voltage electricity pylons, and telecommunications masts:

> We may not welcome such structures, but there seems little chance of avoiding them; what is essential is to prevent them becoming nuclei for the spread of other develop-ment and to remove or otherwise screen the surrounding clutter they engender. To keep them in fact remote non-human presences in the large-scale upland landscape.[1]

Sylvia Crowe's *The Landscape of Power*, published in 1958, considered the spread of energy infrastructure as the defining feature of the post-war British countryside.[2] In 1970, Fairbrother posed a central conundrum of landscape management: how should modernising technology and economy accommodate public concerns about the impact of built infrastructure on the British countryside? The modernist response was proportion: as Fairbrother noted here, the size of pylons and masts needed to reflect the 'large-scale' lines of the landscape. The views of modernist planners and landscape architects converged with countryside preservationists in their preference for ordering and scale over the intrusion of urban 'clutter' into rural scenery. The state drive for reconstruction and modernisation served the country-side preservation movement with several challenges, not least the expansion and intensification of such infrastructure.

This chapter examines debates between preservationists, landscape architects, and utility providers about the meaning of amenity and landscape change in upland

---

[1] Nan Fairbrother, *New Lives, New Landscapes* (London, Architectural Press, 1970), p. 133.
[2] Sylvia Crowe, *The Landscape of Power* (London, Architectural Press, 1958).

Proceedings of the British Academy, **256**, 92–114, © The British Academy 2023.

England, specifically in the Pennine moorland of south-east Lancashire and the West Riding of Yorkshire. With the establishment of National Parks and Areas of Outstanding Natural Beauty (AONB) as part of the post-war national social-democratic settlement, countryside preservation was focused on landscapes classed for their aesthetic value, as unspoilt areas worth saving for the nation. As we will see, it often excluded areas that were not regarded as 'naturally beautiful'. Preservationist discourse about rural infrastructure was not unified, and the fault lines could be seen along the boundaries of the National Parks. This chapter looks beyond the chronologies of 20th-century modernism to consider the earlier large-scale construction of reservoirs and canals in the rural landscape. It then charts three interventions raised by preservationists in the region, with evidence derived from the public local inquiries engendered by their challenges.[3] The controversies took place in the era of technological modernisation and nationalisation of utilities: first, the expansion of military requisitioning of moorland; second, the construction of networks for high-voltage electricity and television communications; and third, the contested route of the Pennine Way long distance trail. These landscape interventions exacerbated tensions between national and statutory definitions of amenity, within the preservationist movement between local and central committees, and between northern and southern interests. The conclusions of the debates ultimately rested on different interests' interpretations of amenity value and the impact of large-scale infrastructure for local residents.

Rural modernisms

Rural modernism was shaped by the countryside preservation movements' negotiation with utility companies and local authorities over the siting of regional infrastructure projects. The regional bounds of these contests are central to this narrative. Denis Cosgrove, Simon Rycroft, and Barbara Roscoe's study of the construction of Ladybower Reservoir in the Peak District in 1945 and Rutland Water in the 1970s is a starting point. They argue that, rather than a homogeneous national Englishness, landscape design 'varied together with attitudes to environmental access and conservancy according to the "reading" of the different regional landscape types'.[4] Matthew Kelly's examination of landscape change in Dartmoor National Park in Devon similarly underlines the key role of preservationist bodies in defending a

---

[3] The Museum of English Rural Life, University of Reading (MERL), SR CPRE C/1, Council for the Preservation of Rural England (CPRE) archives; Lancashire County Record Office (LCRO), Lancashire branch of the CPRE records; Parliamentary Archives, FCP, Forests and Commons Preservation Society records; The National Archives (TNA), POWE, Ministry of Fuel and Power records.

[4] Denis Cosgrove, Barbara Roscoe, and Simon Rycroft, 'Landscape and identity at Ladybower Reservoir', *Transactions of the Institute of British Geographers*, 21:3 (1996), 537; David Matless, 'Regional surveys and local knowledges: The geographical imagination in Britain, 1918–39', *Transactions of the Institute of British Geographers*, 17:4 (1992), 464–480.

special regional landscape and moulding the incursions of new infrastructure as well as the excesses of requisitioning of the moorland by utility companies and the military.[5] The Ladybower scheme demonstrated the post-war Labour government's technocratic-led reconstruction effort that characterises much of rural modernist infrastructure built in this period. These schemes implemented large-scale facilities for urban utilities, including water and electricity, by harnessing the power of nature and its ecosystems services on a national scale. But these impulses were not new. They formed part of a much longer schema of modernisation. Victorian and Edwardian engineers and city fathers thought of themselves as modern, pushing forward civilisation through municipal projects. Modernist initiatives following the Second World War differed in that they were instigated by a socialistic and state-centred government programme of redevelopment, replacing the more speculative and laissez-faire private sector initiatives that local councils had adopted at the end of the 19th century. But the outcomes were, in many respects, aesthetically and technocratically, rooted in the earlier age.

There were other precedents of mass infrastructure in the uplands. In the 1870s, the controversy over Manchester Corporation's construction of Thirlmere reservoir in Cumberland was arguably the prototype for later environmental confrontations over the building of mass infrastructure. Harriet Ritvo notes the 'almost routine' level of contestation over large-scale public works projects undertaken by municipal authorities in the late 19th century, not least other reservoir projects and railway expansion. What the Thirlmere case did in particular was to promote the idea of a pristine Lake District as a landscape antithesis to artificial reservoirs, even though it was widely accepted that the region was already scarred with quarries and mines and altered by commercial forestry.[6] And as with the later National Trust and National Park designations, the Thirlmere case entrenched a preservationist ideal of a national landscape, which had to be defended against compulsory purchase by commercial or non-local interests not merely for the benefit of local inhabitants but for the whole public who would use the landscape as an amenity and view it as a visual amenity.[7] The construction of Ladybower reservoir in 1945 should therefore be understood as a continuation of 'the later Victorian vision of human conquest of nature', as begun by the municipal authorities at Thirlmere and other reservoir and dam building projects.[8]

Although the preservationists sought to depict the southern Pennine moors as wilderness, in which the urban had intruded by quarrying and mines in the

---

[5] Matthew Kelly, *Quartz and Feldspar: Dartmoor: A British Landscape in Modern Times* (London, Jonathan Cape, 2015).

[6] Harriet Ritvo, 'Manchester v. Thirlmere and the construction of the Victorian environment', *Victorian Studies*, 49:3 (2007), 463.

[7] Ritvo, 'Manchester v Thirlmere', 457; Harriet Ritvo, *The Dawn of Green: Manchester, Thirlmere and Modern Environmentalism* (Chicago, University of Chicago Press, 2010); Kelly, *Quartz and Feldspar*, p. 278.

[8] Cosgrove *et al.*, 'Landscape and identity', 537.

substructure, and textile mills on its waterways and valleys, they did so by conveniently glossing over other industrial constructions in the moorland landscape.
Blackstone Edge is an isolated outcrop of millstone grit on the Lancashire–Yorkshire
border near Rochdale. The landscape had been altered with major communications
networks long before the erection of electricity pylons and other features of post-
war energy infrastructure. The Rochdale Canal Act was passed in 1794, enabling
a new, extensive and completely artificial supply system.[9] There were 20 miles
of feeder channels, built using local gritstone, linking a series of reservoirs along
the moors. The early 19th-century maintenance track alongside the feeder channel
linking Blackstone Edge to Light Hazzles reservoirs became part of the Pennine
Way in 1965.[10] Hollingworth Lake, constructed on the valley shelf in 1797, soon
became a leisure resort for the local working classes in the 19th century. It is this
designation as a public amenity that, as we will see, also fed into later debates about
the value of the landscape.

Defining landscape amenity value in areas like the southern Pennines involved
a distinction between aesthetic norms of 'natural beauty' and the more pragmatic
defence of such areas as public amenities. Ecology and nature conservation were
late to the decision-making process. This is not to say that naturalists and artists
in the southern Pennines had a completely different view of 'natural beauty' or
ecology. The political radical Samuel Bamford published *Walks in South Lancashire*
in 1844, in which he nostalgically depicted the picturesque elements of the rapidly
vanishing footpaths, flora, and fauna of his local environment.[11] But the association
between bare moorland and 'wilderness' with public access was also celebrated as
the campaign to save commons and footpaths from enclosure grew apace during
the 19th century.[12] Wilderness was appreciated both from afar in landscape painting
and from within through literary culture (Emily Brontë's *Wuthering Heights* was
published in 1847). Various groups, from nonconformist religious sects and the
Chartist democratic movement holding mass rallies on the moors, to pedestrianism
and fell runners and Clarion cyclists, cemented an association between the Pennines
and ideas about the working class being able to escape the problems of urban
industrial life.[13] Melanie Tebbutt has shown how Derbyshire ramblers around the
turn of the century promoted the wildness of the Dark Peak to prove a sense of
masculinity in an era of social and imperial crisis.[14] Ben Anderson argues that the

---

[9] Manchester Archives, MISC Papers/5 (32652)/59, Ralph Shuttleworth papers, 1797.

[10] Keith Parry, *TransPennine Heritage: Hills, People and Transport* (Newton Abbot, David and Charles, 1981), pp. 62–69.

[11] Samuel Bamford, *Walks in South Lancashire and on its Borders* (Manchester, 1844), https://minor
victorianwriters.org.uk/bamford/b_walks.htm [accessed 30 October 2022].

[12] Wendy Darby, *Landscape and Identity: Geographies of Nation and Class in England* (Oxford, Berg, 2000), p. 130.

[13] Katrina Navickas, 'Moors, fields and popular protest in South Lancashire and the West Riding of Yorkshire, 1800–1848', *Northern History*, 46:1 (2009), 93–111.

[14] Melanie Tebbutt, 'Rambling and manly identity in Derbyshire's Dark Peak, 1880s–1920s', *Historical Journal*, 49 (2006), 1125–1153.

Manchester Ramblers' Federation employed the rhetoric of freedom in the fells to regulate and order urban users of the countryside.[15] But, wilderness was also associated with poverty. As Paul Readman suggests, by the later 19th century, the aesthetic concern with upland moorland scenery in art and literature increasingly reflected a middle-class preoccupation with investigating social problems. 'Dreary' landscapes provided 'appropriate settings for depictions of hardships of rural life and labour at a time of agricultural depression'.[16]

In the 1940s, 'wildness' and wilderness became central characteristics upon which natural landscape value was categorised. Discourses of national landscapes in the 1920s and 1930s were based on the preservationists' desire to preserve a variety of geographical features. But ecologists and writers in the 1940s promoted the value of wildness and natural ecology of uncultivated uplands, notably Arthur Tansley, in his 1945 book *Our Heritage of Wild Nature*. He noted in the case of upland hill country unsuited to arable farming that it was 'unlikely that all the areas which should be protected from defacement and exploitation will be covered and the scheme of National Parks should be supplemented by a number of Scheduled Areas'. Tansley was appointed to the government's Wildlife Conservation Special Committee in 1945, which made the case for National Nature Reserves. He became the first chairman of the Nature Conservancy in 1952.[17] The mass trespass on Kinder Scout in 1932 had also raised the profile of the issue of public access to grouse moors and mountains, and the unsatisfactory provisions of the 1939 Access to Mountains Act were ameliorated by the 1949 National Parks and Access to the Countryside Act. Yet the focus on these specific uplands therefore resulted in the exclusion of lowland and southern landscapes such as the South Downs in Sussex and the Norfolk Broads from the Act, as they were regarded as too cultivated or altered by human intervention (despite the long history of farming and extraction in the Lake District).[18] This shift to protection of 'wild' uplands made the lack of protection for the southern and western Pennines even more frustrating for local preservationists, as in their view, expressed at all the public inquiries, areas such as Blackstone Edge and Belmont Moor were clearly made of the same landscape as those of the nearby Peak District moorland.

The southern and western Pennines were initially considered as one of 30 regional reserves proposed by John Dower at the Standing Committee on National Parks, in 1943. Dower did not solely advocate aesthetic beauty over everyday

---

[15] Ben Anderson, 'A liberal countryside? The Manchester Ramblers' Federation and the "social readjustment" of urban citizens, 1929–1936', *Urban History*, 38:1 (2011), 81–102.

[16] Paul Readman, *Storied Ground: Landscape and the Shaping of English National Identity* (Cambridge, Cambridge University Press, 2018), pp. 54–55; Howard Rodee, 'The "dreary landscape" as a background for scenes of rural poverty in Victorian paintings', *Art Journal*, 36:4 (1977), 307–313.

[17] Arthur George Tansley, *Our Heritage of Wild Nature* (Cambridge, Cambridge University Press, 2013 [1945]), p. 50; Peter G. Ayres, *Shaping Ecology: The Life of Arthur Tansley* (London, Wiley, 2012), p. 9.

[18] Cosgrove *et al.*, 'Landscape and identity', 542; Gordon Cherry and Alan Rogers, *Rural Change and Planning: England and Wales in the Twentieth Century* (London, Taylor & Francis, 2003).

amenity for local residents. In a lecture he gave in July 1939 to the Lancashire branch of the Council for the Preservation of Rural England (CPRE), Dower considered preservation needs in what he termed the 'ordinary' countryside that characterised much of the landscapes outside the 'extraordinary' and 'wilder' areas he sought to designate as National Parks.[19] Kelly notes how the 'wilderness' attributed to National Parks was not drawn from their North American precedents of pristine nature unpeopled (by settler-colonists), but rather were conceived as heritage or cultural landscapes.[20] The resulting Dower Report of 1945 termed the area of moorland bordering what became the Peak District National Park, as 'the Industrial Pennines'. This term classified the landscape in relation to the textile producing towns and villages in the Irwell, Ribble, and Calder valleys below the moors. During the nationalising, modernising, and centralising impulses of the post-war Attlee government, however, Dower's holistic aims for the English and Welsh countryside were subsumed by other economic and agricultural imperatives.[21] The planning and designation process for areas outside the new National Parks were driven by interests both inside and outside the new government, not least the ministries of Defence, Housing and Local Government, and Agriculture, the Forestry Commission, and the newly nationalised water and electricity companies.

Fifty-two smaller Conservation Areas were then proposed in 1946, but by 1947, the Hobhouse report on National Parks narrowed down the list of areas to be designated. The plans eventually resulted in a smaller number of AONB established in 1951.[22] Even these AONB, as Margaret Anderson has pointed out, were less broadly supported than the 10 National Parks that formed the backbone of the 1949 National Parks and Access to the Countryside Act, and were regarded merely as designations for the county council planning authorities to manage as amenity spaces.[23] Dower concluded that not all the 'relatively wild' areas were suitable for designation as they were not beautiful enough, such as the industrial Pennines, or were used for quarrying, military use, forestry or 'other purposes which cannot be successfully combined with National Park requirements'.[24] So the southern and

---

[19] John Sheail, 'John Dower, National Parks and town and country planning in Britain', *Planning Perspectives*, 10 (1995), 12.

[20] Kelly, *Quartz and Feldspar*, p. 220.

[21] David Wilkinson, *Fight for It Now: John Dower and the Struggle for National Parks in Britain* (London, Signal Books, 2019), p. 207; Matthew Kelly, 'Conventional thinking and the fragile birth of the nature state in postwar Britain', in Wilko Graf von Hardenberg, Matthew Kelly, Claudia Leal, and Emily Wakild (eds), *The Nature State: Rethinking the History of Conservation* (Abingdon, Routledge, 2017), p. 116.

[22] HMSO, *Report of the National Parks Commission, England and Wales*, July 1947, pp. 51–52; Wilkinson, *Fight for It Now*, p. 119.

[23] Margaret Anderson, 'Areas of Outstanding Natural Beauty and the 1949 National Parks Act', *The Town Planning Review*, 61:3 (1990), 313, 316.

[24] Michael Dower, 'AONB – the formative years, 1945 to 1988' (talk at NAAONB Conference July 2006), transcript, p. 1, https://landscapesforlife.org.uk/application/files/7615/8928/8605/Dower._M_-_Report_to_the_NAAONB_Conference_2006.pdf [accessed 30 October 2022].

west Pennines outside the boundaries of the Peak District National Park were left outside any national designation of protection.[25]

The term 'Industrial Pennines' was a contested designation that continued to be a bone of contention for the preservation and amenity bodies throughout the rest of the 20th century. Much of the internal conflict involved questions of authority and agency in dealing with the legacy of 19th-century industrialisation in an era of, first, technological modernisation, and then deindustrialisation. As Fairbrother and other critical commentators recognised, local authorities and residents faced the problems of a post-industrial economy and of managing the legacies of industrial, fossil fuel, and infrastructural infrastructure on areas with damaged ecologies. The (post-)industrial Pennines reveal tensions and divisions within different interest groups.

The debates – and the archives – were dominated by the two secretaries of the Lancashire and the Sheffield and Peak District branches of the CPRE. Philip Barnes of the Lancashire branch was a veteran Sheffield mass trespasser.[26] His counterparts in south Yorkshire were Lieutenant Colonel Gerald Haythornthwaite and his wife Ethel. Colonel Haythornthwaite was an architect, planning consultant, and national president of the Ramblers' Association. Ethel Haythornthwaite was the only woman to sit on the Hobhouse Committee on National Parks in 1945–1946.[27] These branches of the CPRE and its affiliated groups clearly saw themselves as different from the southern branches. They were more defensive of working-class participation in the landscape and its activities, and often came into conflict with the central executive committee because of their ideas of what the rural landscape was and how amenity should be both defined and defended. Doubts had been raised both at the time by electricity and water boards, and more recently by historians, about the extent to which preservationist groups were representative of public opinion. Arguably – and Barnes and the Haythornthwaites made this defence at the various public inquiries – their branches of the CPRE, through their federated structure, represented the wide range of working-class memberships involved in rambling, mountaineering, cycling, and naturalist clubs, and co-operative holiday fellowships, more so than the more middle-class concerns of the central executives and aristocratic patrons.[28]

A statutory and administrative separation was enforced between preservation for amenity and for nature between the National Parks Commission and the Nature Conservancy, which also impacted on the ability of northern preservationists to

[25] Karl Spracklen, 'Millstone grit; Blackstone Edge: Literary and heritage tourism in the South Pennines', in Glenn Hooper (ed.), *Heritage and Tourism in Britain and Ireland* (London, Palgrave Macmillan, 2017), p. 73.
[26] David Hey, 'Kinder Scout and the legend of the mass trespass', *Agricultural History Review*, 59:2 (2011), 214.
[27] See *Sheffield Telegraph*, 1 November 1952, for a profile of the Haythornthwaites; Wilkinson, *Fight for It Now*, p. 171.
[28] TNA, POWE 14/1886, public inquiry, Barnsley, October 1963, report.

make the case for protection. The concept of 'natural beauty' in the National Parks Act and in the designation of AONB associated the aesthetics of preservation with particular types of landscape. By excluding the 'Industrial Pennines' from the preservation areas, the result of the National Parks Act, combined with the rationalisation of planning authorities in the 1947 Town and Country Planning Act, was to keep planning relating to preservation on a regional level. This was not necessarily a bad outcome, as it offered the potential for local knowledge to direct local policy. Zoning was mandated by regional plans developed by the county or county borough planning authorities. But often the more pressing priorities of developing large estates of residential housing took precedence over protecting green space or ameliorating post-industrial sites. And by the 1960s, the mid-century technocratic and somewhat abstract visions of land utilisation surveys and regional plans were becoming evident as outdated and not workable in a changing economy.[29]

Wirescapes

The Electricity Act 1957 was the first major piece of legislation to include an amenity clause, section 37, which mandated electricity companies to 'take into account any effect which the proposals would have on the natural beauty of the countryside or on any such flora, fauna, features, buildings or objects'.[30] The insertion of the clause gave a national statutory effect for measures that had already been implemented in the Highlands and North Wales in the acts. The amenity clause was then considered in further legislation regarding coal and water from 1958 to 1963, and finally became a key element of the Countryside Acts of 1967 and 1968.[31] Again, the legislation cemented the association of aesthetic appreciation within amenity considerations. These tensions and parallel responsibilities were arguably still enshrined by the 1974 Sandford Report on National Parks policy, which established the Sandford Principle that 'the preservation of natural beauty' should take priority over the 'promotion of public enjoyment' in cases where public access might negatively affect conservation in National Parks.[32] Ecosystems services were essentially still separate issues for planners. While environmental and ecological concerns began to be appreciated in the later legislation, and perhaps more incrementally in regional planning, the experience of the preservationists in public

---

[29] Simon Rycroft and Denis Cosgrove, 'Mapping the modern nation: Dudley Stamp and the land utilisation survey', *History Workshop Journal*, 40:1 (1995), 102.

[30] https://www.legislation.gov.uk/ukpga/Eliz2/5-6/48/enacted [accessed 30 October 2022].

[31] John Sheail, 'The "amenity" clause: An insight into half a century of environmental protection in the United Kingdom', *Transactions of the Institute of British Geographers*, 17:2 (1992), 152–165; John Sheail, 'The management of wildlife and amenity: A UK post-war perspective', *Contemporary Record*, 7:1 (1993), 44–65.

[32] Kelly, 'Conventional thinking', p. 128.

inquiries illustrated the predominance of aesthetics over everyday use in amenity considerations in the implementation of infrastructure in the southern Pennines.

The construction of the Super Grid high-voltage electricity network posed bigger issues of scale than the initial National Grid erected in the 1930s. The National Parks Commission admitted that though overhead wires, pylons, and transmitters would 'seriously disfigure the landscape in areas of specially vulnerable beauty', it recognised the huge extra cost in placing cabling underground and 'the import-ance of economical electricity supply in National Parks as in other rural areas will call for restraint in making such demands upon the industry'.[33] Preservation for public amenity, meaning access for leisure and recreation, was a debated definition, complicated by the multiplying layers of administrative and legal bodies respon-sible for areas of countryside.[34] In places outside the National Parks and AONB, by contrast, preservationists found it more difficult to argue for aesthetic appearance of the natural landscape as the key feature that would prevent the siting of infrastruc-ture. At a debate at the Royal Society in 1959, Philip Barnes noted:

> I have never described a Super Grid pylon by itself as ugly: individually it may be a graceful thing. But again, what do we find in practice? ... all of different design, of different heights, of different spans. ... Well, that may be the landscape of power, but it shows no respect for the beauty of England.[35]

The influence of Sylvia Crowe and the idea of the wirescape was clearly evident.

A process of negotiation between modernist requirements for function and preservationist concerns for aesthetic 'fit' with the landscape were at play. At Ladybower reservoir, the Sheffield and Peak District branch of the CPRE pushed for use of native gritstone, both crushed in the concrete for the viaducts, and cut and dressed for the control rooms and valve houses attached to the dam. The CPRE claimed that using local materials would achieve a 'fitness of purpose', which, Cosgrove *et al.* argue, 'signified a congruence between locality and form rather than a modern harmony of technique and function'.[36] Transmitter masts for police communications, radio, and now television, were also situated in the same areas. By functionality, they needed to be sited at the highest and unobstructed points of moorland. The BBC chose Holme Moss as the third site in its new public television transmitter network, 1,700 feet above sea level on the moors above Huddersfield, West Riding of Yorkshire. Its transmitting range covered most of west Yorkshire, Lancashire and Cheshire. During its construction in 1949, the Sheffield and Peak

---

[33] HMSO, *Report of the National Parks Commission, England and Wales*, July 1947, paras 143–144; Rosemary Shirley, 'Pylons and frozen peas: The Women's Institute goes electric', in Paul Brassley, Jeremy Burchardt and Karen Sayer (eds), *Transforming the Countryside: The Electrification of Rural Britain* (Abingdon, Routledge, 2017), pp. 139–143.

[34] Katrina Navickas, 'Conflicts of power, landscape and amenity in debates over the British Super Grid in the 1950s', *Rural History*, 30:1 (2019), 87–103.

[35] Christopher Hinton and William Holford, 'Preserving amenities: Power production and transmission in the countryside', *Journal of the Royal Society of Arts*, 108:5043 (1960), 205–206.

[36] Cosgrove *et al.*, 'Landscape and identity', 539–540.

District CPRE negotiated with the BBC to ensure that the base of the transmitter would be in a vernacular style, to 'reduce the effect of the buildings upon their wild setting', and should therefore be constructed in local stone, with dry laid walls, and a pitched roof. The BBC agreed, apart from retaining a pitched roof for technical reasons.[37] The publicity news reel produced by the BBC commented on how the locally quarried stone used for the exterior 'tones it in with the soft colours of the moors'.[38] The base would always, however, be dwarfed by the 750-foot steel mast towering above it.[39] Similar negotiations were undertaken with other companies building communications networks across the country in 1949–1950. Writing to the Ministry of Works about a Post Office television relay station on Windy Hill, Bleakedgate Moor, Littleborough, south of Blackstone Edge (Figure 5.1), Philip Barnes was conciliatory and did not oppose the scheme. He took the example of his colleagues in the Sheffield branch in insisting nevertheless that the buildings should be built in stone to reflect the neighbouring farms and cottages.[40] The public popularity of the new erections should be noted. In July 1963, over a thousand people attended an open day at the Winter Hill transmitter (built by Independent Television in 1956) above Bolton, Lancashire.[41]

Transmitter masts fitted within the grand scale of the moorland environment because they were solitary. The new 400kV pylon network of the Super Grid constructed at the same time to modernise the existing 132kV National Grid erected in the 1930s, by contrast, was more problematic for preservationists. The electricity boards refused on economy grounds to run any cabling underground in sites outside National Parks.[42] The land use categorisations set out by the National Parks Act and regional plans intersected with the geographies laid out by modernising infrastructure, and created fault lines over which areas were designated of national importance. The preservationists accused the electricity board of having 'escaped its obligations under planning laws because they were answerable only to Parliament and they had a close association with the Minister of Power who adjudicated on their proposals'.[43] But even within the terms of the National Parks Act, the National Parks Commission could only negotiate over the appearance of power stations rather than object outright to their siting.[44] Matthew Kelly's study of the public inquiry into the siting of the BBC transmitter on North Hessary Tor on

[37] Annual Report, CPRE Sheffield and Peak District, 1950, p. 10.

[38] BBC online archive, 12 October 1951, https://www.bbc.co.uk/archive/holme-moss-transmitter/z44d rj6 [accessed 19 May 2021].

[39] See the front page of *The Radio Times*, 1456, 7–13 October 1951, https://genome.ch.bbc.co.uk/page/ e9e4e43177be442ba887975e4feec437 [accessed 19 May 2021].

[40] LCRO, CPRE archives, box 16, Barnes to Colquitt, 13 April 1950.

[41] *The Stage*, 20 August 1963.

[42] Shirley, 'Pylons and frozen peas', p. 143.

[43] TNA, POWE 14/1686, public inquiry, Barnsley, October 1963, report, p. 19.

[44] See Christine Wall, '"Nuclear prospects": The siting and construction of Sizewell A power station 1957–1966', *Contemporary British History*, 33:2 (2019), 1–28.

K. Navickas

Figure 5.1 Sketch of Windy Hill transmitter, 1950, Lancashire County Record Office, Lancashire CPRE records, box 16. Reproduced with permission from Lancashire Archives, Lancashire County Council

Dartmoor has shown a similar situation whereby preservationists rapidly became disillusioned with the seemingly toothless powers of National Park authorities.[45]

These conflicts were undercut with differences of class and geography. Tensions were evident not just between the electricity companies and the preservationists, but within the preservationist groups themselves, and indeed between centre and local branches of the main societies, notably within the CPRE. In September 1950, Barnes challenged the priorities laid out by Sir Herbert Griffin, general secretary of the CPRE and a National Parks commissioner. The central committee had issued their opposition to the Super Grid pylons crossing areas of what they termed national significance. Barnes retorted: 'At the end I think the word "national" should not be used. The interference is that only in areas of "national" landscape interest should cables be placed underground.' Barnes vociferously asserted that by focusing solely on National Parks, there would be an inevitable neglect of areas outside their remit, not least the western and southern Pennines:

> Many of your Branches are not concerned with National Parks at all but are concerned with lovely country of regional or local importance. I have never believed that you can so define landscape values and if you do so you run into the grave danger of persuading the official world to spend what little they will on 'amenity' in a few areas only and allowing the great bulk of the countryside to go without any.[46]

In the consultations before the Super Grid public local inquiry at Oldham, Lancashire, in 1959, Barnes wrote to Griffin about his disappointment at 'how extremely unhelpful the National Parks Commission can be when dealing with landscapes which, although in easy reach of millions of people, cannot be labelled of "national" importance'.[47] He reiterated the use value of amenity of the southern Pennines to industrial urban inhabitants, which he defended as just as or indeed more important 'than the more famous places the majority will never see', such as the Lake District or Mount Snowdon.

This thread of defining visual amenity and natural beauty continued into the 1960s. In 1963, at the public local inquiry at Barnsley into the section of the Super Grid that crossed from Stalybridge in Cheshire into the top of the Peak District at Thorpe Marsh, the Central Electricity Generating Board (CEGB) argued that only 'transcendent' landscapes could justify the cost of underground cabling over the erection of pylons. Their representatives insisted: 'It is plainly not enough to justify the incurring of costs of this kind up and down the length and breadth of England that the landscape should merely be something pleasing or interesting or fine. It must be something of transcendent or surpassing value.' Speaking for the CPRE, Colonel Haythornthwaite was incensed that the CEGB had described the Pennine moorland as 'bleak and grim'. The CEGB even questioned the visual amenity of the section of the Peak District that bordered the industrial districts at Stalybridge: 'the

[45] Kelly, *Quartz and Feldspar*, p. 241.
[46] LCRO, CPRE, box 16, Barnes to Griffin, 15 September 1950.
[47] MERL, SR CPRE C/1/62/90, Barnes to Griffin, 9 July 1959.

Board argued that the northern part of the Park which this line would cross was grim and monotonous, quite different in quality from the dales in the south where the real beauty of the Park lay'.[48] Haythornthwaite stressed the need to maintain the areas as a place of adventure and wilderness. His defence directly cited Sir Christopher Hinton's 1959 lecture to the Royal Society, *Preserving Amenities*, and Sylvia Crowe's *The Landscape of Power*, on the difficulties of maintaining integrity in a mass mechanical infrastructure. In part, this was rhetorical flourish, using the chair of the CEGB and its landscape consultant to complicate the debate. But it also reflected his genuine concern for the impact on the rural environment in terms of scale and access. Haythornthwaite lamented: 'The overhead transmission line was a symbol of men's anxiety for security, comfort and convenience, not wanted where man wished to find his full stature in the presence of nature.' In arguing, ultimately unsuccessfully, for underground cabling, he pointed to the previous failures of the National Parks Commission to prevent landscape desecration, and the more effective resistance of the CPRE in negotiating with the government and corporations, notably with the BBC over the appearance of the Holme Moss television mast.[49]

Friction continued between the central executive of the CPRE and its northern branches. In several cases, they feared that Philip Barnes in particular was going directly against central policy in his statements to public inquiries on all kinds of landscape change, and in their publicity. One such case was in 1962, in relation to the public inquiry into the siting of a power station in Holme Pierrepont, Nottinghamshire. The massive increase in demand for power for industry and new housing encouraged the electricity boards to invest in developing a huge power plant network integrated with nearby coal mines and the River Trent, that quickly became known as 'Megawatt Valley', producing a quarter of the UK's power.[50] CPRE assistant secretary M. V. Osmond wrote to Barnes about comments in the Lancashire branch's annual report that railed against the new power stations: 'If the CPRE goes on record as opposing an application to which there are clearly no objections on rural amenity grounds whatever, it will make it almost impossible for us to oppose any coal fired power station in a rural setting ever again – or for that matter many other industrial undertakings.' It is evident that the central executive saw the urban base of the Lancashire branch in particular as a problem.[51] Barnes typically defended himself and the branch in his reply, arguing that CPRE branches in industrial areas 'must think along broader lines than that of strict rural

[48] TNA, POWE 14/1686, Public Inquiry, Barnsley, October 1963.

[49] TNA, POWE 14/1686, Public Inquiry, Barnsley, October 1963, p. 20, citing Christopher Hinton, *Preserving Amenities* (London, CEGB, 1959), p. 7; Crowe, *Landscape of Power*, pp. 20–21.

[50] Historic England, *20th Century Coal and Oil-Fired Power Generation: Introduction to Heritage Assets* (Swindon, Historic England, 2015), pp. 7–8, https://historicengland.org.uk/images-books/publications/iha-20thcentury-coal-oil-fired-electric-power-generation/heag056-electric-power-generation-iha/ [accessed 30 October 2022].

[51] MERL, SR CPRE C/1/34/18, Osmond to Barnes, 6 September 1962.

preservation'. Again he emphasised their wider definition of amenity: 'I am confident that the CPRE time and time again, has stressed "amenity" objections which are not "visual" objections – such as the likelihood of smells, noise and public safety.'[52] The divide over the meaning of amenity began with questions of aesthetic value, but fractured over whether an association dedicated to 'rural England' should include defending landscapes they regarded as too urban or industrial to have value for local (working-class) inhabitants.

Military requisitioning

Military requisitioning of land remained a significant issue after the Second World War. The Requisitioned Land and War Works Act 1945 allowed for Compulsory Purchase Orders for land deemed suitable for military service requirements, and its passage was contested by the preservation societies. In 1946, the armed services controlled nearly a million acres, but were calling for the acquisition of a further three million acres.[53] Although moves towards greater sensitivity to the landscape were considered in the establishment of the Nature Conservancy in 1949, as Paul Readman's chapter in this volume illustrates, the impact of military infrastructure and activity on the ecology and environment of such sites was intense and prolonged.[54] The CPRE were at the forefront of opposing further expansion of the military estate in new areas. At a joint conference with the Town and Country Planning Association in 1947, 'The Countryside Today and Tomorrow', the CPRE assistant secretary noted the tension in the proposals for military uses of areas in the proposed National Parks. By definition, these were 'extensive areas of relatively wild country' and were therefore better suited for the purpose than 'equally extensive areas of productive agricultural land'. Public inquiries had already been raised to consider proposals on Dartmoor and Ashdown Forest.[55]

Outside the National Parks, the issue was entangled in the control of large swathes of moorland by water companies for reservoirs and catchment areas, the

[52] MERL, SR CPRE C/1/34/18, Barnes to Osmond, 11 September 1962.

[53] David Evans, *History of Nature Conservation in Britain* (London, Routledge, 1992), p. 72.

[54] See Marianna Dudley, *An Environmental History of the UK Defence Estate* (London, Continuum, 2012); Marianna Dudley, 'Traces of conflict: Environment and eviction in British military training areas, 1943 to present', *Journal of War and Culture Studies*, 6:2 (2013), 112–126; John Sheail, 'War and the development of nature conservation in Britain', *Journal of Environmental Management*, 44:3 (1995), 267–283.

[55] Gary Willis, 'An arena of glorious work: The protection of the rural landscape against the demands of Britain's Second World War effort', *Rural History*, 29:2 (2018), 261, 273–274; Kelly, *Quartz and Feldspar*, pp. 309–311. London Metropolitan Archives, CL/PK/1/46, CPRE and TCPA conference, 1947. Willis argues however that in participating in the 1946–1947 Inter Departmental Committee on Service Land Requirements, the CPRE ended up ultimately in aiding the government and the Ministry of Defence in their requisitioning schemes. Nor did the CPRE challenge wholesale felling of woodland and open cast mining until late in the war (276).

continuing legacy of the 19th-century rural infrastructure servicing the industrial cities. In 1948, the Ministry of Defence proposed to requisition 3,000 acres of moorland in the west Pennines near Bolton for a territorial training ground. The Army's justification for using the site was that the whole area had been used extensively by US troops during the war, including employing abandoned farmsteads for target practice.[56] The chosen site in the western Pennines was part of the catchment area of Liverpool Corporation's waterworks at the Anglezarke reservoir. It was also within sight of the line that would be proposed for the Super Grid over Belmont Hill, and near to Winter Hill, where the police and television transmitter towers were being erected at the same time. The preservationist bodies and local authorities' planning committees proposed an alternative site of Hailstorm Hill, 1,580 acres in the Rossendale valley in east Lancashire, which was in the catchment area of Heywood and Middleton Water Board. A second alternative site was located at the foothills of Blackstone Edge, part of the gathering grounds of Oldham and Rochdale Water Joint Board (Figure 5.2). The Lancashire branch of the CPRE opposed the plan for the sites at both Anglezarke and Blackstone Edge. They argued that the rifle shooting and tank manoeuvres would disturb the leisure facilities at Hollingworth Lake, which Philip Barnes described as 'one of Lancashire's most popular playgrounds, where the ordinary working folk of the nearby towns congregate at weekends'. Another objection feared that military vehicles would endanger the nearby 'Roman Road' (actually a 17th-century paved packhorse route) over the top of the moor, which the Council of British Archaeology had designated of specific interest.[57]

Much of the language surrounding the opposition sought to define the Pennine moorland as a place of both natural beauty and local amenity. All three moorlands were classified as commons with a general public right of access under section 193 of the 1925 Law of Property Act, as they lay within the boundaries of urban district councils. Barnes further pointed out with regard to Blackstone Edge that 'all of the area lies within the boundary of the South Pennines Conservation Area recommended in the National Parks Report' (although this was a rhetorical guise, given that the recommended area was not implemented).[58] A comparison of the three sites in a CPRE document of May 1949 exemplified their categorisations of types of natural beauty and amenity. Anglezarke Moor was classed as 'of high scenic and amenity value being in a unique position in the heart of industrial Lancashire'. Hailstorm Hill was 'not of high scenic or amenity value', and 'the natural contours have been spoiled to some extent by quarrying and the scenery is certainly not of the same grandeur and popularity as on Anglezarke'.[59] Blackstone

---

[56] http://www.lancashireatwar.co.uk/rivington-at-war/4594325800 [accessed 19 May 2021].
[57] LCRO, Lancashire CPRE annual report, 1950–1; *Manchester Evening News*, 9 September 1950.
[58] LCRO, Lancashire CPRE files, box 14, 1951, statement by Barnes, 10 March 1950.
[59] LCRO, Lancashire CPRE annual report, 1947–1948.

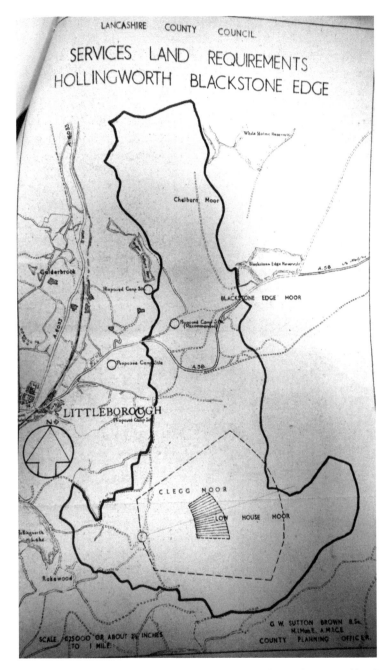

Figure 5.2 Map of service land requirements, Blackstone Edge, 1949, Lancashire County Record Office, Lancashire CPRE records, box 14. Reproduced with permission from Lancashire Archives, Lancashire County Council

Edge was classed as 'more attractive than Hailstorm Hill', and as stated, had high amenity as a leisure destination for local residents.[60]

A public local inquiry was held at Chorley in January 1951. The War Department and Ministry of Health advised that the Hailstorm Hill area was unsuitable owing to possible pollution of water supplies. Anglezarke Moor was chosen, and despite an appeal, was approved by the government as the site for the territorial army training ground and mortar range.[61] Throughout the debates, the question of amenity had been channelled to the potential impact on the main landowners' ecosystems services, that is on the purity of the water in the gathering grounds of the water boards. The leisure and beauty definitions of amenity put forward by the preservationist groups were a secondary consideration in the decision. The debates differed from those related to National Parks areas because public access was intended for local (and predominantly working-class) residents of the industrial towns and villages, rather than considering these as 'national' landscapes visited by all. Any impact on the ecology of the moorland, other than pollution of the drinking supply, was also a secondary consideration. It would take the implementation of large-scale energy and communications infrastructure to alert planners to environmental amenity concerns, though again there was always a difficult negotiation over economic efficiency and the rights of private landowners. Yet it was not long until the military priorities began to change. Following a Defence White Paper in 1957, demilitarisation of some formerly requisitioned sites and the transformation of others to deal with the nuclear threat created new modernist installations, not least the 'golf balls' radomes on RAF Menwith Hill, north Yorkshire.[62]

The Pennine Way

Proposals for the route of the Pennine Way, the first long distance National Trail, also stoked tensions within the preservationist movement, notably leading again to central executive committees seeking to rein in their local branches. The 250-mile route of the Pennine Way stretched from Edale in the Peak District along the Pennine ridge to the Yorkshire Dales and on through Northumberland to the Scottish border. Tom Stephenson lobbied for the proposals upon taking up the secretaryship of the Ramblers' Association after the Second World War. The concept of the Pennine Way was approved in 1950 by Hugh Dalton, then Minister of Town and Country Planning and president of the Ramblers' Association.[63]

---

[60] LCRO, Lancashire CPRE files, box 14, 1951, report of May 1949.
[61] *Manchester Evening News*, 28 December 1951.
[62] David Wood, 'Territoriality and identity at RAF Menwith Hill', in Andrew Ballantyne (ed.), *Architectures: Modernism and After* (Oxford, Blackwell Publishing, 2004), pp. 142–162.
[63] Tom Stephenson and Mike Harding, *Forbidden Land: The Struggle for Access to Mountain and Moorland* (Manchester, Manchester University Press, 1989), p. 70.

But the exact route was not yet fixed and it was not officially opened until 1965. Part of the reason for the delay was due to negotiations with water boards and electricity companies where the route passed through their gathering grounds and pylon wayleaves respectively.

In 1954, the waterworks committee of Manchester Corporation raised objections about the route going through gathering grounds between two of their reservoirs at Longdendale, Cheshire, on the north-western edge of the Peak District. The reservoirs dated from the 1840s. Huddersfield Corporation similarly objected to the route crossing feeder streams to its reservoir at Digley, near Holmfirth in the West Riding of Yorkshire, construction of which was only just being completed in 1954. Both corporations claimed that the Pennine Way would 'lead to the pollution of the reservoirs', a claim that was strenuously denied by the Commons Open Spaces and Footpaths Society.[64] The Ramblers' Association pointed out that the Longdendale Estate was 'over 10,000 acres of fine moorland scenery which belong to the people of Manchester', and therefore access should be granted.[65] Following public inquiries, the government rejected the corporations' objections, and the route was confirmed.[66]

Dower's report into the National Parks complained about 'considerable interference – amounting in some instances to a virtually complete depopulation of the whole catchment area by prohibition of rambling, closing of footpaths and elimination of resident farming – where the water is surface gathered and relatively untreated'. He pointed to the inconsistencies of approach by the water companies and landowners who restricted public access, particularly in grouse shooting areas, in gathering grounds where the water was then fully treated, whereas in other prominent sites such as Thirlmere in the Lake District, access had never been an issue, despite the water being untreated.[67] The Institution of Water Engineers were more hesitant of widening the public amenity of their members' landholdings. In their 1963 report, 'Recreational Use of Waterworks', summarising the results of a survey of 73 local authority water engineers, they expressed cautious encouragement for expanding organised leisure activities on reservoirs, such as sailing clubs and fishing, but were much more hesitant about public access to gathering grounds due to concerns about water pollution, particularly on the moorlands of northern England.[68]

[64] Parliamentary Archives, FCP 2/591–595, Williams to Boulger, 12 February 1954; *Manchester Guardian*, 22 January 1954; *Bradford Observer*, 20 May 1954, 19 July 1954; *Manchester Evening News*, 31 December 1954.
[65] MERL, SR CPRE, C/1/35/8, Ramblers' Association statement, 'Public access to the Longdendale Moors', 1954.
[66] *Halifax Evening Courier*, 19 July 1954.
[67] Wilkinson, *Fight for It Now*, p. 155; TNA, HLG 93/56, Rambling and Water Supply Catchment, 11 January 1945, paras 44–47.
[68] Institution of Water Engineers, *Final Report of the Council on the Recreational Use of Waterworks* (London, Institution of Water Engineers, 1963), p. 11.

Another reason for the delay lay in the necessity for public local inquiries to be held over the route, which acted as magnets for opposition raised by members of the preservationist groups. The Haythornthwaites and Philip Barnes raised concerns about the section across Kinder Scout Plateau. Obviously Kinder Scout held totemic symbolic significance for the Right to Roam movement.[69] But Barnes and the Haythornthwaites feared that by designating a route as a national right of way, the landscape risked spoliation. They argued the way would have to be clearly signposted with new signs, and potentially the path would have to be improved with paving to make it more accessible for inexperienced hikers. Here lay the contradiction in the position of the local branches of the CPRE about the politics of access. Barnes tabled a motion at the Annual Council of the Ramblers' Association in April 1951 claiming that the Pennine Way was detrimental to the landscape of Kinder Scout. Tom Stephenson had to rein Barnes in, tabling an amendment that removed most of the wording of the motion, including that the signs and the path would endanger, as Barnes put it, 'one of the wettest, wildest and most primeval wildernesses in Britain'.[70] This was not the official position of the Ramblers' Association executive.

The local branches' opposition to the route did not reflect the position of the central CPRE, nor that of other amenity societies. The argument between Stephenson and Barnes took place publicly within the letters to the editor pages of the *Manchester Guardian*. It climaxed in a tense encounter between them at a conference arranged by the Haythornthwaites at Edale in September 1951.[71] Stephenson accused the local branches of hypocrisy as they had not raised opposition to the 'serious desecration' of the Hope Valley Cement Works built in the Peak District National Park (Barnes retorted 'that is a lie').[72] Again the issue of the impact of the route was about the relationship between class, amenity, and the idea of the moor as a 'wilderness'. But in this case, the local CPRE branches argued for restricting access to the site. Stephenson wrote to Herbert Griffin, general secretary of the CPRE, in March 1952:

> I certainly agree that there should be the least possible interference with the wild state of Kinder Scout and similar areas. On the other hand, there is a tendency to be overmuch concerned with the preservation of natural beauty and a reluctance to allow facilities for enjoying it. It is no use designating areas as natural parks if one wishes to keep them unvisited except by a few privileged people.[73]

Kinder Scout was an obvious location to defend, and it was within the National Park remit. But Barnes also sought to oppose the route going across areas outside

---

[69] Hey, 'Kinder Scout', 199.
[70] MERL, SR CPRE C/1/35/8, Stephenson to E. Haythornthwaite, 12 April 1951.
[71] *Manchester Guardian*, 17 September 1951.
[72] MERL, SR CPRE C/1/35/8, verbatim report of the conference at Edale, 15 September 1951.
[73] MERL, SR CPRE C/1/35/8, Stephenson to Griffin, 1 March 1952.

Figure 5.3 Design for Pennine Way sign, 1952, Museum of English Rural Life, CPRE archives, SR CPRE C/1/35/8. Reproduced with permission from the Museum of English Rural Life, University of Reading

these designations, not least the potential impact on Blackstone Edge.[74] Following the local public inquiry, Barnes wrote:

> I feel strongly that it is a waste of public money to 'improve' a route across wild moorland country. ... To put up signposts, cairns, etc, cannot make Blackstone Edge any more accessible than it is now, and they may well detract from that quality of wildness and complete unsophistication in which lies the essential appeal of this type of scenery.[75]

The signpost design (Figure 5.3) was produced in 1952, approved by the Royal Fine Art Commission, Ministry of Transport, and local authority associations, 'made of unpainted oak with the words Pennine Way in raised lettering'.[76]

Unlike the debates over the siting of the Super Grid and power stations, where the tensions between local branches and the central committee was an issue over amenity, the conflict touched on one of the core principles of access and the right to roam. Compromise had been the general strategy from the centre as they navigated

[74] MERL, SR CPRE C/1/35/8, Barnes to Griffin, 8 May 1951.
[75] LCRO, Lancashire CPRE, box 15, 1951, Barnes statement, 15 March 1951.
[76] MERL, SR CPRE C/1/35/8, design for Pennine Way sign, 1952.

the complex and entrenched interests of landowners and government. The more radical members of the movement nevertheless maintained a deep attachment to principles from their involvement in Mass Trespass activism in the 1930s. The backing of the state for the establishment of National Parks and national paths was a major step in the preservation of open space and rights of way. But for the more adamantly purist of the right to roam movements, these measures were a compromise not a victory of their ultimate aims of public access to all countryside. Barnes and the Haythornthwaites certainly thought so. But the official policy voted by the Ramblers' Association was to work with the state to achieve rights of way; blanket public access was not the primary aim as it was still unachievable. The further split between the local branches and the national executive committees lay on class and provincial grounds; mistrust of the metropolitan intentions of the executive combined with a belief they did not really know the landscapes of the Pennines.

Conclusion

Landscape change is not a short-term phenomenon, however quickly new structures are erected or political imperatives are suggested by incoming governments or their agents. The 'Industrial Pennines' had long been a site for human intervention, extraction of minerals, and enclosure for agriculture, though mainly on a local or regional scale. The reservoirs, water channels, and dams built by canal companies from the early 19th century onwards were the first kind of rural modernism. They were interventions of large-scale energy infrastructure constructed on the basis of form and efficiency for national needs. Nationalisation of the water and electricity industries after the Second World War, and the quickly spreading reach of the BBC and Independent Television networks, enabled modernisation of technology and expansion of national networks of power and communications. But these infrastructures were not entirely new either. The National Grid of the 1930s offered the blueprint for the Super Grid of the 1950s. Every era saw these changes as modern and improving with technology.

   Different readings of northern upland landscapes were closely related to contested definitions of land use and public amenity. The preservationist mistrust of urban 'wirescapes' intruding in the countryside were overcome by negotiation and conciliation as well as the need for economic and technological improvement. Many of the same issues stirred the preservationist associations hefted to the landscapes of National Parks, and much of the same contests were enacted between these groups and the planning authorities as well as utility companies and the Ministry of Defence. But unlike the National Parks from 1949, the landscapes adjoining industrial centres were not classed officially as nationally significant in terms of amenity. The dominance of an aesthetic of 'natural beauty', encapsulated in the amenity clause of legislation and especially the focus on National Parks by the central executive of preservationist bodies, hampered the efforts of local activists to protect local residents' access and use of the west and southern Pennine foothills for everyday leisure or, somewhat contradictorily, preservation of the moors as an imagined wilderness.

The designation of the 'Industrial Pennines' persisted. And as the textile and mining industries of northern and midland England faced economic collapse and government policies of deindustrialisation, the term came to signify *post*-industrial landscape degradation. In 1970, Nan Fairbrother pictured upland areas in England as failing, held back economically by old practices in agriculture.[77] She proposed an expansion of forestry as one solution. The Forestry Commission appointed Sylvia Crowe as a consultant, whom Fairbrother hoped would engender a more sensitive approach to mass sylviculture. Economic imperatives how-ever often surpassed growing ecological awareness about planting. Fairbrother's second solution for the uplands was tourism and leisure. She argued that the new Rural Development Boards, introduced under the 1967 Agriculture Act to push forward economic development in upland areas, should 'accept urban recreation as a potentially valuable land use'.[78] Ensuring access for ramblers passing through was less of a driver for her plan than holidaymakers spending time (and money) in the area, which contrasted with the views of countryside preservation and access groups. Afforestation with conifers continued to be resorted to as both an eco-nomic driver and a quick fix to degradation of moorland. As noted in Ysanne Holt's chapter in this volume, by the 1980s, the Forestry Commission and Nature Conservancy had reconsidered the ecological impact of conifer planting, moving towards a preference for more mixed deciduous woodland. In October 1988, how-ever, the Minister for Agriculture and the Secretary of State for the Environment announced a loosening of their previous policy, suggesting that 'conifers may have a role to play in ameliorating the environment of the industrial areas of the Pennines'. Significantly, the plans designated the area that could be afforested as the 'Industrial Pennines', the term that Dower had employed in his 1943 report.[79] The secretary of the Derbyshire branch of the Ramblers' Association wrote to the executive, complaining:

> The use of the term 'industrial Pennines' is very misleading. It gives the impression that the areas regarded as potential coniferous planting areas are suffering from indus-trial dereliction. For the most part, this is simply not true. ... There is no reason why these upland areas, which provide attractive landscapes and valuable wildlife habitats, should be subjected to a forestry policy which is any different from that now applied to other upland areas in England.

[77] Kelly, 'Conventional thinking', p. 130.
[78] Fairbrother, *New Lives*, pp. 118, 136; Guy M. Robinson, *Conflict and Change in the Countryside* (Chichester, Wiley, 1990), p. 285. Only one Rural Development Board, for the North Pennines, was established in England. It was abandoned after the election of the new government in 1969.
[79] LMA 4287/02/252, Ramblers' Association files, 'Industrial Pennines', Department of Environment Circular, 15 June 1990; *Halifax Evening Chronicle*, 14 November 1990.

The director of the Ramblers' Association then wrote to the Department of the Environment, noting: 'the committee considered that the adjective "industrial" was inappropriate and denigratory, and suggested "southern" or "south central" or "mid" as acceptable alternatives'. The CPRE also opposed the term, suggesting it provoked connotations of 'dark Satanic hills', a sardonic twist on William Blake's phrase often associated with the industrial north. Despite focus on national bodies and frameworks created by statute legislation, in effect landscape was shaped by regional planning imperatives, and pursued by the efforts of individuals and local groups, often in conflict with their own central executives. Coming to the surface in public local inquiries, the tensions rested on the local and the personal.

By the end of the 20th century, environmental evaluation was part of considerations of land use, amenity value, and ecosystems services in landscape change and planning. But amenity still encompassed definitions of aesthetic value and the deleterious effects of post-industrialisation still blighted the Pennines. Continued debates about access to grouse shooting moors, and the impact of wind turbines erected on the same sites as the pylons, exemplify how amenity in terms of class, aesthetics and public use, remains an unsettled issue.[80] Any future infrastructures implemented nationally will have to negotiate with the needs of local economies and community understandings of amenity.

---

[80] 'Plans refused for England's largest onshore wind farm on Scout Moor', BBC News, 8 July 2017, https://www.bbc.co.uk/news/uk-england-manchester-40532195 [accessed 30 October 2022]; Tom Mordue, Oliver Moss, and Lorraine Johnston, 'The impacts of onshore-windfarms on a UK rural tourism landscape: Objective evidence, local opposition and national politics', *Journal of Sustainable Tourism*, 28:11 (2020), 1882–1904.

6

The Post-war Power Station
and the Persistence of an English
Landscape Tradition

IAN WAITES

IN 1953, AN *Architectural Review* article on the design of power stations stated that 'Five years from now enormous generating stations must stud the landscape … as windmills once studded the Dutch and English fens'. When this does happen, it continued, 'we shall find that engineer-architect co-operation, lay-out, structural techniques and economics are woven into one fabric … the artifact will stand clean metallic in the landscape'. However, 'No generating station yet built has that kind of unity'.[1] Four years later, in 1957, a major step towards achieving that unity came when the Central Electricity Generating Board (CEGB) was formed in order to further improve the organisation and efficiency of the nationalised electricity supply in England and Wales. The CEGB had two principal statutory duties. The first was evident: to develop and maintain an efficient, coordinated, and economical system of electricity supply. The second, however, was new, and introduced an aesthetic thread to be woven into that 'one fabric' of power station design: to minimise the impact of power stations and overhead lines on scenery, flora, and fauna.[2] Several recent historical studies of post-war English culture have noted how the state-driven, technocratic vision of the future that emerged in the immediate decades following the Second World War was often rooted in the rural environment.[3] Indeed, and as Katrina Navickas suggests elsewhere in this volume, the construction of mass

[1] R. Furneaux-Jordan, 'Power stations', *The Architectural Review*, 113 (April 1953), 229.
[2] Jonathan Clarke, *'High Merit': Existing English Post-war Coal and Oil-fired Power Stations in Context* (London, Historic England, 2013), p. 12.
[3] Kristen Bluemel and Michael McCluskey (eds), *Rural Modernity: A Critical Intervention* (Edinburgh, Edinburgh University Press, 2018); Verity Elson and Rosemary Shirley (eds), *Creating the Countryside: The Rural Idyll Past and Present* (London, Paul Holberton, 2017), David Matless, *Landscape and Englishness*, 2nd edn (London, Reaktion Books, 2016).

Proceedings of the British Academy, **256**, 115–137, © The British Academy 2023.

energy infrastructure in rural landscapes drew on longer, more nuanced, currents of past cultural knowledge that were held to be in dialogue with modernity, rather than being in opposition to it. The remit of the newly founded CEGB clearly reflected this framework.

This was made tangible with the creation of the two power stations that are the subject of this chapter: West Burton, built in Nottinghamshire beside the River Trent between 1961 and 1969, and Didcot in Oxfordshire, which was completed in 1970. First, the chapter will demonstrate how West Burton was designed in an attempt to 'naturalise' this modern, but otherwise quite alien, structure within the flat, grass, and arable environment of the Trent Valley. From there, however, the chapter will add further detail to our general understanding of those 'currents of cultural knowledge' that were at play during the post-war period, by identifying two key elements of an English artistic landscape tradition which inspired new and experimental approaches towards the concept and design of these power stations. Initially, that the manner in which West Burton was planned, designed, and represented in contemporary journals like the *Architectural Review*, was defined by a working awareness of the traditions and principles of 18th-century picturesque theory, and borne out of the modernist revival of the picturesque that was championed by Nikolaus Pevsner during the 1950s. Pevsner's belief that the aesthetic potential of functional building planning could be enhanced by a picturesque attention to site and viewpoint will be specifically assessed with regard to West Burton. From then on, it will be shown that the design principles initiated at West Burton were further developed in a neoromantic, and almost metaphysical manner at Didcot, where the cooling towers were carefully arranged so that their modernist forms could mirror key, ancient landscape features within its hinterland. In essence, it will be seen that the design and siting of these power stations was underpinned by the persistence of a landscape tradition revived in the context of a peculiarly English modernist notion that past, present, and future could be united – by using the English countryside as the *mise-en-scène* for a new and forward-thinking, socially democratic, technocratic, nation.

'Variety is necessary; so is contrast': West Burton as a rural picturesque ornament

West Burton is an iconic power station: not only was it the first 2,000MW coal-fired station in Britain, it was also a radically innovative piece of power station design both in itself and in relation to its surrounding landscape. In respect of that second statutory duty, the chair of the CEGB, Christopher Hinton, stressed the importance of amenity, which he described as 'the conditions in landscape which the public as a whole wishes to see and enjoy'.[4] As a consequence, the CEGB established

---

[4] Christopher Hinton and William Holford, 'Power production and transmission in the countryside: Preserving amenities', *Journal of the Royal Society of Arts*, 108 (February 1960), 181.

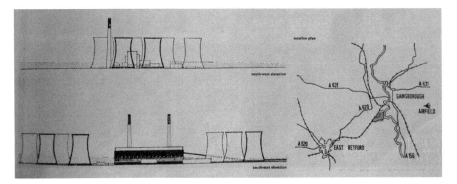

Figure 6.1 Diagram of various elevations of West Burton power station.
© The Architectural Press

an architectural liaison and development group under the aegis of the nationalised industry's first architect, Michael H. Shepheard. Between 1959 and 1970, Shepheard developed an office that came to consist of some 18 architects and up to 20 landscape architects and designers. The sway that this office held in relation to the production of new power stations across the country is exemplified by the fact that landscape architects were often first to advise on initial design development stages before the appointment of architectural or civil engineering consultants.[5] Designed by Rex Savidge and John Gelsthorpe of Architects' Design Group, West Burton was to be the pioneer of this new approach in that it 'represented the first attempt to predict, in a comprehensive and systematic manner, the visual impact of a power station'.[6] Careful thought was given not only to the orientation and layout of the station, but also to the landscaping of the site itself and, indeed, the improvement of the wider, surrounding countryside.

First, the cooling towers were carefully positioned in a varied, asymmetrical manner, split into two groups at either end of the station (four in lozenge formation and four in a slightly waving line) in order to present a variety of arrangements and effects when viewed from different vantage points across the surrounding countryside. A diagram from a January 1962 report on West Burton in the *Architectural Review* (Figure 6.1) shows how the elevations were composed in order, as the report put it, 'to avoid the tendency of shapes to coalesce when viewed at a moderate distance'.[7]

The extent to which the visual impact of the cooling towers was considered in relation to their place in the wider landscape was also typified by the use of a heliodon, a lighting device where an artificial beam of light could be adjusted to

---

[5] Clarke, *High Merit*, p. 13.
[6] Clarke, *High Merit*, p. 46.
[7] 'Power station, near Gainsborough', *Architectural Review*, 131 (January 1962), 64–66.

mimic latitude, date, and time of day, and which was then shone onto an architectural model of the station, so that it could be determined how a particular grouping of the cooling towers might appear under the sun at different times of the year. But perhaps the most radical design feature of West Burton lay in the colouring of the concrete on the cooling towers. In this case, the 'artifact' stood not 'clean metallic in the landscape', but with clean, *coloured*, concrete. A photograph of the power station on the cover of a 1969 CEGB brochure, shows how Savidge and Gelsthorpe used dark grey cement for two of the four towers in the lozenge group to provide tonal contrast to their neighbours and to prevent the group from coalescing, or 'blocking', in conditions of haze or mist, which would have increased their visual bulk (Figure 6.2).

More daringly, an intense yellow was used to colour the most northerly cooling tower (this can just be seen beyond the four towers in the centre of Figure 6.2), which was also slightly offset from the others so as to act as a 'nodal point' of reference visible from multiple viewpoints around which the rest of the station could articulate and cohere. The colour and tonal range of these cooling towers also

Figure 6.2 West Burton power station on the cover of a 1969 CEGB brochure.
© Ian Waites

related closely to the surrounding environment of arable fields, the characteristic grey-green colour of the Trent waters, and the extensive skies so characteristic of the eastern Midlands. In June 1963, the *Times* reported that 'the great new power station at West Burton will be the first in Britain to have a yellow cooling tower 375ft high'. The piece quoted Rex Savidge, who confidently explained that 'At first we thought of trying to hide the power station, we went to the armed services to try to gather some ideas about camouflage. We finally decided to take the opposite alternative and to try to make the individual units stand out. We think it is going to look pretty good.'[8] Today, the towers have mostly lost this colouring but the concrete nevertheless still seems to take on the hue of the prevailing natural conditions of the day. As Nan Fairbrother neatly put it in *New Lives, New Landscapes*, 'the parabolic shapes of cooling towers are beautiful in all lights and all weathers'.[9]

The use of coloured concrete for the cooling towers in combination with the careful positioning and orientation of the station complex as a whole earned West Burton a Civic Trust award in 1968, when it was commended as 'An immense engineering work of great style which, far from detracting from the visual scene, acts as a magnet to the eye from many parts of the Trent Valley and from several miles away.'[10] Indeed, when Fairbrother argued that 'The large, simple shapes' of a nuclear power plant in a National Park seemed to be 'at home in the large hill landscape', she might well have suggested that the large, simple shapes of a coal-fired power station could also be 'at home' in the lowland landscape, with its typical features – trees, telegraph poles, parish church towers, pylons – complementing the station's own vertical features and its 'white swing of sculptured concrete'.[11] More crucially still, and in the case of the flat expanses of the Trent flood plain where West Burton stood, Fairbrother also suggested that power stations had the potential to 'give weight and focus to what might otherwise be indeterminate scenery'.[12]

Statements like this might seem overly rhetorical, especially in relation to the presence of such otherwise large-scale and incongruously modern structures within a rural environment. But the idea that a power station could give 'weight and focus' to a more 'ordinary' stretch of English countryside resonates with a train of thought that nevertheless underpinned the planning and design of West Burton: a working knowledge of the picturesque, the aesthetic ideal which shaped the development of the English landscape painting genre in the late 18th and early 19th centuries.

The picturesque was principally introduced into English cultural debate in 1782 by William Gilpin in his book *Observations on the River Wye, and Several Parts of South Wales, etc. Relative Chiefly to Picturesque Beauty; made in the Summer of the Year 1770*. Essentially, this was a practical manual intended to instruct

---

[8] 'Making power station look good', *The Times*, 11 June 1963.

[9] Nan Fairbrother, *New Lives, New Landscapes* (London, The Architectural Press, 1970), p. 218.

[10] *Keeping the Lights On: Celebrating 40 Years of Electricity Production at West Burton* (West Burton, EDF Energy, 2009), p. 18.

[11] Fairbrother, *New Lives*, pp. 132, 147.

[12] Fairbrother, *New Lives*, p. 129.

England's leisured travellers on how to examine 'the face of a country by the rules of picturesque beauty', by giving guidelines on selecting, using, and adapting elements in a landscape so they could be made into a picture. The picturesque related to scenes that were neither sublime nor beautiful. Instead, it championed scenes containing commonplace things – trees, rivers, fields, cottages, church steeples – that could nevertheless be made aesthetically interesting if certain moods and compositional rules were followed. An interesting and pictorially worthy landscape could be created by arranging these elements in such a manner that new associational effects – in particular, surprise, variety, and contrast – could be fashioned for the viewer. Nature, Gilpin reckoned, is always 'great in design' but 'seldom correct in composition as to produce a harmonious whole'. The 'artist, in the mean time, is confined to space. He lays down his little rules, therefore, which he calls the *principles of picturesque beauty*, merely to adapt such diminutive parts of nature's surfaces to his own eye, as comes within its scope'.[13]

From this, we can see how the designers of West Burton were themselves working with space, adapting the mass of a power station, and its range of unfamiliar forms and shapes, to the 'diminutive' parts of nature's surfaces. Picturesque compositional principles also relied on additional elements that were deemed necessary to aid the perception or comprehension of a scene, for instance by introducing varied and contrasting tones of light and shade, especially where a track might be illuminated by sunlight, in order to 'guide the eye' into the scene. The colouring of the cooling towers was intended to do just that, aided by the use of the heliodon, which in this case was as much of an aesthetic instrument of its time as the 18th-century Claude glass, a small, tinted mirror used by artists and connoisseurs of the landscape who could turn their back on the scene and observe a reflected, framed view which gave the effect of reducing and simplifying the colour and tonal range of a scene in order to give it a painterly quality. The colour scheme of West Burton's cooling towers, however, was not that of the Old Masters. It was bold and modernist, almost to the point that it would have only taken one more of these towers to be coloured a bright red in order to complete a Mondrian-like effect.[14] At the same time, however, this bold use of colour in relation to its surroundings was also understood to be in line with picturesque thinking: 'It is the aim of picturesque description to bring the images of nature, as forcibly, and as closely to the eye, as it can; and this must often be done by high-colouring; which this species of composition demands.'[15]

---

[13] William Gilpin, *Observations on the River Wye and several parts of Wales, etc., relative chiefly to Picturesque Beauty* (London, 1782), p. 18. Emphasis in original.

[14] Not so outlandish as it might seem: at the Drakelow 'C' power station in Staffordshire (1961–1963), one of the towers in each triangular group of three were coloured red to visually accentuate their presence in the landscape. Clarke, *High Merit*, p. 19.

[15] William Gilpin, *Observations, Relative Chiefly To Picturesque Beauty, Made in the Year 1772, On several Parts of England, Particularly The Mountains, And Lakes Of Cumberland, and Westmoreland* (London, 1792), p. xxii.

As the picturesque became popular towards the end of the 18th century, Uvedale Price's series of *Essays on the Picturesque* (1794–1798) extended Gilpin's original principles to include, for instance, a notion of picturesque architecture: 'Were an architect with a painter's eye to have the planning of the whole, he would have the opportunity of producing the richest effects … by varying the characters of the buildings … according to the place which they were to occupy.'[16]

In his pioneering 20th-century revivalist celebration of the picturesque, Christopher Hussey summed up Price's approach thus: 'Just as the picturesque is a mode of vision, so picturesque architecture can be defined as building and design conceived in relation to landscape, whether as a setting, or as the source of certain qualities and features reflected in the architecture.'[17] From the perspective of the architect, Hussey quoted Robert Adam's assertion that the quality essential to great architecture is 'the magnitude and movement of parts':

> Movement is meant to express the rise and fall, the advance and recess with other diversity of form, in the different parts of a building, so as to add greatly to the picturesqueness of the composition, for the rising and falling, advancing and receding, with convexity and concavity and other forms of the great parts, have the same effect in architecture that hill and dale, foreground and distance that swelling and sinking, have in landscape; that is, they serve to provide an agreeable and diversified contour that groups and contrasts like a picture, and creates a variety of light and shade which gives great spirit, beauty and effect to the composition.[18]

This broadly reflects all that was considered in relation to the design of West Burton, where the form, arrangement, and colouring of the cooling towers was intended to produce an effect of advance and recess, creating variations in form, light, and shade in an 'agreeable and diversified' manner, and from all points in the surrounding countryside. The spirit of this was visually articulated in a drawing of West Burton included in the 1962 *Architectural Review* article (Figure 6.3). The artist is uncredited in the article, but the drawing was almost certainly made by the landscape architect, Derek Lovejoy, who was commissioned by the CEGB to produce a landscaping scheme both for the station and for the countryside immediately surrounding it. He began by producing a large number of sketches, illustrating views of the station from nearby roads and from viewpoints further afield, and so it can be reliably presumed that this study is one of those. This is a remarkable drawing, not only because it purposely imagines West Burton before it was yet to appear in the landscape, but also because it presents a clear example of Gilpin's notion of the picturesque artist laying down his 'little rules'. In this case, Lovejoy adapted the component parts of both nature's surfaces, and those of

---

[16] Sir Uvedale Price, 'On architecture and buildings &c', in *Sir Uvedale Price on the Picturesque: with an essay on the origin of taste, and much original matter, by Sir T. D. Lauder, Bart* (Edinburgh, 1842), p. 348.

[17] Christopher Hussey, *The Picturesque: Studies in a Point of View* (London, GP Putnam, 1927), p. 187.

[18] R. Adam, *Works*, Introduction to Part I, 1773, quoted in Hussey, *The Picturesque*, pp. 189–190.

Figure 6.3 1962 drawing of West Burton power station taken from the A156 Lincoln to Gainsborough Road. © The Architectural Press

the man-made forms of the power station, 'to his own eye', as it appeared 'within his scope'.

According to Gilpin, an ideal landscape composition could be framed and enlivened by a variety of objects such as rocks, trees, the towers of a ruined castle, or of a parish church. 'Variety', he stated, in a manner that could easily be applied to West Burton and its surrounding countryside as it appears in this drawing, 'is necessary; so is contrast'.[19] Compositionally, the man-made verticals of West Burton – its cooling towers and chimneys – are deliberately linked with the vertical forms of the natural world: in this case, different species of tree. It is almost suggested here that while the artificial and minimalist forms of the modern power station might not be fully able to compete with the diversity of the natural world, they can be ordered in such a manner to at least fulfil the picturesque ideal of variety and contrast. Given the various diagrams of the different elevations and configurations of West Burton, it can be assumed that the architects were also applying the same ideal in relation to a number of other vantage points. The linearity of the skyline emphasises the sense of variety and surprise, but also creates a simple harmony suggestive of the notion that West Burton could 'nestle' in the

---

[19] William Gilpin, *Three Essays: On Picturesque Beauty, On Picturesque Travel, and on Sketching Landscape* (London, 1792), p. 20.

landscape, and that the landscape in turn could incorporate it, almost as if it had always been there.[20]

Moreover, and as the drawing's caption states, the view was taken from the A156 road from Lincoln to Gainsborough. At this point however, West Burton is also being shown from within the 18th-century ornamental parkland of the Gate Burton estate. Nikolaus Pevsner alluded to the picturesqueness of this spot, when he stated that 'the delight of Gate Burton is the landscaping of the park, across the Gainsborough road to the Trent-side'.[21] The drawing echoes this by making specific vertical features both of the plantation of cedars of Lebanon to the right of the scene, and the traditional, iron estate fencing directly in the foreground.[22] This view of West Burton has therefore been carefully – artfully – chosen and composed by a trained landscape architect who would almost certainly have knowledge of picturesque theory and convention. It is a highly evocative but nevertheless calculated attempt to treat this very modern structure as a pictur-esque ornament within an already artificially composed and created landscape setting: an English power station retroactively established as a part of a continuous English landscape tradition.

Modernity and the post-war picturesque revival

This was no anachronistic peculiarity. The picturesque had a sustained revival amongst post-war debates on architecture, planning, modernity, and the landscape. This was most notably fuelled by Nikolaus Pevsner in his work entitled *Visual Planning and the Picturesque* that was began in the mid-1940s, but which remained incomplete and unpublished until 2010.[23] Pevsner intended this work to highlight 'Britain's unacknowledged contribution to planning history, to prove the funda-mental role of picturesque principles in Britain's cultural production and artistic dispositions, and to show the commonalities of these fundamentals with the mod-ernist architecture of his own day'.[24] More specifically, in his foreword to *Visual*

[20] In relation to the same view today, it also appears that Lovejoy deliberately removed a hedgerow that runs across the middle ground of the field between the fencing and West Burton, probably in order to prevent the viewer's eye from stalling in perceiving the almost perfect linearity and harmony of the skyline.

[21] Nikolaus Pevsner and John Harris, *Lincolnshire* (Harmondsworth, Penguin, 1989). p. 303.

[22] Gilpin discussed the character of different species of tree in terms of their picturesque utility within the ideal landscape, and he gave pre-eminence to the Cedar of Lebanon 'on account of its own dignity', and of the 'respectable mention that is everywhere made of it in scripture'. William Gilpin, *Remarks on forest scenery, and other woodland views, (relative chiefly to picturesque beauty)* (London, 1791), p. 73.

[23] Nikolaus Pevsner and Mathew Aitchison (eds), *Visual Planning and the Picturesque* (Los Angeles, The Getty Research Institute, 2010).

[24] John Macarthur and Mathew Aitchison, 'Pevsner's townscape', in Nikolaus Pevsner and Mathew Aitchison (eds), *Visual Planning and the Picturesque* (Los Angeles, The Getty Research Institute, 2010), p. 2.

Planning, Pevsner described the work as 'a florilegium of English planning theory – that is, the theory of the Picturesque and ... an account of how this theory and this tradition ... *might influence the twentieth*' [my italics].[25] Pevsner published aspects of the argument and text otherwise intended for *Visual Planning* on several occasions in the *Architectural Review*, and much of this work contributed to the development of a long-running campaign primarily developed by the *Review*'s editor and publisher, Hubert de Cronin Hastings, which came to be known as 'Townscape'.[26] This represented an attempt to balance the 'striking visual qualities of modern architecture and its placement within a more traditionalist mode of urban planning': for Pevsner and Hastings, the use and adaptation of 18th-century picturesque principles and theory in this was key.[27] Hastings pointed out that,

> a national picture-making aptitude exists among us, and has done for centuries. In Picturesque Theory, evolved on this island early in the eighteenth century and imitated all over Europe around 1800, a quite unmistakable point of view asserted itself. It was expressed first exclusively in landscaping improvements of private grounds and country estates. ... What we really need to do now ... is to resurrect the true theory of the Picturesque and apply a point of view already existing to a field in which it has not been consciously been applied before: *the city*.[28]

The end objective of this statement is of course unrelated to a discussion on rural modernity and the presence of modern power stations in the countryside, but its wider significance to the general debate on the nature of modernism and modernity in post-war English culture and aesthetics cannot be ignored. We have already seen how that 'national picture-making aptitude' could continue to 'exist among us' in Derek Lovejoy's drawing of West Burton nestling within the outskirts of the designed 'private grounds' of the Gate Burton estate. For *the city* then, also read *the modern countryside*. Advocating for the picturesque in the light of 'landscaping improvements of private grounds and country estates' might be conventionally held as conservative – reactionary even. For Hastings and Pevsner, however, it was 'explicitly modernist', and provided a 'direct connection between Hussey's description of eighteenth-century picturesque theory and the work of [modernist] architects that the *AR* admired'.[29] As Erden Erten has made clear in his studies of the editorial character of the *Architectural Review* during these years of a modern, English post-war social consensus, 'the cultural issues around

[25] Pevsner and Aitchison, *Visual Planning*, p. 49.
[26] For example, 'Price on picturesque planning', *Architectural Review*, 95 (February 1944), 47–50, and 'C20 picturesque: An answer to Basil Taylor's broadcast', *Architectural Review*, 115 (April 1954), 227–229. In 1949, under the pseudonym of 'Ivor de Wolfe', Hastings himself had written on the picturesque in a piece entitled 'Townscape: A plea for an English visual philosophy founded on the true rock of Sir Uvedale Price', *Architectural Review*, 106 (December 1949), 354–362.
[27] Macarthur and Aitchison, 'Pevsner's townscape', p. 19.
[28] The Editor [Hastings], 'Exterior furnishing or sharawaggi: The art of making urban landscape', *Architectural Review*, 95 (January 1944), 3.
[29] Macarthur and Aitchison, 'Pevsner's townscape', p. 14.

Modernism were paramount, especially its relationship to national history and the way the environment both looked and functioned'.[30] This is true with regard to the design and situation of West Burton, and in the way it was represented in the *Architectural Review*. Moreover, this also required 'the coexistence of the new and the old, the modern and the traditional, and with an eye that safeguarded the coexistence of difference'.[31]

'Difference' particularly characterised Uvedale Price's extension of the scope of Gilpin's picturesque principles in his first *Essay on the Picturesque, as compared with the Sublime and the Beautiful; and, on the Use of Studying Pictures, for the purpose of Improving Real Landscape* (1794). Crucially, the subtitle of the essay clearly aimed to steer Gilpin's ideas away from merely creating compositionally ideal pictures towards more practical purposes by applying them to that 'purpose of improving real landscape'.[32] In this, Price particularly asserted that qualities such as 'sudden variation, joined to that of irregularity, are the most efficient causes of the picturesque'.[33] Both Pevsner and Hastings looked to Price for their ideal version of the picturesque, interpreting sudden variation and irregularity to suggest that a unity could be made out of 'disparate elements, particularly modern, historic, and vernacular buildings that were in themselves aesthetically disjunct and ideologically antagonistic'.[34] Pevsner believed that revisiting the picturesque could reveal to us in the modern age the aesthetic potential of functional building planning, arguing that this was not just about formal variation, but that it was also essentially conditioned by an attention to new, modernist forms, as well as site and viewpoint. In *Visual Planning*, he paraphrases Robert Adam's adaptation of picturesque principles to architectural form:

> of variety, of intricacy, of the connection of the building with nature, of advance and recess, swelling and sinking, and of contrasts of texture, you will find that a great many of these principles are principles which you would apply to the idiom which has developed over the last twenty to thirty years.[35]

That 'idiom' was, of course, high modernism. Here, Pevsner is explicitly relating modernism to the picturesque understanding of form, composition, and situation by citing key examples of the architecture that had developed over the 1920s and 1930s and which, Pevsner argued, presented 'a valid argument in favour of the Picturesque in the c20'. 'If one looks', he went on, 'at the work of the pioneers of twentieth century architecture, say as early as about 1925, Gropius's Bauhaus

---

[30] Erdem Erten, 'I, the world, the devil and the flesh: Manplan, Civilia and H. de C. Hastings', *The Journal of Architecture*, 17:5 (2012), 703.

[31] Erten, 'I, the world', 708.

[32] Uvedale Price, *Essay on the Picturesque, as compared with the Sublime and the Beautiful; and, on the Use of Studying Pictures, for the purpose of Improving Real Landscape* (London, 1794).

[33] Price, *Essay*, p. 45.

[34] Macarthur and Aitchison, 'Pevsner's townscape', p. 15.

[35] Pevsner and Aitchison, *Visual Planning*, p. 177.

at Dessau or better still Le Corbusier's Stuttgart houses of 1927 ... what are their aesthetic qualities? First those that everyone is familiar with; cubic shapes, no mouldings, large openings and so on'. We can pause there to relate this to Fairbrother's opinion on cooling towers, which, she asserted, are 'neither genteel nor vulgar but functional shapes indisputably valid, forms of abstract sculpture large enough to register on the landscape scale'.[36] The manner in which Pevsner consolidates his theory of picturesque modernism could almost lead on from this:

> the free grouping of the individual buildings, a mixture of materials, synthetic and natural, rough and smooth, and, beyond that, the free planning of a whole quarter, with differentiation of levels ... interaction between landscape and building ... between buildings of different shapes and heights. Do not these qualities ... show that, albeit unconsciously, the modern revolution of the twentieth century and the Picturesque revolution of a hundred years before had all their fundamentals in common?[37]

In a modern/modernist sense then, the picturesque can be described as a visual formalism in which objects and their relations are subsumed into relations of pictorial composition from particular points of view: with new architectural forms like power stations, the design and visual planning of West Burton was intended to make a pictorial unity out of alien and disparate elements within the English countryside. Conversely, that line from the *Architectural Review*'s report on West Burton, which stated that the arrangement of the cooling towers was intended to avoid the 'tendency of shapes to coalesce when viewed at a moderate distance', could almost be taken from any 18th-century essay on the picturesque. Pevsner's ideas on a new, modernist form of the picturesque had already been outlined by Christopher Hussey in 1927, when he argued that a Cezanne-like sense of significant form, solidity, and plasticity could be applied to a picturesque sense of pictorialism and composition.[38] This was the climate in which the otherwise strictly functional design, siting, and production of new power stations became suffused with an idealistic aestheticism, based on earlier precedents of the English landscape tradition. This came to colour much architectural and landscape writing well into the 1960s, for instance in Fairbrother's caption for a view of Skelton Grange power station looking across the outskirts of the country park of Temple Newsam: 'Contrasting styles in sculpture for the modern landscape' (Figure 6.4).[39]

---

[36] Fairbrother, *New Lives*, p. 220.

[37] Pevsner and Aitchison, *Visual Planning*, p. 168.

[38] Hussey, *The Picturesque*, p. 249. 'Significant form' was a term coined by the British art critic Clive Bell in 1914 to describe the idea that forms within an artwork can be expressive, even if they are largely or completely divorced from a recognisable reality. Clive Bell, *Art* (London, Chatto & Windus, London, 1916).

[39] Fairbrother, *New Lives*, p. 220.

Contrasting styles in sculpture for the modern landscape. Temple Newsam, Leeds—

Figure 6.4 View of Skelton Grange power station from Temple Newsam.
© The Architectural Press

Beyond the picturesque: the power station in an ancient landscape

As Hastings noted, the English landscape tradition was first expressed in the landscaping improvements of country estates from the late 17th century onward. A similar attempt to 'improve' the landscape was also made in relation to the planning of West Burton, when the CEGB commissioned the landscape architect, Derek Lovejoy, to produce a scheme which sought to creatively landscape the site in a manner akin to picturesque principles of framing, variety, contrast, and so on. It was immediately recognised, however, that any attempt to screen the enormous structural elements of West Burton was, of course, impossible, and that it would be more advantageous instead to relate them to their surroundings. Rather than trying to obscure views of West Burton in what was a predominantly flat agricultural landscape, a decision was made instead to enhance the countryside around it, and in relation to the component parts of the station itself: new native trees were planted in the centre of existing hedgerows, along roadside verges, and in fields so as to compose and create new vistas across three miles of countryside around the station. The CEGB therefore instigated what amounted to a regional landscape plan, based on the continuation of an English landscape tradition, but one that boldly shifted the prominence away from the private and aristocratic to a publicly funded post-war social democratic remodelling of the countryside on a scale not seen since the days of Capability Brown and Humphry Repton.[40]

As the 1960s progressed, however, the creative ambition in marrying national infrastructural development with the range of ideologies, aesthetics, and traditions associated with the English landscape extended into newer realms as various forms of popular, counter-cultural thinking came to dominate, producing what has been described as a 'parallel dreamtime of alternative British history and legend'.[41] Architecturally, this reached its apotheosis in the early 1970s, when a team of young, idealistic architects was given the task to create central Milton Keynes. For this, they drew deeply (and fashionably) on a heightened mystical/mythical landscape tradition, particularly when they revised their plans for the town's main road, so that it would frame the rising sun on Midsummer Day in order to 'relate this other-wise cultureless object to the cosmos'.[42] The acknowledgement of a deeper land-scape history and tradition was also reflected in the planning of the power station at Didcot in Oxfordshire, designed by Sir Frederick Gibberd between 1964 and 1968. It should be obvious of course that Gibberd, born in 1908, and the master planner of Harlow New Town, was no doyen of the 1960s counter-culture. When he wrote about the design of Didcot, as in a 1974 piece written for the *Architectural Review*, entitled 'Power and potash', Gibberd did so from a strictly functional standpoint. It is clear that he followed West Burton's lead when he noted that 'cooling towers can be modified in forms, colour and texture in relationship to the particular land-scape against which they are seen'.[43] At the same time however, he also privately dismissed West Burton's use of colour 'as too arty, too trivial, too mannered and too inconsequential'.[44]

Gibberd's rationale however can still be considered in picturesque terms of variety and surprise, as Didcot's appearance was intended to vary as the observer moved around the Thames Valley. A diagram from Gibberd's *Architectural Review* piece (Figure 6.5) shows how he experimented with the arrangement of Didcot's six cooling towers, creating what he referred to as a 'visual study of the effects of functional layout on the environment', and in a manner similar to the elevations produced for West Burton (Figure 6.1).[45] Gibberd finally arranged Didcot's cooling towers into two triangular groups, using the station's chimney to act as a fulcrum around which the towers were intended to move and change in number and in scale from different viewpoints.

[40] Nottinghamshire County Council carried out the work and remained responsible for its maintenance. Tony Aldous and Brian Clouston, *Landscape by Design* (London, Heinemann, 1979) p. 55.

[41] Rob Young, *Electric Eden: Unearthing Britain's Visionary Music* (London, Faber, 2011) p. 476.

[42] Patrick Barkham, 'Story of cities #34: The struggle for the soul of Milton Keynes', *The Guardian*, 3 May 2016, https://www.theguardian.com/cities/2016/may/03/struggle-for-the-soul-of-milton-keynes [accessed 28 July 2021].

[43] Frederick Gibberd, 'Power and potash', *The Architectural Review*, 156 (August 1974), 89.

[44] Clarke, *High Merit*, p. 47.

[45] Gibberd, 'Power and potash', 90.

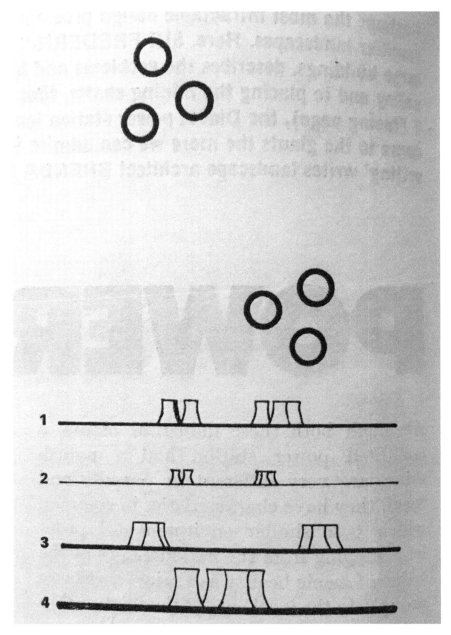

Figure 6.5 Arrangement of the cooling towers at Didcot power station.
© The Architectural Press

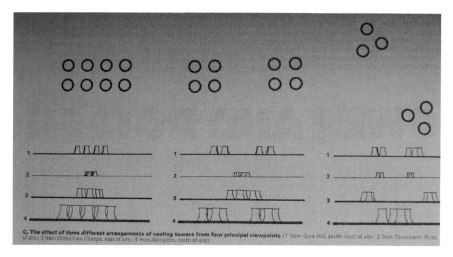

C, The effect of three different arrangements of cooling towers from four principal viewpoints (1 from Gore Hill, south-west of site; 2 from Crowmarsh Road, of site; 3 from Wittenham Clumps, east of site; 4 from Abingdon, north of site)

Figure 6.6 Three different arrangements of the cooling towers at Didcot power station from four principal viewpoints. © The Architectural Press

Didcot was also landscaped in a similarly extensive manner to West Burton: Gibberd had five blocks of woodland planted around the site, each one placed in relationship to the structures of the station, and to further compose its visual impact from the surrounding countryside. Once the trees reached maturity, they would create a series of distinct compositions as the viewer moved around the landscape.[46]

In contrast to the relatively 'featureless' landscape of the Trent Valley, however, Didcot's 'environment' was much different. The power station was to be situated within a 'deeper England' that was dominated by other, more ancient, but similarly monumental man-made inscriptions on the landscape, being in the near-vicinity of the prehistoric Ridgeway, the White Horse at Uffington, and the Wittenham Clumps close to the River Thames. Gibberd was obviously aware of this deep history because he took considerable trouble to consider critical viewpoints of Didcot not just in general relation to the surrounding countryside, but also to those particular ancient local landmarks. The two triangular groups of cooling towers were positioned half a mile apart and laid diagonally across the site on a north-west–south-east axis so as to leave space for views to the Ridgeway to the south-south-west and, in particular, towards the Wittenham Clumps to the east (Figure 6.6).

Wittenham Clumps are a pair of wooded chalk hills, Castle Hill and Round Hill (Figure 6.7). Castle Hill is the site of an Iron Age hill fort. Both hills have a prominent appearance, each crowned by a plantation of beech trees that are thought

---

[46] Clarke, *High Merit*, p. 22.

Figure 6.7 Wittenham Clumps. © Marathon, licensed for reuse under Creative Commons CC BY-SA 2.0, creativecommons.org/licenses/by-sa/2.0

to have been planted in the early 18th century.[47] In the first half of the 20th century, this ancient site was frequently immortalised in the work of the neo-romantic landscape painter, Paul Nash (Figure 6.8). Neo-romanticism was another strand of English landscape aesthetics contemporary to Pevsner's modernist revival of the picturesque, and with roots also dating back to the late 18th and early 19th centuries. It was not a movement as such, but rather a term applied to a variety of expressive artistic and literary works where landscape was the core motif, from the paintings of John Piper to the films of Michael Powell and Emeric Pressburger, and including writing such as Jacquetta Hawkes' imaginative history of Britain's geology, *A Land* (1951).

Artistically, neo-romanticism was modernist, with surrealism as a major influence. Like most strains of creative thinking that emerged out of the Second World War, it looked to the future, but one that was written in terms of 'a projected past which found its origins in the land'. Consequently, it developed a narrative that was poetic and visionary, 'coiled and involuted, with King Arthur and William Blake twined close to Picasso and Andre Masson as points of cultural reference'.[48]

[47] Wessex Archaeology, *Round Hill, Wittenham Clumps, Oxfordshire: An Archaeological Evaluation and an Assessment of the Results* (Salisbury, Wessex Archaeology, 2004), p. 7, https://www.wessexarch.co.uk/our-work/round-hill-wittenham-clumps#main-content [accessed 29 July 2021].

[48] David Mellor (ed.), *A Paradise Lost: The Neo-Romantic Imagination in Britain 1935–55* (London, Lund Humphries, 1987), p. 16.

Figure 6.8 Paul Nash, *Landscape of the Moon's Last Phase*, c. 1940. Public domain

In 1911, Nash described the prehistoric earthworks at Wittenham Clumps as 'Grey hollowed hills crowned by old old trees … a beautiful, legendary country haunted by old gods long forgotten'.[49] Later, in his 1949 autobiography, *Outline*, he praised the site in very different terms: 'I felt their importance long before I knew their history. … This was due almost entirely to their formal features.'[50] In a post-war culture that was suffused with 'ideal definitions of British landscape which celebrated unbroken historical continuity and the ideal of heritage as a mystical binding force and repository of national identity',[51] Gibberd would have surely been familiar with Nash's work, and aware of the cultural connections, old and new, that would have been made by taking this ancient site into consideration when planning the orientation of Didcot's cooling towers. The Wittenham Clumps had been a significant feature of this landscape for thousands of years, from the Neolithic period through

[49] Quoted in David Fraser Jenkins, *Paul Nash: The Elements* (London, Dulwich Picture Gallery, 2010), p. 37.
[50] Paul Nash, *Outline: An Autobiography and Other Writings* (London, Faber, 1949), pp. 122–123.
[51] Lauren Piko, 'Mirroring England? Milton Keynes, decline and the English landscape' (PhD thesis, University of Melbourne, 2017), p. 286.

to the romantic era, and now into the modern period. Gibberd responded to this with the notion that the cooling towers of Didcot should also be seen as a coherent and enduring group in relation to the timeless group of trees at Wittenham: simple massed forms where modernity could mirror the ancient, and vice versa.

'A valid, new twentieth-century experience of landscape'?

The historic, aesthetic, and symbolic references and meanings implicit in the design and planning of massive post-war infrastructural sites such as the power stations at Didcot and West Burton continue to be plentiful, and are representative of the persistence of a landscape tradition in English modernist culture. In his book on the picturesque, Christopher Hussey noted that a key aspect of Capability Brown's landscaping involved the planting of 'circular clumps' of trees, which 'dotted' his landscapes, and displayed the 'sublimity' of 'rotund forms.'[52] Elsewhere, Hussey quotes 'Mr Milestone' from Thomas Love Peacock's *Headlong Hall* (1816) extolling the virtues of his design for a new country park in a manner that can be seen to echo Gibberd's scheme for arranging and composing Didcot's cooling towers in relation to the Wittenham Clumps: 'majestic circular clumps, disposed at equal distances with wonderful symmetry'.[53] It is remarkable how the design and engineering complexities in creating these massive infrastructural sites were also fundamentally influenced and shaped by a profound appreciation of the connections between past and present, the romantic and the practical. In the immediate post-war years, it was widely held that energy infrastructure projects were becoming the new defining feature of the British countryside.[54] But this was only made possible because principled attempts were made to develop these projects while giving due consideration to the impact on the countryside. Scale and ordering were paramount but this was also tempered by an aesthetic sense of the visual, of compositional integration and balance in relation to rural scenery that was clearly borne out of an artistic English landscape tradition.

Nevertheless, the success – or otherwise – of these massive aesthetic experiments was bound to be up for debate. With regard to West Burton, the local newspapers of the time show no trace of any opposition to its development either on aesthetic grounds, or in relation to its physical impact upon the surrounding countryside and its communities. In March 1960, the *Times* reported that Nottinghamshire County Council had 'no serious planning objections' to CEGB proposals for new power stations at West Burton and nearby Cottam.[55] In contrast however, the council

[52] Hussey, *The Picturesque*, p. 141.
[53] Hussey, *The Picturesque*, p. 171.
[54] See Fairbrother, and Sylvia Crowe's book, *The Landscape of Power* (London, Architectural Press, 1958). It should be noted that Crowe, alongside fellow landscape architect, Barbara Colvin, fundamentally helped to shape the CEGB's attitude and approach to landscape design in the development of power stations during the 1960s. Clarke, *High Merit*, pp. 18–19.
[55] 'Plan for four new power stations', *The Times*, 10 March 1960.

declared itself to be 'shocked' at another plan to build a power station at Holme
Pierrepont near Nottingham, in amongst what the *Times* pointedly described as
'the heart of the county's green belt' with 'its considerable rural amenities'. The
different reactions here are a clear indicator of the deep-rooted and complex social
and cultural forces that could arise with regard to proposals such as these. In the
case of Holme Pierrepont, its 'considerable rural amenities' consisted of an early
16th-century, Grade I listed hall that was situated amongst 270 acres of country
park and extensive ancient water meadows, and which was home to the Pierrepont
family and the successive Dukes of Kingston from the late 13th century until the
late 1960s. The inference here was that a power station could never be built within
a parish so historically and aesthetically significant as Holme Pierrepont. On the
other hand, no 'serious' objections could be found with respect to that at West
Burton – the implication being perhaps that a power station was always permissible
within what was implicitly assumed to be a purely agricultural, lowland landscape
with little historic, aesthetic, or 'rural amenity' value at all.[56]

A more incisive, if somewhat journalistic, aesthetic critique of West Burton was
given by the *Times* in May 1965, in a report entitled 'Rival "works of art" costing
£70M each'. The piece described 'the nation's biggest artistic controversy', which
was being waged over 'two competing works of art'. Either would cost 'more than
£70m to buy', even though 'Thousands of people' would nevertheless 'have no
option but to look at the Cottam and West Burton power stations once they are
built'. The article then went on to describe the artistic differences between the two
structures, particularly of the more dispersed layout and the distinctive colouring
of West Burton in relation to Cottam's 'eight plain concrete cooling towers ... laid
out in two parallel lines'. As such, both would come to 'bear massive witness to the
fact that the campaign to make power stations look attractive has run into aesthetic
disagreement'. The two sides in the disagreeing schools of thought argued, on the
one hand, that the eye would find it difficult to sort out a group of cooling towers
from different angles, unless if one or more is coloured: then they will appear as
'a group of clearly defined structures'. The other school argued that to colour a
cooling tower would simply make it 'stand out from the landscape'. An unnamed
'supporter' of the latter option reckoned (quite perceptively given West Burton's
present condition) that plain concrete towers would better reflect 'the variations
in weather and the light. ... If you put a positive colour on it then it does not live
in the countryside'. The controversy would continue, the article predicted, after
1969 when both stations were completed: 'Will not the avant garde at West Burton
stare out with disdain at the drab enormity of Cottam's uncolourful bulk. Must
not the Cottam purist regret the pretentiousness of West Burton's yellow tower?'[57]

[56] The proposal for a power station to be built at Holme Pierrepont eventually went to a public inquiry
in February 1961, and was rejected on the basis of it being in conflict with proposed Green Belt plans,
and that it would depress local property values. John Sheail, *Power in Trust* (Oxford, Clarendon Press,
1991), pp. 153–155.
[57] 'Rival "works of art" costing £70M each', *The Times*, 14 May 1965.

Either way, the piece demonstrated the seriousness with which these ideas were taken at the time.

When West Burton was officially opened on 25 April 1969, *The Retford, Gainsborough and Worksop Times* declared the design to be a successful combination of 'beauty with economy', and proof that 'a large organisation can be human and manage to reconcile with aesthetic principles rapid technological progress'.[58] By the time Gibberd wrote about his work at Didcot in 1974 however, mid-century English modernist concerns with planning, aesthetics, 'the visual', and the 'picturesque' were all declining in importance as new, 'post-modern' and therefore individually subjective values of communication and meaning supplanted the idea of merely gaining aesthetic pleasure from good form and composition.[59] The formalist modernism employed in the service of a socially democratic sense of progress increasingly became incompatible with new considerations of individually lived experience, a consequent anti-essentialism, and a more critical-historical discourse suspicious of over-dominant 'conservative' or 'establishment' narratives, such as that of 'The Picturesque'.

Nan Fairbrother inadvertently acknowledges this shift when she justifies the presence of these new power stations in terms of individual sensation, where 'fast-moving cars' in particular could present 'a valid, new twentieth-century experience of landscape'. In this context, the 'forms of the cooling towers', and of their abstract shapes 'large enough to register on the landscape scale', were once again seen to be ideal within a 'bold and uncluttered composition of wide views and clearly-defined effects'. From there however, this all becomes newly defined as 'The best landscape for fast travel'.[60] At this point the careful, compositional planting of trees around these sites and beyond; the expressive colouring of the cooling towers, and their alignment with the wider historical landscape, comes to count for little against the single, swift experience of catching them out of the corner of your eye as you passed at speed. In this new 'Autopia', even monumental cooling towers became a mere adjunct – a picturesque ornament indeed – reduced to arranging themselves only in relation to the perception of the individual as they drove by. As such, and in this new, a-historical and perpetual present, it could be considered that the design and planning of these power stations therefore worked: that they did become naturalised within the landscape, almost as if they had always been there, but only now in terms of a fleeting glance taken from within an accelerated culture. As a further consequence, their aesthetic standing was immediately compromised and reduced: 'their design is no longer a fine art but an applied art, and though the function of design in applied art is still to give pleasure, it does it by making *use* pleasant'.[61]

---

[58] *The Retford, Gainsborough and Worksop Times*, 2 May 1969.
[59] Macarthur and Aitchison, 'Pevsner's townscape', p. 29.
[60] Fairbrother, *New Lives*, pp. 245–246.
[61] Fairbrother, *New Lives*, p. 212. Emphasis in original.

By the early 1970s however, other, newer, but even more pressing social and cultural concerns regarding the situation of these power stations within the landscape were emerging. In her 1974 *Architectural Review* critique of Didcot, Brenda Colvin noted 'the damage to the environment ... at the hands of any monolithic power sources' that 'lead to further questions affecting the future of our land and its landscape'. Should we not 'be seeking a variety of power sources, especially unlimited ones such as sun and wind? Should we not try to distribute our installations in small-scale units which could be available at least in emergency, rather than sinking more capital into faster use of our reserves of fossil fuel?'[62]

At this time, the *Architectural Review*'s 1953 prediction that 'enormous generating stations' would come to 'stud the landscape ... as windmills once studded the Dutch and English fens' had been fully realised across the Trent Valley. West Burton was one of three power stations built along a 15-mile stretch of the Trent between Gainsborough and Newark-on-Trent, with High Marnham (1954–1959) to the south, and Cottam (1964–1968) in between. Along with a number of other power stations built downstream towards Stoke-on-Trent, the region became popularly known as 'Megawatt Valley'. Since then, Colvin's concerns have developed into a full-blown, global, climate emergency, where rapid decarbonisation is now seen as a necessity if our planet's ecology is to survive. Consequently, all of these coal-fired power stations are presently being decommissioned and demolished: High Marnham was decommissioned in 2003, and finally demolished in 2012, while Cottam ceased production in 2019, and is set to be demolished in the near future.

Didcot was demolished in a somewhat piecemeal and ultimately tragic manner between 2014 and 2020.[63] Historic England had already declined to give listed building status to Gibberd's power station in 2013. According to Wikipedia, the report, currently unavailable on the Historic England website, recognised that while Didcot had some interesting features, for example the 'carefully designed setting', there were 'better examples elsewhere'. As a power-generating site, West Burton will remain in some form because a gas turbine generating plant has been built alongside the original coal-fired station, but its once aesthetically respected cooling towers are under threat, and there is little hope of them being preserved because the operator, EDF Energy, was granted a certificate of immunity for the site by Historic England in 2017. This guarantees that the station will not be statutorily heritage listed or be served with a Building Preservation Notice by the local planning authority. The certificate expired in August 2022 but EDF has since deferred closure until the end of March 2023.[64]

[62] Brenda Colvin, 'Power station, Didcot, Berkshire: Criticism', *The Architectural Review*, 156 (August 1974), 100.
[63] 'Didcot power station's chimney has been demolished', *BBC News*, 20 February 2020, www.bbc.co.uk/news/uk-england-oxfordshire-51403221 [accessed 2 August 2021].
[64] https://historicengland.org.uk/listing/the-list/list-entry/1448823 [accessed 3 August 2021].
'West Burton closure update', 14 June 2022, www.edfenergy.com/media-centre/news-releases/west-burton-closure-update [accessed 25 January 2023].

Within the grounds of West Burton are the remaining earthworks of the now deserted West Burton village, which was finally abandoned in 1886 when the village church was demolished. A 2010 archaeological survey suggested that the site offers a 'rare example of a link between the medieval and the modern'.[65] Once the almost certain demolition of the coal-fired power generating station at West Burton is carried out, that archaeological link between the medieval and the modern will be deepened as new earthworks appear: the circular footprints of the two sets of cooling towers, one in a lozenge shape, the other in a waving line. In the end, these will form the abstract traces of yet another moment in West Burton's history, but this time from the post-1945 age of social democracy in England, and a period when governments used to effectively plan for our future with diligence and artistic flair.

---

[65] Andy Gaunt, *A Topographic Survey of the Deserted Village of West Burton, Nottinghamshire* (Nottinghamshire County Council, 2010), unpaginated. Before the power station was built, West Burton could therefore be considered to be just as historically important as Holme Pierrepont.

7

England and the Isovist

MOA CARLSSON

DURING THE LATE 1950s and 1960s, when the harsh encroachment of industrialisation in rural areas reached a new peak, landscape architecture, design, and urban planning were sought out by industrialists as means to improve deteriorating public relations. Facing the contentious task of integrating large industrial structures – coal and nuclear power stations, pylons and power lines, coal mines, spoil heaps, motorways and oil terminals – the hired practitioners were asked to put their design skills and sensibilities to use in new ways. Their assignment was not simply to reduce the perceived erosion of rural landscapes but to find a more acceptable (to local communities, preservationists, and conservationists) mode of continual industrial expansion. This chapter recounts the efforts by landscape architects and planners in this pursuit. It tells of how, after numerous attempts at trying to reach consensus for shared aesthetic values of the countryside, methods of perceiving, recording, and describing scenery rationally and geometrically came to the fore in the siting of industrial projects, and in landscape planning more broadly. Geometry and abstraction offered landscape architects and planners, first, a new way of understanding the changing landscape, which corresponds with a broader turn to systematic and science-based planning during the post-war period. It also offered the practitioners a new way of capturing landscape change geometrically in charts and diagrams. The chapter traces how this new way of assessing scenery abstractly with properties and relations between points and lines, manifested in new ways of graphically simulating, predicting, and ultimately controlling landscape change during the 1960s and 1970s.

Negotiating the tensions and contradictions that emerged during this period, landscape architects and planners began to blend concepts of 18th-century picturesque theory, military calculations of lines-of-sight and intervisibility, and computer simulation. One method in particular gained traction in these pursuits, the isovist method of landscape analysis. Developed by landscape architect Clifford Ronald Vivien Tandy, who in turn had borrowed it from military surveys, the isovist method provided a lens through which to observe and record scenery that

Proceedings of the British Academy, **256**, 138–155, © The British Academy 2023.

was disinterested, structured, and seemingly free of bias. To many, the abstract diagrams seemed to present a clear picture of planning issues that were often highly political and riddled by conflicting views and positions. As a number of case studies will demonstrate, the isovist method was used in attempts to better integrate new industrial developments in their surroundings. It was also used in land reclamation projects to make improvements in areas that were already scarred by industry. As the Durham motorway study will show, resonating with the progressive views of Nan Fairbrother on cars and motorways, planners also deployed the isovist to design entirely new visual experiences of rural Britain that were unique to the motorist travelling through the countryside at great speed.

The chapter ends by showing how, in the hands of creative practitioners hired by local government and industrialists – the Central Electricity Generating Board (CEGB), the National Coal Board, British Gas, and oil companies operating in the North Sea – these analytical drawings practices, later augmented by computing technology, facilitated a new way of planning and designing the rural-industrial landscape. This new planning approach was goal-driven yet eclectic. From it, a stream of projects materialised on the ground, including power stations, power lines, motorways, coal mines, and oil terminals that helped shape the image of Britain's rural modernity during the 1960s and 1970s.

Seeing landscape aesthetically and geometrically

During the years following 1950, vast stretches of rural Britain changed rapidly as a consequence of agricultural intensification, industrial expansion, and increased appetite for rural leisure pursuits.[1] The competing interests in the countryside often placed the visual landscape at the heart of planning debates. The fear of irreversible damage to rural landscapes was not new, having occupied conservationists and preservationists for centuries.[2] But as post-war reconstruction efforts began in earnest, and England began its long process of post-war physical and cultural recovery, some social critics and preservationists grew increasingly alarmed at what they saw to be a deterioration not only of the rural landscape but of public taste for building and design in general. The realisation that unregulated development, including both urban growth and modern agriculture, could

[1] See Paul Brassley, Jeremy Burchardt, and Karen Sayer (eds), *Transforming the Countryside: The Electrification of Rural Britain* (Abingdon, Routledge, 2017); John Sheail, 'The "amenity" clause: An insight into half a century of environmental protection in the United Kingdom', *Transactions of the Institute of British Geographers*, 17:2 (1992), 152–153; and Katrina Navickas, 'Conflicts of power, landscape and amenity in debates over the British Super Grid in the 1950s', *Rural History*, 30:1 (2019), 87–103.
[2] David Evans, *A History of Nature Conservation in Britain*, 2nd edn (London, Routledge, 1997); Alun Howkins, *The Death of Rural England: A Social History of the Countryside Since 1900* (London, Routledge, 2003).

erode the countryside triggered a series of attempts, by the Campaign to Protect Rural England (CPRE) and other groups and individuals campaigning against threats to rural areas, to teach people how to see the countryside in particular ways, which in turn, it was hoped, would raise the standard of public taste. In 1942, the CPRE formed a committee dedicated to incorporate the teaching of design appreciation in general education. The Committee for Education in the Appreciation of Physical Environment was formed with town planner Patrick Abercrombie as chairman and architect Clough Williams-Ellis as vice president. The idea was to cultivate cultural values that the committee (renamed the Council of Visual Education in 1942) regarded to be essential in shaping modern Britain. The founders believed that appreciation of the physical environment, including architecture, town and country planning, and the fine and industrial arts, were topics that should be taught to all school children in secondary and art schools. As cultural geographer David Matless has explained, citing W. J. Morris of the Council, 'the council asserted that children should be taught impatience with things unnecessarily drab or sordid and should be inculcated with a desire to remove or improve them'.[3] The judgments of such visually enabled citizens, the CPRE believed, would ultimately influence policy.

To promote another kind of visual education, which was intended to fill a perceived gap in the general educational system, the Field Studies Council was formed in 1943 by Francis Butler, a schools inspector of the London County Council. The goal was to establish field study centres in unspoilt country across England and Wales that would provide opportunities for individuals to study environments first-hand. The first field centre opened at Flatford Mill in Suffolk, in 1946, in a former watermill on the River Stour that had featured in John Constable's iconic 1816 painting titled *Flatford Mill (Scene on a Navigable River)*. Like the Council on Visual Education, the Field Studies Council was part of a wider post-war reconstruction programme for education that was founded on the ideas that first-hand interaction with the natural world constituted a method of acquiring *an eye for the country*, that is, an understanding of the evolution of landscape founded on both aesthetic and scientific principles. In the words of Butler, the goal was to make the field study centres 'genuinely scientific institutions'.[4]

The idea that aesthetic sensibility and appreciation of unspoilt country, and systematic knowledge of the physical or material world go together, would soon also come to influence landscape planning. This happened because by 1960 it had become apparent that official measures of urban containment and agricultural support – for example, the founding of National Parks, Areas of Outstanding Natural Beauty, National Nature Reserves, Site of Special Scientific Interest, and the codification of Green Belt policy – which had been key strategies for protecting

---

[3] David Matless, *Landscape and Englishness* (London, Reaktion, 1998), pp. 351–354.
[4] Thomas W. Freeman and Philippe Pinchemel (eds), *Geographers: Bibliographical Studies*, vol. 2 (London, Bloomsbury, 2016).

rural landscapes, did not sufficiently prevent the encroachment by modern development. It was generally agreed that a more effective approach to landscape planning was needed.

In 1967, a group called the Landscape Research Group (LRG) was formed to promote landscape research as an interdisciplinary activity, and to encourage the exchange of knowledge and ideas concerning landscape.[5] Its founder was Francis Butler, the founder of the Field Studies Council, and its first Chairman was Keith Coleborn, the Joint Principal of the Ravensbourne College of Art and Design.[6] While membership of the professional body of the Institute for Landscape Architects (currently the Landscape Institute) was granted only to those with a degree in landscape architecture, the LRG welcomed and engaged researchers and practitioners from any discipline concerned with landscape. Its membership included representatives of a wide range of disciplines, including architecture, landscape architecture, town planning, surveying, civil engineering, meteorology, geography, and ecology. In addition, the group intended to recruit members from the fields of economics, sociology, psychology, biology, physiology, botany, and agriculture.[7]

According to Allen Fionn Holford-Walker of the CPRE, the LRG was 'a worthwhile if rather high-flying body'.[8] With a broad understanding of landscape, the LRG had two main objectives: to develop a comprehensive plan for coordinating landscape studies that were tied with actual work programmes, and to establish a landscape laboratory intended to be both 'a scientific device' to predict the effects of design proposals, and an 'instrument of use in teaching of, and research into, planning and landscape design'.[9] The idea of a landscape laboratory aligned with the agenda of the Field Studies Council. This link suggests that aesthetic and scientific observation and experimentation, as advocated by the Field Studies Council, were promoted as central aspects also of the emerging brand of landscape research. While the landscape laboratory was never realised, during the following years pioneering LRG members, including Tandy, Alan Murray, John Higgins, and Alex Hardy, freely crisscrossed the line between pragmatic design, art, and science. Through drawing, photography, mathematical graphing, and, later, computing, they experimented with methods of modelling and representation, often involving

[5] The Museum of English Rural Life Special Collections, University of Reading (hereafter MERL) SR CPRE C/1/196/2, Landscape Research Group, Council for the Protection of Rural England. Alan C. Murray, 'Landscape research: Memorandum by A. C. Murray ARIBA', April 1967, p. 2. See also Steven Shuttleworth, 'Fifty years of Landscape Research Group', Landscape Research, 42 (2017), s5–s64.

[6] MERL SR CPRE C/1/196/2, Landscape Research Group, Council for the Protection of Rural England. Alan C. Murray, 'Landscape research: Memorandum by A. C. Murray ARIBA', April 1967, p. 2.

[7] MERL SR CPRE C/1/196/2, Landscape Research Group, Council for the Protection of Rural England. Alan C. Murray, 'Landscape research: Memorandum by A. C. Murray ARIBA', April 1967, p. 2.

[8] MERL SR CPRE C/1/196/2, Landscape Research Group, Council for the Protection of Rural England. Letter from A. F. Holford-Walker to R. G. Alexander, 5 June 1969.

[9] MERL SR CPRE C/1/196/2, Landscape Research Group, Council for the Protection of Rural England. Letter from A. F. Holford-Walker to R. G. Alexander, 5 June 1969.

techniques that approximated human behaviours, particularly visual behaviour, in systematic methods of design and planning.

This search for new and more precise methods of modelling and analysis was also a response to the direction set by a series of conferences dedicated to the implications of urbanisation, industry, agriculture, forestry, and recreational pursuits in the countryside. In 1963 and 1965, two conferences in the 'Countryside in 1970' series were held to discuss future sustainable relationships between the countryside, new developments, and recreational activities. The conferences were organised by the Council for Nature and the Nature Conservancy and, to communicate the importance of the gatherings, had selected as president Prince Philip, Duke of Edinburgh. The first conference was held in London in November 1963 and was attended by 200 delegates from 90 different organisations. The event is significant because it brought disparate parties together and initiated conversations between major stakeholders and practitioners involved in shaping the countryside: landowners, developers, amenity and scientific bodies, industry and government officials, the nature-conservation bodies, the planning and design professions, and the monarchy.[10] As Matthew Kelly has discussed elsewhere, the outcomes of these debates significantly influenced British planning policy during the 1960s and 1970s.[11]

In many panel sessions of the 1963 conference, the ongoing development in the countryside was construed as a process in which citizens were deeply implicated yet had limited possibility to influence decision-making. Addressing industrial expansion, CEGB Chairman Christopher Hinton queried whether new industrial premises were being built in rural or semi-rural areas largely because their 'advent is feared and resented to an unwarranted extent by urban residents, who are in any case more numerous, vocal, and better organised than the country-dwellers to resist development?'[12] Calling for change, the CPRE argued that local communities' perception of the landscape must be taken into account in questions concerning development. Town planner William Holford – hired by the CEGB to spearhead questions of landscape and amenity – similarly lamented that those asked to make assessments and assertions had no agreed 'yardstick' to deploy when measuring the value of amenity.[13] Discussions within the conference's individual Working Parties led to the conclusion that more effective coordination was needed among those involved in landscape development, administration, and research.

---

[10] The Nature Conservancy, *The Countryside in 1970: Proceedings of the Study Conference held at Fishmongers' Hall, London, E.C.4, 4–5 November 1963* (London, HMSO, 1964).
[11] Matthew Kelly, 'Conventional thinking and the fragile birth of the nature state in post-war Britain', in Wilko Graf von Hardenberg, Matthew Kelly, Claudia Leal, and Emily Wakild (eds), *The Nature State: Rethinking the History of Conservation* (Abingdon, Routledge, 2017), pp. 114–131.
[12] The Nature Conservancy, *The Countryside in 1970*, p. 17.
[13] The Nature Conservancy, *The Countryside in 1970*, 6–7. Cited in Kelly, 'Conventional thinking', p. 120.

In November 1965, the second 'Countryside in 1970' conference commenced, an event that helped bring rational and systematic methods in landscape planning and policy work to the fore. A shared understanding among those gathered at the conference was that planning and care of the natural environment 'must be based on science as well as practical experience'[14] – an approach understood to 'require systematic and continuing research'.[15] At the closing of the conference, Prince Philip encouraged participants to reflect on the identified needs and to take appropriate action to conceive of new means with which to develop and manage the modern landscape.[16] The LRG was established in part to respond to two general goals agreed upon at the 1965 conference for finding a sustainable balance between modern needs and rural appearance: to promote better coordination between the disparate professions concerned with rural land use planning, and to develop new methods of unbiased visual appraisal.

Analysing visual encroachment geometrically

After the 1965 conference, both the working methods and the terminology of landscape planning began to change. In response to Prince Philip's call for increased coordination of landscape research and new systematic working methods, a new era of landscape research developed. This was evident at the first conference organised by the LRG. The Methods of Landscape Analysis symposium was held in May 1967 at the CEGB's offices in London.[17] It was chaired by Holford, and was a clear indication that systematic design methods, operational research, and information science were permeating landscape planning and research. Human visual perception and its potential roles in landscape assessment commanded particular attention. Five of the nine papers presented directly concerned visual analysis of landscape, whereas the remaining papers discussed the broader topic of landscape quality evaluation, aerial photography, information science, and classification of environmental information.

The symposium presentations relayed numerous systematic working methods for landscape design and planning, many of which re-described visual aspects of landscape as a resource that would be measured and expressed numerically. Such methods were however no novelty in military reconnaissance, and several of the symposium presenters had encountered such during military service years earlier. One drawing method used for capturing terrain intelligence would resonate especially strongly with the landscape architects, architects, and planners present: the

---

[14] The Council for Nature, The Royal Society of Arts, and The Nature Conservancy, *The Countryside in 1970: Second Conference, London 10–12 November 1965, Proceedings* (London: HMSO, 1965), p. vii.
[15] The Council for Nature *et al.*, *The Countryside in 1970*.
[16] The Council for Nature *et al.*, *The Countryside in 1970*, pp. 138–143.
[17] MERL SR LI AD1/8/1, Folder 1. ILA Research Committee, 'Minutes of a meeting of the Research Committee held on 30th June', 30 June 1966.

isovist method of landscape survey.[18] It seemed to many that this simple and seemingly objective method could be a productive tool with which to address the pressing planning problems that landscape planners were facing.

Drawing on his experiences from military service before and during the Second World War, Tandy presented a new mode of seeing and analysing landscape that was encoded in abstract line drawings that he called 'isovists'.[19] An act of re-presentation of a military survey method for a new audience, Tandy's isovist promised to capture the limit of human vision either as a single 'vision contour' or as a series of 'limit-of-vision' plots.[20] To draw an isovist in practice, a surveyor positioned in the field would use a pen to draw, on a cartographic map, the unbroken limit line of the area in view from his or her location, covering a 360-degree panorama. In this way, the isovist was meant to record not what can be seen, such as trees, buildings, or roads, but the *extent* of uninterrupted vision. The isovist was a precise hand-drawn diagram that was readily available for analysis and reproduction. To give his idea a 'crisp' name, Tandy coined the term 'isovist', meaning 'line-of-equal vision', which he based on the existing terms isobar and isotherm. The method, he explained, rendered visible information about human visual perception that would otherwise remain within an observer's memory and personal experiences. The military origins of the technique was present in the terminology of it: 'dead ground', 'lines of sight'. To know precisely what areas of a terrain would be 'in view' from a location was considered essential knowledge not only for planning reconnaissance and concealing troops and military equipment from the enemy, but also for establishing the reach of weapons, assessing the performance of weapon systems, and for siting radio communication equipment.

But Tandy was not alone in making the connection between military mapping and visual analysis of rural areas. Immediately after the First World War, Williams-Ellis saw opportunity to make the mapping techniques he had developed available to a wider audience. In 1919, under the pseudonym Graphite, he published a pamphlet titled *Reconography: Simplified Reconnaissance Sketching*.[21] It described methods he had developed for recognising enemy dispositions – largely by sketching with frozen hands in an open cockpit over or near enemy lines. It offered, in short, a system for codifying observation. Published shortly after the end of the First World War, Williams-Ellis made the pamphlet available to the Boy Scouts – set up by his friend Robert Baden-Powell – who used it to educate scouts about systematic field observation.[22]

---

[18] Clifford Tandy, 'The isovist method of landscape survey', in Alan Murray (ed.), *Landscape Research Group Symposium: Methods of Landscape Analysis, London, 3 May 1967* (London, LRG, 1967), pp. 9–10.

[19] MERL SR LI AD2/2/1/60. Letter from Clifford Tandy to Mrs Douglas Browne, 14 October 1950, Clifford Tandy, ILA Membership Files, Landscape Institute Archive.

[20] Tandy, 'The isovist method of landscape survey', p. 9.

[21] Graphite (pseud.), *Reconography: Simplified Reconnaissance Sketching* (London, Hodder & Stoughton, 1919).

[22] Arnold Rattenbury, 'Come and stay', *London Review of Books*, 19:23 (1997), 13–16.

Sylvia Crowe, President of the Institute for Landscape Architects between 1957 and 1959, was another pioneering practitioner with extensive wartime experience, and a prominent voice in the debate about the place of industry in the countryside. During the Second World War, Crowe served as an ambulance driver in northern France with the Polish Army. From 1940 until the end of the war, she served with the Auxiliary Territorial Service in England where she was promoted to Sergeant. In 1945, when Britain's rebuilding efforts began in earnest, Crowe set up a landscape architecture firm dedicated to landscaping for the public sector. She proved capable of handling landscapes of hugely diverse scales, from small garden details to hundreds of acres of new towns, forests, and sites for power stations, gasometers, sewage works, crematoria, airfields, and large-scale reservoirs. She was the first ever landscape consultant for the Forestry Commission and one of the first landscape architects to be hired by the CEGB, where she remained a consultant between 1948 and 1968, a period during which the National Grid was developed into the largest in the world.[23] Advising on the siting of power stations and their fit in the countryside – years before Holford was recruited by the CEGB – Crowe used a technique that was nearly identical to Tandy's isovist method. In her 1958 book, *Landscape of Power*, she wrote that each power station casts around it 'a zone of visual influence',[24] what Tandy later termed isovist.

Planning and constructing the rural-industrial landscape

The geometric way of seeing landscape, and the abstracted isovist plots that captured that perspective, contributed to a new culture of planning and constructing industrial projects. Throughout the 1960s and 1970s, large-scale industrial infrastructure, planned and shaped with the isovist method of analysis, materialised across the UK, from Dungeness to Orkney. Despite intensive and continuous campaigning by the CPRE and other interested parties, industrialisation had not abated, but had rather begun to take a different direction.

Continuing the work on power station siting pioneered by Crowe and others, landscape architect Ronald Hebblethwaite managed a small team of landscape architects at the CEGB during the early 1960s.[25] Because it would often take several years to complete detailed landscape quality maps from first-hand observations, Hebblethwaite proposed that one should limit qualitative studies to the area in which a power station made a discernible visual impact. Like Crowe, Hebblethwaite called the area impacted a 'zone of visual influence' or 'ZVI'.[26] The fundamental method

[23] MERL SR LI AD2/2/1/25. Sylvia Crowe, Membership files sub-series.

[24] Sylvia Crowe, *Landscape of Power* (London, The Architectural Press, 1958), p. 27.

[25] Archive of the University of Liverpool, UK. D147/EB11. CEGB, Holford Papers. 'Landscape architects (1958–1968)'.

[26] MERL AR THO B/8, Marian Thompson Collection. 'Landscape quality assessments and zones of visual influence with quantitative assessment', unpublished manuscript for the ILA (1969), pp. 1–10.

for establishing such zones was Tandy's isovist method of analysis. A draftsman would draw sections through the landscape based on elevation heights read off contour maps. These sections were then laid out radially around the power station under analysis. To define the ZVI plot of a 2,000MW station, a section would be drawn at five-degree intervals within three miles of the power station, and every two and a half degrees from three to five miles distance. By drawing a line of sight across each section drawing, parts of the cross-section in view or out of sight could be identified. To cover a 360-degree field around a power station required constructing hundreds of section drawings, which was time-consuming and expensive: to carry out a study would often take three to four days of work. Because of the cost of this labour Hebblethwaite and the CEGB team began to experiment with mainframe computers to analyse landscape visibility conditions.

The first computer application for power station siting, developed at the CEGB, was written in the FORTRAN programming language. The application would, in effect, carry out line-of-sight calculations using two inputs: the height of an 'an average man' and a numerical description of topography generated from contour maps.[27] These elevation heights were configured as a square matrix, and the computational procedure worked by comparing the height of the observer with the elevation heights stored at each location in the matrix along a line of sight. These calculations also considered the curvature of the earth and light refractions found to influence views over a certain distance. Hebblethwaite explained that, in the application, a line of sight from the observer location would read, for example, '000111000000111111000000000111', where 1 indicated a grid cell 'in sight' and 0 one in 'visual shadow'.[28] As can be seen in Figure 7.1, the results of calculations were printed out as schematic maps, and lines were drawn around groups of 0s and 1s to create defined zones. The edges of areas were then re-examined by photogrammetry to correct for varying heights of surface mantle features such as buildings, woodlands, and hedgerows. Provided with sufficient topographic data, the computer application allowed for momentous time and cost savings, compared to drawing the sections by hand. Invented to aid comparison between alternative power station configurations, Hebblethwaite's 'economical' method assisted not only creative design work but managing resources, including staffing cost and project budgets.[29] The analogue and computer-based methods were used in several power station projects during the 1960s and 1970s, and were used to select sites, design buildings and their configurations, surrounding landscapes and screening features.

One of the first projects in which the technology was used was the West Burton power station, the first 2,000MW station to be approved for construction. Here,

[27] MERL AR THO B/8. Marian Thompson Collection, 'The determination of zones of visual influence by computer and photogrammetry', *CEGB Technical Disclosure Bulletin*, 255 (December 1975), p. 2.
[28] Marian Thompson Collection, 'The determination of zones of visual influence'.
[29] Marian Thompson Collection, 'The determination of zones of visual influence'.

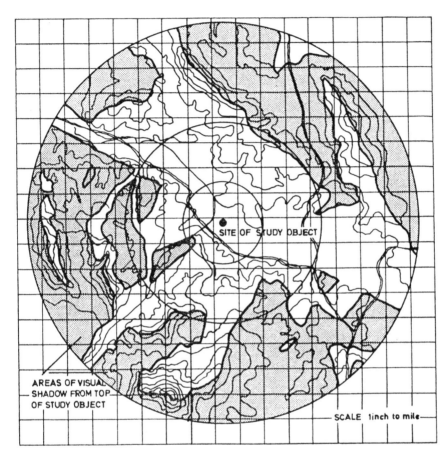

Figure 7.1 Output from Ronald Hebblethwaite's computerised view analysis program at the CEGB. Courtesy of The Museum of English Rural Life Special Collections, University of Reading. AR THO B/8. Marian Thompson Collection. Hebblethwaite, 'The determination of Zones of Visual influence by computer and photogrammetry', 1975

Hebblethwaite assisted landscape architect Derek Lovejoy on the landscaping of the station. As discussed by Ian Waites elsewhere in this volume, based on various visual analyses, the project architects (The Architects Design Group) separated the cooling towers into two groups at either end of the facility to prevent the power station from forming a bulky mass that blocked views of the landscape.[30] Another station project which employed Hebblethwaite's computer application was the Didcot A power station in Oxfordshire. Designed by architect Frederick Gibberd,

---

[30] Jonathan Clarke, *'High Merit': Existing English Post-war Coal and Oil-fired Power Stations in Context* (English Heritage/CEGB, 2013), p. 8.

its 650 feet tall chimney was surrounded by six cooling towers 375 feet high. Viewpoints scattered across the valley were drawn up and it is these views, as Waites explains, that help us understand why the power station came to have its unusual layout.[31] But the isovist method was not only used to integrate new infrastructure in rural areas. It was also used to design new kinds of visual experiences that lacked a historical tradition.

In the mid-1960s, landscape architect Brian Clouston used the isovist method to formulate a policy for the general setting of a new motorway proposed through County Durham.[32] The 22-mile-long Durham Motorway was built in four sections and opened in September 1969. Different from the way that it was used at the CEGB, the isovist method was here used, not to decide the actual alignment of the motorway – this had already been decided – but to analyse, improve, and control the landscape views that would be available to motorists travelling along the route. The idea that the car fundamentally changes how one uses rural areas was also picked up by Nan Fairbrother in her 1970 book, *New Lives, New Landscapes*. In the chapter titled 'Roads as new environment', Fairbrother envisions a future where roads are carefully routed and specifically laid out for the landscape.[33] But should new roads be routed to leave the landscape undisturbed or be laid out so that as many people as possible can enjoy scenic views from their car windows? For Fairbrother, roads were not a threat but rather a key constituent element of Britain's modern landscape. According to her, the large-scale patchwork of rectilinear fields that characterises modern agricultural landscapes make most sense from a moving vehicle. Encouraged by what she observed to be the growing design skills and sensibilities of road-designers, Fairbrother saw the visual integrity of the fast-moving car and modern agricultural landscapes as an almost organic expression of a technological modernity. In the Durham motorway study we can observe how that expression is deliberately manipulated to create certain effects on the motorist viewer.

Carried out by Clouston and members of the landscape section of the Durham County Council planning department, the objective of the study was to determine the quality and character of the rural landscape visible from the motorway and to determine how improvements could be made to 'the visual image' of the landscape in view from the route.[34] The project drew in part on a study carried out in the early 1960s at the Joint Centre for Urban Studies at MIT and Harvard University in the United States. This project, titled 'The View from the Road', was developed by urban planners Kevin Lynch and Donald Appleyard with architect John Myer, and sought to explore the aesthetics of highways, which to the researchers was a

[31] John Sheail, *Power in Trust: The Environmental History of the Central Electricity Generating Board* (Oxford/New York: Clarendon Press/Oxford University Press, 1991).

[32] James Richard Atkinson, *Landscape and the Durham Motorway* (Durham County Council, 1965).

[33] Nan Fairbrother, *New Lives, New Landscapes* (London, The Architectural Press, 1970).

[34] Brian Clouston, 'The Durham motorway landscape study', in Alan Murray (ed.), *Methods of Landscape Analysis* (London, Landscape Research Group, 1967), p. 11.

neglected opportunity in urban design.[35] Clouston argued, however, that the Durham project was unique in its focus on rural environments, which differed from the MIT project's focus on urban contexts. One of the main objectives of the Durham project was to determine where landscape improvements and reclamation efforts into the land visible from the motorway would make the greatest difference. The project was aimed, in other words, both at improving views of the rural area through which the motorway passed and about maximising the benefit from the allocated resources and funds.

In order to plot the extent of land visible from the motorway, Clouston and the project team defined station points along the route. At each point, an isovist recording was made on trace paper over an Ordnance Survey map. While the full stretch of land along the route would be visible, some areas would remain visible for much longer than others due to fluctuation in topography and other features. To better understand which areas would be most visible from the motorway, once all station isovist plots had been drawn, the different tracings were overlaid to determine the number of times each part of the visual corridor was seen from the road: a measure the team referred to as 'visual frequency'.[36] In addition, a graphic notation system was devised to record the visual character along the motorway, including ridges, focal points, eyesores, and prominent skylines. A detailed survey was carried out of derelict and unsightly land and 'eyesores', which identified 54 intrusions including pit heaps and collieries, quarries, piggeries, prefab housing, refuse tips, and other structures.[37] To appreciate the variation in visibility of these features, and to determine which features were most frequently obscured or blurred by fog and other weather phenomena, the team also made field observation of the structures daily over a period of two months. The diagrams resulting from these analyses were then correlated to the frequency map in order to identify the areas that were most in need of remediation and improvement.

Based on these findings a number of recommendations were formulated, many of which were later acted upon in the physical landscape. Areas determined of low landscape quality, possessing numerous unsightly features, were prioritised for remedial actions. Tree planting was the preferred means to improve the appearance of scarred areas and for screening off or redirecting views towards preferred sights. Along a stretch of the motorway near West Rainton south of Newcastle upon Tyne (see Figure 7.2) two pit heaps were reshaped and planted, and minor eyesores in form of industrial sites were tidied and screened off with trees. The method of forming a visual barrier by carefully positioning clusters of trees was also used to screen off views of an area with prefabricated housing deemed unsightly. Still today, when studying aerial photos of the A1 motorway through County Durham

[35] Donald Appleyard, Kevin Lynch, and John R Myer, *The View From the Road* (Cambridge, MA, MIT Press, 1964).

[36] Clouston, 'The Durham motorway landscape study', pp. 13–15.

[37] Clouston, 'The Durham motorway landscape study', p. 13.

Figure 7.2 Aerial view of West Rainton and Leamside in County Durham (white arrows added for emphasis)

it is clearly visible how sites that were judged unsightly are flanked by trees in designed formations that block views, not from all sides of the inferior structures but specifically from the point of view of the motorway. These deliberate design interventions, which resulted in views that appear natural though were highly controlled and framed for particular effects, also become apparent in the parts of the route where only one side of the motorway is densely planted whereas the other side is open, allowing far reaching views into the landscape.

As a result of this and other early demonstrations of the effectiveness of the isovist method in analysing, controlling, and manipulating the visibility of certain infrastructure, many industrial leaders were convinced that the method would enable more efficient landscape planning. As a result of this optimism, during the first half of the 1970s, applications for isovist view analysis gained a favourable reputation across Britain's industrial sector. British Gas adopted the isovist method, and in Scotland, the South of Scotland Electricity Board began using the computerised isovist analysis methods to assess visual intrusions caused by pylons and power lines, notable those of the Torness Nuclear Power Station, doing so in conjunction with the so-called Holford Rules.[38] The isovist method also became an

---

[38] William Holford, *Guidelines for the Routing of New High Voltage Overhead Transmission Lines* (London, CEGB, 1959).

important assessment tool for the National Coal Board (NCB) where it was used both to assess the location of new schemes and in landscape remediation.

As principal landscape consultant to the NCB, Tandy and the firm Land Use Consultants (LUC) – founded in 1966 by Tandy, conservationist Max Nicholson, and John Herbert – worked on many land reclamation schemes commissioned by the NCB. One of the first commissions for the LUC, and the project that made Tandy perhaps the most influential landscape consultant to the NCB during this period, was the tragic Aberfan disaster of 1966. After this catastrophe, in which 28 adults and 116 children died as a result of the collapse of a colliery spoil tip located on the slope just above the town, Tandy advised the NCB on the restoration of the disaster area. However, and as has been well documented by Iain McLean and Martin Johnes, the removal of the spoil heaps became a major source of contention in the aftermath of the disaster.[39] NCB Chairman Alfred Robens was reluctant to admit responsibility, and in the end, some of the funds to remove the final spoil were taken from the Aberfan Disaster Memorial Fund, which had been raised by public appeal. Most of the spoil was shifted to a plateau further up the mountain towards Mynydd Merthyr, and was terraced and sown with grass following the design proposals developed by Tandy and the LUC. Their work at Aberfan marked the beginning of a number of commissions by the NCB involving the remediation of scarred landscapes and perceived eyesores, among which some of the most renowned projects were located around Stoke-on-Trent in Staffordshire and in neighbouring Derbyshire.[40]

An article published in *The Illustrated London News* in 1975 describes 'new capabilities' being used to turn a large stretch of industrial land in Stoke-on-Trent into a park.[41] Formerly the home of England's pottery industry, Stoke-on-Trent had more wasteland within its boundary than any other English town. In the mid-1960s, 1,746 of the city's total 22,927 acres were officially classified as derelict. The phrase 'new capabilities', coined by an architectural journalist, was a deliberate invocation of Lancelot 'Capability' Brown – one of the most renowned landscape gardeners of the 18th century.[42] A true visionary, Brown was known for building seemingly naturalistic parks on an immense scale by creating vistas, moving hills, planting thousands of trees, and making lakes and serpentine rivers. Because carefully constructed views were central to his designs, contemporary and later critics considered the parks built by Brown and his followers to be quintessentially picturesque. It was, in fact, after observing Brown's landscape garden at Stowe in Buckinghamshire that English clergyman, artist, and writer William Gilpin (1724–1804) defined the picturesque as 'that kind of beauty which is agreeable

---

[39] Iain McLean and Martin Johnes, *Aberfan: Government and Disasters* (Cardiff, Welsh Academic Press, 2000).

[40] See also John Barr, *Derelict Britain* (London, Pelican, 1969).

[41] Tony Aldous, 'New capabilities', *Illustrated London News* (December 1975), 47.

[42] Dorothy Stroud, *Capability Brown* (London, Faber & Faber, 1975), pp. 49–53.

in a picture'.[43] As Waites discusses in more detail in his chapter in this volume, to Gilpin and Brown, a landscape vista constituted a framed picture to be viewed and appreciated from a defined viewing location. Tandy's efforts to reinvigorate Stoke-on-Trent and Derbyshire during the 1970s were arguably motivated by such 'pictorial appreciation of nature', and relied on 'capabilities' that could turn his vision of the modern landscape into reality.[44]

In 1969, the Stoke-on-Trent City Council found a 'new Capability Brown'[45] in the LUC and Tandy, who was also the president of the Institute for Landscape Architects at the time. To construct landscape views, as Brown had, was also Tandy's forte. At his disposal were drawing utensils, maps, and a camera but also the isovist method for drawing the precise boundary of a person's field of view from a defined position. For seven years, Tandy worked to develop an overall strategy for Stoke-on-Trent that ultimately comprised a green way system of pedestrian footpaths, linking six towns together along the lines of old railways. In addition, he designed an 87-acre Central Forest Park that drew inspiration from London's Hampstead Heath and Amsterdam's Bos Park.[46] At the outset, large black mounds of coal slag were visible from most of the surrounding areas, which at the time was home to more than 260,000 people. Using his isovist method – an example of which can be seen in Figure 7.3 – Tandy refashioned the wasteland into a stretch of landscaped country with carefully crafted views that gave an appearance of rolling countryside.

Using his isovist method as a tool for both management and design, Tandy re-sculpted the slag mounds into landforms, sowed them with grass and planted saplings. As a management tool, it helped him to identify smaller areas within the vast landscape that required special attention. He envisioned that focusing on the areas most frequently viewed by the local community, and allocating resources accordingly, would allow the council to reclaim a much larger total area. At the time, the city councils responsible for landscape clearance could manage on average a modest 30 acres a year. Tandy's Central Forest Park alone spread out over 87 acres.[47] As a design tool, the isovist method allowed Tandy to make changes and additions to the landscape according to what the geometric figures reported was 'in' or 'out' of view' from particular locations. Once completed, the project was reported as a success. Residents and visitors were pleased with the sweeping country views that had replaced the bleak industrial landscape. With this scheme, Tandy persuaded the Stoke-on-Trent councillors to adopt a comprehensive approach to landscape planning and move away from piecemeal funding of land reclamation. It was one of the largest and most successful landscape reclamation projects of the 1960s and 1970s and

[43] William Gilpin, *An Essay on Prints*, 5th edn (London, A. Strahan, 1802), p. xii.
[44] Christopher Hussey, *The Picturesque: Studies in a Point of View* (London, Frank Cass & Co., 1927), p. 17.
[45] Aldous, 'New capabilities', 48.
[46] Aldous, 'New capabilities'.
[47] Aldous, 'New capabilities', 47.

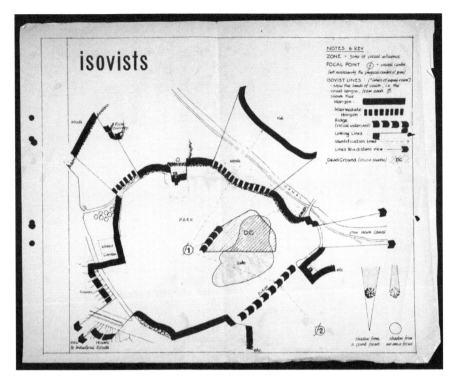

Figure 7.3 Isovist diagram by Clifford Tandy. The Museum of English Rural Life Special Collections, University of Reading. AR THO B/8. Marian Thompson Collection. Hebblethwaite, 'The determination of Zones of Visual influence by computer and photogrammetry', nd

became a precedent for many later projects.[48] From 1970 to 1974 Tandy continued working in the area and transformed the Shipley Colliery into a park memorialising the area's mining history. Here, as in Stoke-on-Trent, he used the isovist methods to transform spoil heaps, derelict buildings, polluted lakes, and 30 abandoned mine shafts into what is still known as the Shipley Country Park (see Figure 7.4).

A new planning culture

This chapter has shown that a new approach to landscape planning would in part be defined by pioneering practitioners deploying the isovist method of landscape

---

[48] Clifford R. V. Tandy, G. A. Jones, and A. D. N. Penman, '7 industrial spoil tips', in *Civil Engineering Problems of the South Wales Valleys: Proceedings of a Conference Held on 15–17 April 1969 at Cardiff*, (London, Institution of Civil Engineers, 1970), pp. 81–91.

Figure 7.4 Shipley Hill, Derbyshire © Garth Newton, licensed for reuse under Creative Commons CC BY-SA 2.0, creativecommons.org/licenses/by-sa/2.0

assessment. During the 1960s and 1970s, the practice of analysing, designing, and manipulating views with isovist plots evolved into an increasingly mathematical (later computerised) practice that in many ways served industrial expansion. The method was adopted by design and planning practitioners working in the electricity, coal, oil, and other industries, where it was used to capture visual aspects of landscape in the language of geometry, and used to communicate information about visual landscape change in structured line diagrams. The resulting industrial projects changed both the functioning and the appearance of rural Britain, and the isovist became a tool to manage what Crowe called the visual encroachment by these projects on landscapes. The developments had a profound impact on the landscape, visually, environmentally, and culturally. Still, when constructed, many of the projects (for example, power stations and power lines) met with substantial resistance.[49] Curiously, the decommissioning of this infrastructure in recent years has also spurred a widespread public interest, sometimes even a tendency for resistance.

---

[49] See, for example, Navickas, 'Conflicts of power', 87–103; Matthew Kelly, *The Women Who Saved the English Countryside* (New Haven and London, Yale University Press, 2022).

In August 2019, thousands of people came to Oxfordshire to witness the controlled demolition of Didcot A's three remaining cooling towers. In August 2021, another power station was erased from Yorkshire's skyline as two chimneys and the boiler house at the Ferrybridge C power station were demolished. That same month, four of eight cooling towers were demolished at the Eggborough power station in North Yorkshire. In 2022, the Hunterston B and the Hinkley Point B nuclear power stations started decommissioning, and more will follow. The dismantling of this infrastructure follows a 2015 statement by the government announcing that the UK's remaining coal-fired power stations would be shut by 2025. In social media groups and other online forums, communities discuss what the erasure of this infrastructure means, and what (if any) new development may take its place. With a visual reach of up to 50 miles on a clear day, these landmarks have dominated the British landscape for half a century, which means that communities in their vicinity have grown accustomed to their presence. Over time, it seems that life on the *inside* of the isovist plot is not always considered visually inferior to the rural scenery it was deployed to manage almost six decades ago.

8

The View from the Land, 1947–1968: 'Modernity' in British Agriculture, Farm, and Nation

KAREN SAYER*

Introduction

> The problem of the future of the whole land area of the British Isles is one of the most urgent and difficult which we have to face today. I say 'today' deliberately, because this problem cannot be put off. The process of development is virtually irreversible, which means that we cannot afford to let things happen by chance or accident, only to be regretted later.[1]

IN 1966, COMMAND Paper No. 2928, *Leisure in the Countryside*, grappled with the challenges posed by the apparently competing aims of 'modern farming', the new leisure cultures enabled by mass car ownership, and the maintenance of what J. Noel White, Deputy Director of the Council of Industrial Design, called 'a countryside which is a delight to the eye'.[2] The government response, in the Countryside Act 1968, gave new countryside committees responsibility for developing access to the countryside and securing it for recreation by establishing and managing country parks, lakes and waterways, and planting schemes, facilitated via provisions

---

* This research was funded in whole or in part by the Wellcome Trust Grant 209818-E-17-Z. For the purpose of Open Access, the author has applied a CC-BY public copyright licence to any author accepted manuscript version arising from this submission.

[1] H.R.H. Prince Philip, in Garth Christian, *Tomorrow's Countryside: The Road to the Seventies* (London, John Murray, 1966), Foreword.

[2] *Leisure in the Countryside, England and Wales*, Cmnd. No. 2928, Vol. XIII.223, 1965–66, Permalink https://parlipapers.proquest.com/parlipapers/docview/t70.d75.1965-053883?accountid=13651 [accessed 29 September 2021]; J. Noel White, 'Concern for the countryside', *Farm & Country* (March 1969), 38–40 at 38.

for compulsory and voluntary action. As White reassured the readers of *Farm and Country*, farm grants would ensure that farmers and landowners required to enhance the amenity value of their holdings, such as by establishing footpaths or erecting gates, would not be out of pocket. This was because, as White phrased it, 'the population requires *both* home grown food production and a pleasure park. Consequently, a policy and programme were urgently needed which would avoid defeating either or both'.[3]

In 1968, *Agriculture*, the journal of the Ministry for Agriculture, Fisheries and Food (MAFF), reported that the focus of the 22nd Oxford Farming Conference was to have been the increasing pressure on domestic food production for a growing population. Britain's population was expected to increase from 54¾ million in 1968 to more than 60 million by 1980. Though the conference was cancelled due to a Foot and Mouth outbreak, the conference papers were published as normal and of sufficient significance to be disseminated through the specialist press. According to Philip Bolam, a district MAFF official,[4] increased population pressure, combined with changing patterns of land use, were 'the teeth gnawing away at our farm acres'. New housing, 'fast roads', 'new centres of industry', and 'all the amenities of a society that finds itself with a great deal more leisure than earlier generations ever knew' had led to the expectation that the relationship of 'farm and country' would need to go through a significant step change.[5] In a similar vein, Garth Christian had already argued in *Tomorrow's Countryside: The Road to the Seventies* that:

> The shape of tomorrow's countryside will depend upon the attitudes and outlook that dominate public opinion in the immediate future. … We must obviously accept the need for more towns and cities, modern industrial installations including nuclear reactors and oil refineries, more pylons and Post Office towers. But many of the visual consequences of change need not spoil the landscape, and some may even improve it. We now possess the knowledge and the technical resources to direct the programme of urban and rural renewal in a way that could produce profound improvements in our environment.[6]

In sum, Command Paper (No. 2928), the Countryside Act 1968, Garth Christian's evocatively titled book, and the 22nd Oxford Farming Conference envisioned a future British landscape in which its rural component would be re-conceived as

---

[3] White, 'Concern', 38–39. Emphasis in original.
[4] At the time, a district agricultural advisor for MAFF's National Agricultural Advisory Service (NAAS) in Hexham; in 1969, the year after the 22nd Oxford Farming Conference, he was appointed a deputy regional advisor for the South West; in 1973 he joined Barclays Bank and advised on agriculture in several Commonwealth countries, and in 1980 became involved with the Royal Agricultural Societies of the Commonwealth; in 1982 he was elected to the National Sheep Association. See obituary: Michael Pollitt, 'Philip Bolam, former Norfolk County farm adviser became top Barclays banker', *Eastern Daily Press*, 19 April 2014.
[5] Philip Bolam, quoted in S. R. O'Hanlon, 'Land: Use or abuse?', *Agriculture*, 75:8 (August 1968), 385–386 at 385 – the 22nd Oxford Farming Conference, scheduled January 1968, was cancelled 'in view of the foot-and-mouth epidemic'.
[6] Christian, *Tomorrow's Countryside*, p. 1

a holistic 'British Countryside' planned on a national scale for agriculture *and* for leisure. This planned countryside would continue to utilise new technologies, and methods for efficient agricultural production as had been the case since 1947, but also be much more open. The new car-owning public would want to come, it was assumed, alongside the cyclists and walkers who had already started to visit between the wars, and the wider spaces of the countryside beyond the National Parks would welcome anyone from a town or city with sufficient financial or physical means to get there.[7] As the Command Paper argued, the National Parks Commission, established by the National Parks and Access to the Countryside Act (1949), had created a 'valuable national asset' by designating 10 National Parks and a series of long-distance footpaths alongside negotiating numerous access agreements, but these provisions were no longer adequate. In the future, many more so-called 'townspeople' would want to access much more of the countryside and ways were needed to enable this 'without', it stated, 'spoiling what they go to the countryside to seek'. These claims were based on the assumption that they would have 'more leisure; and that in future they will be able to buy cars and boats and otherwise spend their money on their weekends and holidays'.[8] The post-war British citizen was expected to have both disposable income and time to spend at their discretion, and it was assumed they would want to spend both in the countryside at large.

Here was a rural modernity shaped not only by the new post-war British infra-structure, of nuclear reactors and pylons, reservoirs and roads, but one that also built on agricultural practices that were already aiming at improved production for greater efficiency, and better animal and human health. With new techniques such as grazing cattle on leys rather than permanent pasture, Sir George Stapledon had argued in 1944, 'the fertility and health of the soil will be maintained' and therefore the 'health of the animals', while 'milk, vegetables and eggs cannot possibly be of too high a quality or too fresh'.[9] As David Matless has observed, these landscapes continued to be celebrated as they had come to be pre-war: for their appearance, and for being at the service of the body and future wellbeing of the British citizen, a vision that informed the period of reconstruction that had taken shape in the war.[10] The tracts of productive agricultural land and built environments of farming

---

[7] There was a normative presumption of physical capability at the time, which persisted with little review until the turn of the 20th and 21st centuries. Nicola Burns, Kevin Paterson, and Nick Watson, 'An inclusive outdoors? Disabled people's experiences of countryside leisure services', *Leisure Studies*, 28:4 (2009), 403–417.

[8] *Leisure in the Countryside*, Cmnd. No. 2928, pp. 3–4.

[9] Sir R. George Stapledon, 'General trends', in Laurence Frank Easterbrook (ed.), *The Future of Agriculture* (London and New York, Todd Publishing Co., 1944), p. 17.

[10] David Matless, 'Visual culture and geographical citizenship: England in the 1940s', *Journal of Historical Geography*, 22:4 (1996), 424–439. Matless adopts the use of 'citizen' in addressing the ways in which landscape was regarded/looked at by those who visited it, and the physical expression of this, David Matless, *Landscape and Englishness* (London, Reaktion Books, 2016 [1998]), pp. 94–144, 296–312. The National Parks are not the focus of this chapter, but reference points include John Sheail, *An Environmental History of Twentieth-Century Britain* (Basingstoke, Palgrave, 2002); John Sheail,

lying *between* were just as intrinsically modern as the eye-catching large-scale projects. By 1947, agriculture was systematised with a clear goal and underpinning objectives, with strategy and policy, knowledge generated, and knowledge assets managed through advice and education. Indeed, we might read the immediate post-war British landscape as a whole as belonging to a sociotechnical imaginary: a scientific, technological agricultural future made manifest in farmers whose prosperity was one facet of a national imaginary of food security and plenty grown within a harmonious productive countryside. In post-war Britain, this vision was expressed as part of a series of interconnected policy threads, concretely sponsored through government grants, and enthusiastically articulated by the National Farmers' Union (NFU).[11] Yet, I will argue, respect for the past, in the form of a heritage of progress, was also integrated into this for the citizen to benefit from in their journeys to the country. Fields and farms were tasked with a complex of duties beyond food production. This was itself, as we will see, grounded in a tradition of the idea of what was termed 'the Land'. The idea of the duty of stewardship captured by Prince Philip, not just mastery of nature, was what generated the modern British landscape.

This chapter focuses on the acres of Britain, the agricultural land and buildings, that were tasked with increasing food production after the Agriculture Act of 1947. Starting first with the land, its organisation and its management, then moving to a consideration of the vision for agriculture and the land, it argues that these elements of the British landscape were significant components in the representation of Britain as a modern nation state, involving the integration modern environments of production and of leisure for the good of the British body. This stance meshed with the arguments made by agriculturalists in favour of the sustained increase of home food production following the Second World War. But rather than agricultural intensification and conservation necessarily being in tension with each other, as environmentalists often argued in the 1970s and 1980s, this chapter examines how policy initiatives between 1947 and 1968 sought to reconcile these differences so that agricultural modernity might be harmonised with vernacular rural structures, wildlife, and amenity. The strand of thinking, less noticed by historians than contemporary narratives of environmental decline, posited that agricultural landscapes, enriching and feeding the modern British citizen, epitomised 'natural England' as

---

Nature's Spectacle: The World's First National Parks and Protected Places (London and New York, Earthscan, 2010); Craig Pearson and Judith Nasby, *The Cultivated Landscape: An Exploration of Art and Agriculture* (Montreal and Kingston, London, Ithaca, McGill-Queen's University Press, 2008); Harriet Ritvo, *The Dawn of Green: Manchester, Thirlmere and Modern Environmentalism* (Chicago and London, University of Chicago Press, 2009); Matless, 'Visual culture and geographical citizenship', 424–425.

[11] Following Jasanoff, we should note that this was revised during the 1992 BSE crisis, when the British public's confidence in the NFU and agriculture's associated sponsoring structures (MAFF) were tested and as a result restructured. See Sheila Jasanoff, *Science and Public Reason* (London and New York, Routledge, 2012), pp. 64–68, 71–76. See also Sheila Jasanoff and Sang-Hyun Kim (eds), *Dreamscapes of Modernity: Sociotechnical Imaginaries and the Fabrication of Power* (Chicago, University of Chicago Press, 2015).

a central component of post-war British national identity. What often now appear to be competing, quite disparate rural modernities (agricultural, environmental, and touristic) were married. Opponents of scientific and nuclear modernisation such as W. G. Hoskins may well have celebrated the post-war British countryside as a historical palimpsest, but in successive Acts between 1947 and 1981, post-war British governments represented the countryside as a rich yet changing tapestry of modernised agricultural practice, tradition, and natural resource alive to emerging European environmental policy and global questions of sustainability.[12]

As Brassley *et al.* have observed, the standard narrative of agricultural change after the Second World War has been dominated by the centre and the official, a focus on rapid and highly impactful technological innovation in farm methods, and a commensurate step change in production supported by government politics and policymaking.[13] The Agriculture Act of 1947 emerged in response to policies used to drive up and sustain domestic agricultural production in the Second World War, and a commitment to the sector that had not been carried through after the First World War and the 1921 so-called 'Great Betrayal'. According to this narrative, the 1947 Act resulted in increased specialisation, mechanisation, and use of chemical products (pesticides, fungicides, herbicides, fertilisers), off the back of an increased application of scientific research and technological development, widening formal systems of education, reduced labour input, and increasing use of state and private financial tools.[14] Similar accounts have addressed comparable histories worldwide, framing these changes within critical assessments of the Global North's progressivist politics, as exercised via land reform, technology, and sponsorship of production excess, often interpreted as attempts at what James C. Scott has called 'the catechism of High-Modernist agriculture'.[15]

---

[12] William George Hoskins, *The Making of the English Landscape* (London, Hodder & Stoughton, 1955), pp. 231–232. Well-known as the originator of the point about its being a 'palimpsest', Hoskins only uses the word once (p. 211), in reference to the pleasures of studying the landscape history of towns. He could also be critical of too stultifying and decaying an atmosphere, see Oliver Creighton, Penny Cunningham, and Henry French 'Peopling polite landscapes: Community and heritage at Poltimore, Devon', *Landscape History*, 34:2 (2013), 61–86 at 62. For more on Hoskins, see Charles Phythian-Adams, 'Hoskins' England: A local historian of genius and the realisation of his theme', *Trans Leicestershire Archaeol. And Hist. Soc.*, LXVI (1922), 143–159; David Matless, 'One man's England: W. G. Hoskins and the English culture of landscape', *Rural History*, 4 (1993), 187–207.

[13] Paul Brassley, David Harvey, Matt Lobley, and Michael Winter, *The Real Agricultural Revolution: The Transformation of English Farming 1939–1985* (Woodbridge, The Boydell Press, 2021), p. 2.

[14] Edith Whetham, 'The Agriculture Act of 1929 and its repeal – the "great betrayal"', *Agricultural History Review* 22:1 (1974), 36–49; John Martin, *The Development of Modern Agriculture: British Farming since 1931* (New York, St Martin's Press, 2000); Nicola Verdon, *Working the Land: A History of the Farmworker in England from 1850 to the Present Day* (Basingstoke, Palgrave Macmillan, 2017); Pearson and Nasby, *The Cultivated Landscape*, pp. 90, 108.

[15] James C. Scott, *Seeing Like a State: How Certain Schemes to Improve the Human Condition Have Failed* (New Haven and London, Yale University Press, 1998), p. 270; David D. Vail, *Chemical Lands: Pesticides, Aerial Spraying, and Health in North America's Grasslands since 1945* (Tuscaloosa, University of Alabama Press, 2018); Venus Bivar, 'Agricultural high modernism and land reform in postwar France', *Agricultural History*, 93:4 (2019), 636–655; Carin Martin, 'Modernized farming but

Writing evocatively soon after the 2001 Foot and Mouth crisis, for example, Alun Howkins described an increasingly industrialised landscape of production, of lost labourers, and cottages inhabited by commuters, retirees, and second homeowners, which he argued became foundational to Britain's nascent 20th-century movements for environmental protection.[16] Yet, the policies behind these changes were part of a project to secure and increase food production which had their origin in the 1920s and 1930s, and were only fully realised after the Second World War, scaffolded by its War Agricultural Committees and wholesale state control of food supply.[17] While in one era, what has been called the 'production paradigm' looks like the pursuit of a damaging superfluity in the name of food security and cheap food, it may look quite different in another that has experienced the food scarcity of Depression, austerity, rationing, or shortage.[18] As Tom Williamson has more recently observed, though it is empirically valid to offer an environmental critique of this period's impact 'we should also remember … the deprivations of the wartime years, the continued threat of hunger during the peace, and the political attitudes which these engendered right across Europe'.[19] It is this perspective that will allow us to see how and why modernisation of agricultural practice after 1945 could be celebrated nationally, and why rural modernity was not seen as at odds with the wider aesthetic/cultural or even historical appeal of the countryside.

Context: the land, ownership, policy, and advice

'What', asked J. Scott Watson in his 1957 foreword to *Agriculture in the British Economy*, 'will the future historian have to say about these, our own times?'[20] Such was the significance of post-war change that the period has come to be referred to as 'the Second Agricultural Revolution', even if its extent and rate varied depending on the region, size of farm, its produce, and structure. Indeed, so extensive was this

---

stagnated production: Swedish farming in the 1950s emerging welfare state' *Agricultural History*, 89:4 (2015), 559–583; Nicola Gaberllieri, 'California dreamin': Rural planning and agricultural development in Italy's Grosseto Plain, 1949–1965', *Agricultural History*, 94:2 (2020), 224–250; John Agar and Jacob Ward (eds), *Histories of Technology, the Environment and Modern Britain* (London, UCL Press, 2018); Pearson and Nasby, *The Cultivated Landscape*, pp. 102–126.

[16] Alun Howkins, *The Death of Rural England: A Social History of the Countryside since 1900* (London and New York, Routledge, 2003), pp. 156–157, 172–173, 190–191, 193–206; Howkins' account of the farm worker has been cogently added to using oral and autobiographical accounts; see Verdon, *Working the Land*, pp. 223–244.

[17] David Matless, 'Visual culture and geographical citizenship: England in the 1940s', *Journal of Historical Geography*, 22:4 (1996), 424–439 at 436. A related point is made of the science by Dominic Berry, 'Agricultural modernity as a product of the Great War: The founding of the official seed testing station for England and Wales, 1917–1921', *War & Society*, 34:2 (2015), 121–139.

[18] Pearson and Nasby, *The Cultivated Landscape*, p. 126.

[19] See Tom Williamson, *An Environmental History of Wildlife in England 1650–1950* (London, New Delhi, New York, Sydney, Bloomsbury, 2013), pp. 184–185.

[20] J. Scott Watson, 'Foreword', in *Agriculture in the British Economy* (London, ICI, undated, c. 1957)

transformation that Brassley *et al.* refer to it as 'the real Agricultural Revolution', arguing that the sum of its impacts surpassed the 'agricultural revolution' of the mid-18th to 19th centuries.[21] To understand the drivers of this change, we must understand the social imaginary of the modern countryside, and that means recognising that such a revolution is exactly what was imagined.

Core to this new vision were changes in the fundamental issues of land ownership and land use, both of which governments sought to direct through policy. Despite a Labour manifesto commitment to land nationalisation in the general election of 1945, the existence of County Farms owned by Local Authorities, and frequent reference to the National Farm as a productive unit, landownership remained largely private.[22] In fact, many of the grants, credit facilities, and other forms of investment available to farmers derived from fiscal and agricultural policy linked to owner-occupancy, so that the distribution of land during the period saw owner-occupiers become the majority relative to tenant farmers. Until new policy contexts emerged as the post-war settlement broke down in the 1980s and 1990s, the shift away from tenancy underpinned the post-war farm modernity that forms our focus here.[23]

The grants and policy framework also encouraged significant changes to agricultural land use, including farming practice and management, all promoted by the large-scale and commercial operations represented by the NFU. Not that all possible tools for more efficient farming went uncriticised by the British state, especially when it came to weed and pest control. Indeed, environmental historian John Sheail has traced the evolution of concerns about pesticides among government agencies from their emergence as an issue of workplace health and safety in the 1950s, through conflicts within the farming sector, to arrive at broader concerns

---

[21] Brassley *et al.*, *The Real Agricultural Revolution.*

[22] County Farms/County Council smallholdings emerged from the late 19th century in Acts from 1892, 1980, and 1925, and peaked during the 1930s–1940s with a shift towards fewer but larger holdings after the Agriculture Act 1970. In 1936 there were 459,103 acres held in 29,071 holdings; in 1974 there were 427,650 acres held in 10,319 holdings. Since the 1970s they have declined, but were still seen by the industry as an important first step into farming. For a detailed exploration of the County Farms, see Nick Prince, 'Agricultural property rights and the county farms estate in England and Wales' (PhD thesis, University of Gloucestershire, March 2012). As a subject of continued political activism, they are mapped by G. Shrubsole and A. Powell-Smith, 'How the extent of county farms has halved in 40 years', *Who Owns the Land?*, 8 June 2018, https://whoownsengland.org/2018/06/08/how-the-extent-of-county-farms-has-halved-in-40-years/ [accessed 25 January 2023].

[23] Olivia J. Wilson, 'Land ownership and rural development in theory and practice: Case studies from the north Pennines in the 19th and 20th centuries' (Durham theses, Durham University, 1990), pp. 30, 50–54, 60–65, http://etheses.dur.ac.uk/6250/ [accessed 25 January 2023]. Significant changes to the context in which agricultural policy was designed and implemented included: (a) the financial sector was increasingly buying up land for investment; (b) in response to the Council of Europe's Convention on the Conservation of European Wildlife and Natural Habitats/'Bern Convention' 1979, a new Wildlife and Countryside Act was enacted in 1981; (c) around 1984 the European Community's Common Agricultural Policy significantly changed tack after it was found to have resulted in excess food production; and (d) the 1992 Rio Earth Summit established the idea of Sustainable Development.

about persistent chemicals and public health by the early 1960s.[24] This new civic epistemology through which the state and other national agencies ascertained environmental risk on behalf of the British citizen in terms of both food production and pleasure comprised another facet of rural modernism.

During the 1950s, and some years before the publication of Rachel Carson's land-mark *Silent Spring* in 1962, government and parliament began to address the poten-tial risks attaching to the use of chemicals in agriculture. For example, in 1959 John Farr, Conservative MP for Harborough in Leicestershire, concerned to maintain 'the balance of nature', made a plea for a Royal Commission to examine the increasing use of 'toxic sprays' in agriculture, which had doubled in his estimate over six years. Citing examples of failures, including an insecticide and the arsenate 'Stemmex' used to kill potato tops, Farr argued for an investigation considering possible side and long-term effects on humans, domestic animals, rivers, fish, soil, insects, and other wild-life, and for a research centre dedicated to improved development, technical design, and education. His motion was seconded by Colonel Tufton Beamish, Conservative MP for Lewes and council member of the Royal Society for the Protection of Birds, who argued for immediate field trials and 'ecological research', alongside greater co-ordination between the Medical Research Council, the Agricultural Research Council, and Nature Conservancy. Beamish drew on questions already raised in the Commons on this theme by himself and other MPs, and cited the specialist press, such as the *British Farmer*, on advice issued to farmers and labourers, mainstream print media, including reports in the *News Chronicle* on meetings of the Council of Nature, and indeed the government's own Working Party's Report on Residues of Toxic Chemicals in Food (the 'Zuckerman Report' of 1953) to strengthen his case.[25] MPs on both sides of the House supported the case for further investigation, highlighting the possible dangers of substances such as DDT and organo-phosphorus sprays.

In his response, Joseph Godber (Joint Parliamentary Secretary to the MAFF) did his best to deflect concerns, outlining the range of experts already involved in man-aging the existing voluntary scheme that aimed at managing use and the valuable role played by the Advisory Committee established in 1954 after the publication of the Zuckerman Report. The House was assured that the Minister for Agriculture had initiated discussions with the Ministers for Science and of Health and 'the Association of British Manufacturers of Agricultural Chemicals, the Association of British Sheep and Cattle Dip Manufacturers, the National Association of Corn and Agricultural Merchants, the National Farmers Union, the National Association of Agricultural Contractors and the British Chemical and Dyestuffs and Traders Association (Importers)'.[26] This complex of attitude, approach, and organisation,

---

[24] John Sheail, 'Pesticides and the British environment: An agricultural perspective', *Environment and History*, 19:1 (2013), 87–108.

[25] *British Farmer*, 5 September 1959; *News Chronicle*, 10 October 1959.

[26] Mr John Farr (Harborough), Colonel Tufton Beamish (Lewes), 'Agriculture (Toxic Sprays)', *Hansard*, 1959–60, Fifth Series, Vol. 613, cc. 1568–1585. NB Natural Resources (Technical) Committee, chaired by Solly Zuckerman, was formed in 1950.

including the commitment to voluntary rather than statutory controls, typified the response of those invested in productive land to apparent environmental threat. It was thus no coincidence that in 1958 the Council for Nature was formed as an umbrella organisation representing nature conservation organisations boasting a combined membership of more than 100,000 people. According to Garth Christian, the Council reflected a new determination by nature conservation organisations to work together to inform public debate and opinion in parallel to the government body, the Nature Conservancy. These bodies were part of expanding organisational network committed to the 'welfare of wild plants and animals' in the British countryside, whose 'concern for the protection of the rare plant and animal' species would evolve 'into a growing awareness of the importance of the habitat, and the complex problems involved in its management'.[27] Such was the complex expert, policy, legal, scientific, and commercial landscape modern agricultural interests had to navigate a decade or so after the Agriculture Act (1947).

The Ministry of Land and Natural Resources, formed by the Labour government in March 1965, was an attempt to manage these differing perspectives politically, but its dissolution just 18 months later indicated how difficult the task was. Not only was this small, under-resourced ministry tasked with establishing a Land Commission to address leasehold reform and land ownership, but it also had strategic oversight of all aspects of functional land use and natural resources, as well as managing information and advice via the Natural Resources Advisory Committee. Its vast portfolio included forestry via the Forestry Commission, tree preservation, registration of Common Land, allotments, access to the countryside, National Parks and the National Parks Commission (which became the Countryside Commission in 1968), Water Resources Board, and the Ordnance Survey. Despite the ministry's failure to make significant political progress – there was considerable clamour about the abandoned Land Commission Bill and the Leaseholders' Bill – it played an important part in planning and legislation relating to rural amenity at a pivotal moment, perhaps best remembered for the seminal 1966 White Paper on *Leisure in the Countryside*.[28,]

The agricultural sector was further challenged by increasing labour shortages alongside pressure to raise output.[29] The way to tackle this, the agricultural advisors

[27] Christian, *Tomorrow's Countryside*, p. 3.
[28] Minister of Land and Natural Resources, House of Commons debate, *Hansard*, 1965, Fifth Series, Vol. 707, 1st March 1965, cc. 1065–93, https://parlipapers.proquest.com/parlipapers/docview/t71. d76.cds5cv0707p0-0006?accountid=13651; Ministry of Land and Natural Resources (Dissoloution) Order, *Hansard*, 1966–67, Fifth Series, Vol. 740, Tuesday 7th Feb 1967, cc. 1459–1516, https://parl ipapers.proquest.com/parlipapers/docview/t71.d76.cds5cv0740p0-0007?accountid=13651; *Leisure in the Countryside*, Cmnd 2928, p. 4; Anon, 'Obituary Mr Frederick Willey, PC: stalwart Labour moderate', *The Times*, 16 December 1987, p. 16; Mr Hugh Gardner, 'The green debate', letter to the editor, *The Times*, 21 January 1986, p. 17; Michael Ratcliffe, 'State of the nation', *The Times*, 14 June 1976, p. 10; Anon, 'Land planning brought under unified control', *The Times*, 8 February 1967, p. 14; Anon, 'Corridors of economic power', *The Times*, 12 April 1967, p. 22; Leader, 'An unfairly drawn bill', *The Times*, 24 February 1967, p. 13.
[29] Verdon, *Working the Land*, pp. 230–232.

suggested, was through improved productivity, which, if necessary, must be independent of human labour input. Advertising in the specialist press at the time therefore frequently referenced key terms such as profitability, progress, modernity,
efficiency, scientific and modern methods in its body text and used modernist
visual imagery. Advertisements like the one for Wolseley Engineering (1957, see
Figure 8.1) depended on a technocratic readership that was looking for opportunities to grow and extract ever greater value from their labour and land, despite the
central human figures in its advert at one with, and ready to work through, sun
and harvest, and depended for its explicitly modernist visual references on a presumption of the cultural connections that existed across Continental Europe and
North America. These concepts, the energised, the technocratic and the modern, had
become interlinked discursively with the state policies operationalised by MAFF (as
represented in *Agriculture*) and were clearly considered by the ancillary trades who
authorised the copy and designs as crucial to their marketing. Alongside the official
advice, products were being imagined commercially for farmers that smoothed the
way to better, more profitable futures rooted in High Culture as well as in effect a
new form of high-input, high-output High Farming: high agri-*culture* if you will.[30]

But, as well as the products offered by ICI and other agri-chemical producers,
and the energising technological solutions offered up to address the pains of labour
shortage by manufacturing companies like Wolseley, the focus post-war on 'farm
management' focused primarily on the management of farm land as managed space,
or built environment. This can perhaps be seen most clearly in advice gleaned from
work-time study management techniques. These had become commonplace and
were intended to shape the way that labourers were directed to undertake tasks,
leading to an efficient whole farm system approach. That approach could shape
the whole plan of the farm and in application to its built structures reveals the
ways in which the idea of the farm was conceptualised as whole system (including
buildings, labourers, and beasts).

'[B]uildings must make a positive contribution to the farming system',
Agriculture argued, advocating 'an integrated layout'. Focused on the reduction
of labour, the article set out the 'basic principles of handling' feed and livestock,
recommending in its text designs that made use of a combination of gravity,
ready-cut feed (that is, chopped hay) and the normal movements of livestock as
they fed to encourage flow without intervention.[31] Written by a Senior Assistant

[30] See, for example, 'Modern farmers rely on ICI – and profit by experience', 'Modern farmers choose
from this well-proved range', ICI Compounds advert, *Agriculture*, 71:1 (1964), viii; 'Martins Bank
understands the farmer's problems: The hazards of weather and prices and the need for modernization',
Martins Bank Ltd advert, *Agriculture*, 71:2 (1964), vii; 'The Bedford [van]'s engine … is *designed* to
operated with maximum efficiency on low-cost petrol', Better Buy Bedford advert, *Farmers Weekly*,
1 January 1965, p. 69.
[31] John Troon, 'Handling and building design', *Agriculture*, 71:4 (April 1964), 177–180.

Figure 8.1 Wolseley Engineering Company, of Birmingham, 1957. Courtesy of Grace's Guide to British Industrial History. Wolseley Engineering began in Australia, manufacturing mechanised sheep shearing equipment, and moved to Birmingham, UK in 1889.[32]

---

[32] Advert for Wolseley Engineering Ltd., (1957), www.gracesguide.co.uk/File:Im1957BIF-Wols.jpg [accessed 25 September 2022].

Land Commissioner within MAFF's Agricultural Land Service (who was awarded a Kellogg Fellowship for the study of agricultural mechanisation and farm buildings), the article was typical of the sort of advice being disseminated to the sector.[33] Work-time study, as a new form of modern farm management, and a knowledge asset, fitted into the professionalisation of agriculture promoted elsewhere in the literature, as taught at all levels through full- and part-time courses by the Agricultural Colleges and University Agriculture Departments.[34] But it also resulted in a broader encouragement to revise agricultural practice on the farm (looking in detail at every component and every material on the farm, even the feed), the adoption of farm mechanisation, and new forms of farm layout, promising to materially alter the agricultural landscape through more efficient land use, according to what was conceived to be 'modern farm practice and principles'.[35] Whereas intensified use of new technologies such as pesticides, herbicides, and artificial fertilisers, or powered equipment, that directly impacted the landscape were continuous with existing approaches to commercial agricultural production, the emphasis on the more efficient and profitable use of time within the managed space of the farm itself was new and impactful. Alongside the adoption of the Standard Man Day, work-time studies on farms ensured that the farm was reimagined, as I have argued elsewhere, for labour and time (the Man Day) rather than space (acreage), and this had a material effect on the labourer and on the land.[36]

The vision

Throughout the period, while the space-time of labour and farm was being reconceptualised for agricultural modernity, there was an ongoing fascination in Britain with country life, wildlife, and nature. This fascination was continuous with much earlier periods,[37] but, popular representations of 'amenity' focused on a countryside innocent of modern agricultural processes, and an environment and wildlife

---

[33] Troon, 'Handling', p. 80n.

[34] Graham Boatfield, 'Part-time students', *Agriculture*, 71:2 (1964), 71–74.

[35] Boatfield, 'Part-time', 73.

[36] Karen Sayer, 'The changing landscape of "labour": Work and livestock in post-Second World War British agriculture', *History*, 103:363 (2019), 911–940. http://dx.doi.org/10.1111/1468-229X.12920

[37] The literature on the earlier forms that this focus took, and meanings attaching to them, is extensive and includes Raymond Williams, *The Country and the City* (London, The Hogarth Press, 1985); Roger Sales, *English Literature in History; 1780–1830, Pastoral and Politics* (London, Hutchinson, 1983); Ann Bermingham, *Landscape and Ideology: The Rustic Tradition, 1740–1860* (London, Thames & Hudson, 1987); S. Daniels, *Fields of Vision, Landscape Imagery and National Identity in England and the United States* (Cambridge, Cambridge University Press, 1994); Jeremy Burchardt, *Paradise Lost: Rural Idyll and Social Change since 1800* (London, I. B. Tauris, 2002).

at risk from them. Consequently, the increasing use of the countryside for leisure by urban visitors and the focus by policymakers on raising home food production have often been characterised as representative of distinct, competing, interests. The National Parks, for example, sought to preserve traditional farming practices as part of their wider effort at conservation, and these landscapes through those efforts have become woven into key concepts of heritage.[38] Yet, if 'traditional' in their management/oversight – or at least in the visible presentation of farming (in the form of conserved buildings, or preferred breeds of sheep) – the National Parks were nevertheless farmed landscapes harnessed to a very particular modern public purpose. Indeed, in the 1980s, 40 per cent of the members of the committees with oversight of the English National Parks were farmers or landowners, 30 per cent in Wales. Neither local tourist organisations, nor representatives from the urban areas that many tourists came from, were represented, because from the interwar period through to 2000 (the period in which he was writing), governments as Howkins observed had 'seen farming as protecting the countryside'.[39]

The vision of the future for the British countryside captured in Command Paper 2928, in the new Countryside Act (1968) or the 1966 White Paper on *Leisure in the Countryside*, articles like White's, books about 'tomorrow's countryside', and events in this period such as the 'Countryside in 1970' conferences, all worked from the common foundation of the socio-economic, political, planning, and legislative impacts of changes following on from the National Parks and Countryside Act 1949 and its eventual formation of 10 National Parks. As argued by Sheail, the 1949 Act represented a new and powerful force coming to prominence in the management of rural space post-war, and the Countryside Act 1968 followed through on much of the original intent.[40] However, in addition, because the 1968 Act extended many of the key components of the 1949 Act beyond the National Parks, it was also linked to the socio-economic, political, planning, and legislative frameworks associated with farming, agricultural production, and the agricultural landscape in the same period. It was here that the 1968 Act attempted to synthesise what often now appear to be competing, quite disparate rural modernities (agricultural, environmental, and touristic). The 1968 Act, responding to the impacts of the Agriculture Act 1947 and extending the principles of conservation beyond the National Parks, had its roots as much in the foundations of policy intended to increase food production as in policy designed to enable the non-farming population to take their leisure time seriously and responsibly in newly conserved, 'natural', 'wild', safe, and accessible rural

[38] Matthew Kelly, 'Conventional thinking and the fragile birth of the nature state in post-war Britain', in W. Graf van Hardenberg, M. Kelly, C. Leal, and E. Wakild (eds), *The Nature State: Rethinking the History of Conservation* (London, Routledge, 2017); Harriet Ritvo, 'Counting sheep in the English Lake District: Rare breeds, local knowledge and environmental history', *Nobel Cows and Hybrid Zebras: Essays on Animals in History* (Charlottesville and London, University of Virginia Press, 2010).
[39] Howkins, *Death*, pp. 190–191.
[40] John Sheail, 'Leisure in the English countryside: Policy making in the 1960s', *Planning Perspectives*, 16:1 (2001), 67–84 at 68–69.

landscapes across the British countryside in its entirety.[41] Operationally this was grounded in a fundamental expectation, despite the changes sought by the Labour government, that landowners and farmers would deliver on the pre-existing belief in landlords as timeless custodians of the land. This belief persisted through the 20th century, just as it had persisted through the 18th century alongside the idea of the improving landlord who invested in the technologies, techniques, and alterations of land use and ownership that came to be called the first Agricultural Revolution.

Farmers and landowners were therefore called on to continue to preserve the whole of the countryside, and not just the National Parks. This is not as inconsistent as it might at first appear. Certainly, the modern underpinnings of agricultural production were less important to the promotors of farm visits than images of rural felicity, and the imagery of rural felicity was often characterised by the farming practices and structures representative of the previous century. Moreover, older forms of agricultural improvement, such as hedges planted during the 18th-century Enclosure Movement, came to be characterised as timeless, and interwoven with the aesthetics of heritage and wildlife conservation. What had once been cutting-edge agricultural equipment was preserved in farming/rural life museums, displayed alongside the old crafts. And, by the 1970s, 'improved' livestock that had been bred to meet the demands of consumer preferences in the 18th and 19th centuries were on display in rare breed visitor attractions. But rather than a strict binary opposition, what this demonstrates is that the British countryside is and was a landscape resulting from a continuous history of usage,[42] with agricultural land capable of working rhetorically as 'Natural' and conserved for wildlife or heritage, and bona fide heritage or wildlife landscapes (inside and outside the National Parks) similarly contributing to debates about contemporary agricultural practice. As discussed below, agricultural publications and advisory services frequently drew out past stories of success from these materials, and brought to the fore an established narrative of successful progress: the history of agricultural improvement. Modernity in this sense was always already present, that is, it operated as a constant, a standing wave within the British countryside, as can be seen in Figure 8.2, an advertisement for Fisons in *Farmers Weekly*, 8 July 1960. The text stresses that avoiding waste saves money, and the technology on sale (the 'Fisons 40 Range' brand of fertilisers) will address that, but by focusing from soil level on a large image of careful ploughing at sunset it adds a visual emphasis to its message, stressing the traditional precision and hard work of preparing the land. The saturating red light of the setting sun (which functionally asks the reader to stop and read) underlined the way that farmers worked through the whole day, the whole year, to get as much work done as possible, to grow as much as possible in the service of the country and its citizens. A visual reference to

---

[41] There was national guidance issued on how to behave. See *Joe & Petunia – Acceptance of the Country Code* (Central Office of Information for the National Parks Commission and the Countryside Commission, 1971), www.nationalarchives.gov.uk/films/1964to1979/filmpage_country.htm [accessed 25 November 2021]; see also David Matless, 'Action and noise over a hundred years: The making of a nature region', *Body & Society*, 6:3–4 (2000), 141–165.

[42] A related point is made by Williamson, *An Environmental History of Wildlife*, p. 186.

Fisons 40 Range

The purpose of Fisons 40 Range of compound fertilizers is to enable you to match the plant food supplied to the needs of your crop and soil conditions. If you make full use of the 40 Range you avoid wasting plant foods, and you save money.

Figure 8.2 *Farmers Weekly*, 8 July 1960. Courtesy of The Museum of English Rural Life, University of Reading. Fisons were a British company that like many in this period (including *Farmers Weekly*) owned experimental farms for research and development

work-time efficiency, but also to the timeless character of the land and the timeless progress of agriculture, as mid-ground we see some green and a chalk downland path, open to access and suggestive of a deeper history that is always present in the country against that red light of the setting sun.

The supposedly intrinsic aesthetic appeal of this, what we might call 'the well farmed functional landscape',[43] was itself not new. It can be found consistently within the established appreciation of an older agri-*cultural* landscape that was orderly, tidy, and neat, dating back to the period of what is conventionally considered to be the first Agricultural Revolution. A representative mid-19th-century example combines tidiness with economy and productiveness. Of rye straw John Wilson said 'it is a good plan to cut the truss or bundle in half ... this gives a more neat and tidy appearance to the stable, greatly economises the litter and makes better dung'.[44] Grounded in arable practice, this was a visually framed appreciation of harmony through perfected planning and management of the land, its products and the control of nature. Twentieth-century rural landscapes similarly made of productive farmland (and parklands) were the result of constant making and remaking, innovation mixed with continuity, over centuries. Farms were cultivated artefacts, but clearly capable of providing solace for all that. As V. C. Fishwick put it in the Second World War teach yourself book *Good Farming* (1944):

> To many readers there is much in this book which may come as a rude shock, for to them the glory of the British countryside has been its genial, kindly country folk and its peace. Must these be sacrificed on the altar of progress? Must the genial country folk give place to the jostling business men, and the peace of the countryside be broken by the throb and roar of internal combustion engines.
>
> Fortunately that is not likely to be the result of progress.
>
> The worst threat to its peace come from holiday makers who at times invade the countryside in an endless stream of noisy cars, but even that only touches the fringe. Education certainly does not cause a deterioration in the character of the countrymen, why should it? And the noise of internal combustion engines is muffled by distance. Normally they sound no louder than the drone of an insect. I write only five miles from one of the busiest coast roads – but a mile away on the top of a hill it is possible to look over one hundred square miles of the adjoining countryside, which is normally as peaceful as anyone could wish. Any night you can stand there at sunset without hearing a sound other than the song of the birds, the drone of insects, or the lowing of cattle, and in truth can echo the words of Gray:-
>
> > 'The curfew tolls the knell of parting day,
> > The lowing herd winds slowly o'er the lea,
> > The ploughman homeward plods his weary way,
> > And leaves he world to darkness and to me.'[45]

[43] ADSS leaflet no. 517, published by the ADAS (HMSO, Winter 1979).
[44] J. Wilson, *Our Farm Crops (1.2) Barley, Oat, Rye, Canary Seed, Buckwheat* (London, Blackie & Son, 1859), vol. 1, p. 178.
[45] Victor Charles Fishwick, 'Foreword', in *Good Farming* (London, Hodder & Stoughton, 1944).

What we see in the 20th century is a rush at least at first to celebrate the National Farm off the back of this type of Second World War discourse, as an element of a new British modernity in continuity with an older countryside already imagined ('peaceful', full of birdsong and insects). Here the reader, who is positioned outside the landscape looking in, therefore as a tourist, standing with the farmer listening to the coast road, is offered reassurance and a gentle direction to look to 'progress' as a boon. It is not farming 'progress' that disrupts the peace of the countryside, nor the cars of rural tourists, it is the cars driven to the coast. And to the modern countryside still comes 'darkness', quietly contented cattle 'lowing', and the Anglican church bell audibly manging the end of the working day. Progress, Fishwick argues, does not destroy the country; education is a good thing, and even if the tourists do come, still moving with the times will not overwrite Gray: there is continuity within change, and so solace remains.

With *Good Farming* offering a relatively standard, if simplified, example of modern farm textbook for the period, it is not surprising that the advice on offer from MAFF did not just outline the latest production techniques or farming methods but also encompassed the modern management of the well-farmed historical landscape. One booklet (one of several editions) advising Norfolk's farmers how to manage land that included archaeological remains was predicated on reducing 'interference' with farm production while simultaneously avoiding damage to the sites. The leaflet opened by stating that most farmers and landowners, like archaeologists, wanted to preserve archaeological sites 'for posterity', as 'most farmers understand the concept of being guardians of the land'. It then described how the county's rich landscape was produced by 10,000 years of human occupation, 2,000 of those involving cropping, and the many riches found in Norfolk over the years, especially at Sutton Hoo, Snettisham, and Mildenhall. It went on to set out the legal framework that could be used to protect remains if required, and landowners' obligations. The several contributors navigated, on the one hand, the need to get farmers' attention as custodians of 'the land' via a celebration of the deep history of the county, and, on the other, the need to provide information on their duties as framed by the relevant legislation, advice, grants, and compensation, and the threat of sanction to achieve compliance. This guidance it stated was particularly needed in East Anglia, 'one of the great food-producing' regions, because of the 'increasing rate and scale' of destruction, due to 'the increasing size and work rates of modern farm machinery' and the adoption of 'new and improved agricultural techniques … to increase crop yields'. *Good Farming* noted that since 1935 around half of '570 known upstanding burial mounds have been obliterated' because the 'new improved form of sub-soiler can lead to the almost total fragmentation of archaeological remains within a few hours'. Farming over hundreds of years might have already destroyed ancient monuments, but the sheer speed of modern agricultural processes now necessitated better communication between farmers and archaeologists to ensure 'the preservation of archaeological remains under our farmland'. That meant the involvement of five named contributors to a leaflet of barely 20 pages, from bodies as diverse as the

NFU, the Agricultural Development and Advisory Service, the Ancient Monuments Inspectorate, and the Norfolk Archaeological Unit.[46] Throughout, the pamphlet was directed to a recognition of the underlying continuity of occupation and food production, and the importance of preserving the evidence of that as part of the deep heritage of the county alongside the practices then shaping the modern landscape. The advice rested on the established idea that the landowner's duty as 'custodian' or 'guardian' of the landscape acted in concert with their duty as producer.

This was founded on the understanding that the post-war agricultural landscape existed in continuity with the past, and this was framed explicitly as linked to the nation, rhetorically seeking to strengthen its political importance. Specialist publications directed at farmers frequently alluded to the landscape's historical context and their place in the history of agriculture. Notably, in 2000 *Farmers Weekly* ran an anniversary edition celebrating its foundation in 1934, which compared conditions for farmers at the millennium to those in the interwar period. As an editorial decision to capture readership and secure 70-years' worth of authority this made sense, but *Farmers Weekly* regularly ran reflective historical or semi-autobiographical pieces, and articles linked to traditional practices through the 20th century. Characteristic of the *Farmers Weekly* outlook was a statement by the independent-minded A. G. Street, who in 1955 had reflected on the past year and hoped-for shifts in approach to the state's oversight of farmers and farming: 'British agricultural history', he stated, 'is national history'.[47] This historical outlook is equally evident in the advisory services' publications. The Introduction to the ADAS booklet, *Norfolk Farming Over Two Centuries, 1778–1978*, by W. R. B. Carter, Divisional Agricultural Officer, produced for the Holkham Sheep Shearings Bicentennial (23–4 June 1978), explained that it was important to understand 'the contribution of history to the contemporary scene', because 'the history of agriculture in Norfolk is part of the story of the British people at large. Changes in farming were inextricably bound up with changes in our national life – sometimes cause, sometimes effect'.[48] Contributions to the slim volume came from the Royal Norfolk Agricultural Association, the Norfolk Agricultural Station, the Norfolk College of Agriculture and Horticulture, and MAFF as well as Norwich Central Library. This offers us both a snapshot of the key institutions working in agriculture at the time, and a sense of the value that they placed on maintaining a historical record. The historical story that Carter then chose to tell, based on these institutions' archives and

[46] Anon, *Farming on Ancient Monuments in Norfolk*, ADAS, MAFF with the Department of the Environment, National Farmer's Union and Norfolk Archaeological Unit (undated, c. 1973), pp. i, 1–4, 5–6, 9.
[47] John Nix, 'What life was like on the farm in 1934', *Farmers Weekly*, January 2000, p. 60; Anon., 'Old-fashioned way', *Farmers Weekly*, 4 January 1985, p. 58; John L. Jones, 'I knew a pond', *Farmers Weekly*, 2 January 1970, p. 75; Arthur George Street, 'And so to 1955', *Farmers Weekly*, 7 January 1955, p. 47.
[48] Ray Carter, *Norfolk Farming Over Two Centuries, 1778–1978: The Holkham Sheep Shearings Bicentennial (23rd and 24th June 1978)* (ADAS, MAFF, 1978).

library holdings, was one focused on the formation of Norfolk's most progressive agricultural bodies, its agricultural shows, which celebrated improvement, and its relationship to national action taken, such as in response to a Foot and Mouth outbreak in 1881 or requests to government to 'extend teaching of Scientific Principles of Agriculture' in 1883.[49]

In texts like this we see the historical sources being put to work in the service of the dominant post-war rhetoric of agricultural progress, and British national identity. In consequence the agricultural past became evidence of the integral nature of improvement and progress to British agriculture, and therefore of the inherent modernity of agriculture at all times and of agricultural landscapes as a national feature. The same process was at work in *British Farming: An Illustrated Account of all the Branches of Agriculture in England, Scotland, Wales and Northern Ireland. A Story of Progress in Providing Food from Britain's Fields* (1951) by W. B. Mercer, Provincial Director of the West Midland Province of the National Agricultural Advisory Service. Produced by the Ministry of Agriculture for the Central Office of Information, it included collaborators who were agricultural researchers, inspectors, officers, and advisors. The booklet reaches back to the ice age and weaves history into the celebration of British agricultural food production with an eye on the present modern condition of the industry. In its first chapter, a historical narrative, it name-checked the key protagonists and events associated with British agricultural improvement in the 18th and 19th centuries, such as Lord Townshend (turnips), Robert Bakewell (stockbreeding), and John Bennet Lawes (artificial fertilisers/Rothamsted). Throughout the whole booklet (97 pages) there are subsequently further moments of historical comparison and reference, for example, setting the scene for the chapter on Scotland.[50] Though there is mention of the late 19th-century 'declining prices' experienced in the arable sector, the weight of the story, as suggested by the subtitle, is placed on 'agricultural progress' alongside improving food production, which chimed with the wider Festival of Britain project with which the booklet's release coincided. Its publication also coincided with the launch of the Agriculture Gallery at the Science Museum in London, opened in 1951, described by David Matless as 'agricultural progress wrought in iron', a gallery that was itself 'a powerful conjunction of science, landscape and modernity'.[51]

[49] Carter, *Norfolk Farming*, pp. 4–5.

[50] Wilfred Bernard Mercer, *British Farming: An Illustrated Account of all the Branches of Agriculture in England, Scotland, Wales and Northern Ireland. A Story of Progress in Providing Food from Britain's Fields* (Ministry of Agriculture, Central Office of Information, 1951), p. 64.

[51] David Matless, 'The Agriculture Gallery: Displaying modern farming in the science museum', in Jon Agar and Jacob Ward (eds), *Histories of Technology, the Environment and Modern Britain* (London, UCL Press, 2018), pp. 101–122 at pp. 101, 102; to access a film of the gallery, which closed in 2017, visit the Science Museum's blog by Mary Cavanagh, https://blog.sciencemuseum.org.uk/celebrating-the-past-present-and-future-of-agriculture/ [accessed 12 November 2021].

With detailed maps, graphs, and photographs on almost every page, and in contrast with the Science Museum gallery's English focus, the booklet offered a richly illustrated account of the landscape of modern agricultural production for the whole of the UK. What is most striking about this is that, like the Science Museum's Agriculture Gallery, it offered a representation of British agriculture that was a synthesis of established and the innovative or newly adopted practices. In the photographic plates describing potato production in the Fens we see hand work, work from horse-drawn carts, and work using a tractor. The booklet also offered an account that was in many respects transparent, and expected an audience like that for *Good Farming* to be familiar with agriculture and its travails.[52] British readers, still under rationing, might have been reassured by descriptions of the development of new weedkillers, spraying techniques, and artificial fertilisers, that addressed some of the problems that farmers encountered, though the booklet also explained the persistent difficulties, such as eelworms in areas where potatoes were trad-itionally grown, which were still 'challenging scientist and farmer alike'.[53] This fitted into a national narrative that recognised continuity of practice as a part of the new techniques that characterised the modernity of the British landscape and emphasised the heroic national effort in food production that drew on the skill of farmers and labourers combined with scientific expertise. The underlying message was the importance of adhering to and working for 'the rules of good husbandry', a concept, Mercer admits, that was perpetually ill-defined, but whose plasticity made it adaptable to new techniques or discoveries, and therefore as important in the 1950s as it was in the 18th century.[54]

The focus in this period was on the so-called National Farm, i.e. all of the farms of the nation of Britain were conceived of as a unified whole, producing food for the whole population. The British public depended on the same infrastructure as the farmers who produced their food: improved roads, new reservoirs, and the roll-out of mains electricity. Farmers used this infrastructure to support production and distribution whereas the public, as in part, used it to access the countryside. Though attracted by ideas of rural felicity grounded in heritage, the concrete man-agement of leisure that was evident in easy road access, also of visitor safety and comfort that required some sympathetic adaptations (signage, picnic benches and car parks), therefore largely overlapped with the same on- and off-farm built envir-onment required by food producers. Both needed newly surfaced farm roads or tracks linked up to the national road network, reliable electricity supplies, and piped water from bore holes or reservoirs, and both were supported and guided by policy,

---

[52] The BBC radio broadcast regularly on agricultural topics from before the Second World War, some of these were captured in W. S. Mansfield, *Farming Talks by W. S. Mansfield* (Worcester, Littlebury & Company Ltd, undated, c. 1938).

[53] Mercer, *British Farming*, pp. 60–63.

[54] Mercer, *British Farming*, pp. 2–15.

advice, and grants from the state's advisory services and bodies. The overall project was both modernising in the infrastructure and in its shared purpose. This was despite the kinds of tensions described in a text like *Methods of Charging at Rural Car Parks* (1969), which offered guidance on how to manage the inconvenience to 'the countryman' of the urban visitor within the countryside:

> [T]he rapid growth in recent years of leisure motoring in the countryside has led to a related demand for car parking spaces. Demand, however, has outstripped the provision of rural car parks. This is most apparent on fine summer weekends when cars are parked in narrow lanes, farm roads and gateways, on roadside verges and common land, in most cases to the detriment of the appearance of the countryside, often to the inconvenience and annoyance of the countryman, and frequently to the impediment and danger of moving traffic.

> The car park in the countryside, if suitably designed, may actually be the place that people visit, the place in which they picnic and look at the view. ... There are aesthetic issues: machinery that is quite acceptable in an urban setting may be thought incongruous or even offensive in the countryside.[55]

We are perhaps reminded of the fear that the noise of the visitor's car will drown the voice of the curlew here, and this had to be managed. The Countryside Act 1968 made provision for sites to be recognised as picnic sites and country parks, and local authorities and private individuals could get grants to establish car parks like these in adjacent rural areas. The task was then to contain the visitors, and simultaneously to erase the 'incongruous', 'urban' modernity of equipment such as barriers and pay-stations, and to ensure that the structures in car parks were fashioned to conform to the aesthetics of the picturesque, in order that the countryside would retain the pastoral calm that had attracted the visitors in the first place. If the car park adhered to the prescriptions in *Methods of Charging at Rural Car Parks*, then apparently the modern British citizen would be sufficiently charmed not only to come to the country, escaping the 'machinery of the city' to enjoy the heritage of parks and pastures, but also to spend their leisure time in its pockets of adjacent service space.

The land, vital, energised, managed, farmed, producing food, meanwhile needed its own dedicated structures that had to sit well in the landscape of heritage, its own progressive history protected and celebrated. To this end dedicated agricultural advisors provided guidance on farm buildings, with additional information made available through publications such as *The Farm Buildings Digest: A Cumulative Information Service*, as if the National Farm should have a specific look and feel, its own standardised architecture in sympathy with the British landscape. Farm buildings it was thought ought to sit comfortably in the countryside,

---

[55] Introduction, *Methods of Charging at Rural Car Parks: A Report Prepared by the Countryside Commission with the Aid of their Consultant, Mr Robin J. Reip, Managing Director of Parking Management Ltd.* (London, Countryside Commission, HMSO, 1969).

respectfully nodding to past building materials, blending in in colour and form (even if the techniques were drawn from other countries), and there was much debate about sympathetic paint finishes and the impact of moss and lichen growing on new corrugated asbestos roofing sheets.[56] New builds first had to be assessed for cost and direct value to the farm. Adaptations to existing buildings, such as live-stock housing, were assessed, for example, could they be re-arranged internally to take a new herringbone parlour? Sometimes old buildings were integrated into the farm plan with additions, extensions, and mergers to ensure that the flow of work went smoothly as suggested above. But, when new structures were built, these increasingly came in a standard pattern of a picturesque mix of old (wood panels) and new (breeze blocks), associated with landscape assessments that looked at the aesthetic issues as well as underlying services. What was key, it was established by the end of our period, is that the whole site had to be considered for its visual appeal as well as its practical and economic elements. As Victoria J. Haigh put it at an advisory conference in 1983, '[c]ollecting this breadth of information at this stage so that aesthetics and the visual qualities of the site are included in decisions regarding the siting and early scheme design' was as 'important as the buildings' "functionality".' She therefore argued that a range of scales had to be considered, namely, 'site', 'farm' and 'locality', in order to 'establish the "landscape context" of the site'. Assessors were therefore encouraged to look out from buildings as well as in, to take photographs and to make sketches. Thoroughness was required, and while later assessment, Haigh said, could 'be a mental thing', she offered a matrix to support evaluators balance all aspects of the site in question (access, microcli-mate, drainage and aesthetics, and so on) when selecting the optimal position for a new build.[57] To support this detailed work, books and grey literature were published that set out the history of farm buildings by period in different landscapes, to ensure that whatever was placed in the country during the 20th century would be in some sympathy with its predecessors.[58] The agri-*culture* wanted by Prince Philip equated to a synthesis of the control of nature through technology, science, and knowledge for increased production *with* stewardship, heritage, and natural history. This was expected, if newly monetised for the car-owning public. This was the norm of the relationship between farmer or landowner and the land, and it generated the modern landscape within which equally modern 20th-century infrastructure grew.

---

[56] Anon, *Colour Finishes for Farm Buildings: Report to the Design Council by its Farm Buildings Advisory Committee on Colour Finishes for Factory-made Cladding used in Farm Buildings* (London, Design Council, May 1975). Miscellaneous materials held by the Yorkshire Museum of Farming include: Anon, 'Architects in Agriculture', Information Leaflet No 2, August 1983 and 'Ferrous Oxide Treatment of Asbestos-Cement Roofs'.

[57] Anon, 'A landscape management plan for a farm enterprise', unpublished paper, Yorkshire Museum of Farming, 26 (G); B. Dempsey, 'Summary of talk delivered at Farm Buildings Group Conference 1985 (internal circulation only)', summary of unpublished paper by V. J. Haigh, Yorkshire Museum of Farming, 26 (G).

[58] Mary Roadnight, *Farm Buildings* (1979), grey literature, Yorkshire Museum of Farming, 26 (4).

Conclusion

The Agriculture Act (1947) in Britain was designed to increase food production in line with reconstruction, shaped by international policy,[59] and underpinned the programmes of food production in the UK until the end of rationing in Britain in 1954. The industry itself was nevertheless still complex, as diverse in its politics as it was in the size and type holding (tenancy/ownership), location, or market orientation. It was perhaps therefore no surprise that, following the end of rationing, the extent of official oversight that had been in situ in effect since the Second World War was immediately questioned. Men and women like author and farmer A. G. Street who sought greater independence from what was perceived as state control,[60] contested the Act in the Courts. And adjustments were made, for example to the ability to remove farmers from their farms when they failed to meet specified standards. But it delivered significantly on many of its intentions, and as Brassley *et al.* have argued, the period saw a significant step change in agriculture.[61]

The goal of this work, of the agricultural system, was to produce good-quality and plentiful food that would sustain the British subject. Policies sought to ensure maximum output through grants, while knowledge generated by (state and commercial) agricultural institutes and on experimental farms was distributed via (state and commercial) advisors and by agricultural educational bodies to farmers, managers, and workers. It was the Marketing Boards that then secured the food supply, through managed payments and distribution systems, and sold it to the British subject as consumer. Commissioned by the Marketing Boards, messy consumer bodies at that time seem strikingly to have offered advertisers an opportunity to sell British agricultural products as a modern, standardising corrective, as exemplified by the British Egg Marketing Board (BEMB) 1957–1971. The BEMB typically represented British agricultural products at the service of the so-called 'Housewife', for example.

The Housewife was a Cold War icon which, like Wolsey's images of Peasant Modernity, had its European and US paradigms. As Sean Nixon has argued, through the period advertising 'was an important conduit for the circulation in Europe and beyond of [a] common standard of domestic modernity and the model of Mrs Consumer'.[62] Certainly, Mrs Consumer was very visible in the imagery of the BEMB. As we see her in Figures 8.3 and 8.4, which were published in the national press including the *Glasgow Daily Record*, *Daily Express*, and the *Daily Mail*, she ranged across their publicity in a number of guises, from aspirational

---

[59] See Sayer, 'The changing landscape of "labour"', and for the founding arguments in tension within see Federico D'Onofrio, 'Agricultural statistics in their international aspect: The International Institute of Agriculture, the Economic Conferences of Genoa (1922) and Geneva (1927) and the 1930 census of agriculture', *Agricultural History Review*, 65:2 (2017), 277–296.

[60] Street, 'And so to 1955', p. 47.

[61] Brassley *et al.*, *The Real Agricultural Revolution*.

[62] Sean Nixon, 'Life in the kitchen: Television advertising, the housewife and domestic modernity in Britain, 1955–1969', *Contemporary British History*, 31:1 (2017), 70.

Issued by the British Egg Marketing Board

how you should be!

HOW MUCH WOULD YOU GIVE TO BE SLIM?

BUT it's not money that's needed. It's not even suffering. It's common sense, optimism, and eggs for breakfast.

Eggs are the slimmer's best friend. A couple boiled for breakfast will fill but not fatten, will nourish, sustain and see you happily through a nibble-free morning.

After that, with your morale sky-high, it's an easier matter to cut down the carbohydrates through the rest of the day, step up the proteins, and look forward to a newer, slimmer you.

For slimmers more than anyone the egg-for-breakfast rule holds good; *you know you ought, and aren't you glad when you do!* Go to work on an egg slim, svelte, and serene.

PETULA CLARK says: 'I believe in breakfast! I always have eggs. I love them. And if I'm going to have to miss lunch (life's so hectic it quite often happens) I treat myself to something special like poached eggs on haddock.'

Figure 8.3 British Egg Marketing Board, 'How you should be', 1965. Courtesy of The History of Advertising Trust, Raveningham[63]

bikini-wearer ('How you should be!') to custodian of food and family life ('Have a better breakfast: be a better mum!'). In its campaigns, the BEMB nipped and tucked the ideal female British consumer through its nutritional advice and

[63] History of Advertising Trust, British Egg Marketing Board – How you should be (OM_1_1_12_6).

Have a better breakfast, be a nicer mum

or
Did you get your egg this morning?

If you don't have a proper protein breakfast, you are more irritable through the day than you need be. You are less efficient than you can be, and more tired in the evening than you like to be.

A proper protein breakfast means an egg breakfast. Because eggs are packed with the protein you must have to sustain you after a night without food. And because eggs are quick to cook. Simple to serve. Cheap to buy. And wonderfully, delectably, good to eat.

The truth is this – a breakfast that is not centred round eggs is hardly worthy of the name. It's a snack. No more. And it won't keep you going for long. *So, go to work on an egg every morning.*

Figure 8.4 British Egg Marketing Board, 'Have a better breakfast', 1965. Courtesy of The History of Advertising Trust, Raveningham[64]

---

[64] History of Advertising Trust, 1965 British Egg Marketing Board – Have a better breakfast (OM_1_1_12_6).

calorie-controlled recipes.[65] Though the slogans such as 'how you should be!' and 'be a better mum' were there to write large what were assumed to be the reader's deepest desires/fears, they read as imperatives, as instructions curating bodies and behaviours. Trust was at the heart of these campaigns. This was a trust that it, like other agricultural producers, had to live up to through the delivery of a safe, as well as a consistent, product – at the risk of real harm to the British body if it failed. That trust relied on innovations in the technology of food production and distribution,[66] was sold through the reassurance that the British consumer's body was not just safe in its hands, but much improved (by the lights of the period) in appearance and demeanour.

For nearly 40 years, the British state seemed intent on peacetime objectives through which the citizen would be made and remade physiologically, even behaviourally, by the consumption of foods that were produced by modern agricultural processes, sourced via modern supply chains. Alongside these acts of consumption lay the managed performances of visiting, of driving, cycling, or walking through a landscape rich in a *longue durée* heritage of perpetual agricultural progress that guaranteed to put good food on the table back home. Rather than a site of conflict, 'Tomorrow's Countryside' promised a synthesis of what often now appear to be competing, quite disparate rural modernities (agricultural, environmental, and touristic) in which the construction of a modern countryside would permit modern agricultural production and the pleasures of rural amenity to co-exist in agri-*culture*.[67] The modern British citizen was made by the land within which pylons, nuclear reactors, and Post Office towers sat as part of a much greater, and seamlessly modern, whole.

---

[65] For example, BEMB, *Glasgow Daily Record*, 26 October 1962, History of Advertising Trust, archive ref 21978/3.

[66] Karen Sayer, ' "His footmarks on her shoulders": The significance and place of women within poultry keeping in the British countryside, c. 1880-c.1970', *Agricultural History Review*, 61:2 (Autumn 2013), 301–329.

[67] Foreword by H.R.H. The Duke of Edinburgh, in Christian, *Tomorrow's Countryside*.

9

Landscapes of Military Modernity:
From 'Eyesores' to National Heritage?

PAUL READMAN

ROBERT ARBIB ARRIVED in Britain in summer 1942. A sergeant in an American
Engineer battalion, he and his unit went into Suffolk to construct a military
aerodrome. Arbib was struck by the beauty of the landscape – what he called its
'pastoral sweetness' – which he attributed to many centuries of continuous human
habitation. He was struck, too, by the destructive impact of war on this landscape.
He was not thinking so much of German bombs, but of military installations like
the airfield he had helped to build:

> there is nothing quite as final, quite as levelling, as an aerodrome. Every growing
> stick was beaten down and uprooted. Every patch of cover for rabbits and partridges
> was flattened. Every graceful contour, softened and smoothed by centuries of wear by
> little brooks and by wind and rain, was hacked and shoved and levelled. Whatever had
> stood there before was now lost.

One afternoon, Arbib found himself by the River Stour at Sudbury, gazing out
over the meadows on the town's edge, thinking of Constable. As dusk fell, he was
transported from the 20th to the 18th century. But the spell was broken when, looking
across the meadows again, he saw, 'white and ugly under a copse of willows, like
one monstrous overgrown mushroom, a concrete pillbox. Perhaps some day soon',
he reflected, 'they will uproot those ugly mushrooms, spaced almost every hundred
yards down the river valley all the way to the sea, hiding behind knolls, lurking in
the underbrush, under the willows. Perhaps they will be left there, to gather moss
and then grass and then to be split by the roots of trees, as relics of an age, a strange,
incongruous footnote to Suffolk history'.[1]

---

[1] Robert S. Arbib, Jr., *Here We Are Together: The Notebook of an American Soldier in Britain* (London,
Longmans & Co, 1946), pp. 18–19, 94.

Proceedings of the British Academy, **256**, 182–207, © The British Academy 2023.

Figure 9.1 Pillbox near Sudbury, Suffolk. Photograph © Chris Hamer

Arbib's remarks were prescient (see Figure 9.1). About 28,000 pillboxes were constructed in Britain during the Second World War. Where not demolished, the vast majority were left to decay: by 2009 only about 2,000 remained unruinous.[2] A similar fate befell the tank traps, radar stations, coastal batteries, and myriad other defence installations: most have disappeared, the 9,000 miles of aerodrome hardstanding proving particularly useful in constructing the post-war motorway network.[3] The last few decades, however, have seen growing interest in such sites. Along with other 20th-century military landscapes – not least those associated with the Cold War – they are now seen in a more favourable light, at least by some. Organisations such as English Heritage and the National Trust have been involved in their preservation. With the National Trust as my focus, what follows tracks and evaluate this shift in attitudes to English landscapes of military modernity. How, and to what extent, have we come to value them as heritage?

[2] William Foot, *Defence Areas: A National Study of Second World War Anti-Invasion Landscapes* (York, Archaeology Data Service, 2009), pp. 21–22.
[3] Paul Francis, Richard Flagg, and Graham Crisp, *Nine Thousand Miles of Concrete: A Review of Second World War Temporary Airfields in England* (London and Swindon, Historic England, 2016), p. 24.

Hostility to modern-day military landscapes

Distaste for the militarisation of the English landscape is deep-rooted. It can be found in William Cobbett's protests at the early 19th-century fortification of the heights around Dover, which made, as he put it, 'a great chalk-hill a honey-comb' in which to hide British soldiers from Frenchmen.[4] It can be found in late-Victorian hostility to the use of common land, such as that of the New Forest, for military training – hostility that led to the prohibition, in 1892, of the appropriation of commons for rifle ranges without parliamentary consent.[5] It can be found, later still, in opposition to the stationing of cruise missiles on British soil, anti-nuclear campaigners sharing Arbib's sense that the England emblematised by Constable Country was affronted, desecrated even, by the appurtenances of war. This was nicely caught in Peter Kennard's *Haywain with Cruise Missiles* (1980), reproductions of which gained considerable popular currency in the 1980s (see Figure 9.2).[6]

As with Kennard's adaptation of Constable, this distaste could be a vehicle for oppositional and radical Englishness. But its wider significance should not be underestimated. For an island nation, war amid the heartland landscape of England had a real shock factor, one played on by the sensational invasion fiction of the late 19th and early 20th centuries. In G. T. Chesney's famous scare story of 1871, *The Battle of Dorking*, the moment of vanquish for the British army comes amid the Surrey hills – a landscape celebrated for its beauty, tranquillity, and associations with an organic, settled Englishness.[7]

In the event, the fears expressed in Chesney's tract led to the militarisation of this same landscape: in the 1880s and 1890s a ring of forts was built on high ground around London, including Box Hill. But with the coming of the Dreadnought these were abandoned before the Great War. When in 1913 the National Trust acquired Box Hill, it did so to preserve the beauty the military installations were seen to have impaired.[8] As late as 1973, the Trust opposed the scheduling of the fort, the Chairman of the Trust's Box Hill Committee thinking it to be 'neither of historic nor of architectural interest' and 'merely a monument to someone's stupidity'.[9]

---

[4] William Cobbett, *Rural Rides*, ed. G. D. H. and M. Cole, 2 vols (London: Peter Davies, 1930), vol. I, pp. 227–230.
[5] Military Lands Act 1892 (55 & 56.Vict.43); G. Shaw Lefevre, *Commons, Forests, and Footpaths* (London, Cassell & Co., 1910), p. 168.
[6] Peter Kennard and Ric Sissons, *No Nuclear Weapons: The Case for Nuclear Disarmament* (London, Pluto, 1981); Peter Kennard, *Dispatches from an Unofficial War Artist* (London, Lund Humphries, 2000), p. 83.
[7] [G. T. Chesney], *The Battle of Dorking: Reminiscences of a Volunteer* (London, 1871).
[8] National Trust Archives, National Trust, *Annual Report* (1913–1914), p. 5.
[9] Note by Sir Raymond Jennings on letter from the Trust's south-east regional director, I. F. Blomfield, 11 January 1973, National Trust Archives, box SE04:85 (ID 5987169); also Blomfield to W. James Hawkins, 26 July 1973, National Trust Archives, box SE04:85 (ID 5987169).

Figure 9.2 Peter Kennard, *Haywain with Cruise Missiles* (1982). © Peter Kennard.
Photo: Tate

This position reflected a long-established hostility to modern-day military landscapes. Unlike those of ancient and medieval times, they seemed jarringly intrusive, incompatible with the natural environment – and with the integrity of the longer continuities of history embodied in the storied ground of England, the preservation of which was central to the Trust's patriotic agenda. A particularly egregious example was the airfield established at Stonehenge during the First World War.[10] The National Trust led a campaign of protest: it badgered the government to relinquish the airfield, purchased the land, and finally removed the offensive traces of prematurely senescent modernity from a place 'before which', as the appeal letter to *The Times* had it, 'our ancestors have stood in awe throughout all our recorded history'.[11]

Across the interwar period, the National Trust and its supporters maintained a hostile attitude to the contemporary military presence in landscape of significant amenity value. Surrey commons, much coveted by the British Army in the 1920s, provide one case in point, for all that compromise with service

---

[10] Martin Barber, *Stonehenge Aerodrome and the Stonehenge Landscape* (London, English Heritage, 2014).
[11] National Trust Archives, National Trust, *Annual Report* (1927–1928), pp. 12–13 and *Annual Report* (1928–1929), p. 6; *The Times*, 5 August 1927, p. 7.

demands was sometimes required.[12] But deep into the 1930s, even as international tensions mounted, the Trust's Council was quite strenuous in resisting government requests to use its holdings for military training. It also protested when land near but not actually on its property was proposed to be so used, as in March 1938, when the Air Ministry suggested siting a practice anti-aircraft range close to Blakeney in Norfolk – a proposal that drew a commitment from the Trust, in the pages of its *Bulletin*, to 'use all its energies to ensure that land preserved at some cost from building for the benefit of the nation is not taken advantage of in this way'.[13]

The National Trust's patriotism was of a peaceable sort. It welcomed the donation of landscape as memorials to wartime sacrifice, the summit of Great Gable in the Lake District being a notable example.[14] But few of the Trust's post-1918 properties commemorated fallen soldiers. This reflected a wider disinclination to mark the war dead with gifts of land. On the evidence of the War Memorials Archive, there are just 17 such memorials across all Great Britain.[15] War and the military – even heroism for King and Country – was not as readily associated with valued landscape as might be expected. To a significant extent, the relationship was one of antithesis.

This antithesis became especially apparent during and because of the Second World War. It is hard to exaggerate the impact of the war on the English landscape. By February 1944, around 11.5 million acres – 20 per cent of Britain's total land area – were under military control for military purposes. These purposes included 740 airfields, a thousand army camps, hundreds of training areas, mile upon mile of concrete obstacles and anti-tank ditches, coastal and anti-aircraft batteries, radar and searchlight installations, and of course the near-ubiquitous pillboxes.[16] This militarisation of the landscape ran alongside patriotic and often propagandistic invocations of it as an emblem of home, of something worth dying for. Examples include Harry Batsford's *How to See the Country*, published in 1940, or J. B. Priestley's celebration of 'the unusual loveliness of our gardens and meadows and hills' in his radio broadcasts of the same year.[17] And, of course, there was the iconic 'Your Britain: Fight for it Now' series of posters, designed by Frank Newbould and issued in 1942 (see Figure 9.3).

[12] 'Surrey Commons: Case against acquisition by War Office', *Manchester Guardian*, 12 October 1927, p. 5; 'More Surrey schemes', *Saturday Review*, 15 October 1927, p. 497; 'Army Council and Surrey Commons', *The Times*, 10 January 1928, p. 17.
[13] *National Trust Bulletin* (March 1938), pp. 5–6.
[14] Jonathan Westaway, 'Mountains of memory, landscapes of loss: Scafell Pike and Great Gable as war memorials, 1919–29', *Landscapes*, 14 (2013), 174–193; National Trust Archives, National Trust, *Annual Report* (1923–1924), pp. 4–5.
[15] Westaway, 'Mountains of memory', 187.
[16] John Schofield, *Combat Archaeology: Material Culture and Modern Conflict* (London, Duckworth, 2005), p. 47.
[17] Harry Batsford, *How to See the Country* (London, B. T. Batsford, 1940), J. B. Priestley, *Postscripts* (London, Heinemann, 1940), pp. 5–7.

Figure 9.3 Frank Newbould, *Your Britain: Fight for it Now*. Poster, 1942. © Imperial War Museum (Art.IWM PST 14887)

The patriotic appeal of an unspoilt rural landscape helps explain reactions to its militarisation, which was tolerated, though not without some resentment. Hostile reactions were especially acute in places where communities were evacuated to make room for military training grounds, places where 'the land had changed its face' – as one farmer recalled of the countryside of the South Hams in Devon, its hedgerows flattened, its trees splintered and flayed, its fields pitted with shell-holes.[18] But they were much in evidence elsewhere, too. Certainly, with the cessation of hostilities there was a widespread desire to heal what the National Trust's first post-war *Annual Report* called 'the scars of war'.[19] Between 1946 and 1953, the Ministry of Works spent £3.5 million on the removal of defence installations.[20] Later, local authorities carried out their own clearance programmes. In the 1960s and 1970s, Kent County Council was still removing what it called 'incongruous … ugly and conspicuous' pillboxes, gun emplacements and other 'grim eyesores' that were 'obtrusive foreign elements'

[18] Grace Bradbeer, *The Land Changed its Face: The Evacuation of the South Hams 1943–44* (Dartmouth, Harbour Books, 1993 [1973]).

[19] National Trust Archives, National Trust, *Annual Report* (1946–1947), p. 11.

[20] William Foot, *Beaches, Fields, Streets, and Hills … the Anti-invasion Landscapes of England, 1940* (York, Council for British Archaeology, 2006), p. 4.

in the natural landscape.[21] Their efforts were supported by local and national amenity organisations, including the National Trust.

Indeed, the National Trust was especially assiduous in applying balm to wartime scarring, pressing government and the armed services for resources to remove military installations from its properties. It also drew on its own membership and volunteers from groups like the Youth Hostels Association and the Civic Trust to tidy up places such as its holdings on the Cornish coast – places which it felt were 'debased and disfigured' by wartime eyesores.[22] In some cases, the work of demolition became a festive affair. At St Catherine's Point near Fowey, in 1955, the use of gelignite to dismantle concrete gun emplacements and pillboxes – described as 'beastly' and 'hideous' by Trust officials – was an occasion worthy of announcement by the Town Crier (who happened to be the Champion Crier of England; his yelling notice of the impending spectacle could be heard in Polruan, across the Fowey estuary).[23] Four years later the blowing up of what the Trust called 'an ugly bomb-proof strongpoint' at Hor Point, near St Ives, provided a similarly gratifying spectacle. As the Trust's *News Letter* noted, 'chunks of concrete rose three hundred feet into the air in a single memorable blast'.[24]

The National Trust was hostile to the built environment of military modernity: it did not regard it as worthy of preservation as heritage. This perspective was consistent with a more general opposition to the depredations of the 20th century, one reflected in the preoccupations of figures such as James Lees-Milne, whose zeal for saving English stately homes did much to shape the Trust's activities in the immediate post-war decades. In perhaps less reactionary vein, it was also reflected in the Enterprise Neptune appeal, launched to great patriotic fanfare on St George's Day 1965, and to date the Trust's most effective fundraising campaign.[25]

Neptune's focus was the coastline, which it sought to protect from caravan and bungalow developments, mass tourism, extractive and other industries, and – not least – the armed services. Evidence presented to the 1971–1973 Defence Lands Committee (the Nugent Committee) claimed that up to two-thirds of the derelict structures defined as 'eyesores' by local planning authorities were of military origin.[26] At Dungeness, for example, the armed services' use of the beach both

---

[21] 'Schedule of works and structures between Langdon, near Dover and the Dover Patrol Memorial, St Margaret's-at-Cliffe: First priority for removal', Appendix I to Chief Planning Officer's Report to a special meeting of the Development Subcommittee of Kent County Council, 24 September 1969.

[22] National Trust Archives, National Trust, *Annual Report* (1947–1948), p. 8.

[23] Letters from George Senior to L. G. G. Ramsey (21 October 1948) and to National Trust Chief Agent (13 April 1951): National Trust Archives, 'St Anthony Head', box DC01:97 (ID 6108632); National Trust, *News Letter* (Spring 1955), p. 7.

[24] National Trust, *News Letter* (Spring 1959), p. 15.

[25] National Trust, *News Letter* (Spring 1965), p. 7. As of 2015, Neptune had raised £65 million: Merlin Waterson, 'Neptune's story: How it begun', *National Trust Magazine*, 136 (Autumn 2015), 27–29.

[26] Michael Hanson, 'Countryside opens up more of its gates to the public', *The Times*, 18 January 1974, p. 11. Appreciation of the ecological benefits of the military presence in at least some landscapes was a later development: see Marianna Dudley, *An Environmental History of the UK Defence Estate, 1945 to the Present* (London, Continuum, 2012).

during and after the Second World War was seen to have had environmental and scenically destructive effects. According to one local, 'that blooming army has devastated the place'.[27]

High-profile acquisitions made under the aegis of Enterprise Neptune included substantial sections of the Cliffs of Dover, where the continued presence of modern-day military remains was a source of public complaint.[28] As recently as the late 1970s, National Trust management plans for its clifftop holdings recommended removing wartime structures – to enhance the view.[29] When the Trust bought the 270-acre Bockhill Farm in 1974, which included nearly one mile of the white cliffs, it was a matter of satisfaction that 'most of the scars' of war had been removed, as had 'all visible sign' of a radar station built there in the 1950s.[30]

Just a year after the National Trust acquired Bockill Farm, more visually striking chalk coastline fell into its hands, in the shape of the Needles headland on the Isle of Wight. The Trust's *Annual Report* called the landscape 'as familiar and as English as the White Cliffs of Dover'.[31] Like them, it was associated with a great figure in the national literary pantheon – in this case Tennyson (for the white cliffs, it was Shakespeare).[32] Also like the Dover Cliffs, it had been occupied by the armed services – indeed it had only recently been relinquished by the Ministry of Defence, having been used for military purposes since the establishment of a gun battery there in 1860. A further set of weapons emplacements and related buildings – the so-called New Needles battery – was constructed in the 1890s and was operational throughout the Second World War.[33]

For some years concern had been expressed about the unsightliness of the defences on the Needles headland, and indeed on the coast of the Isle of Wight more generally. Even one of the gunners who served there during the war remembered the scene as 'desolate', while in the 1950s *The Times* thundered against the 'offensive structures' that littered a place of whose beauties Tennyson had sung.[34] When the Trust took over the site in 1975 it set out dismantling the New Needles battery, leaving only the magazines and command post. Interestingly, however, it also began restoration work on the older, mid-Victorian battery, disused since the late

[27] Brian Ferry and Dorothy Beck, *Dungeness before 1960: The Landscape and the People* (Peterborough, English Nature, 2004), pp. 20–21.
[28] See, for example, *The Times*, 18 April 1968, p. 2.
[29] Email from Jon Barker (National Trust) to author, 26 March 2019.
[30] Press Release, 24 July 1974, National Trust Archives, 'White Cliffs of Dover', box 266:56 (ID 8719).
[31] National Trust Archives, National Trust, *Annual Report* (1975), p. 9.
[32] Shakespeare's Cliff, near Dover, was associated with Act IV of *King Lear*, in which the blinded Gloucester is led to the edge of 'a Cliff whose high and bending head / Looks fearfully in the confined deep'. See Paul Readman, '"The cliffs are not cliffs": The cliffs of Dover and national identities in Britain', *c.*1750–*c.*1950', *History*, 99 (2014), esp. 259–260.
[33] For the architectural history, see Anthony Cantwell and Peter Sprack, *The Needles Defences* (Ryde, Redoubt Consultancy, 1986).
[34] British Library, National Trust Sound Archive C115=68/84 T1-T3: Needles Battery, Isle of Wight, Gunner George Brown – life story; 'Spoiling of the Needles', *The Times*, 9 August 1952, p. 2.

19th century – and this nearly two decades before it was listed. With the completion of the restoration work in 1982, the site was opened to the public by the Prince of Wales, and for a few years it was one of the National Trust's most visited attractions (around 40,000 people came in 1984).[35]

Changing attitudes? Brean Down, Studland, Orford Ness

The Trust's treatment of the Needles Old Battery reflected shifting attitudes to modern-day military remains; Victorian fortifications could now count as heritage. Much of the running here was made by archaeologists, many of them associated with what in 1983 would become English Heritage. But National Trust archaeologists also played a significant role. One of these was David Thackray, the Trust's first professional archaeologist and later its Head of Archaeology. From early on in his time with the Trust, Thackray took an active interest in landscapes of military modernity. One property that occupied much of his attention was Brean Down in Somerset. It provides a revealing case study for my purposes here, and its story is worth telling in some detail. At the western end of the Mendip Hills, Brean Down is a limestone headland that extends for about two kilometres into the Bristol Channel. A naval fort was built at its western end in the 1860s (see Figure 9.4). Occupied until 1900, when a suicidal gunner blew himself and part of it up, the fort was used as a tearoom in the early 20th century, before being remilitarised at the outbreak of the Second World War, when it became home to an Emergency Coastal Defence Battery.

The headland had been presented to the National Trust in 1951.[36] The fort, however, was owned by Weston-super-Mare Borough Council, with restrictive covenants over its four-acre site later being secured by the Trust. The aim of this arrangement was to prevent the fort's development without the Trust's consent, and preserve its immediate environs as 'open space'.[37] There seems to have been a worry that the site might be transformed into a commercial mass tourist attraction, to the detriment of the natural environment of Brean Down as a whole; certainly, the covenants did not imply any recognition of the heritage value of the fort itself. In March 1973, Weston-super-Mare Council, who had previously considered turning the fort into a casino, finally offered it to the National Trust, but this offer was refused, and the property was instead transferred for a nominal sum to Axbridge Rural District Council, whose members had little enthusiasm about their

[35] Tony Soper, *The National Trust Guide to the Coast* (Exeter, Webb & Bower, 1984), p. 181; National Trust Archives, National Trust, *Annual Report* (1984), p. 34.
[36] National Trust Archives, National Trust, *Annual Report* (1951–1952), p. 23.
[37] National Trust Archives, National Trust, *Annual Report* (1963–1964), p. 12; Nicholas van der Bijl, *Brean Down Fort: Its History and the Defence of the Bristol Channel* (Cossington, Hawk Editions, 2000), p. 127.

Figure 9.4 Brean Down Fort. © David Martin, licensed for reuse under Creative Commons CC BY-SA 2.0, creativecommons.org/licenses/by-sa/2.0

new acquisition. One councillor thought the fort was 'an eyesore ... and should be demolished and the land allowed to go back to nature'.[38]

Thus neglected, the fort decayed (see Figures 9.5 and 9.6). Over time, buildings and installations were demolished. Sometimes the army was brought in, the work providing good training opportunities for the sappers who blew up the crumbling roofs of Second World War gun emplacements; in other cases the job of so-called 'eyesore clearance' was done by archaeologists excavating the plentiful pre-modern evidence of human occupation on the headland.[39] Showing uncanny foresight, one student involved in the 1958 excavation of a Romano-British Temple on Brean Down was quoted in a newspaper as saying:

> When we demolish a building we spread the rubble out and one of the councils will cover it over with earth so it can grow back to nature. Then I suppose in a few hundred years time those archaeological chaps will come along and dig it all up again.[40]

Yet at least until the later 1970s, the fort was treated as a blot on the landscape, a nuisance that detracted from the amenity value of the headland as a place of wild

---

[38] Van de Bijl, *Brean Down Fort*, p. 127.
[39] Van de Bijl, *Brean Down Fort*, pp. 125–128.
[40] Cited in Nick Hanks, *Brean Down, Somerset* (London, National Trust Archaeological Survey, 2000), p. 54.

Figure 9.5 Brean Down: interior of gun emplacement. Photograph © Paul Readman and Martha Vandrei

Figure 9.6 Brean Down: Second World War observation post. Photograph © Paul Readman and Martha Vandrei

nature. The 1975 National Trust Management plan for Brean Down recommended that 'the local authority should be encouraged to level the site' – that is, to remove the whole complex.[41]

It was around this time that Thackray became involved. He opposed demolition, his efforts in this regard benefiting from the Department of the Environment having added the fort to the schedule of Ancient Monuments in May 1977. But Thackray's senior colleagues continued to see the fort as a problem: in the words of a memorandum issued by the regional land agent in 1978, 'it has a totally unreasonable influence on the character of the down as a whole'.[42] When in the 1980s Axbridge council offered to give the fort to the Trust, the answer was once again no. 'At present no-one wants to own the fort', was the pithy assessment of the Trust's Land Agent for Somerset and Avon in 1986.[43] And when in 1989 a Fortress Study Group report, commissioned by Thackray, recommended the restoration of the fort and its development as a heritage attraction, the response from the Trust's Regional Agent for Wessex was uncompromisingly blunt. '[W]e should do nothing', he felt, 'to encourage visitors to Brean Down, the importance of which lies in its relatively isolated and difficult access [sic]'. 'It is a magnificent landscape', he went on, 'and I feel strongly that we should resist all pressure for more public access'.[44] Wild nature came first.

Thackray was disappointed by the resilient scepticism about the fort's value as heritage, telling correspondents that he had had 'to do battle … unsuccessfully' with Trust colleagues over the matter.[45] Indeed, it was not until the mid-1990s that the Trust accepted there was a case for taking over the fort; and this only after persistent pressure from Thackray, various reports and surveys, and two Heritage Lottery Fund (HLF) applications – the first of which, made (unsuccessfully) by Sedgemoor District Council, the Trust refused to back.[46] Only at the turn of the millennium did the Trust actually acquire the fort – the acquisition being supported by funds from Enterprise Neptune, the considerable resources of which might have been used for this in previous years, had there been the willingness to do so.

[41] 'Management Plan, Brean Down, Somerset', p. 20: National Trust Archives, 'Brean Down: Property Information', box CIR 1159 (ID 6073013).
[42] W. J. B. Thorneycroft to D. Dodd, 20 November 1978, National Trust Archives, 'Brean Down: Archaeology', box CIR 1201 (ID 55274).
[43] 'Memorandum by Land Agent Somerset and Avon—January 1986', National Trust Archives, 'Brean Down', box 89:59 (ID 6215078).
[44] Memorandum by J. Cripwell, 24 April 1989, National Trust Archives, 'Brean Down Fort: General Correspondence', box CIR 1159 (ID 55643); Victor T. C. Smith, Images of Brean Down Fort: A Report to the National Trust on the possibilities for the Restoration and Presentation to the Public of this 19th-20th Century Artillery Fort (February 1989), in National Trust Archives 'Brean Down Fort: Feasibility Study', box CIR 1161 (ID 62501419).
[45] Thackray to Victor T. C. Smith, 6 April 1989, National Trust Archives, 'Brean Down Fort: General Correspondence', box CIR 1159 (ID 55643).
[46] Van der Bijl, Brean Down Fort, pp. 131–136.

Figure 9.7 A pillbox at Redend Point, Studland. © Mike Searle, licensed for reuse under Creative Commons CC BY-SA 2.0, creativecommons.org/licenses/by-sa/2.0

The story of Brean Down is one of slow, halting recognition of the heritage value in modern-day military landscapes. Similar stories could be told for other places. One is Studland in Dorset. Four thousand acres of coastal downland and heath, it was acquired by the National Trust in 1981. It included environmentally significant nature reserves and a popular sandy beach, which by 1990 was drawing about one million people a year – including, to the disgruntlement of some Trust officials, significant numbers of naturists and homosexuals. (The Warden at Studland was unhappy that 'a good deal of soliciting and sex goes on among the gays'; his approach – as 'an ex-copper' – was to apprehend them and hand them over to the police.)[47] Studland also contained the sites of many Second World War-era coastal defence installations, at least some of which had been demolished in the 1970s to prevent their use by 'undesirable elements who frequent the dunes around the nudist beach'.[48] The extant structures included pillboxes (see Figure 9.7), gun emplacements, observation posts, anti-tank obstacles, and most notably 'Fort Henry', a concrete bunker built in 1944

[47] Charlie Pye-Smith, *In Search of Neptune: A Celebration of the National Trust's Coastline* (London, National Trust, 1990), p. 74

[48] Martin Papworth, *The National Trust Archaeological Survey: Studland, Purbeck, Dorset* (London, National Trust, 1995), p. 75.

to shelter General Eisenhower, Field Marshal Montgomery, and other military bigwigs when they visited to view Operation Smash, the elaborate D-Day
rehearsals staged on Studland Beach. But it was not until the mid-1990s that
the Trust began to take a serious interest in this military heritage, as evidenced
by the archaeological survey undertaken by Martin Papworth in October 1995.
Where they had not been demolished, many of the defence works had become
overgrown, decayed, and difficult to access. Since having acquired the property
in 1981, the Trust had not undertaken any significant preservation work on them;
nor had it applied for any to be listed – not even Fort Henry – and although
Papworth's survey did recommend that it and a gun emplacement be designated
Grade II, this did not happen until 2012.[49]

By the mid-1990s, however, the National Trust's increasing interest in
the modern-day military heritage in the landscape reflected broader trends. An
important landmark was the 1995 launch of the Defence of Britain Project.
Organised by the Council for British Archaeology with funding from English
Heritage, this was a nationwide survey of 20th-century military sites. By the
time it concluded, in 2002, it had created around 14,000 records, with follow-up
projects pushing this above 20,000.[50] It revealed the extent of the militarisation of
the landscape during the Second World War, but also how far the remains of this
militarisation had fallen into decay – eloquent testimony of the degree to which
such remains had not previously been thought worth preserving. Of the 1,000
heavy anti-aircraft gun sites dating back to 1939–1945, just 10 survived in their
original form – and no trace at all was left of 94 per cent of such sites not subsequently adapted for post-war use.[51]

Tellingly, the Defence of Britain Project included consideration of Cold War
sites, the conflict between the capitalist west and the communist east now being
thought to have passed into history. It was in this context that the Trust showed
an interest in the post-war history of the New Needles battery, which had been
acquired in 1975. Here, in the late 1950s, the propulsion units of a proposed
nuclear-armed ballistic missile had been tested. In 2003, the Trust began restoring
the underground rooms associated with these tests, opening them to the public
four years later.[52]

But the supreme example of the Trust's engagement with the Cold War landscape is Orford Ness, a nine-mile stretch of shingle on the Suffolk coast. Occupied
by the military across two world wars, in the 1950s the Atomic Weapons Research
Establishment (AWRE) built massive concrete structures there. These were the

---

[49] Papworth, *National Trust Archaeological Survey: Studland*; 'Gun emplacement and Fort Henry',
Historic England Listing database, https://historicengland.org.uk/listing/the-list/list-entry/1411809
[accessed 9 October 2020].
[50] Schofield, *Combat Archaeology*, p. 57; Rachel Woodward, *Military Geographies* (Oxford, Wiley-
Blackwell, 2004), pp. 146–147.
[51] Schofield, *Combat Archaeology*, p. 83.
[52] David Mattin, 'Hush-hush missile site reveals its secrets', *The Times*, 21 April 2007, p. 4 [S4].

Figure 9.8 Laboratories numbers 4 and 5 at the former Atomic Weapons Research Establishment, Orford Ness. © Tony Lockhart, licensed for reuse under Creative Commons CC BY-SA 4.0, https://creativecommons.org/licenses/by-sa/4.0, via Wikimedia Commons

so-called 'pagodas', beneath the protective canopies of which the components of nuclear bombs were subjected to environmental tests (see Figure 9.8). The Ness was used by AWRE until 1971, with the last service personnel moving out in 1987.[53] After much behind-the-scenes wrangling, and assisted by large public grants, the Trust bought the property in 1993.[54]

   In making the decision to go ahead with the acquisition, the Trust acknowledged the heritage value of the military legacy in the landscape, including that associated with the Cold War. A report to the Properties Committee in November 1991 formally assigned an 'A' grade – the highest – to the 'historic associations' of the place, making it clear that 'With the recent dramatic changes in the Soviet Union and Eastern Europe, the uses to which Orford Ness was put by the Ministry of Defence already seem remote', and thus 'even very recent structures have entered the domain of history'. From the outset, then, the pagodas and other AWRE buildings were presented as heritage sites; as what the same 1991 report called 'monuments

---

[53] For the military history of Orford Ness, see Paddy Heazell, *Most Secret: The Hidden History of Orford Ness*, 2nd edn (Stroud, The History Press, 2013).

[54] For a good concise account from the perspective of a senior Trust official closely involved in the acquisition, see Merlin Waterson, *The National Trust: The First Hundred Years*, rev. edn (London, National Trust, 1997 [1994]), pp. 256–259.

to the Cold War', they were replete with symbolic power.[55] According to Angus Wainwright, Trust archaeologist for the East of England and chief architect of the original Orford Ness management plan, the landscape 'symbolize[d] the role of technology in ... late twentieth-century warfare and the awesome destructive forces it unleashed as well as the political, moral and social repercussions'.[56] The AWRE buildings were relics of an important part of the nation's past; Wainwright even compared them to the medieval 'castles of Wales and the Scottish borders'.[57]

Preservation and its limits

Orford Ness seems to demonstrate the extent to which 20th-century military landscapes have become valued as heritage. Along with modern ruins more generally, interest in such places has certainly grown in recent years, as well as providing inspiration to visual artists – such as Dennis Creffield, in the case of Orford Ness (see Figure 9.9).[58] Yet this interest has grown from a low base: whether edgily counter-cultural and subversive, or motivated by a reverential archaeological concern for understanding the history of place, 'bunkerology' remains a distinctly specialist avocation.[59] Furthermore, and in contrast to other modern ruins (for instance derelict industrial plants), military landscapes remain uncongenial to many – precisely on account of their martial associations. Their presence in rural contexts is often seen as especially rebarbative and incongruous, where the broken concrete and rusted metal detritus of war-making appears to jar with the conventional and long-established aesthetic language of English pastoralism, with its connotations of peace and tranquillity.[60] Their ruination is not perceived as graceful, the product of centuries of gradual decay, but as disturbingly abrupt, the almost futuristic modernity of their structures suggestive as much of violent vicissitudes to come as of those now happily overborne. It was in these terms that W. G. Sebald saw the pagodas in his semi-fictional account of ruminative wanderings along the Suffolk coastline, *The Rings of Saturn*: appearing to be troubling harbingers of destruction, they provoked Sebald to imagine himself 'amidst the remains of our own civilization after its extinction in some future catastrophe'.[61]

---

[55] 'Report by the Regional Director [Merlin Waterson] and the Regional Land Agent [Simon Garnier], East Anglia, to the Properties Committee of the National Trust, 7 November 1991', National Trust Archives, 'Orford Ness: Conservation', box CIR 269 (ID 57274).

[56] Angus Wainwright, 'Orford Ness', in David Morgan Evans, Peter Salway, and David Thackray (eds), *'The Remains of Distant Times': Archaeology and the National Trust* (London, Boydell, 1996), p. 207.

[57] Wainwright, 'Orford Ness', p. 202.

[58] Dennis Creffield, *Paintings and Drawings of Orford Ness* (London, Connaught Brown, [1995]).

[59] Luke Bennett, 'Bunkerology', *Environment and Planning D: Society and Space*, 29 (2011), 421–434; Tim Edensor, *Industrial Ruins: Space, Aesthetics and Materiality* (Oxford, Berg, 2005).

[60] For the 19th-century origins of this language, see Malcolm Andrews, *A Sweet View: The Making of an English Idyll* (London, Reaktion, 2021).

[61] W. G. Sebald, *The Rings of Saturn*, trans. Michael Hulse (London, Vintage, 2002 [1998]), p. 237.

Figure 9.9 Dennis Creffield, *Lab 4 (Pagoda)* (1995). © Artist's Estate/Portland Gallery.
Photo: Imperial War Museum, Art.IWM ART 16589

Robert Macfarlane has also emphasised what he calls Orford Ness's 'militarising influence upon one's vision'. When he visited with his friend Roger Deakin, 'everything I saw seemed bellicose, mechanised. A hare exploded from a shingle divot. Bramble coiled and looped like barbed wire. Geese landed with their undercarriages down. Green and orange lichen camouflaged the concrete of pillboxes'. Nature itself had become warlike. Having returned to 'the woods and fields of Suffolk', Macfarlane looked back on an apocalyptic sight: 'A single mushroom-cloud of cumulonimbus dominated the eastern sky, and it was soaked in the red fission light of the late sun'.[62] Such imagery recalls Creffield's paintings of the Ness, the eerie and vacant buildings of which – in Creffield's own words – 'clatter in the wind and smoke with imaginary radiation'.[63]

Not everyone shares the sensibilities of Sebald, Macfarlane, or Creffield, but their reactions do testify to the negative associations of modern-day military landscapes – for all that such places also provide a potent source of creative inspiration. Despite the powerful presence of the Second World War in late 20th- and

[62] Robert Macfarlane, *The Wild Places* (London, Granta, 2007), pp. 257, 262–263.
[63] From Creffield's commentary on his *A General View of 'The Island' with Laboratories and Magazine: Midday, Summer, 1994*, in Creffield, *Paintings and Drawings of Orford Ness*.

early 21st-century memory cultures, including those transatlantic in nature,[64] these negative associations have proved enduring. As we have seen, the physical impact of the temporary defence works, airfields, and training areas that were instituted in 1939–1945 stirred regret at the time, even if their necessity was usually unquestioned (except, perhaps, by some farmers).[65] In the course of the clear-up of the later 1940s and 1950s, nobody argued that wartime military installations and buildings should be preserved for the sake of their historic interest – an exception being the machine gun emplacements installed within the medieval and Roman fabric of Pevensey Castle walls, which were seen as a constituent and congruous element of a longer history of defence at the site.[66] Similarly, few objections were made against the later 'eyesore' clearance programmes of the kind carried out by Kent County Council in the 1970s on the Cliffs of Dover. While the white cliffs were certainly imbued with sentimental meaning in the post-war decades (Vera Lynn's famous song inevitably springs to mind), their iconographic force as emblems of the national home and its defence was rooted in their physical attributes as ramparts walling Britain off from foreign threats; it was not enhanced by the decaying debris of recent war.[67] For this reason, on the chalky heights above Dover as elsewhere across Britain, bunkers, coastal batteries, and other such structures were not seen as worthy of preservation until comparatively recently. To adapt Nikolaus Pevsner's verdict on bicycle sheds, while cathedrals (and castles) were architecture, pillboxes were not.[68]

And in part because they lacked value as architecture, when not knocked down by government agencies or amenity bodies, military installations and buildings were demolished by private individuals or simply left to decay.[69] Dunsfold airfield in Surrey is a case in point. Occupied by the RAF between 1942 and 1946, its abandoned buildings and runways later attracted 'squatters' and 'gypsies', provoking local pressure for demolition; as recently as 1992, even one Second World War aviation enthusiast could declare its overgrown 'trackways, paths, shelters and hut bases' to be 'dark and dismal places'.[70] Farmers sometimes used military

---

[64] See for example Lucy Noakes and Juliette Pattinson (eds), *British Cultural Memory and the Second World War* (London, Bloomsbury Academic, 2014); Sam Edwards, *Allies in Memory: World War II and the Politics of Transatlantic Commemoration in Europe c.1941–2001* (Cambridge, Cambridge University Press, 2015).

[65] See, for example, A Norfolk Woman [Lucilla Reeve], *Farming on a Battleground* (Wymondham, Geo. R. Reeve, [1949]), esp. pp. 47–50, 62–64, 75–78.

[66] Foot, *Beaches, Fields, Streets, and Hills*, p. 4.

[67] Readman, ' "The cliffs are not cliffs" '.

[68] 'A bicycle shed is a building; Lincoln Cathedral is a piece of architecture ... the term architecture applies only to buildings designed with a view to aesthetic appeal': Nikolaus Pevsner, *An Outline of European Architecture*, new and enlarged edn (London, John Murray, 1948 [1943]), p. xix.

[69] Foot, *Defence Areas*: 'Landowners see little to commend in structures so evidently abandoned by responsible authority, and will be unconcerned about their future survival: indeed, just the opposite, they may be motivated to remove them as a lure to undesirable elements entering their land' (p. 22).

[70] Paul McCue, *Dunsfold: Surrey's Most Secret Airfield 1942–1992* (New Malden, Air Research Publications, 1992), pp. 203, 276–277.

buildings to store equipment or animal feed, but many more found them a nuisance, and as lately as 2009 the Council for British Archaeology was reporting the 'recent destruction' of defence structures, mainly for the purposes of field clearance.[71] When English Heritage began work in 1994 to identify a sample of modern defence sites for statutory protection, it did so acutely conscious of the fact that wartime remains were 'today widely neglected'.[72]

It was just such neglect that prompted the late 20th-century preservationist reaction, one of the most notable expressions of which was the Defence of Britain project. From the outset, this project had an avowedly educational intent. It did not reflect widespread popular concern about modern-day military remains; it sought, rather, to inculcate such concern. It aimed 'to promote people's understanding and enjoyment of these defence landscapes ... to ensure greater recognition of the[ir] value ... and the need to conserve the components they include'.[73] The archaeologists and others associated with the project seem to have had a sense in which doing so might be an uphill task, or somehow counterintuitive in heritage terms. They were aware that 'Questions will continue to be asked about whether these sites should be preserved at all'.[74]

So far as the National Trust was concerned, by the 1990s, for all that its main preoccupations lay elsewhere, 20th-century military landscapes had established at least some claim on its attention. They were routinely included in archaeological surveys; their interpretation was discussed in management plans; their features were formally graded on a scale of heritage 'importance'. (Thus, for example, an overgrown bombing decoy at the western end of Brownsea Island in Dorset was of 'local importance'; Second World War concrete gun emplacements at Brean Down were of 'national importance'; and, at the other end of the scale, the demolished remains of machine-gun posts on Studland Heath were of 'minimal importance'.[75]) As with the Defence of Britain project, such surveying activity was stimulated by a new appreciation of the vulnerability of these military sites; also like this project, it was actuated by a desire to educate a largely unknowing public as to their heritage value. This is clear from the management plans and other internal documentation produced by the Trust. Those relating to Studland emphasise the need for the provision of interpretative material to help visitors make sense of the defence works that still littered the property.[76] At Brean Down, having finally determined that the

[71] Foot, *Defence Areas*, pp. 11–12.

[72] Colin Dobinson, 'Twentieth-century fortifications in England: The MPP approach', in John Schofield (ed.), *Monuments of War: The Evaluation, Recording and Management of Twentieth-Century Military Sites* (London, English Heritage, 1998), p. 2

[73] Foot, *Defence Areas*, p. 1.

[74] John Schofield, 'Concluding remarks', in Schofield, *Monuments of War*, p. 22.

[75] Martin Papworth, *National Trust Archaeological Survey: Brownsea Island, Dorset* (London, National Trust, 1992), p. 25; Hanks, *Brean Down*, p. 58; Papworth, *National Trust Archaeological Survey: Studland*, p. 67.

[76] Papworth, *National Trust Archaeological Survey: Studland*, for example, p. 58.

fort was worthy of acquisition, the Trust's plans stressed the importance of making its history more legible. As a 1998 conservation statement lamented, visitors were supplied with 'no printed information'; most came upon the buildings 'by accident' and had 'no idea about the importance or meaning of the structures and their cultural or social significance'.[77]

Emphasis on education ran alongside greater concern with preservation, and here the Trust's approach repays closer examination. Since it began taking an interest in things such as pillboxes, searchlight emplacements and Second World War gun batteries, its policy has typically been to 'preserve in current condition' – to invoke a form of words frequently used in archaeological surveys and property management plans. In practice, this has often implied an acknowledgement that the process of decay might be slowed but should not be stopped. The Trust was clear that modern military remains were of sufficient merit to be monitored, stabilised, and made safe; but doing more than this was not often countenanced, and in many cases, nature was to be left to take its course. Large-scale restoration was impermissible; indeed, the reason why the Trust refused to support Sedgemoor Council's original Brean Down HLF application in 1995 was because it proposed just that. By contrast, the second – and successful – HLF application, this time made with the backing of the National Trust, was much less ambitious, asking for around £360,000 for the consolidation of the fort before transfer to Trust ownership.[78] The Trust's policy, as set out in the conservation statement written to accompany the bid, was 'to retain as much of the existing fabric as possible', with remedial work to be undertaken 'only if a *substantial* loss of an *individually significant* part would result otherwise'.[79] For some critics such as Nicholas van der Bijl, a military historian and former soldier, this amounted to a 'policy of "ruinisation" '.[80]

Views such as van der Bijl's were not representative of mainstream opinion, however. Indeed, Brean Down provides evidence of the enduringly limited public appeal of modern-day military landscapes. As acknowledged even in van der Bijl's account of the affair, the ill-fated 1995 HLF proposal encountered significant local hostility. The Brean Residents Association voted overwhelmingly against it, one member suggesting that the fort should be 'razed to the ground'. Somerset and North Somerset County Councils also opposed the scheme: it was a 'cock-eyed idea', said one councillor.[81] And when it came to the second HLF application three years later, the answers to the questionnaire that accompanied a public exhibition

---

[77] Tracey Hartley and Adrian Woodhall, *Brean Down: A Conservation Statement* (London, Sedgemoor District Council/National Trust, 1999), p. 17.

[78] Tracey Hartley and Adrian Woodhall, *Brean Down Fort: Project Proposals* (London, Sedgemoor District Council/National Trust, 1998). English Heritage also provided some funds (£100,000): Van der Bijl, *Brean Down Fort*, p. 136.

[79] Hartley and Woodhall, *Brean Down*, p. 20. Emphasis added.

[80] Van der Bijl, *Brean Down Fort*, p. 136.

[81] Van der Bijl, *Brean Down Fort*, pp. 134–135.

detailing the scheme confirmed that Brean Down as a whole was valued less for its military heritage than for its 'tranquillity', 'natural beauty', and 'wilderness'. It was a 'special unspoilt place' for 'quiet reflection', somewhere 'to walk in solitude', take in sea views and 'enjoy [a] peaceful relationship with [the] natural environment' away from the 'rush of modern day life'. So far as the fort was concerned, one respondent suggested that some of its remains might be 'bricked up' so as to prevent their use 'as drinking dens, lavatories, etc.'; another thought the whole complex 'a mess of derelict concrete and bricks and would be best demolished'. In general, however, the consensus pointed to what many respondents termed a 'low key' approach. There was strong opposition to restoration of the fort, which should be left 'to nature', or 'more or less as it is'.[82]

Still lower key was the approach at Orford Ness. The primary rationale for taking on the property was ecological and scientific: the nine-mile stretch of coast was a Grade I Site of Special Scientific Interest and one of the most important shingle spits in the world.[83] As Wainwright told a BBC World Service programme in April 1995, 'The site was really acquired for its landscape and nature conservation value, rather than the historic side'.[84] Indeed, some senior officers in the Trust were 'appalled at the squalor and ugliness' that were 'the legacy of seventy years of military occupation' and needed considerable persuading to agree to the purchase in the first place.[85] Once the go-ahead had been given, however, the question remained as to what to do with the derelict buildings and installations. The Trust's original architectural survey recommended that more than 60 buildings be demolished,[86] and while some were indeed pulled down, removal of the AWRE testing labs was not an option, since the forcible removal of these massive concrete structures would have damaged the fragile ecosystem of the shingle. In general, what Wainwright called a 'philosophy of non intervention' underlay the approach taken; once the site had been made safe – though not 'tidied up' – the remaining ruins would be left standing.[87] Their decline neither arrested not accelerated, they would be left to 'gently deteriorate'.[88]

---

[82] Hartley and Woodhall, *Brean Down*, Appendix 6: Documentation Supporting the Public Consultation, n.p.

[83] Derek Ratcliffe (ed.), *A Nature Conservation Review: The Selection of Biological Sites of National Importance to Nature Conservation in Britain*, 2 vols (Cambridge, Cambridge University Press, 1977), vol. II, p. 9 ('of outstanding physiographic and botanical interest'). The Trust's own assessment relied heavily on a report commissioned from the leading environmental scientist, Professor Keith Clayton: 'Report by the Regional Director and Regional Land Agent', esp. pp. 2–3, 12–13, National Trust Archives, 'Orford Ness: Conservation', box CIR 269 (ID 57274).

[84] British Library, National Trust Sound Archive C1168/808.

[85] 'Report by the Regional Director and the Regional Land Agent', p. 3.

[86] Sophia Davis, *Island Thinking: Suffolk Stories of Landscape, Militarisation and Identity* (London, Palgrave Macmillan, 2020), p. 250.

[87] Angus Wainwright to David Thackray, Memorandum on 'the aesthetics and history of Orfordness', 1 May 1994: National Trust Archives, 'Orford Ness: Conservation', box CIR 269 (ID 57274).

[88] 'Orford Ness Management Policy', c. March 1995: National Trust Archives, 'Orford Ness: Conservation', box CIR 269 (ID 57274).

The geographer Caitlin DeSilvey has described this approach as an example of 'palliative curation', reflecting a recognition that dilapidation and disintegration are part of the normal lifecycle of buildings – processes that should be worked with, not against.[89] But at Orford Ness such an approach was determined less by any general principle relating to buildings *qua* buildings, and more by the site's specific associations. The pagodas were inextricably linked to what Merlin Waterson, the National Trust's Regional Director for East Anglia, called 'the futilities of the Cold War', to nuclear weapons and – by extension – to humanity's capacity for mass destruction; as such they exercised 'a powerful, if chilling fascination'.[90] But it did not follow from this that they ought to be preserved; rather, given these connotations, it was seen to be appropriate that they should decay. And the Trust was clear that 'nature' – so vulnerable against the Bomb – should be enlisted as an 'ally' in this process. The harsh but ecologically fragile environment of the Ness was to have its revenge on its defilers: in contemplating the acquisition of the property in 1991, the Trust's committee-men anticipated that 'If allowed to, the sea and the savage climate would in a surprisingly short time restore Orford Ness to a state of wild, natural beauty'.[91] The intention was to emphasise the regenerative capacities of the natural world, even in the face of the awesome potential of nuclear fission to wreck devastation on that same world. As Wainwright explained, in their ruined state '[t]he buildings at Orford Ness ... say a lot about our confrontation with the forces of nature and the ability of these forces to adapt our structures, and given time, destroy them'.[92] And while the abandoned AWRE buildings have proved quite resilient, over the past several decades wind and saltwater have been slowly dismantling them, the process of decay being assisted by high levels of salinity in the concrete out of which they were built. Given the management philosophy of the Trust, it is fitting that this structural weakness derives from the fact that shingle from the Ness itself was used in the original composite mix. Increasingly colonised by plants and other wildlife, the pagodas can thus be seen as returning, albeit slowly, to the natural environment from which they were raised.

It is possible that the National Trust may change its approach to Orford Ness.[93] But its non-interventionist philosophy has aligned with wider cultural attitudes to military heritage of this kind. Unlike that of some other countries, France being one notable example, the British experience of post-war nuclear culture centred on envisioning the destruction that might be caused by nuclear

---

[89] Caitlin DeSilvey, 'Palliative curation: Art and entropy on Orford Ness', in Bjørnar Olsen and Þóra Pétursdóttir (eds), *Ruin Memories: Materiality, Aesthetics and the Archaeology of the Recent Past* (Abingdon, Routledge, 2014), pp. 79–91; see also Caitlin DeSilvey, *Curated Decay: Heritage beyond Saving* (Minneapolis, University of Minnesota Press, 2017).

[90] Waterson, *National Trust*, p. 259.

[91] 'Report by the Regional Director and the Regional Land Agent', p. 12.

[92] Wainwright, 'Orford Ness', p. 202.

[93] It has even been suggested that site might qualify for UNESCO World Heritage status: Desilvey, 'Palliative curation', p. 87.

weapons: by and large, atomic technology had negative connotations, at least for the wider public.[94] The pagodas of Orford Ness embodied such connotations. Standing exposed on the shingle, in what Wainwright called 'violent contrast' to their wild natural surroundings,[95] they did much to make the Ness the uneasy and unsettling landscape described by Sebald, Macfarlane, and others. As the National Trust well knew as it pondered whether or not to take on Orford Ness, many people who saw the place, including senior figures in the organisation, found its military structures repellent (according to one account, the top brass were only won round when, at a crucial committee meeting, an appeal was made to the cultural associations of that part of the Suffolk coast – specifically the links with George Crabbe and Benjamin Britten).[96] And once the decision was finally made to acquire the property, Wainwright and others who saw value in its military heritage had to work hard to counter the fact that 'Many who visit Orford Ness dislike it on first meeting'.[97]

For all its significance and interest, Orford Ness is unusual, of course. As Rachel Woodward has noted, in common with other Cold War sites, it appeals to 'enthusiasts' but defies 'easy marketing' to a wider public for whom the negative connotations of the nuclear age still loom large.[98] Other 20th-century military landscapes are less problematic. Among these are the acoustic mirrors erected in coastal locations between the First World War and the late 1930s.[99] A failed forerunner of radar, these concrete structures were designed to detect the noise of incoming aeroplanes, so providing advance warning of bombing raids. The most notable examples are to be found amidst old quarry workings at Denge, near Dungeness, in what is now an RSPB nature reserve (see Figure 9.10), and these – as well as others including one on a National Trust-owned stretch of the Cliffs of Dover – have recently been the focus of successful preservationist efforts.[100] Much of the appeal of sound mirrors seems to derive from their military uselessness, their status as 'spectacular remnants of a dead-end technology',

[94] As Jonathan Hogg has concluded, 'For the vast majority of the British people following 1945, imagining the devastation of nuclear weapons was at the root of how they experienced British nuclear culture': Jonathan Hogg, *British Nuclear Culture: Official and Unofficial Narratives in the Long 20th Century* (London, Bloomsbury Academic, 2016), p. 173. Compare the French experience, where nuclear power was – by and large effectually – harnessed to a patriotic programme of post-war regeneration, one that extolled 'technological prowess ... as a basic element of French national identity': Gabrielle Hecht, *The Radiance of France: Nuclear Power and National Identity After World War II* (Cambridge, MA and London, The MIT Press, 1998), p. 329.
[95] Wainwright, 'Orford Ness', p. 198.
[96] Waterson, *The National Trust*, pp. 257–258.
[97] Wainwright, 'Orford Ness', p. 199.
[98] Woodward, *Military Geographies*, p. 148.
[99] For the history, see Richard N. Scarth, *Echoes From the Sky*, 2nd edn (Bromley, Independent Books, 2017 [1999]).
[100] 'Fan Bay Deep Shelter', https://www.nationaltrust.org.uk/the-white-cliffs-of-dover/features/fan-bay-deep-shelter-an-excavation-of-epic-proportions [accessed 15 February 2019]; Scarth, *Echoes from the Sky*, pp. 409–418.

Figure 9.10 The Denge sound mirrors. © Julian P. Guffogg, licensed for reuse under Creative Commons CC BY-SA 2.0, creativecommons.org/licenses/by-sa/2.0

in the words of a website dedicated to them.[101] Known colloquially as 'concrete ears' or 'listening ears', they are suggestive less of conflict than communication, and many of the art projects they have inspired have reconceptualised them as emblems of dialogue between people and nations.[102] (One of the more ambitious of these projects, by the Danish artist Lise Autogena, envisaged the construction of two new mirrors, one at Dungeness and one at Boulogne, the idea being to create a working sonic link between them; perhaps unsurprisingly, it has not come to fruition.)[103]

[101] 'Sound Mirrors', http://www.andrewgrantham.co.uk/soundmirrors/ [accessed 16 July 2019]. This aspect of the mirrors – as 'defunct out of date technology' – has also appealed to artists. See, for example, Ian Chamberlain, 'Mirror I and Mirror II selected and hung for the Royal Academy Summer Show 2015', http://ianchamberlainartist.blogspot.com/2015/05/mirror-i-and-mirror-ii-selected-and.html [accessed 16 July 2019].

[102] Claire Barrett, 'Building of the month' (October 2003) https://c20society.org.uk/botm/sound-mirrors-greatstone-kent/ [accessed 16 July 2019].

[103] 'The Sound Mirrors Project', https://www.autogena.org/work/sound-mirrors [accessed 11 October 2020]; Tom Dyckhoff, '"I'm on the beach!" Who needs phones when you've got giant concrete "sound mirrors"?', *Guardian*, 13 June 2001, p. A15. At a different level of artistic endeavour, the inspiration behind a music video for the R&B singer Nicki Minaj, set at the Denge sound mirrors, was also affected by the site's association with communication – or so it seems. As its director explained, despite battling 'shitty' English weather his crew was able to shoot 'super hot shit': 'the wall we are standing next too

Yet the appeal of even such relatively benign structures should not be overestimated. Despite being scheduled in 1979, until recently they had been left to rot, suffering what one local historian and sound mirror enthusiast described as 'long years of neglect'.[104] The English Heritage-financed intervention in 2003 to preserve the Denge mirrors came only just in time to save them (two of the three were on the verge of collapse), and was only possible through an experimental pilot scheme: as one English Heritage inspector explained, 'We couldn't have found the funding' otherwise, since 'in the order of national priorities' the mirrors were not 'high enough up the agenda'.[105] Even now their celebrity is of a fairly recherché sort, being confined to certain constituencies of people: military history buffs, archaeologists, 'urban explorers', the concrete cognoscenti,[106] artists and musicians, and, more generally, the often rather self-conscious seekers of 'alternative' heritage experiences.[107]

Conclusion

The Denge sound mirrors thus provide an *a fortiori* illustration of the restricted appeal of 20th-century military landscapes. So far as more typical such landscapes are concerned, the story is similar. As we have seen in the cases of Brean Down, Studland, and elsewhere, their heritage value was only hesitantly recognised – even by the National Trust. Indeed, it is notable that those sites seen as most valuable have often been those with long histories of military use. Continuity of military occupation over decades and centuries (and not, for example, just in the crisis of world war) conferred a reassuring sense of appropriateness, diminishing the frequently reported sense of incongruity provoked by the sight of concrete pillboxes in the peaceful fields and meadows of England's green and pleasant land. In 1995, the Trust's archaeological survey of Studland made much of the fact that 'Enemy attacks

that's super curved was an old sound satellite they built back in the day that was supposed to receive messages from England to Paris .... kinda awesome. If you stand on one end and whisper the person on the other end can hear as if you are next to each other' [*sic*]. Stephen Gottlieb, 'Director Colin Tilley on Nicki Minaj "Freedom"', *Videostatic*, 27 November 2012, https://www.videostatic.com/content/direc tor-colin-tilley-nicki-minaj-freedom [accessed 16 July 2019].

[104] Roger Bowdler, 'The 200 foot sound mirror: Denge, district of Sheppey, Kent', *[English Heritage] Reports and Papers*, 19 (London, English Heritage, 1999), pp. 9–10; Scarth, *Echoes From the Sky*, p. 397.

[105] Barrett, 'Building of the month'. The scheme was the Aggregate Levy Sustainability Fund (ASLF); originally introduced as a two-year pilot in 2002, it was axed in 2011. The mirrors were eligible for help under this scheme due to their location in an area previously subject to the environmental depredations of quarrying.

[106] Christo Hall, 'The second life of concrete: Brutalism's renaissance', *The Quietus*, 10 July 2016, https://thequietus.com/articles/20558-sound-mirrors-raw-conrete-this-brutal-world-concrete-concept-brutalism [accessed 18 July 2019]; Barrett, 'Building of the month'.

[107] For the tastes of the latter, see, for example, Robin Halstead, Jason Hazeley, Alex Morris, and Joel Morris, *Bollocks to Alton Towers: Uncommonly British Days Out* (London: Michael Joseph, 2005).

on the Studland coast have been recorded since the Danish raid of 877AD': thus the machine gun posts, tank traps, and so on were just the latest in a line of shore-line defences, elements of which included Napoleonic-era gun emplacements and signal stations, a 16th-century battery at Redend Point and the now-vanished medi-eval Studland Castle.[108] Similar considerations supported arguments assertive of the heritage value of the modern-day military remains on the Needles headland, the Cliffs of Dover, Brownsea Island, and Brean Down, all of which also had long his-tories as fortified sites.[109] Where such histories did not exist, these arguments were harder to make, and very often not made at all.

The relatively marginal status of 20th-century military landscapes as heritage perhaps explains why, as recently as 2005, the archaeologist John Schofield felt the need to deny that only 'anoraks' were interested the material culture of such places; that he thought this was still a view requiring rebuttal is itself telling.[110] Visitors to Brean Down or the Needles come primarily for the natural landscape, not the military relics. For all that 20th-century Britain may have been a 'warfare' quite as much as a 'welfare' state,[111] these and other similar monuments to the nation's mili-tary experience remain incompletely integrated into mainstream understandings of national heritage. With the partial exception of the Cliffs of Dover, which since the early 19th century have exerted a symbolic power quite independent of the defence installations – Roman watchtower, medieval castle, pillboxes and all – that cluster on the chalky heights, they have not established themselves as icons of nationhood. Across the 20th and into the 21st century, understandings of the archetypal landscapes of Englishness remained of a rather different order. These understandings were governed by established ideas of natural beauty, and a felt sense of the longer continuities of history – history as it was congealed in the fields, hills, valleys, villages, and streetscapes of the storied ground of England.[112]

---

[108] Papworth, *The National Trust Archaeological Survey: Studland*, p. 23.

[109] Offering what the Trust's 1998 Conservation Statement called 'a wide range of archaeological remains … dating from the Neolithic period to the Second World War', the military heritage of Brean Down encompassed 20th-century coastal defences, Victorian gun batteries, and an iron-age hillfort; while that of Brownsea Island included a Tudor blockhouse with 19th- and 20th-century gun emplacements, a searchlight building, and a bombing decoy (Hartley and Woodhall, *Brean Down*, p. 14; Papworth, *National Trust Archaeological Survey: Brownsea*).

[110] Schofield, *Combat Archaeology*, pp. 86–87.

[111] See David Edgerton, *Warfare State: Britain, 1920–1970* (Cambridge, Cambridge University Press, 2005).

[112] On this theme, see Paul Readman, *Storied Ground: Landscape and the Shaping of English National Identity* (Cambridge, Cambridge University Press, 2018). For the idea of landscape as 'history congealed', see Tim Ingold, *The Perception of the Environment* (London, Routledge, 2000), p. 150.

10

Nuclear Narratives: Rural Modernity, Identity, and Heritage in the Highlands and Islands

LINDA M. ROSS

Introduction

WRITING IN 1960, a Caithness commentator considered the Dounreay Experimental Research Establishment (DERE) 'a prize which any tourist-minded county would jump at'.[1] Capitalising on this enthusiasm, the United Kingdom Atomic Energy Authority (UKAEA) opened the site's airfield control tower as a viewing platform and visitor centre that June, taking a different view from those who believed that development in the Highlands would deter visitors.[2] The Scottish Tourist Board reported on bright prospects for Scotland's tourist season and congratulated the UKAEA for 'being so quick to realise the tourist possibilities of nuclear power', recognising the attraction not only of the county's scenery and beaches, but also 'the spectacular spheroid construction at Dounreay'.[3] Such a positive response was justified: 8,000 visitors to the control tower over the three-month tourist season in 1960 had risen to 20,000 by 1966.[4] Recognising the significance of this unexpected by-product of the nuclear industry, Caithness County Council selected Dounreay as the location for its tourist information service.[5] Notably, it was chosen over

---

[1] *John O'Groat Journal*, 24 June 1960, p. 4.

[2] This was something faced by the proponents of the North of Scotland Hydro-Electric Board in the 1940s and 1950s, when opponents to the building of its schemes 'expressed grave anxieties concerning the scenic beauty of the Highlands', Peter L. Payne, *The Hydro* (Aberdeen, Aberdeen University Press, 1988), p. 48.

[3] *John O'Groat Journal*, 24 June 1960, p. 4.

[4] *John O'Groat Journal*, 30 September 1960, p. 5; The National Archives (hereafter TNA), AB61/68 E40, F. Levens, Caithness County Council, to D. M. Carmichael, UKAEA, 6 June 1966.

[5] TNA, AB61/68 E40, F. Levens, Caithness County Council, to D. M. Carmichael, UKAEA, 6 June 1966.

Proceedings of the British Academy, **256**, 208–233, © The British Academy 2023.

Figure 10.1 A local farmhand works the land as Dounreay's fast breeder reactor takes shape in 1957. Credit: Copyright Nuclear Decommissioning Authority

the established tourist draw of the famous John O'Groats: evidence of changing patterns within a transformed county.

In the six years between the Dounreay project's announcement in 1954 and the decision to present the site and its history as a visitor attraction in 1960, Caithness had changed from a region whose economy was dominated by agriculture and fishing to one which prioritised technological innovation (see Figure 10.1). Caithness of the early 1950s was the product of the former, with the coast and hinterland looking towards one of the two burghs – Wick, the larger county town, in the east, and Thurso in the west – for markets and services. The UKAEA's arrival to Scotland's north coast brought nuclear science to this rural landscape, distant from major population centres, at a time when road travel to Edinburgh took 10 hours and London 20.[6] The chosen site was close to Thurso, the population of which grew by 147 per cent as a result of the UKAEA 'importing' scientists and engineers from the south.[7] This necessitated

---

[6] D. Carmichael, 'Nuclear fission and social fusion', a paper on local relations submitted on behalf of the United Kingdom Atomic Energy Authority, World Congress of Public Relations, Venice, 24–27 May 1961, p. 1.

[7] HMSO, *Census 1961, County Reports, Vol. 1 Part 12, County of Caithness* (Edinburgh, 1963), p. 11; TNA, AB8/644 123A, Mr Shirlaw to Mr Parkin, 19 February 1955.

the planning and construction of a new architecture for a new community, a set of circumstances which is unique in terms of patterns of inward-migration to the Highlands and Islands. In 1970, Nan Fairbrother called for 'new landscapes for our new lives' to be realised by 'positive and clear-sighted adaptation of the habitat to our new industrial condition'.[8] This chapter shows how, 16 years prior, co-operation between the UKAEA, local authorities, and the incumbent and incoming populations achieved exactly that, making Caithness a stand-out example of technologically induced social development within a rural area. It also highlights the value of re-examining the traditional history of the Highlands and Islands in the mid- to late 20th century, in particular showing how nuclear cultural heritage can contribute to the 'much overlooked, and misunderstood' history of the region.[9]

Dounreay was not a conventional nuclear power station: it was the site of Britain's first full-scale fast breeder reactor, designed to 'breed' large quantities of fissionable man-made plutonium from natural uranium, creating more plutonium than is used and generating power. This plutonium could be reprocessed and used as reactor fuel in place of uranium. It was an experimental system designed to test the viability of the technology for future power generation. The Dounreay site grew to include five reactors – the materials test reactor (DMTR, operational 1958), the fast reactor (DFR, operational 1959), the prototype fast reactor (PFR, operational 1974) and two pressurised water reactors at the Admiralty's adjacent Vulcan naval reactor test establishment, which was commissioned in 1963. The site's civil reactors were decommissioned in the late 20th century as nuclear technology developed. The final reactor to be taken offline was the PFR in 1994, with the commercial reprocessing of spent nuclear fuel and waste ceasing in 1998. The Admiralty reactors were shut down in 1987 and 2015, with decommissioning expected to begin in 2026. Despite the highly technical nature of the process, this chapter will show that it has heritage at its centre. Adding to the complexity of both, although a product of modernity Dounreay does not represent mass industrialisation. It is, as the site's heritage strategy states, 'a bespoke place; tailored to fit a very particular need'.[10] The site's distinct purpose, alongside its place in the community, help us understand why a strategy for nuclear cultural heritage has been pioneered at this site.

---

[8] Nan Fairbrother, *New Lives, New Landscapes* (London, The Architectural Press, 1970), p. 8.
[9] For a study of Dounreay-associated change see Linda M. Ross, 'Dounreay: Creating the nuclear north', *The Scottish Historical Review*, 100:1 (2021), 82–108; Andrew Perchard, 'A little local difficulty? Deindustrialization and glocalization in a Scottish town', in Steven High, Lachlan MacKinnon, and Andrew Perchard (eds), *The Deindustrialized World: Confronting Ruination in Postindustrial Places* (Vancouver, UBC Press, 2017), p. 290.
[10] DSRL, *Dounreay Heritage Strategy: Delivering a Cultural Legacy Through Decommissioning* (DSRL, 2010), p. 45.

Once decommissioned, the visible remains of Dounreay will not be technical but social. Although the site itself will be largely cleared, its legacy will remain in Thurso, situated nine miles to Dounreay's east, where large housing estates were built to accommodate the atomic workforce. As part of the site clearance process, the distinctive fast breeder reactor containment sphere, alongside all other buildings on site, will be demolished: an act which garners a mixed response ranging from those who believe 'it should stay and it should become some sort of museum' to those who favour the practicality of 'just taking it down'.[11] Under these circumstances the need to address heritage whilst the site is still extant is increasingly time-critical. Tackling this in 2010, Dounreay Site Restoration Limited (DSRL) published the 'Dounreay Heritage Strategy', which sets out the best means of creating a cultural legacy for the site based on evidential, historic, aesthetic, and communal values.[12] 'Dounreay' is responsible for the safe and secure clean-up of the site, with DSRL acting as the site licence company. Since 2021 it has been a wholly-owned subsidiary of the Nuclear Decommissioning Authority (NDA), which funds it to deliver the closure programme, of which heritage is a part.[13] This chapter will put this legacy in context before exploring the ways in which the site's heritage has been captured over the past decade; it will also look to the future, addressing the challenges the country faces as much of its nuclear estate moves from being home to innovative technology to the preserve of heritage within a generation. It sits within a growing body of work addressing the 'expansive concept' of nuclear cultural heritage. This crosses professions and disciplines, and can be broadly defined as 'anything that has come into contact with nuclear science and technology: a vast and hybrid field'.[14] Although the decommissioning of nuclear sites across the country is underway, the Dounreay heritage strategy is the first of its kind in the United Kingdom. As Karly Kehoe and Chris Dalglish argue in their work on history, heritage, and sustainable development in the Highlands, heritage is both 'a living process which comes from and draws on the past' and 'an active and dynamic part of the present': much like decommissioning itself.[15] With this in mind, the very fact that Britain's nuclear heritage approach was pioneered at this site stands as testament to its place in shaping present-day Caithness.

---

[11] David Broughton, interviewed by James Gunn, 14 August 2014; Morris Pottinger, interviewed by James Gunn, 16 September 2013; The James Gunn recordings are available at Nucleus: The Nuclear and Caithness Archive, Wick, ref. P778/8.

[12] DSRL, *Heritage Strategy*, p. v.

[13] www.gov.uk/government/organisations/dounreay/about [accessed 15 June 2022].

[14] Eglė Rindzevičiūtė (ed.), 'Nuclear cultural heritage: Position statement', AHRC Research Networking Project, AH/S001301/1 (Kingston upon Thames, 2019), p. 4.

[15] S. Karly Kehoe and Chris Dalglish, 'History, heritage and sustainable development: A position statement on the Scottish Highlands', *Northern Scotland*, 9:1 (2018), 1–16 at 11.

Creating the nuclear north

To appreciate why heritage is so important to the site's decommissioning, one needs to understand Dounreay and its place within Caithness. Central to this is the sense, outlined perfectly in the strategy, that 'beyond its fences, Dounreay is part of the dynamic growth of Thurso and almost every layer of the town's social and economic existence'.[16] This potential was recognised as soon as the original project was announced in 1954, with the *Caithness Courier* predicting that Dounreay was 'a name destined to become famous', filling 'Caithness homes with a new hope for the future'.[17] Following a national search, the government had chosen the disused Admiralty-owned airfield nine miles west of Thurso because it met a specific set of geologic and geographic requirements, not least that a UKAEA representative considered Caithness 'the most remote locality in the UK', a belief which brought opportunities and challenges.[18] As the government privately conceded, the Dounreay experiment was not without risk. The consequences of a nuclear accident were unknown, the relatively small population in the surrounding area therefore a plus, but still officials questioned 'how remote a "remote" site should be'.[19] Despite this, the available evidence suggests that local reaction was overwhelmingly positive, although as a government establishment exempt from planning protocols it was sited without consultation. This meant that there was no official channel for voicing dissent, which itself impacts on the historic record.[20]

The largely positive reaction was based on its expected economic impact. By the time Dounreay reached its predicted manpower ceiling of 2,500 in 1962, it employed approximately 1,300 local staff from Caithness and Sutherland, and Thurso's population had almost trebled: achieving goals like these was at the forefront of minds in 1954.[21] Whilst the geology and geography provided the ideal location, other factors of influence were also at play: principally those of Sir David Robertson, Conservative MP for Caithness and Sutherland. He was a proponent of a boosted economy stemming from nuclear development, and considered it 'the greatest event that has ever occurred in the Far North of Scotland'.[22] A year before the project's announcement Robertson told parliament that he believed the Highlands would never be able to 'fulfil its destiny' unless there were alternative industries available.[23] This lack of opportunity triggered an 'economic compulsion' which drove his constituents to leave: almost 19 out of every 20 school children

---

[16] DSRL, *Heritage Strategy*, p. 42.

[17] *Caithness Courier*, 10 March 1954, p. 3.

[18] TNA, AB16/1105 E19, E. J. S. Clarke, DAE, to G. F. Humphreys-Davies, HM Treasury, 14 December 1953.

[19] Stan Openshaw, *Nuclear Power: Siting and Safety* (London, Routledge & Kegan Paul, 1986), p. 98.

[20] For more on siting see Ross, 'Dounreay', 92–96.

[21] *The Scotsman*, 16 October 1962, p. 7.

[22] TNA, SUPP16/33, D. Robertson, MP, to D. Sandys, Minster of Supply, 17 December 1953.

[23] Parliamentary Debates (hereafter Parl. Debs.), vol. 511, cols. 2105–220 at 2136, 25 February 1953.

had 'no chance' of remaining. He called for the situation to be tackled with 'imagination and vigour'; one year later he was rejoicing at the decision to site the reactor at Dounreay.[24]

Dounreay's impact was immediate and all-encompassing, playing out in the social make-up of Thurso and its environs. Between 1955 and 1963 the UKAEA constructed 1,007 houses for its employees, situated in the Pennyland and Mount Vernon estates in Thurso and in smaller settlements in Castletown and Scrabster. All town-based development was undertaken within the requirements of the Town and Country Planning (Scotland) Act 1947, which ensured that expansion was controlled in a manner which Joseph Westwood, Secretary of State for Scotland, hoped would provide 'that balanced blend of town and country that is so essential to the whole economy'.[25] Fairbrother believed that these national acts resulted in 'the most advanced planning system in the world', regulating land-use and necessitating planning permission while checking 'irresponsible development'.[26] These protocols ensured Thurso's atomic expansion aligned with the burgh's development plan – a document every planning authority had to produce following the 1947 act – which underwent near-continual revision until it was approved in 1960. This plan had to show expected development and expansion over the next 10 years, determined on the results of physical, economic, and sociological surveying of the district. Extensive in-migration triggered by Dounreay meant that Thurso was one of the few areas in the Highlands and Islands where the act had a significant impact in terms of large-scale planning control.

The UKAEA considered itself a 'reluctant landlord' and had no option but to build accommodation for its workforce due to the lack of available housing in the county. Its in-house architectural team worked alongside local Thurso architect Sinclair Macdonald and Son to deliver the programme, with a focus on inexpensive, quick construction.[27] Accommodating its employees was essential for the operation of the site: without housing, there could be no reactor project in Caithness. Accommodation was provided for those coming into the county, with the size and quality of housing increasing with grade. This polarisation was summarised neatly as being of a 'better class type for higher managerial staff' and being of 'normal council type' for the remaining eligible staff, although the cost per unit and quality was higher than standard local authority builds.[28] Detached and semi-detached timber, brick, and rendered houses of several sizes were built, as were flats and maisonettes. Single employees and apprentices were accommodated in one of the two hostels converted or built for the purpose. Although housing on this scale was a first for the region, the presence of standardised property types, the introduction

[24] Parl. Debs., vol. 524, cols. 844–967 at 871, 1 March 1954.
[25] Parl. Debs., vol. 433, cols. 1713–823 at 1714, 24 February 1947.
[26] Fairbrother, New Lives, p. 161.
[27] TNA, AB16/1427, Authority general notice no. 18/60, housing provision and assistance, 8 June 1960.
[28] TNA, AB8/595 5, D. A. Shirlaw, UKAEA, to R. E. Russell, DHS, 5 April 1954.

of higher-density living, and the use of elements of prefabrication and modern materials resonate with post-war construction across the United Kingdom, in both rural and urban settings. Likewise the application of Radburn principles – such as vehicle access at the rear rather than front of properties – was used to greatest effect in the Mount Vernon estate, where large areas of green space dominated.[29]

Thurso's new citizens were immediately defined as 'atomics', their place of residence as well as their place of work identifying them as newcomers. The term 'atomic' was integral to Dounreay's social 'experiment', a single word with a specific interpretation; it was used exclusively to refer to those who had come 'from the south' to work at the research establishment.[30] Arriving as heterogeneous individuals from different areas, on arrival they became part of a distinct, non-local group. Through their work and housing, they were bestowed with a certain homogeneity unique to the situation and different from anything the Highlands and Islands had ever experienced, particularly in terms of their group permanence.

We do, however, find parallels with other instances of rural development. As Ysanne Holt explains in this volume, expectations were not met in the Forestry Commission settlements at Kielder in Northumbria. People were 'dumped ... in the hilly, exposed, isolated district' with below-par housing and a lack of amenities.[31] With Dounreay, we find similarities born of location. One year after the site commenced operation, *The Scotsman* reported that the scientific and industrial staff who were 'recruited in the south' had to be settled in what was, for the majority, 'a very strange environment'.[32] By situating its fast reactor establishment in 'remote' Caithness, the Authority had accepted 'difficulties at which the ordinary industrial company might boggle'.[33] These ranged from the 'rigours of the Thurso wind' to the expense of contracting removal firms to transport belongings to the far north.[34] Thus, in addition to housing, a suite of incentives were developed to attract and retain staff. These included promotion opportunities, secondment positions, recreation facilities, and financial concessions for travel south, with the hope that these would offset the financial and psychological considerations of such a move. In contrast to the 'discontent' of Kielder's residents, the Dounreay experiment was a success.

As early as 1956, the nuclear had become part of daily life in Thurso. *The Manchester Guardian* reported that in the burgh, 'atomic energy is in every sense a bread and butter affair'; this modern source of employment had quickly found

---

[29] Eugenie Ladner Birch, 'Radburn and the American planning movement', *Journal of the American Planning Association*, 46:4 (1980), 122–151 at 139.

[30] R. D. Nicol, 'Caithness and Dounreay, 1954–1964' (unpublished history, 1977), p. 26.

[31] See Holt, Chapter 11, this volume, p. 245.

[32] National Records of Scotland (hereafter NRS), DD12/2597, newspaper clipping: *The Scotsman*, 10 August 1959.

[33] NRS, DD12/2597.

[34] TNA, AB16/4649, Note by D. A. Shirlaw, DAE, 27 July 1954; TNA AB16/1398 E18/1, UKAEA Group Secretaries' 7th conference: note by D. S. Mitchell.

its place alongside the county's traditional primary industries of agriculture and fishing.[35] From 1949, the Forestry Commission provided additional employment, with a variety of experimental plantations designed to test growth in less-than-optimal conditions.[36] Like the land or sea, atomic energy had become a means of sustaining life in the burgh through occupation, with myriad opportunities arising from the expansion of 'atomland', 'atom town', and 'atomic city'.[37] In June 1959 Sir David Robertson summarised this impact, stating that 'children of the farmer, crofter and fisherman are adapting themselves and taking to industry like ducks to water', a positive step in the UKAEA's aim to increase the local labour employed onsite.[38] In 1956 Dounreay works manager Arthur Parry announced that 'the time would come when the younger generation of Caithness would control and operate the atomic station', with the UKAEA implementing a series of policies designed to reduce the proportion of imported staff.[39] This included the elimination of the outside recruitment of all industrial and 'basic' non-industrial staff, such as scientific assistants, assistant experimental officers, and clerical officers.[40] Central to this was the provision of enhanced training facilities; the UKAEA offered further education from 1956, culminating in the opening of Thurso Technical College in 1959. Building on an increasingly technical curriculum at Thurso High School, where, because of the new courses on offer, 'a larger proportion of children [tended] to study science', the college provided qualifications in technical and scientific subjects.[41] It also catered for secretarial examinations, with Caithnessian Christina Munro starting work as a shorthand typist in Dounreay in 1957.[42] Rather than give up work upon marriage as was expected, Christina and hundreds like her continued in their employment onsite. As the local press commented, 'more than anything else, [Dounreay] provided openings for married women who were glad of the opportunities'.[43] Once the preserve of agricultural traffic and day-trippers, the improved road passing the site soon became subject to the far north's first modern rush-hour as a fleet of buses carried the workforce home at shift-change: a practice which continues today.

It was during the initial phase of Dounreay's development, between the 1954 siting decision and the 1966 announcement that the site was the chosen location

---

[35] *The Manchester Guardian*, 16 October 1956, p. 12.

[36] John McInnes, 'The county of Caithness', in John S. Smith (ed.), *The Third Statistical Account of Scotland: The County of Caithness* (Edinburgh, Scottish Academic Press, 1988), p. 20.

[37] *John O'Groat Journal*, 27 May 1960, p. 2; National Library of Scotland, Moving Image Archive, T1126, *Atom Town* (1966); George Gunn, *The Province of the Cat* (Laxay, Islands Book Trust, 2015), p. 217.

[38] Parl. Debs., vol. 606, cols. 197–322 at 263, 3 June 1959.

[39] *John O'Groat Journal*, 3 August 1956, p. 4.

[40] Robert Hurst, 'The viability of Dounreay report' (UKAEA, 1959), p. 7.

[41] TNA, AB61/68, D. K. Sutherland, 'The educational impact of Dounreay', *The Scottish Educational Journal*, February (1959); *John O'Groat Journal*, 14 October 1960, p. 6.

[42] Anonymous participant (pseudonym used), interviewed by Linda M. Ross, 5 September 2017.

[43] *John O'Groat Journal*, 7 February 1958, p. 4.

for the government's prototype fast reactor, that nuclear development became an indelible part of the far north of Scotland. At the time of writing, a change equally as significant as DERE's arrival is underway: the site will reach its interim care and maintenance end state in the 2030s, at which point decommissioning will be considered complete. Yet the site will not reach its 'final end point' until 2333, when the site can be released for all uses.[44] In the interim, radioactive decay of stored waste will occur during 300 years of passive remediation, which will see nuclear temporalities stretch beyond the plant's commissioning to decommissioning lifecycle. This time period offers an opportunity to consider situations which were not at the forefront of UKAEA thought in the 1950s. The long-term 'deep time' consequences of waste disposal were not planned for; the rise of anti-nuclear awareness and environmentalism was not anticipated; and the effects of a series of health and safety incidents at the plant could not be predicted. All of these aspects contribute to the site's complex history, the study of which needs to combine its social and cultural impact with the growing field of toxic heritage which, as part of the wider heritage of the Anthropocene, confronts 'the landscapes, residues, health impacts, and histories of toxicity and their impacts on affected communities'.[45] When 'cleared', the site will contain low- and intermediate-level waste in near-site and near-surface storage repositories, in accordance with Scottish Government policy: what Tatiana Kasperski and Anna Storm would perceptively consider 'an anthropogenic wound or scar of our shared living environment that we have to care about'.[46]

The 'Faustian bargain' of nuclear energy

The Dounreay narrative is contested, polarised between those who are fiercely critical and those who are intensely protective of the site. This tension is at its most pronounced in the debate over nuclear waste and contamination, a topic subject to increased scrutiny following safety breaches in the late 1960s and 1970s.[47] The matter was compounded by the 1976 report on 'Nuclear Power and the Environment', which termed the acceptance of risk in return for abundant electricity 'the Faustian bargain'.[48] One year later, some of the report's concerns were realised by Dounreay's most serious accident: an explosion in its poorly audited waste shaft. The explosion blew the concrete cap off the shaft and scattered 'hot' radioactive

---

[44] Dounreay Site Restoration Ltd, *Environmental Statement: Phase 3 (2018 – Interim End State), vol. 1 – Non Technical Summary* (2018); these dates are liable to change as decommissioning progresses.
[45] https://toxicheritage.com/ [accessed 29 September 2021].
[46] Tatiana Kasperski and Anna Storm, 'Eternal care: Nuclear waste as toxic legacy and future fantasy', *Geschichte und Gesellschaft*, 46 (2020), 682–705 at 684.
[47] For more on the evolution of the fast breeder reactor programme see Markku Lehtonen and Jenny Lieu, 'The rise and fall of the fast breeder reactor technology in the UK: Between engineering "dreams" and economic "realities"?', project report (University of Sussex, SPRU, 2011).
[48] Brian Flowers, 'Nuclear power and the environment', Cmnd. 6618, (London, HMSO, 1976), p. 85.

particles onto the foreshore and surrounding areas; it was thought to have been caused by sodium and potassium wastes reacting to groundwater which had seeped through rock fissures.[49] Originally sunk to extract rubble from the construction of the site's effluent discharge pipeline in the 1950s, it was unfit for purpose and has long been considered 'one of biggest clean-up challenges in the world'.[50] While this process is party to the relative transparency of decommissioning, the full story of the 1977 explosion, reported in a UKAEA press release as a 'minor incident at solid waste facility', was not revealed until June 1995, when it emerged that contaminated materials had been recovered outwith the site boundary, impacting already precarious public confidence in nuclear communications.[51]

The Dounreay heritage strategy recognises the shaft explosion as a watershed event, evidencing changed attitudes towards the threats posed by the nuclear industry, its operating procedures and accident reporting.[52] From a heritage perspective, responses to this one event can help contextualise the complexity of feeling surrounding any of the site's reported historic safety management errors. Wick-born Donnie Harper, who joined Dounreay as a health physics monitor in 1957, reflected the view of many employed at the site with regard to the disposing of licensed waste down the shaft: 'we were all doing what we were asked to do and what we were expected to do and we were doing a bloody good job'.[53] Likewise Brian Hart, who moved to Caithness from Southampton and worked in various roles in the fuel and maths groups, recognised that 'the place was thought of as a mess, there are particles coming on, on Sandside beach, and possibly along the coast … but if you weigh that against the amount of good that was done, it's no doubt in my mind it was a worthwhile experiment'.[54] Some Caithness locals who did not work at Dounreay took a relaxed view, with farmer Morris Pottinger believing the aftermath of the explosion was 'a big hoo-ha'.[55] Pottinger, who bought farmland at Dounreay in 1953 before selling it to the UKAEA and renting it back, explained away the significance of the accident in farming terms: 'you get the same thing if you are charging a battery for a tractor and the top is off and you are stupid enough to take the plugs off before you put the top on … unbelievable explosion from a wee battery'. John Young, a local councillor and farmer, recalled former Dounreay director Clifford Blumfield claiming that he had told the UKAEA 'not to put stuff down that shaft' but 'was overruled'.[56] Young was adamant that the accident caused

[49] DSRL, *Heritage Strategy*, p. 21.

[50] *The Herald*, 25 January 2007.

[51] George Monbiot, 'Dounreay's catalogue of idiocy is a cautionary tale of nuclear danger', *The Guardian*, 12 September 2006, www.theguardian.com/commentisfree/2006/sep/12/comment.politics [accessed 30 September 2021].

[52] DSRL, *Heritage Strategy*, pp. 36, 40.

[53] Donnie Harper, interviewed by James Gunn, 18 June 2014.

[54] Brian Hart, interviewed by James Gunn, 17 February 2015.

[55] Morris Pottinger, interviewed by James Gunn.

[56] John Young OBE, interviewed by James Gunn, 6 March 2013.

a lot of damage, but considered it 'quite wrong to blame the people who were there, for that. It was others who did it'. Although not Dounreay employees, both he and Pottinger were concerned about the reputational damage. Pottinger was exasperated that 'a lot of folk will not accept' that it was a chemical rather than nuclear explosion; Young was conscious that 'it gave those who were critical of Dounreay an opportunity to use that against them'.

This sentiment is best summed up in the unapologetically pro-nuclear history of the site written by local author Iain Sutherland in 1990. Sutherland recounts how 'until the anti-nuclear movement forced the industry on the defensive, optimism and self-confidence pervaded Dounreay, as in spite of all the frustrations and difficulties with research, all problems had been solved, and there was pride in the achievements'.[57] By contrast, Thurso-born author, poet, and playwright George Gunn, who turned 21 in 1977, saw the accident as a turning point: the explosion and its denial 'put an end to any slight faith I had in the nuclear "project"', causing the 'beginning of the unravelling of whatever tapestry I had woven of Atomic City'.[58] Gunn is not alone, and stands at the sharp end of a wave of criticism started by a lone voice in 1953. In a public letter addressed to Thurso's Provost John Sinclair and read out to the assembled Thurso town council, artist, activist, and Scottish independence campaigner Wendy Wood expressed alarm over the potential hazards of establishing a nuclear reactor in Caithness. The *Aberdeen Evening Express* reported that the letter contained warnings of ' "sociological disturbances" and "radio-active fish" '.[59] Paraphrasing Wood, Sir David Robertson wrote that she 'pictures the horrors and dangers which will overtake the people of Caithness', dismissing her apprehension as 'haverings'.[60] Wood is now lauded as 'a human rights campaigner before people knew what human rights were'.[61] With Dounreay, she pioneered anti-nuclear activism long before ground was broken at Scotland's first nuclear site; her opposition to the atomic project closely aligned with her vociferous support for Scottish nationalism. Hers is one of the few recorded instances of early opposition to the Dounreay project, something which gained traction though local and worldwide events including the increasing number of radioactive particles found on the seabed near Dounreay and international accidents at Three Mile Island (1979) and Chernobyl (1986).[62] Anti-Dounreay sentiment has a complex history in itself, but the strength of feeling is succinctly conveyed by author

[57] Iain Sutherland, *Dounreay: An Experimental Reactor Establishment* (Wick, Iain Sutherland, 1990), p. 116.
[58] Gunn, *Province*, pp. 256–257.
[59] *Aberdeen Evening Express*, 19 December 1953, p. 8.
[60] TNA, SUPP16/33, D. Robertson, MP, to D. Sandys, MP, 21 December 1953.
[61] Hamish MacPherson, 'Wendy Wood: A Scottish patriot to her very core', *The National*, 21 April 2020, www.thenational.scot/news/18392801.wendy-wood-scottish-patriot-core/ [accessed 12 September 2021].
[62] For more on the discovery of radioactive particles see Rob Edwards, 'Lid blown off Dounreay's lethal secret', *New Scientist*, 23 June 1995, www.newscientist.com/article/mg14619830-600-lid-blown-off-dounreays-lethal-secret/#ixzz74TxILNwX [accessed 30 September 2021].

and environmental campaigner George Monbiot, who considered the site's operation as a 'catalogue of idiocy' which served to highlight the inherent dangers of
nuclear power.[63] Dounreay's heritage strategy does not shy away from this debate,
recognising it as simultaneously factual, rational, and emotional. These issues, it
states, 'affect how people value and judge Dounreay'.[64]

The challenge of nuclear waste

This discourse sits alongside the narrative of opportunity which has always been
part of the Dounreay story: from increased prospects during Dounreay's early
years to its present decommissioning role as 'an inadvertent growth centre' which
continues to employ upwards of 1,000 people directly, with a similar number in
supporting supply chain roles.[65] As early as 1961 rumours that the UKAEA was
to abandon the fast breeder project were circulating.[66] Such concerns reflected the
new-found anxiety caused by an enlarged population now largely dependent on one
employer; something brought to the fore following the 1988 announcement that the
site was to be run-down and closed, with the PFR funded until the end of financial year 1993–1994 and the reprocessing of spent reactor fuel until 1996–1997.
Although the fast breeder reactor technology developed at Dounreay proved viable,
the fact that commercial applications were not developed coupled with the low-cost
availability of uranium meant that the technology was uneconomic.[67] This news
was met with the campaigning of the Dounreay Action Group, which called for
Caithnessians to 'support Dounreay – it's your future'.[68] The site's future, therefore,
was as much a consideration at the end of the project as it was at the start.

As one study observes, 'Dounreay as it stands today is a result of fluctuating
strategies, timescales, and structures'.[69] The Dounreay decommissioning plan, originally set out in 2000, has evolved through several iterations with the eventual goal
of site remediation, by which point the site's sealed waste stores will be passively
safe and require no human intervention. In the UK, radioactive waste management
is a devolved issue, with responsibility for policy, in the Dounreay case, resting
with the Scottish Government. There is no High Level Waste (HLW) in Scotland,
with the term Higher Activity Waste (HAW) used to encompass Intermediate Level

---

[63] Monbiot, 'Dounreay'.

[64] DSRL, *Heritage Strategy*, p. 43.

[65] Niall G. MacKenzie, 'Chucking buns across the fence? Governmental planning and regeneration
projects in the Scottish Highland economy, 1945–82' (PhD thesis, Glasgow, 2008), p. 215; https://doun
reaycareers.com/benefits-and-rewards/ [accessed 13 September 2021].

[66] *John O'Groat Journal*, 24 February 1961, p. 4.

[67] Parl. Debs., vol. 137, cols. 1302–11, 21 July 1988.

[68] William A. Paterson, *50 Years of Dounreay* (Wick, North of Scotland Newspapers, 2008), p. 80.

[69] Cara Mulholland, Paul W. Chan, and Kate Canning, 'Deconstructing social value in
decommissioning: Industrial heritage at Dounreay, UK', in Ani Raiden, Martin Loosemore, Andrew
King, and Chris Gorse, *Social Value in Construction* (Abingdon, Routledge, 2019), p. 194.

Waste (ILW) and certain types of Low Level Waste (LLW).[70] Spent reactor fuel is transferred from Dounreay to Cumbria for consolidation at Sellafield's plutonium management facility. Much of this fuel will be reprocessed into its component parts of uranium and plutonium for re-use and waste, which will be placed into storage (alongside remaining unprocessed fuel) pending a decision to dispose of it in a still-to-be-sited Geological Disposal Facility (GDF).[71] Here, Scottish and UK government policies diverge. The Scottish Government does not support deep geological disposal of radioactive waste, as Richard Lochhead, former Cabinet Secretary for Rural Affairs and the Environment, argued in 2012, 'this out of sight out of mind policy should not extend to Scotland'.[72] In-line with the Scottish National Party's anti-nuclear stance, Lochhead was firm in his belief that the government could not impose such a facility on any community. Much had changed since the community's enthusiasm for the nuclear imposition 60 years earlier.

This chapter has outlined both pro- and anti-Dounreay sentiment with the aim of showing that both are part of its complex past, present, and future. The distinction between the two is far from black-and-white and one issue unites them: the ambiguity surrounding 'closure'. Arguably, neither those in favour nor against nuclear power can be completely satisfied with the site's run-down. For the former, although decommissioning provides jobs, it is effectively a situation where people are working themselves out of a living.[73] For the latter, although it signals the reduction of accident-associated risk and the end of waste production, it means the storage and management of material which will remain radioactive for hundreds of thousands of years, depending on the radionuclides contained within. As Kasperski and Storm relate, keeping this matter isolated while remembering where it is as society and language inevitably change, is 'one of the most fundamental challenges of our time'.[74] Speaking to this uncertainty, the NDA acknowledges that 'indefinite, long-term storage leaves a burden of security risks and proliferation sensitivities for future generations to manage'.[75] Its aim, it states, is 'simple': the clean-up of its legacy sites and their release for 'beneficial reuse'. For all its 'simplicity', the

[70] High Level Waste is nuclear waste which may rise significantly in temperature due to its radioactivity. Less than 1 per cent of waste is in this category, and it is produced as a liquid by-product of reprocessing spent reactor fuel. Six per cent of waste is considered Intermediate Level Waste. It does not produce a lot of heat and is mainly comprised of reactor components, graphite, and sludges. Low Level Waste makes up 94 per cent of nuclear waste, including items such as metal, paper, or plastics, alongside waste from hospitals and universities. For further details see https://ukinventory.nda.gov.uk/about-radioactive-waste/what-is-radioactivity/what-are-the-main-waste-categories/ [accessed 15 June 2022].
[71] NDA, 'Strategy: Effective from March 2021' (NDA, 2021).
[72] www.no2nuclearpower.org.uk/scotland/scotlands-radioactive-waste-management-policy/ [accessed 16 September 2021].
[73] Dounreay is dedicated to 'supporting staff to plan their futures beyond decommissioning and supporting the community to diversify its economic base', DSRL, *Dounreay 2021: Your Guide to Scotland's Centre of Excellence in Nuclear Decommissioning* (DSRL, 2021), p. 16.
[74] Kasperski and Storm, 'Eternal care', 683.
[75] NDA, 'Strategy', p. 60.

NDA recognises the unpredictability of its task, listing changes in social attitudes, science, regulation and the supply chain over time as among the trials it faces. The UK is not alone in this challenge. The Organisation for Economic Co-operation and Development (OECD) Nuclear Energy Agency's Radioactive Waste Management Committee tackled the problem in a landmark 2019 report. Responsible radioactive waste management, it states, requires the preservation of records, knowledge and memory (RK&M), handing down a message which must be kept 'interpretable, meaningful, credible and usable over time'.[76] It lists memory institutions (archives, libraries, and museums) and culture, education, and art as two of the nine broad approaches it recommends for preserving RK&M. Most importantly, alongside impeccable record-keeping, the NDA is making valuable progress in building relationships with organisations and individuals dedicated to retaining its cultural heritage. The remainder of chapter will examine how these principles are being applied at Dounreay.

Nuclear cultural heritage: from the past to the future

For the nuclear industry, cultural heritage is therefore preserved and communicated for reasons that go beyond a desire to record and understand the technological, political, and social past. It is a 'process during which social values and knowledges are shaped and transmitted to the future'.[77] Applying this to the nuclear context foregrounds the role of cultural heritage in preventing the loss of knowledge: information about nuclear technology and its toxic legacy will be passed on in ways which far exceed the capabilities of data management systems. Reflecting an increasing public awareness of this, a recent radio feature explored the question of how to leave an unambiguous warning message 'for a society which may be utterly different from our own', where even the recognisable nuclear trefoil warning symbol may have lost its meaning.[78] Pioneering work in this regard has been done by the French nuclear agency Andra, whose Manche disposal facility (CSM) in Normandy is the first radioactive waste disposal facility to enter the post-closure monitoring stage. Its Memory for Future Generations programme has resulted in a comprehensive system based on technical and regulatory information and the important role of local residents in ensuring that nuclear memory is passed on through the generations.[79] When Dounreay is considered alongside this, the potential of the community to act as nuclear tradition bearers becomes clear.

---

[76] NEA, *Preservation of Records, Knowledge and Memory (RK&M) Across Generations: Final Report of the RK&M Initiative* (Paris, OECD Publishing, 2021), p. 13.

[77] Rindzevičiūtė, 'Nuclear cultural heritage', p. 7.

[78] BBC Radio 4, 'The Nuclear Priesthood', broadcast 7 September 2021.

[79] https://international.andra.fr/index.php/existing-facilities/manche-disposal-facility-csm   [accessed 30 September 2021].

In Caithness, Britain's nuclear programme had a transformative societal effect which extended beyond the quantifiable impacts of an increased population, reduced unemployment, and an expanded built environment towards impacts which are less tangible. This long-term impact is best described by former Thurso teacher Heather McLean, who explained that people felt 'great pride' at 'what had been achieved at Dounreay'. Decommissioning, however, has triggered 'disillusionment' and a need to review the life of the community; with the ultimate effect of 'having to find another identity'.[80] This situation, in terms of the closure of industry, is well-explored by scholars investigating deindustrialisation worldwide. Dounreay was unique in the context of the Highlands and Islands, but common ground can be found elsewhere with other industries, particularly mining and shipbuilding, where narratives of community-building and identity are bound up with governance and economy in the post-war years.[81] Industrial restructuring impacted on the 'existential identity as well as the material well-being of workers and communities affected'; the 'Clydesider' identity was 'embedded in life and work in the shipbuilding community'; and 'the destruction of working-class communities following the contraction of industry' shaped a Scottish narrative.[82] Much of this was happening whilst Dounreay was on the ascendancy in an area where conventional industrial class divisions did not necessarily exist. During this period, it was argued that the overarching Caithness 'character' was bound up with agricultural employment; the identity of its people rested on a historic tie to the land which, according to local councillor Robin Sinclair, accounted for its 'strength'.[83] Sinclair utilised this to demonstrate that the Caithness character would survive the onslaught of 'new people and new occupations': essentially the introduction of a professional and scientific class to the area. Three years later, the character of Caithness's 'crofting stock' was being used to attract further industry, with the local authorities of Caithness and Sutherland touting the crofting class as 'well educated and extremely adaptable'.[84] Local labour was drawn from this group, comprising people who were 'accustomed to turning their hands to any task which comes their way and have an inherent manual dexterity not normally found amongst the

[80] BBC Radio Scotland, 'Our Story: Dounreay', series 11, episode 3, broadcast 15 August 2017.

[81] For more see studies of deindustrialisation including Shelley Condratto and Ewan Gibbs, 'After industrial citizenship: Adapting to precarious employment in the Lanarkshire coalfield, Scotland, and Sudbury Hardrock Mining, Canada', *Labour/Le Travail*, 81 (2018), 213–239; Ewan Gibbs, *Coal Country: The Meaning and Memory of Deindustrialization in Postwar Scotland* (London, University of London Press, 2021).

[82] Jim Phillips, Valerie Wright, and Jim Tomlinson, *Deindustrialisation and the Moral Economy in Scotland since 1955* (Edinburgh, Edinburgh University Press), pp. 36, 154; Andy Clark, ' "Stealing our identity and taking it over to Ireland": Deindustrialization, resistance, and gender in Scotland', in Steven High, Lachlan MacKinnon, and Andrew Perchard (eds), *The Deindustrialized World: Confronting Ruination in Postindustrial Places* (Vancouver, UBC Press, 2017), pp. 332–335.

[83] *John O'Groat Journal*, 25 November 1960, p. 3.

[84] TNA, AB61/68, Outline of statement to be made with reference to the visit of industrialists, 13 May 1963.

classes from which labour is drawn in the industrial area'. This was something also espoused by the Crofters Commission, which praised the associated work of crofters as providing 'an opportunity in the Highlands of working towards a new form of industrial society which will be healthier and more stable than any community which is completely urbanised': creating a specific form of industrial life in the region.[85]

Dounreay, via decommissioning, now represents a form of deindustrialisation which, as outlined above, cannot be adequately compared with the loss of traditional industry. A more apt comparison from the Highlands and Islands can be found in the closure of the British Aluminium Company's Invergordon smelter in 1981. Andrew Perchard's insightful exploration of the topic reveals that local narratives of closure 'developed in contradistinction to lowland Scotland'.[86] Here, the 'significance of locality and regionality was greater ... than in the predominantly occupational and national narratives seen in the coal, steel, and shipbuilding communities'.[87] This partly resulted from the 'regional motif of Highland otherness and peripheralization'; similarly, much of the Dounreay narrative is bound up with the UKAEA considering it an 'unconventional' location, which itself taps into the dialogue of Caithness as 'a place apart': the 'Lowlands beyond the Highlands'.[88] Like Caithness, Dounreay is different: for one, the lengthy process of decommissioning means that although the spectre of closure looms large, it has not yet happened. As with Invergordon and the smelter closure, Dounreay has created and will continue to create its own situation-specific narrative.

At the heart of this is the construction – and current deconstruction – of Jeff Hughes's 'nuclear citizen': whether directly affected or not, the Caithness population became part of Britain's nuclear story.[89] Central to this is a sense of a prevailing collective memory among those who experienced Dounreay's development. This reflects Maurice Halbwachs's belief that the memories which predominate are those which are commonly agreed upon.[90] This can be seen in the repetition of stories which 'were heard', 'rumoured', or joked about: the DFR sphere, for example, was shaped like a golf ball so it could be rolled into the sea in the event of disaster; in shops there was 'one price for atomics and one price for locals'; an

---

[85] 'Crofters Commission Report for 1966', p. 11, quoted in James Hunter, *The Claim of Crofting: The Scottish Highlands and Islands, 1930–1990* (Edinburgh, Mainstream, 1991), p. 129. As Hunter notes, there were few industries providing large levels of employment in the Highlands and Islands: Dounreay, the Fort William pulp mill, and the later smelter in Invergordon were the exceptions.

[86] Perchard, 'A little local difficulty?', p. 288.

[87] Perchard, 'A little local difficulty?', p. 307.

[88] TNA, AB16/1638 E27, Minutes of Scottish physical planning meeting, 16 October 1953; Donald Omand, 'Introduction to the county', in Donald Omand (ed.), *The Caithness Book*, rev. edn (Inverness, Highland Printers Ltd., 1973), p. xv.

[89] Jeff Hughes, 'What is British nuclear culture? Understanding *Uranium 235*', *British Journal for the History of Science*, 45:4 (2012), 495–518 at 518.

[90] Lynn Abrams, *Oral History Theory*, 2nd edn (Abingdon, Routledge, 2016), p. 96; collective memory is common in industrial (and deindustrialisation) studies – for an example see Gibbs, *Coal Country*, p. 16.

engineering apprenticeship at Dounreay would guarantee you a professional foot in the door anywhere in the world; the waste shaft is commonly termed 'infamous' or 'notorious' in personal testimony and newspaper coverage alike.[91] In a sense, such shared recollections have become part of a new Caithnessian folklore; passed via the oral tradition identified as one of Caithness's 'own forms of cultural expression'.[92]

Heritage strategy: a nuclear first

It is clear to see why Britain's first nuclear heritage strategy was devised at this site, where 'nuclear fission and social fusion' was at its most marked, impacting not only on employment but on identity.[93] The genesis of the strategy came in 2007, following discussions between Historic Scotland and the UKAEA about Dounreay's legacy. Unlike many industrial closures, which often involved a 'grab-and-run' approach to saving heritage documents or objects amid 'a "body count" of lost factories and jobs', Dounreay's lengthy decommissioning has allowed for a more considered approach.[94] Addressing questions such as those relating to the preservation of buildings, structures, or objects within the context of contamination; the preservation and display of artefacts, records, and photographs; and the historic status of a site which may not be publicly visitable for generations, the strategy provides a framework for a complex case of NDA-funded heritage protection. Developed in accordance with best practice methods of conservation management, it is 'founded on a robust understanding of the site and its cultural values and on a clear recognition of the issues and external factors relating to decontamination, waste management and decommissioning'.[95] The strategy was compiled by Atkins Heritage, with contributions from a range of bodies including Historic Scotland, National Museums Scotland (NMS), Caithness Horizons, English Heritage, and, representing the local community, the Dounreay Stakeholder Group. Recognising the magnitude of the task, it saw the appointment of a heritage officer to oversee the implementation of its recommendations, and the formation of the Dounreay Heritage Advisory Panel to ensure that heritage issues receive a focused review.

This chapter began with a discussion of the site's visitor centre, located 500 metres from the nuclear licensed area in the former airfield's control tower.

---

[91] John Macrae, interviewed by James Gunn, 6 February 2013; Anonymous participant (pseudonym used), interviewed by Linda M. Ross, 5 September 2017; Brian Hart, interviewed by James Gunn; David Broughton, interviewed by James Gunn; Alistair Fraser, interviewed by James Gunn, 11 November 2013; Morris Pottinger, interviewed by James Gunn; *The Herald*, 25 January 2007.

[92] James Miller, *Caithness* (London, Skilton and Shaw, 1979), p. 81.

[93] The term 'nuclear fission and social fusion' is taken from the title of an address given by Dounreay's general secretary Donald Carmichael at the World Congress of Public Relations, Venice, in 1961.

[94] Gibbs, *Coal Country*, p. 4; For a full discussion of the process of developing the heritage strategy see James B. Gunn, 'A unique journey in preserving nuclear industrial heritage', in Celia Clark and Carlos A. Brebbia (eds), *Defence Heritage and Future* (Southampton, WIT Press, 2012).

[95] DSRL, *Heritage Strategy*, p. v.

Its closure, mooted in 2001 and finalised with the building's demolition in 2007, offered a new opportunity for engagement with the opening of the Caithness Horizons museum in Thurso in 2008.[96] In a collaboration funded by The Highland Council and the UKAEA, with additional funding from local, national, and international bodies, artefacts related to the Dounreay site were brought together to form a permanent exhibition, the first public exhibition to preserve the history of a nuclear establishment in the UK.[97] Pre-dating the heritage strategy, this partnership paved the way for the display of objects relating to Dounreay's social and cultural history; as work onsite developed this remit has expanded to the site's technical history, with the wall panels and operator desk from the Dounreay materials test reactor (DMTR) forming a display centrepiece following their transfer in 2014. Given the significance of Dounreay, objects for potential museum acquisition are of national interest, with certain retention decisions made in partnership with NMS. Between 2008 and 2021, 448 objects had been collected, with the acquisition programme continuing as decommissioning progresses.[98]

Using the example of the Manhattan Project Preservation Initiative, which developed a system for identifying objects of historic significance, the heritage strategy determined that it 'is technically feasible and desirable to develop and curate a diverse collection of material from Dounreay'.[99] Its structured approach recognises that, taking practical and safety considerations into account, not everything can or should be collected. Radioactivity means that some historically significant material cannot be collected and many items are recorded and photographed before being treated as nuclear waste. As well as visual recording, emphasis is put on the capturing of intangible cultural heritage: 'the practices, representations, expressions, knowledge, skills – as well as the instruments, objects, artefacts and cultural spaces associated therewith – that communities, groups and, in some cases, individuals recognize as part of their cultural heritage'.[100] These aspects are passed from generation to generation, with oral traditions identified as a vehicle of intangible cultural heritage. The NDA itself recognises its importance for the nuclear

[96] Beki Pope, Joanne Howdle, and James Gunn, 'The Dounreay Heritage Partnership Project: An innovative approach to developing successful museum partnership working activities', TICCIH conference paper (2015), p. 4; Caithness Horizons closed in 2019 following financial difficulties. It re-opened in late 2021 under the 'North Coast Visitor Centre' name, operated by High Life Highland on behalf of the Highland Council. Highland Council and DSRL will provide funding for an initial three-year period.
[97] Pope *et al.*, 'Dounreay Heritage', p. 7.
[98] Reflecting an even broader appeal, the DFR control room equipment was jointly acquired by NMS and the Science Museum in 2015. A subsequent review, however, determined that it was more appropriate for ownership to lie with NMS, with the title transferred in 2021; DSRL, 'Dounreay Heritage Initiative 2020/21 annual report' (2021).
[99] DSRL, *Heritage Strategy*, p. 61; as well as the Manhattan Initiative, the strategy compilers looked to other international heritage examples, such as the Musée de l'Atome, housed in a decommissioned reactor containment sphere in Chinon, France (pp. 47–50).
[100] UNESCO, *Basic Texts of the 2003 Convention for the Safeguarding of the Intangible Cultural Heritage* (Paris, UNESCO, 2020), p. 5.

industry 'given its unique evolution, practices, peculiarities, sensitivity, industry language and its workforce existence'.[101] In a situation where little physical evidence will remain, it is fitting that the Dounreay heritage strategy prioritises oral history as a key way of retaining evidential material about the site, building on work previously collected in an 'ad hoc' manner.[102]

By formalising the recording of oral history, DSRL is proactively capturing information that encompasses all phases of the site's history, relating not only to occupation-based knowledge, but also to social and cultural aspects. The opportunity to record personal testimony with the site's heritage officer has been embedded into the protocol for staff leaving the site with the recordings and transcripts made available for public consultation, moving its value beyond the requirements of the nuclear industry. Recognising that it needed to keep its records securely for an indefinite period of time, the NDA opened Nucleus: The Nuclear and Caithness Archive in Wick in 2017. This unique facility serves as the repository for both the UK civil nuclear industry and the county of Caithness.[103] As part of its socio-economic remit, the NDA considered sites within four regions where nuclear closures were predicted to have extensive impact, with Caithness selected as the area most likely to benefit from a facility which, at present, employs approximately 70 people. Wick, situated 20 miles from Thurso on Caithness's east coast, did not experience the latter's Dounreay-related population and economic growth, largely due to distance. Nucleus will eventually contain the records from across the NDA's estate, with Dounreay's records – including almost a third of a million photographs and 200 tonnes of documents – already transferred: a milestone that will contribute to the site retaining its evidential value, a heritage strategy priority. The full transfer of records from sites to Nucleus is expected to take several years, with the aim of the preservation of records relating to decommissioning, waste storage, and historic NDA material. While this is underway, its nuclear records are largely inaccessible; the practicalities of an archive with an operational and business focus as well as public interest are still to be played out. As a partnership facility, the site-related oral histories are deposited with the Caithness Archive, operated by High Life Highland. This makes them immediately accessible, foregrounding their place in Caithness's heritage and serving as an exemplar of the enduring connection between the nuclear industry and the community.

At the time of writing, Dounreay continues to innovate in capturing site heritage, with a community engagement project set to be trialled to enhance the photographic record. By gathering a group of former employees to discuss and review

[101] NDA, UK Nuclear Heritage Initiative, 'Tier C – Completing Intangible Cultural Heritage Site Reports: A Guide for Industry Authors on the Report Structure and Content of Intangible Cultural Heritage Site Record (ICHSR) Reports', version 0–07C (working draft, 2021), p. 9.
[102] DSRL, *Heritage Strategy*, p. 71.
[103] For further details see www.gov.uk/government/case-studies/nda-archive [accessed 30 September 2021]; the NDA secured Restore as its commercial partner to manage the nuclear archive, working together to achieve 'Place of Deposit' status.

images – the pilot will look at housing and recreation – the project will tap into Dounreay's strong social network as a way of supplementing the official record, with the possibility of recording personal testimonies. Central to this, as the heritage officer explains, is 'a sense of camaraderie, social inclusion and increased well-being' which will help retirees see that their working lives still have value.[104] Here, heritage becomes social action: a form of 'cultural capital' where collective and individual memory influences community and identity.[105] As a joint project (between the NDA, DSRL, Restore Digital and High Life Highland), this demonstrates the value of a partnership approach in nuclear heritage. More pointedly, although driven by the institutional heritage initiative, it speaks to the role of non-nuclear industry heritage professionals and nuclear workers in addressing nuclear cultural heritage from the bottom-up. This is something explored in Eglė Rindzevičiūtė's study of nuclear energy in Soviet and post-Soviet Russia, 'as nuclear power left the laboratories, plants and factories and entered a very different symbolic space: the museum'.[106] Although writing about a different context, Rindzevičiūtė notes neatly that 'the nuclear industry acquired its social past' as a generation of retired nuclear workers 'wanted to secure its place in history by making sure that their stories, and also material culture, were preserved and made available'.[107] This relationship is indicative of nuclear cultural heritage's complex positioning at the intersection of state, industrial, and public realms.

It is this juncture which makes the makes the nuclear industry so well-situated for collaborative working. Indeed, projects led by other organisations are essential in representing a history which resonates beyond the bounds of the nuclear authority. These relationships are crucial in ensuring that a critical heritage approach is foregrounded, in which cultural heritage is emphasised as a political, cultural, and social phenomenon and the relationship between top-down and bottom-up approaches to heritage are investigated.[108] Through this process, heritage is democratised as official or elite narratives make way for 'unofficial voices': something which Jonathan Hogg has written extensively about in regard to British nuclear culture.[109] Returning to Dounreay, the heritage strategy identified several opportunities falling outwith the budget and expertise of DSRL and the NDA, enabling 'heritage organisations to take the lead in implementing substantial elements' of the strategy: making room for studies which move research beyond

---

[104] James Gunn, Dounreay and NDA heritage officer, personal correspondence with Linda M. Ross, 2021.
[105] Rodney Harrison, 'What is heritage?', in *Understanding the Politics of Heritage* (Manchester, Manchester University Press, 2010), pp. 38–39.
[106] Eglė Rindzevičiūtė, 'Nuclear energy in Russia: From future technology to cultural heritage' (preprint of essay published in *Tiltas*, November [2016]), p. 1; see also Eglė Rindzevičiūtė, 'Nuclear power as cultural heritage in Russia', *Slavic Review*, 80:4 (2022), 839–862.
[107] Rindzevičiūtė, 'Nuclear energy', p. 4.
[108] Kynan Gentry and Laurajane Smith, 'Critical heritage studies and the legacies of the late-twentieth century heritage canon', *International Journal of Heritage Studies*, 25:11 (2019), 1148–1168 at 1149.
[109] Jonathan Hogg, *British Nuclear Culture: Official and Unofficial Narratives in the Long 20th* Century (London, Bloomsbury, 2016), pp. 8–11.

the bounds of the nuclear authority.[110] These included academic engagement, with the present author completing an AHRC-funded PhD with the University of the Highlands and Islands and Historic Environment Scotland in 2019. Undertaken independently of the NDA and DSRL – but with their welcome support – this established the extent of Dounreay's impact, revealing its role in creating a mid-20th-century Highland counter-narrative of migration and modernity far removed from traditional discourses of rural depopulation.[111] As a first-of-its-kind in-depth study of one element of the United Kingdom's nuclear estate, its social and cultural focus offers an insight into the rich research potential of atomic sites. In this, and the work of independent networks, we find a significant nuclear research agenda which is increasing in momentum.[112]

Dounreay's sphere: 'a bizarre thing at the end of the land'[113]

This chapter has reinforced the value of capturing heritage in a situation where the onsite remains of a project will be limited. Whilst Dounreay's presence will continue in Caithness – where all houses built by the UKAEA continue to be occupied – all buildings at Dounreay will be recorded and demolished.[114] Whilst the structures onsite number hundreds, the remainder of this chapter will concentrate on Dounreay's one immediately recognisable structure, which informs the site's logo and the identity of the wider area.[115] The Dounreay 'sphere' forms the containment vessel for the DFR, and was constructed to mitigate the effects of an explosion because of the project's 'unknowns'.[116] Sutherland-born Alistair Fraser, who worked at Dounreay in catering, construction, and communications from his teenage years until retirement, considered the sphere a symbol of 'Scottish engineering at its very best', constructed without computers or 'fancy laser gadgetry'.[117] In 1966, *The Illustrated London News* reported that Dounreay's 'pale green sphere of steel' had 'become one of the symbols of British science'.[118] Constructed from bright, modern materials, it stood out in a new landscape for a new, clean industry; the

---

[110] DSRL, *Heritage Strategy*, p. iv.

[111] Linda M. Ross, 'Nuclear fission and social fusion: The impact of the Dounreay Experimental Research Establishment on Caithness, 1953–1966' (PhD thesis, Dornoch, 2019).

[112] Projects include the AHRC research network 'Nuclear Cultural Heritage: From Knowledge to Practice' (completed) and 'NuSPACES – Nuclear Spaces: Communities, Materialities and Locations of Nuclear Cultural Heritage' https://nuspaces.eu/about/ [accessed 12 April 2022].

[113] *The Observer*, 12 May 1957, p. 11.

[114] These houses are now in housing authority or private ownership.

[115] DSRL, *Heritage Strategy*, p. 46.

[116] Christopher Hinton, 'The birth of the breeder', in John S. Forrest (ed.), *The Breeder Reactor: Proceedings of a Meeting at the University of Strathclyde, 25 March 1977* (Edinburgh, Scottish Academic Press, 1977), p. 11.

[117] Alistair Fraser, interviewed by James Gunn.

[118] *The Illustrated London News*, 19 February 1966, p. 8.

circular shape of its reactor containment shell differing from recognised structures. Landscape architect Sylvia Crowe stated that it was a 'cosmic' shape which related 'not to the human scale, but to the sky, the clouds and the mountains': it was an elemental structure which disrupted the landscape.[119] More prosaically, it was a monument to modernity which became quickly synonymous with the site itself.

This sense of synonymity is frequently expressed in personal testimony. Alistair Fraser considered it 'the symbol of Dounreay; whenever you talk about Dounreay the first thing that flashes into your mind is the sphere'.[120] Sydney Pickles viewed the sphere as a 'very important historical monument', likening it to the symbol of Blackpool Tower which was of 'much more importance to its area than its function'.[121] Several former employees, including Owen Pugh, David Broughton, and Christina Munro, described it as 'an icon'.[122] David Crowe stated that 'it's known world-wide'; Willie Sloss believed that 'if you show that to almost anybody, they would say, "that's Dounreay"'.[123] This is reflected in the heritage strategy, which recognises that the sphere 'seems to figure in the collective memory of the UK', acting as either a 'symbol of modernity, progress and discovery' or 'the darker side of human endeavour'.[124] Furthermore, the strategy states that it often appears incorrectly in the media 'as an archetype of the nuclear industry or the nuclear age'.[125] As a unique project within Britain, Dounreay was not typical of the country's nuclear sites: indeed, the fully spherical structure is one of only five similar containments in the world (see Figure 10.2). Yet its visual strength means that it is imbued with significant national meaning, making it an iconic industrial form in a coastal-rural setting.

Over the past 65 years Dounreay's sphere has become a landmark, providing, as Sefryn Penrose elucidates, 'a tool for understanding the journey we've made as individuals and as a society since the end of the Second World War'.[126] Yet this form of general 'tool', she continues, will soon be surpassed by those of the 21st century, much as the prehistoric sites in Dounreay vicinity evidence the evolution of the landscape. In this fast-moving environment, she raises the question of 'whether [we should] address our own heritage while we still possess it', something which, as we have seen, DSRL has embraced. As things stand, Dounreay's sphere, once considered 'Britain's future in a steel ball', will be demolished.[127] Following stakeholder consultation and an assessment of options, it was 'reluctantly' concluded

---

[119] Sylvia Crowe, *The Landscape of Power* (London, The Architectural Press, 1958), p. 40; p. 17.
[120] Alistair Fraser, interviewed by James Gunn.
[121] Sydney Pickles, interviewed by James Gunn, 9 June 2014.
[122] Owen Pugh, interviewed by James Gunn, 12 March 2013; David Broughton; Anonymous participant (pseudonym used), interviewed by Linda M. Ross.
[123] David Crowe and Willie Sloss, interviewed by James Gunn, 13 March 2014.
[124] DSRL, *Heritage Strategy*, p. vi.
[125] DSRL, *Heritage Strategy*, p. 41.
[126] Sefryn Penrose, *Images of Change: An Archaeology of England's Contemporary Landscape* (Swindon, English Heritage, 2007), p. 9.
[127] For more on demolition, see Anderson and Kelly, Chapter 12, this volume, pp. 278–279.

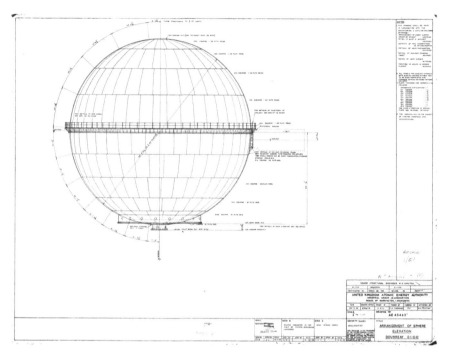

Figure 10.2 A structural drawing of Dounreay's fast breeder reactor containment sphere: a 'cosmic' shape in a flat, coastal landscape. Credit: Copyright Nuclear Decommissioning Authority

that the retention of the sphere as a monument or visitor centre would 'not deliver significant benefits on a local or national scale'.[128] The cost of care and maintenance, the risk of residual radioactive contamination, a loss of authenticity, and security and access issues associated with the proximity of waste stores contributed to a decision not universally well-received: a reminder that safe decommissioning, rather than heritage, will always be the priority. Unlike some other sites related to Britain's atomic or military past, such as the Atomic Weapons Research Establishment testing labs at Orford Ness in Suffolk – discussed by Paul Readman in his chapter on military modernity – Dounreay cannot be left to 'gently deteriorate'.[129] According to Andrew Croft, one of the compilers of the strategy, the dismantling of the sphere 'will mark the end of Dounreay for many people'.[130] This, he

---

[128] DSRL, *Heritage Strategy*, p. 67; p. iv.

[129] 'Orford Ness Management Policy', c. March 1995: National Trust Archives, 'Orford Ness: Conservation', box CIR 269 (ID 57274); see Readman, Chapter 9, this volume, p. 202.

[130] Andrew Croft, 'Dounreay heritage strategy: White heat of heritage', in Sigrid Brandt and Thorsten Dame (eds), *Nuclear Power Stations: Heritage Values and Preservation Perspectives* (Berlin, ICOMOS, 2018), p. 108.

continues, may pose 'the biggest test for the strategy', with public and professional reaction destined to determine whether the 'legacy delivered by the strategy reflects the historic and cultural significance of Dounreay and its sphere'.

During stakeholder engagement, the proposal to demolish all buildings including the sphere garnered a mixed response, with 17 in favour and 21 against.[131] Differing opinions were also recorded in oral testimony, although the majority were similarly against demolition: perhaps unsurprising given that most respondents worked at Dounreay. Recent work by Rebecca Madgin has explored emotional attachments to urban heritage, in which 'communities share emotional responses and attachments to historic urban places based on a combination of context, time, and place'.[132] Transferring this to the Dounreay's rural-coastal context, parallels can be found with Madgin's finding that emotion 'is often only revealed and expressed during times of urban change', with an overwhelming sense of attachment often demonstrated. In an unequivocal letter published in *The Scotsman*, John Little denounced the decision to demolish as an 'act of vandalism' made purely on financial grounds.[133] Peter Higginson considered its potential demolition 'a terrible shame'.[134] Those interviewed were also mindful of the problems associated with retention, with Alistair Fraser summarising this train of thought. He 'would love' to see the sphere kept, though was cognisant of the 'major problems' which would result from its 'contamination and cleanliness and importantly upkeep'.[135] Ernie Lillyman reiterated that 'if there wasn't a maintenance cost, there wouldn't be a question' of retaining it in situ.[136] As 'a very identifiable part of the area', Alastair MacDonald believed that 'it would need to be maintained for a purpose', rather than just a symbol.[137] Sarah Clark, who grew up in Thurso, voiced support for retention and considered the image of the sphere 'a portal to the 1960s', an instant trigger for childhood memories.[138] John Young believed it 'would be nice to see it retained, but if it's too expensive, well, we have to move with the times'.[139] Reflecting this need for progress, Morris Pottinger would 'miss it, make no mistake … but what are you going to do with it? There are very few adults who have saved their toys from when they were bairns'.[140] Donnie Harper looked to the difficulties of information-sharing across generations in his assessment that 'many years down the line people tend to forget, of course they wouldn't forget the sphere itself, but

---

[131] DSRL, *Heritage Strategy*, p. 69.

[132] Rebecca Madgin, *Why Do Historic Places Matter? Emotional Attachments to Urban Heritage* (Glasgow, University of Glasgow, 2021), p. 8.

[133] *The Scotsman*, 11 October 2010, www.scotsman.com/news/opinion/letters/letter-save-dome-1701243 [accessed 29 September 2021].

[134] Peter Higginson, interviewed by James Gunn, 11 February 2015.

[135] Alistair Fraser, interviewed by James Gunn.

[136] Ernie Lillyman, interviewed by James Gunn, 11 July 2013.

[137] Alastair MacDonald, interviewed by James Gunn, 9 November 2011.

[138] Anonymous participant (pseudonym used), interviewed by Linda M. Ross, 5 September 2017.

[139] John Young, interviewed by James Gunn.

[140] Morris Pottinger, interviewed by James Gunn.

they might forget what's in there'.[141] Leslie Rowe was unequivocal in his belief that is should be taken down, and considered preservation 'daft'.[142] Taking a more positive approach, he suggested 'something to mark the spot when it's all finished and gone, rather like a war memorial', reflecting a popular line of thought among interviewees and respondents. This is also outlined in the heritage strategy, which notes that Dounreay has a culture of commemoration which has seen the marking of significant milestones in its past. It proposes a gate guardian, such as those seen at military bases, or a sculpture/marker as among options which could be considered. This decision is one for the future, with DSRL hoping to involve the community in determining the most appropriate form of commemoration. Post-decommissioning, its physicality will become intangible; a commemorative marker, whatever that may be, will ensure that a 'physical manifestation' of Dounreay's activities remains in place.[143]

Conclusion

In personal testimony, Morris Pottinger joked that DSRL should 'turn [Dounreay] back to green fields and sell them back to me'.[144] With the site expected to be released for use in 2333, Morris's tongue was firmly in his cheek. The length of time and dangers associated with decommissioning mean that where nuclear heritage is concerned, standard practices do not apply: the DFR sphere, for example, will not enter the 'official' heritage canon via the listing process; former industrial buildings and their 'gritty appeal' will not be repurposed for housing or recreation; the site will not be subject to ruination, standing as an embodiment of changing policy; the landscape will not bear the spoil heaps or associated scars of extraction.[145] This is something faced by all the UK's civil nuclear sites, each featuring their own social, cultural, and technological histories. The experience gained during the compilation and implementation of Dounreay's heritage strategy is currently being utilised NDA-wide, with the development of the NDA heritage initiative. With Dounreay's heritage officer taking a leading role, this will provide a framework applicable across the board, including potential roll-out to commercial sites outwith the NDA's portfolio.[146] As with Dounreay, heritage contributions

---

[141] Donnie Harper, interviewed by James Gunn.

[142] Leslie Rowe, interviewed by James Gunn, 18 February 2013.

[143] DSRL, *Heritage Strategy*, pp. 67–68; p. 43.

[144] Morris Pottinger, interviewed by James Gunn.

[145] Steven High, Lachlan MacKinnon, and Andrew Perchard, 'Introduction', in S. High, L. MacKinnon, and A. Perchard (eds), *The Deindustrialized World: Confronting Ruination in Postindustrial Places* (Vancouver, UBC Press, 2017), p. 8.

[146] The NDA owns 17 sites across the UK. As well as Dounreay, these include 12 Magnox sites, the LLW Repository, Sellafield, Springfields, and Capenhurst. Commercial sites include the seven power stations operated by EDF Energy.

from national bodies, academia, researchers, and the public will be welcomed: an essential part of preserving the heritage of what Eglė Rindzevičiūtė has identified as a public technology.[147] This standard approach, which will see the production of detailed guidelines covering object selection, intangible cultural heritage, and building recording, will facilitate the creation of site heritage reports. This will result in a definitive national record which is mindful of the nuances of each site. This chapter has explored some of the complexities associated with one site, highlighting the impact of a national project with enduring local consequences. As the NDA moves to record heritage across its estate, Dounreay serves as an example of how technology affected many of the country's rural areas: leaving a heritage which is as much a part of Britain's nuclear history as national policy and practice.

---

[147] Rindzevičiūtė, 'Nuclear cultural heritage', p. 4.

11

'Think Rural: Act Now': The State of the Countryside and Rural Arts Residencies in the 1970s and 1980s

YSANNE HOLT*

AFTER WELL OVER a decade of social and economic decline and growing deprivation across swathes of rural England, in June 1989 the Arts Council published a paper by its then Director of Planning, Sally Stote, in the form of an urgent appeal to *Think Rural: Act Now*.[1] This chapter considers the background from which that paper emerged and its relation to then pressing issues for the arts in rural contexts. More particularly, it traces the nature and significance of one arts association, Northern Arts, in its support for artists in certain rural locations in the north of England through the 1970s and 1980s. To counter still prevalent conceptions of modernity or of 'being modern' as a fundamentally urban experience, the chapter contributes to our understanding of the complex and shifting relations between urban and rural modernity through consideration of forms of cultural production across those decades. To that end it draws on archives relating to English Regional Arts Boards, on contemporary discourse in the regional and national art press, and conversations with individual artists and arts administrators. The Regional Arts Boards frequently found themselves operating at odds or certainly with some diffi-culty within the constraints and demands of centralised Arts Council bureaucracy. Through its accounts of visual arts practices and arts policy, therefore, the chapter challenges still often assumed relations between the urban and rural, the centre and

* First, my thanks to Peter Davies for conversation about his time at Northern Arts and the regional arts context. Particular thanks also to John Kippin for discussions as well as permission to reproduce his photographs, to David Nash, Kate Johnston, and Robin Gillanders, and to the staff at Tyne and Wear Museums and Archive Services. Finally, my thanks to the editors of this publication for their helpful and perceptive comments on various drafts of this chapter.
[1] Stote's paper, 'Think rural: Act now', was summarised in *The Town Planning Review*, 60 (October 1989), 484–485.

Proceedings of the British Academy, **256**, 234–257, © The British Academy 2023.

peripheries, and the position and agency of the regions. It reflects upon the wider social, cultural, and economic implications of engagements with and participation in the arts, and on priorities in provision, in this case in expansive areas of commercial state forestry in Grizedale in the Cumbrian Lake District and Kielder in north Northumberland. Throughout what follows, conceptions of the countryside as predominantly set apart for urban escape, breathing space, and leisure are progressively problematised.

The timeframe begins, appropriately, around the publication of Raymond Williams' celebrated *Country and the City* (1973) with its critique of those persistent notions of rural culture and rural place as static and harmonious rather than processual and conflicted. Through the interests of capital from the later 18th century there emerged in Britain an aestheticised landscape that was principally organised for consumption, with the effect that consistently, and with consequences, a 'real land and its people were falsified'.[2] The implications of Williams's view resonate throughout a disciplinary-diverse literature on the ideological nature of landscape and the negative implications of homogenous and exclusionary understandings of the rural.[3] This chapter reflects on contemporary considerations of the nature of landscape and rural environments, and most particularly the extent to which social and cultural organisations, public bodies and agencies, artists and publics both contributed to and, in instances, challenged evolving representations, identities, and experience.

The Arts Council and Regional Arts Associations

In 1940, the Council for the Encouragement of Music and the Arts was formed under Royal Charter and chaired by John Maynard Keynes between 1941 and 1946. Under the post-war settlement, the body became the Arts Council of Great Britain, whose state sponsorship was more at arm's length, with the government providing 'money, policy and silence'.[4] From 1964 the Labour government and its Minister for the Arts, Jennie Lee, supported a wide national programme of arts associations, largely to expand access to and appreciation of the arts, broadly conceived, mainly via touring programmes of exhibitions and performances. A Northeast England Arts Association had already been established in 1961. This was one of the first

---

[2] Raymond Williams, *Country and the City* (London, Chatto & Windus, 1973), p. 258.

[3] See, for example, William John Thomas Mitchell (ed.) *Landscape and Power* (Chicago, University of Chicago Press, 1994); Paul Cloke and Jo Little (eds), *Contested Countryside Cultures: Otherness, Marginalisation, Rurality* (London, Routledge, 1997); P. de Lima, 'Boundary crossings: Migration, belonging/"un-belonging" in rural Scotland', in Charlotte Hedberg and R. M. do Carmo (eds), *Translocal Ruralism: Mobility and Connectivity in European Rural Spaces* (New York, Springer, 2012), p. 206.

[4] University of Northumbria Library, English Regional Arts Board (ERAB) collection. This chapter also draws on papers relating to Northern Arts Association held in Tyne and Wear Archives and Museums collection.

and indeed a model for the nationwide Regional Arts Associations (RAAs) to follow.[5] As would be the case more widely, its activities were funded by a combination of Arts Council, local authority, and private sponsorship. After the national reorganisation of county boundaries in 1974, that northern region was extended to include the large and diverse counties of Cumberland and Westmorland (henceforth Cumbria), and so with an extensive rural as well as urban remit, became the Northern Arts Association. Northern Arts was consistently challenged in this period by the problem of representing a region of such scale.[6] Nonetheless, it is worth underlining the significant impact of arts and wider government policy here on what, from a cultural perspective, has been termed the 'curation of regions'.[7]

From the mid-1970s, the Arts Council impetus was to work more closely with the RAAs which were the product of their own patch. RAAs were able to stimulate greater activity at the grassroots than what was understood to be the centralised and constrained Arts Council. They could work with multiple constituencies, including amateur and professional artists, and provide a more tailored service to their urban and rural communities through grant aid, promotion, publicity, advising, research, help for artists, and by attempting to provide a 'regional voice'.[8] The diversity as well as the scale of this northern region certainly produced conflict. David Dougan, an early director of Northern Arts, reported endless difficulty with local authorities, notably Durham City Council, who frequently refused to make financial contributions to what were perceived to be Newcastle-centric, or purely urban, activities. These tensions surfaced more widely in debates over devolved resources from the Arts Council too.[9] Nevertheless, Northern Arts operated with dedicated fine art, video and photography, craft, theatre, and literature officers who lobbied hard on behalf of their area.

Tensions were experienced beyond the northern region of course too. One regional lead noted a tendency in the 'Arts Council to see devolution as administratively convenient rather than morally and politically necessary', hence, for example, the need to 'restate the moral justification for giving people a greater

---

[5] The Regional Arts Associations were replaced by a smaller number of Regional Arts Boards in 1990.
[6] Note the existence of a hard geographical border with nearby Scotland, with its own Arts Council and no cross-border mechanism.
[7] See, for example, Penny Fielding, 'Curated regions of the north: Art and literature in the "Scottish Border" and the Transpennine Corridor', *Visual Culture in Britain*, 15:2 (2014), 159–172 and Natasha Vall, *Cultural Region: North East England 1945–2000* (Manchester, Manchester University Press, 2011).
[8] ERAB/1/18 – SCRAA/ACGB 71/72. As Peter Davies noted in our conversations, 'Northern Arts over this period created an innovative artists' support regional model, with a network of schemes, programmes and organisations. Artists' rights (such as Exhibition Payment Right), the crafts and marketplace initiatives (such as Artwork Purchase Scheme) were developed. Gallery, production facilities and services (such as Artists Newsletter) were improved. independent trusts were supported (LYC, Bede Gallery, Sunderland Arts Centre, etc.). Exhibition outside the gallery was explored through residencies, sited commissions and different forms of public art, which underpinned the Northern Region's award of "UK Year of the Visual Arts 1996".'
[9] Vall, *Cultural Region*, p. 100. Vall's study focuses on literature in the north-east.

control over the arts as they affect them, recognising the right of regional communities to influence the spending of national resources'.[10] The RAAs were 'effectively supplicants', dependent on funds and uneasily positioned between the Arts Council as a central government agency 'supposedly' not under direct political control, and the elected local authorities in each region, who were bound by political consideration. Rather than acting as mere agents for Arts Council schemes, it was clear the RAAs required proper devolution of responsibility and finance. The forging of partnerships with other regional bodies and organisations was crucial here too.

Within this partnership context, and with its extensive rural remit, Northern Arts took a significant lead amongst the RAAs from the mid-1970s. It developed two artist residency programmes in association with the Forestry Commission in the diverse landscape settings of Grizedale and Kielder forests, both planted just before but greatly expanded in the immediate post-war period. The distinctive qualities of these programmes and the nature of the artistic practices that became associated with them underlined the impact of social, cultural, and environmental policy changes among regional and national authorities and organisations, as well as shifts in the discourse, ideology, and practice of the artists involved.

The emergence of artist residency programmes in these sites was rooted in a wider concern about the social role of the arts, including artists' participation in and value to local communities. One source of inspiration was the Federal Art Project of the American Depression-era Works Progress Administration (WPA) which was developed to provide economic support for artists and to realise public or community arts projects. In the late 1960s, a group of conceptual artists established the Artist Placement Group (APG), which worked to reposition the artist as a person of use within a wider social context through 'placements' in government, industry, and commerce.[11] This initiative intersected with the rise of the broad-based community arts movement, with community, as Owen Kelly described it in 1984, understood as 'formed through shared social meanings which are constantly created and mutated through the actions and interactions of its members' and wider society.[12] As Kevin Stephens argues, in the early 1970s young arts officers who shared the ideals of contemporary art movements found that arts associations provided a means to realise something of their ambition to 'promote artists of their own generation in a relatively inexpensive way', as well as succeed in taking art out of galleries and making it more publicly accessible.[13]

---

[10] Clive Fox, Director of Lincolnshire & Humberside Arts, ERAB/2/13, 1979.

[11] Relating to the ethos of the Artists Placement Group was the Artists Agency founded by Lucy Fairley (Milton) in 1983 in Sunderland with, from 1987, co-director Esther Salamon. The Artists Agency expanded the idea of connecting artists with industry, business and public bodies, or with diverse and disadvantaged communities to support engagement with social and environmental issues.

[12] Owen Kelly, *Storming the Citadels: Community, Art and the State* (London, Commedia, 1984), p. 49.

[13] Kevin Stephens, 'Artists in residence in England and the experience of Year of the Artist', *Cultural Trends*, 42:11 (2001), 45–47. Kevin Stephens was a young Northern Arts Music Officer in the 1970s.

Grizedale Forest

The first of the forest-based artist residency schemes in the Northern Arts region began in 1976 with the sculpture residency at Grizedale, which then covered 8,700 acres in the Lake District's Furness Fells between Coniston and Windermere. The Forestry Commission had acquired the Grizedale Estate in 1934 after the death of its owner, the Liverpool shipowner and Cunard tycoon, Harold Brocklebank. The estate then comprised some 3,500 acres of rough grazing, ancient woodland and plantations, together with Grizedale Hall, which was to be commandeered to intern captured German officers in the Second World War. Tree planting, thinning, and harvesting (predominantly of spruce trees) was carried out from the later 1940s by a labour force brought from Barrow in Furness, 15 miles away, or by workers living in specially built houses in and around Satterthwaite village. As at Kielder in the 1930s, the hiring of labourers who were often originally from urban or industrial areas for large state-financed schemes such as forestry, provided unemployment relief underpinned by a widespread belief in the value of physical labour and exercise in open-air rural contexts.[14] That sense of the physical and wellbeing benefits to be derived from being in nature, even in heavily managed commercial forests, persisted, but in significantly transformed ways throughout the decades to come.

Following the fifth World Forestry Congress in Seattle in 1960, the focus of forestry schemes moved increasingly from 'mono-functional' forests towards policies of multi-functional or 'multiple use' forestry, emphasising their recreational and environmental value as well as timber production. As Susanne Raum and Clive Potter outlined, this shift coincided with a period in Britain in the 1960s of non-governmental organisations lobbying for greater public access to the countryside in general, and forests in particular. Their concerns culminated in the 1968 Countryside Act, requiring local authorities to have regard 'for the conservation and enhancement of natural beauty and for the benefit of those resorting to the countryside'.[15] The person leading a multiple use strategy at Grizedale from 1963 was Head Forester and originator of the Grizedale Society, Bill Grant. In 1968 Grant was awarded a Winston Churchill Travelling Fellowship to North America to study the educational aspects of wildlife conservation, and from there produced plans that would make 'wise use of fresh air, open space, water and wildlife, linked to people management within the forest'.[16] Benefiting from that experience of US National Parks, Grant at Grizedale developed nature trails, forest walks, and

---

[14] On this point in relation to Kielder see Jill Payne, 'Constructing the Kielder landscape: Plantations, dams and the romantic ideal', in Peter Coates, David Moon, and Paul Warde (eds), *Local Places, Global Processes: Histories of Environmental Change in Britain and Beyond* (Oxford, Windgather Press, 2016), p. 101.

[15] Susanne Raum and Clive Potter, 'Forestry paradigms and policy change: The evolution of forestry policy in Britain in relation to the ecosystem approach', *Land Use Policy*, 49 (2015), 462–470 at 465.

[16] Bill Grant and Paul Harris (eds), *The Grizedale Experience: Sculpture, Arts & Theatre in a Lakeland Forest* (Edinburgh, Canongate Press, 1991), p. 7.

wildlife observation towers to entertain and also to educate visitors on aspects of conservation. Grant's strategy appears to have anticipated the criticisms that the Forestry Commission were to receive more widely through the 1970s and 1980s from environmental and recreational bodies focused on the importance of public goods and non-market benefits from forestry and the countryside more broadly.[17]

Working alongside Grant and the Grizedale Society, from 1977 Northern Arts established a role for the forest as a studio or place for open experimentation in the arts, with a series of funded residencies of three or six months intended to celebrate in sculptural form 'an individual's response to a particular landscape, a large production forest' with its 'local materials, dry stone walls, coppice woods and agricultural buildings'.[18] In its time the scheme, located within a working forest rather than a sculpture park and where planning permission was Crown exempt, was an innovative partnership model with the Forestry Commission, who made materials available, and the support of foresters, rangers, and locally skilled craftsmen such as dry stone wallers. Fundamentally, the site was intended to attract increased tourism to Grizedale; by 1984, with around 150,000 visitors a year, it had given the Commission a national profile. Numerous agenda underlay the scheme therefore which, through time, was progressively shaped, or nuanced, for diverse contexts and interest groups.

The agency of Peter Davies, Northern Arts' Visual Arts Officer from 1974 to 1992, was crucial in the development and success of this partnership. Davies had also spent the late 1960s and early 1970s in the US, in his case teaching at the School of the Art Institute of Chicago where he had been impressed by the legacy of those Roosevelt-era WPA schemes for artists, and by developments in American land or environmental art.[19] In the earlier days of his role at Northern Arts, Davies was required to live in rural Cumbria and was aware of a lack of opportunity to see or participate in the visual arts. Nationally too, as he noted later, 'at that time there was not much evidence of art in the landscape and, for that matter, public art commission was not very evident in the UK'.[20] In our discussions Davies commented that 'Living through the seasons in a small village in the rural Eden valley and criss-crossing the northern region made a profound impact. It influenced my search to find the most effective ways to support the artist, facilitate new work and enable public engagements.'[21]

[17] On these wider circumstances see Raum and Potter, 'Forestry paradigms and policy change'.

[18] Peter Davies, 'The Grizedale Experience' in Grant and Harris, *The Grizedale Experience*, p. 19. The Grizedale Society's interest was in the performing arts centred on the small 'Theatre in the Forest'. There was no involvement or expertise in the visual arts until Davies proposed and raised funds for the sculpture programme, a programme which he curated for the first 10 years.

[19] Examples of the latter from the late 1960s by, for example, the American land artists Robert Smithson and Robert Morris and the British artist Richard Long, were to figure in the survey of practices involving marked sites and impermanent marks in Rosalind Krauss's highly influential article, 'Sculpture in the expanded field', *October*, 8 (1979), 31–44

[20] Davies, *Grizedale Experience*, p. 19.

[21] Davies went on: 'Clearly there was a need for a wider visual support infrastructure for galleries, groups and creative learning situations. A mesh of support schemes for the artist evolved such as loans,

Ten years after the first Grizedale residency, a report commissioned by Northern Arts and Cumbria County Council on arts provision in Cumbria noted continuing out migration of artists from the county in the early and middle years of their careers; on little in the way of gallery space or curatorial staff expert in contemporary art, and virtually non-existent touring exhibitions of contemporary art to small rural towns or villages. Grizedale remained Northern Arts' most substantial achievement in this context, providing 'not merely the aesthetic for exploring the relationship between art and landscape particular to the area, but a practical means of providing patronage to young artists and of building up a contemporary collection unhindered by the constraints of museum conservation'.[22] Observing many artists' resistance to then outmoded traditions of landscape painting, Pratley noted that the relations of sculpture and photography to the landscape was of much greater interest. It was sculpture of course that predominated at Grizedale from the 1970s while photography was the practice for the residency programme at Kielder in the early 1980s.

In common with much contemporary art of the period, partly in defiance of the perceived institutionalisation of art and the dominance of commercial and largely metropolitan galleries, the sited, temporal, and ephemeral nature of the Grizedale sculptures was key, as was the practice of working with free and found materials, primarily wood and the slate stone. Artists were encouraged not to interfere with living trees but, in a spirit attuned to the environment, to work 'with' those trees that had fallen naturally, such as the dismantled oak with which David Nash constructed his *Running Table* (1978) (Figure 11.1). Other works resulted from considered interventions with the essential materials of the forest; water, streams, and spongy surfaces, including Kees Bierman's *the Sound of Running Water* (1986). David Kemp's sculptures, such as *Scale Green Birdman* (1981) were essentially assemblages constructed from discarded and found items. In the wider contemporary context of minimalist art, several sculptures took the form of simple abstract shapes, such as Andy Goldsworthy's *Woven Ash Ball* (1984) and Keir Smith's *Seven Stones before the Old Man* (1980) with an emphasis on careful and relatively inobtrusive integration into the forest space. This was in marked contrast to the earth-shifting, often highly engineered structures of much American land art of that period. A survey of sculptures in the earliest years of the programme reveals a predilection for forest-pertinent themes such as trails and pathways, shelters and enclosures, and in some cases whimsical or craggily carved human figures, including David Kemp's *Ancient Forester* (1988) or figurative forms of wild animals commonly associated with forests, such as Sophie Ryder's *Grizedale Stag*

grants, awards, fellowships, residencies, artists newsletter, exhibition payment right, art purchase plan, travel awards and so on.'

[22] David Pratley, *Quality and Equality: A Strategy for Developing the Arts in Cumbria*, April 1987, p. 64 (ERAB, 256 21-3-95). In a preliminary note attached to this Arts Consultancy report Peter Stark, then Director of Northern Arts, acknowledged it made 'uncomfortable reading … highlighting as it does our past shortcomings and the uneven spread of our funding within Cumbria'. Stark reinforces Pratley's own comment on the singular importance of the Grizedale sculpture programme for the county.

Figure 11.1 David Nash, 'Running Table', Grizedale, 1978. © David Nash. Courtesy of David Nash

(1986) and Sally Matthews' *Wild Boar Clearing* (1987) assembled from twisted roots, brush, and dead wood.[23]

Inevitably, weather took its toll on the sculptures over time. In several cases materials were gradually reclaimed by the forest, or indeed by animals. David Nash's first *Willow Ladder* (1978), for example, was munched by red deer. Another hazard was occasional vandalism. Nash's *Running Table* was one such victim with, in that case, a suspicion of local vendettas amongst the Satterthwaite community, and even visiting 'mods' from Kendal.[24] The transient nature of the works was noted by Eric Geddes, one of the sculptor residents, as entirely appropriate in terms of the cycle of growth and decay within the forest and the particular forestry conditions there. As he recorded, 'the shallowness of root systems against underlying rock' and 'the rotting of felled brushwood' all 'point to the fragility and transformation of what may seem initially to be enduring'.[25]

[23] A number of these Grizedale sculptures can be seen on Amelia Harvey's excellent web resource, https://grizedaleforestsculpturepark.wordpress.com/ [accessed 31 July 2021].

[24] Letter from David Kemp to Peter Davies, 1982, Tyne and Wear Archives and Museums (TWAM)/ GH2.

[25] Eric Geddes in 'Grizedale Forest', *Aspects: A Review of Contemporary Art* (April 1985), n.p. *Aspects* was founded in 1977 and based in Newcastle with financial support from Northern Arts.

The artists had to contend with working alone in a rural context, one not without danger in terms, for instance, of handling chain saws in quite inaccessible parts of the forest. At interview, therefore, as well as plans for their practice, the residency selection committee also assessed whether the artist, who was frequently young and not long out of art school, was independently minded and socially adjusted enough to work in a small community. Within a National Park and a small valley with limited housing stock, accommodation was an issue and various solutions were found over time. Richard Harris, the first sculptor, lived happily in a caravan in the forest, while David Nash and his family lived at a house at the Centre. The next plan was to convert a barn at Force Mill, which explains a cluster of sculpture sited in the south forest. The Forestry Commission at Grizedale chalets proved a longer-term prospect. Such were the considerations of site-based practices emphasising 'embeddedness' in place. That emphasis also extended to what Nash described in 1983 as a sense of needing to impress the more suspicious foresters and wider workforce of his own discipline of hard work and ability to put in long hours.[26] Many preconceptions of landscape and the rural were therefore reassessed through time spent at Grizedale. An archived letter of 1981 from David Kemp (the 1980 resident) records:

> In anticipation I had thought of it as purely an arcadian retreat. But as it is largely a man-made forest planned for timber production, man's presence is constantly in evidence. Thus I have had to consider as well as the 'romantic' aspect of the forest, the forest community who live and work here, the visitors who walk the trails, and the outside world whose reality is echoed in its ordered wilderness.[27]

There is clear awareness here from Kemp of the distance between myth and reality, that any pastoral ideal was essentially an ideological construction or, to return to Raymond Williams, who argued 'a working country is hardly ever a landscape. The very idea of landscape implies separation and observation'.[28] As art critic Paul Overy noted in 1984 in a publication related to the forest sculpture touring exhibition, the sculptural practices at Grizedale were underpinned by recognition of and learning from the distinct skills of the foresters, their ways of working and knowledge of the material. In his terms, a residency there was 'more like an "industrial placement", where the artist spends a period of time in the working environment of a factory, hospital, or some other kind of industrial or commercial enterprise'.[29] This was the essence of course of the APG, referred to earlier, and the model established in the north-east by Lucy Milton and the Artist's Agency from 1983.

---

[26] Grizedale Forest Installations, in *Studio International*, 196:999 (1983), 10.

[27] Letter dated 1981, TWAM, GH2.

[28] Williams, *Country and the City*, p. 149.

[29] Paul Overy, 'Grizedale sculpture', in Peter Davies and Tony Knipe (eds), *A Sense of Place: Sculpture in Landscape* (Sunderland, Ceolfrith Gallery, 1984), p. 64.

Key here was integration with local communities and environment, not separation and distanced observation. As a result, a practice emerged that can be understood as inherently modern.

While the underlying spirit of these sited sculptures of the late 1970s and 1980s was underpinned by democratic belief in locating artworks outside the usual fine art contexts, and by a notion of the artist as one who, however temporarily, was embedded within a working community, there is perhaps less sense in the qualities of the artworks themselves of engaging with the wider ideological complexities and implications of Kemp's 'ordered wilderness'. Rather, 'nature' is for a large part presented unproblematically here as an experience of authenticity, retreat, sometimes of spirituality and, above all, of pleasure.

A comment by Bill Grant in a 1989 film about Grizedale is relevant here:

> This statement might sound like heresy as far as the art world is concerned, but I really don't think that we should allow people to indulge themselves too much in putting very inaccessible types of work into the forest. I think we've got a great responsibility because we're dealing with public money and we've got a big job in educating the public.[30]

Grant's remarks perhaps forecast tensions in the evolution of the Grizedale Society and the programme. His retirement both as its Director and Head Forester inevitably led to change. Grizedale Arts was also significantly reshaped as a contemporary arts organisation in subsequent decades.[31] Tensions were to develop nationally over forms of public art and the political implications of artists' participation in 'culture-led' regeneration schemes, be they urban or rural. The popular success and widespread appeal of this particular northern initiative, as Davies notes, saw Grizedale emerge as a model for other UK forests such as the Forest of Dean, and with wider influence on national agencies, organisations, and programmes, including the first National Garden Festival in Liverpool in 1984. In north-east England in particular it led to what was later termed an 'Urban Grizedale' approach, with artists working on sites in the Rivers Tyne, Tees and Wear valleys, and with walk/cycle (Coast to Coast) and Metro trails through the three major urban areas.[32]

---

[30] From the film directed by Maggie Ellis, *Grizedale: A Sense of Place* (Border Television and ACGB, 1989) quoted in Edwina Fitzpatrick's unpublished thesis 'Artists' geographies of the landscape-archive: Trace, loss and the impulse to preserve in the anthropocene age' (The Glasgow School of Art, 2014).

[31] Under the new leadership of Adam Sutherland from 2000, Grizedale Arts was established as a contemporary arts organisation and subsequently relocated to Lawson Park, a farmhouse on the fells above Coniston. The Forestry Commission (Forestry England since 2019) has consequently taken responsibility for the continuing sculpture programme in the forest. For Grizedale Arts see www.grizedale.org/about/ [accessed 31 July 2021].

[32] Davies in conversation with the author.

Kielder Forest

In the contemporary arts context rather more critical understandings of the constructed nature of landscape itself and the conflictual character and experience of rural modernity emerge in works produced through the second residency programme considered here. This was a small-scale photography-based programme established at Kielder Forest and funded by Northern Arts and the Forestry Commission from 1980 to 1984.

Kielder is some 50 miles from Newcastle upon Tyne and ideally situated for commercial forestry as a sparsely populated site of open moorland, terrain for sheep, grouse-moor, and peat bog with high levels of rainfall. Afforestation at Kielder began from 1926 and developed intensively on land acquired in lieu of death duties from the Duke of Northumberland's estate from 1932. The expanding labour force was supplemented by unemployed workers from north-east mining communities, many of whom were also involved after 1945 in building the long straight forest roads alongside a number of Polish ex-servicemen.

By the time the Forestry Commission published *Britain's Forests: Kielder*, in 1950, the site had extended over 70,000 acres and was intended to include 40,000 acres of growing trees.[33] This was the biggest scheme the Commission had been engaged in, and it lay adjacent to the equally vast areas of forest developing just across the border in Scotland. In 1950 the Commission employed some 210 men at Kielder but estimated it would ultimately provide productive employment for about 2,000 in the woods alone, with additional indirect workers. Hence an urgent need for new forest villages to house a significant proportion of the labour force.

One existing village, Byrness, had been extended and developed from 1946 to the designs of Thomas Sharp. Sharp, who was born in County Durham, was a key figure in mid-20th-century town planning with such influential publications as *Town Planning* (1940) and *Anatomy of a Village* (1946). In the latter, Sharp praised the nucleated form and ordered informality of the traditional village. In his plans for the forest villages of Kielder, Stonehaugh, and Byrness he sought reconciliation between existing and valued character with modernity, in the form of open squares and private gardens in a modern housing idiom with, crucially, good facilities; pub, shops, and village hall.[34] In the Commission's publication, Kielder village (officially opened in 1952) with its final target of 250 houses and some 800 to 1,000 inhabitants, was envisaged as a complete community. Whereas, it noted, 'the local style of building in this part of Northumberland has hitherto been of grey, rather dour and forbidding stone', by contrast, the new village houses 'will

---

[33] Forestry Commission, *Britain's Forests: Kielder* (HMSO, 1950).
[34] On Sharp, see in particular Newcastle University's Special Collections Archive, 'Town and Townscape: The Life of Thomas Sharp'. The archive results from an AHRC project, PI John Pendlebury, completed in 2007.

be white fronted, bright, clean, and new, bringing a fresh and attractive style to the neighbourhood'.[35]

The tone of *Britain's Forests: Kielder* also reveals something of the benign paternalism of Griersonian Documentary Film Movement footage of inter- and post-war inner-city rehousing initiatives, here transplanted to rural Northumberland. As with the rhetoric of the post-1945 new towns movement in general, the future is always clean, fresh, and bright. Drawing further interconnections between the rural and urban, Kielder and its surroundings are seen to be 'opening a new "lung"' for the people of Tyneside as a whole; implied reference to decades there of industrial pollution and working-class poverty.[36] There is resonance here too with sentiments in Nan Fairbrother's *New Lives, New Landscapes*: 'New country workers prefer a new council house to a picturesque old cottage, and so would anyone who considered them at the same level of non-improvement', and more widely in her chapter 'The urban-rural countryside': 'Future town and country must similarly learn to live together, for they are essentially interdependent.'[37]

In this particular context and in spite of that post-war ethos of community renewal and national reconstruction, the rapidly developing mechanisation of forestry work required to speed up productivity and meet demand for wood pulp and cheap timber, alongside growing foreign competition, meant the estimated size of the workforce dropped considerably. The Commission did not build to the quality and extent Sharp had planned, and the villages lacked his intended amenities. His proposed modernity, the best qualities of both rural and urban living, was unachieved.[38] And in 1960, 10 years after the Commission's publication, Rupert Speir, Conservative MP for Hexham, raised the 'legitimate grievances' of his constituents in the forest villages of Kielder, Stonehaugh, and Byrness in a parliamentary debate. Speir spoke of their unrest, discontent, and the poor morale caused by that absence of amenities. It was a severe indictment of the administration of the Forestry Commission, whose acclamation of the designs was 'the most awful nonsense and humbug'. Castle Drive in Kielder looked like 'nothing more than a dockyard settlement'. The villagers, he stated, are 'charged the full economic rent for their houses, although they are tied houses. They are snowed up in winter and for a large part of the summer they are consumed by midges from the forests and trees'. It was, he maintained, 'the duty of any organisation that dumped these people in the wilds – in the hilly, exposed, isolated district of the county of Northumberland to see that at any rate they have a chance to lead reasonably full lives'.[39]

---

[35] *Britain's Forests*, p. 14.

[36] Connections can be drawn here of course to the post-1948 plans for Peterlee, the new town developed in County Durham to provide decent housing for a significant population of mining families.

[37] Nan Fairbrother, *New Lives, New Landscapes* (Middlesex, Penguin, 1970), pp. 86–87, 105.

[38] In his unpublished 1973 autobiography, *Chronicles of Failure*, Sharp described the Commission as his worst client. Newcastle University's Special Collections Archive, 'Town and Townscape: The Life of Thomas Sharp'.

[39] https://api.parliament.uk/historic-hansard/commons/1960/jul/28/forestry-commission-villages [accessed 31 July 2021]. Interestingly, Fairbrother makes the point in relation to Kielder that the forestry

The concerns Speir articulated continued while, in the early 1960s, demand for water across the north-east region began outstripping supply, and extensive areas of forestry were cut down as Kielder became the site of the vast reservoir scheme which opened in 1982 to provide water to the populations and steel and chemical industries of Tyneside, Wearside, and Teesside. At that very moment, of course, those industries were set upon their own long process of decline. In 1980 Northern Arts initiated its Kielder residency scheme. This was led by then Film, Photography and Video officer, John Bradshaw, with a brief that selected residents would develop and explore their own work for a year – a longer period than at Grizedale – to become attuned to the surrounding environment and, ideally, integrate with the local community. The experiences of Murray Johnston, the first Kielder resident in 1980, were documented in a 1983 discussion with the photographer John Kippin (the fourth resident) and recorded by Robin Gillanders.[40] In response to Kippin's queries, Johnston describes the impact of moving from his peer group of photographers based at that time at Spectro Arts Workshop in Newcastle (of which more below), to a 'uni-occupational' and tightly knit community situation at Kielder and an entirely new, to him, type of landscape. The effect of this shift caused Johnston to reconsider the nature of his past work and the formulated way of seeing he had derived from the 'natural' landscapes he had worked in previously. He was now faced with the purely practical, repetitive rows of trees and the long straight roads of the Forestry Commission land. It was a landscape he described as difficult to decode. Either you stood on a hill and took panoramic views, or you were close down in amongst the trees in a space that was restricted and claustrophobic. It was not possible here to produce pictures that were simply in praise of nature, not that this was his ambition, but it certainly prompted more speculation on widespread preconceptions of landscape and nature, and any residual notion of arcadian retreat, as commented on by David Kemp at Grizedale.

Having constructed a dark room and struggled for two months to make work in this alien new context, Johnston hung a series of photographs in the Kielder community centre library and waited to see how local residents would respond. One of these, a black and white close-up image of the forest with several fallen pines leaning on those that remain standing, reveals what is described as his interest in the 'conflicts between human management and the forces of nature', with tall trees that have been planted in shallow soil on bare rock so easily uprooted by the strong winds that often whip through the plantations (Figure 11.2).[41]

---

workers were now housed 'in existing communities instead of the early separate villages. These were not successful, and workers with cars moved to larger centres and commuted to work (even the horses commute by lorry in Kielder Forest)' (*New Lives*, p. 131).

[40] Thanks to John Kippin for sharing the recording with me and for permission to quote from it. Murray Johnston, who went on to be first director of Stills gallery in Edinburgh, died in 1990. The second and third residents were Don Jackson and Justin Monroe.

[41] Johnston's black and white photograph, *Lewis Burn, Kielder Forest* (1980), is in the collection of the National Galleries of Scotland, www.nationalgalleries.org/art-and-artists/54448/kielder-forest# [accessed 31 July 2021].

Figure 11.2 Murray Johnston, 'Kielder Forest', 1980, National Galleries of Scotland, Purchased 1999. © Kate Johnston

Initially there was no particular interest in Johnston's work amongst the Kielder residents. Responses improved over time, however, but it took a while for an outsider to integrate both as an individual and as photographer, and he records feeling that a sculptor may have had an easier reception from the start. To be seen out of doors making work by hand would have resonated with the work ethic possessed by those who spent their days up to their elbows in sawdust. It was harder for forest workers to understand how a photographer could usefully fill up a year. So Johnston stopped making work altogether for the middle-period of his residency. Instead he ran a photography course for eight to ten people, and his darkroom became a community resource. Setting up this course, which outlasted his residency, marked a shift from what he termed the arrogance of a photographer's call to the public to come and see how he or she sees the world, to an approach to communities to ask how making photographs might be of use to them in understanding their own lives. From here the residency evolved with discussions about photography and work with the Kielder school children who used cameras to document their science day activities, such as research experiments in the river.

Johnston remarks that the Kielder community itself could seem claustrophobic and segregated, especially for the wives of forest workers who for whatever reason felt on the edge of the established village grouping. Throughout his own residency year in 1984, John Kippin largely concentrated on images of the everyday lives of this local community at work and leisure; a focus made easier by the fact that Northern Arts rented one of the Thomas Sharp designed white-fronted Kielder village houses from the Forestry Commission for the duration of the residency programme.

From 1979 Kippin had been part of the newly formed Basement Group in Newcastle that was supported by a small grant from Northern Arts awarded under the aegis of Peter Davies.[42] A highly politicised collective of young artists, the Basement Group was located in Bells Court, a run-down back lane in the city, along with Spectro Arts Workshop, and became a focus for innovative forms of performance, video, and installation. In tandem with other Newcastle collectives such as Amber Films and the Side Gallery there was, as Richard Grayson describes, a 'history of experimental activity in the northeast, albeit often heterodox and isolated. The region had maintained a slightly wary distance from metropolitan centres and discourses but fostered innovative practices, often informed by the trajectories of international modernism'.[43] Across the group's diverse forms of practice was a concern with how to address the impact of social and economic power dynamics on individual lives. This was the moment of large-scale deindustrialisation and mass unemployment in the north-east and across the north more generally. 1984, the year Kippin went to Kielder, was of course the period of the miners' strike and the devastation of semi-rural 'pit village' communities in Northumberland and neighbouring County Durham. Of the 190 pits in operation nationally in 1963, only 15 were still in existence in 1987.[44] The social and economic changes of the period therefore were equally evident across urban and rural communities. As Beryl Charlton notes in her study of Upper North Tynedale published that same year, 'The social results of streamlining the [forestry] industry are reflected in the shrinking workforce and in the depopulation of the forestry villages. At Kielder for instance, the empty houses and falling numbers on the school roll bear mute witness to the threat posed by foreign competitors to just one aspect of the British economy.'[45]

[42] John Kippin came to Newcastle from London in 1979 having been part of the artist's collective at Butler's Wharf on the Thames, east of Tower Bridge. Butler's Wharf was a key venue for late 1970s performance and video art. A semi-derelict building with cheap studio space just pre- the large-scale urban property development era of the 1980s onwards, and so a pattern for many artist-led groups in the period.

[43] *This Will Not Happen Without You: From the Collective Archives of the Basement Group, Projects UK and Locus + (1977–2007)* (John Hansard Gallery, Southampton and Hatton Gallery, Newcastle, 2006–2007), p. 39.

[44] The impact of the miners' strike on the Northumberland and County Durham pit villages was documented in photographs by Keith Pattison, Bruce Rae, and Chris Killip for Side Gallery exhibitions throughout the period

[45] Beryl Charlton, *Upper North Tynedale: A Northumbrian Valley and its People* (Newcastle, Northumbrian Water, 1987), p. 146.

Figure 11.3 John Kippin, 'Untitled' from 'The Forest', 1985. © John Kippin. Courtesy of Laura Noble Gallery, London

Throughout his residency, as it was described in the regional arts magazine, *Aspects*, John Kippin's focus was on 'the problems of representing the life of a rural community as being more related to current economic and social realities than to romantic notions of "country life" '.[46] In some instances, as in photographs of social club dances, leek shows, easter bonnet parades, and scenes of children playing in the village and its surroundings, his rural Kielder images compare to those by contemporary photographer Sirrka Lissa Kontinnen, then working in Byker in central Newcastle – another economically marginalised working-class community (Figure 11.3). That connection is all the more relevant here as the results of

[46] The Side Gallery exhibition in 1985 was reviewed by Dave Barden in *Aspects*, 30 (1985), n.p.

Kippin's residency were shown in 1985 at the Side Gallery in Newcastle, where Kontinnen's Byker photographs of that period were also shown. At a moment of critical reassessment of the often clichéd 'documentary tradition' of working-class life, both photographers avoid any tendency towards sentimentality or nostalgia. To large degree, such avoidance came from Kippin's experience of living and working within the community for a sustained period and, like Johnston, engaging with school children in photography workshops (his portrait photographs of the children were also shown at the Side exhibition). Fundamentally, his images underscore what Leona Skelton's much later (2014) oral history investigation at Kielder confirmed. Despite a community undermined by the decreased employment and the impact of newcomers, social cohesion still remained, with regular events, as she lists them, such as leek-growing competitions, bonfire displays, bingo evenings, village dances, and vintage car rallies.[47]

The Side Gallery exhibition was entitled 'Forest', but rather than a romantic image of woodland, as might be expected, the gallery poster image was of a worker with a coal-blackened face and hard hat emerging from nearby Falstone Mine; this was alongside gallery images of fish farm workers and dry stone wallers (Figure 11.4).[48] In a much later, 2017, photo book publication of some of these residency images, the editor's selection and juxtaposition reveals the very particular circumstances at Kielder at that moment when the forestry-work community was declining in numbers and the national focus was on the great technological feat of the seven-mile-long, 2,684 acre covering Kielder reservoir.[49] Kippin's images are predominantly peopled. The co-existence of traditional agriculture and modern industry is registered across scenes of farm workers with lambs and collie dogs, to the heavy chain sawing and mechanical loading of timber. The existence of the nearby Ministry of Defence range at Otterburn is witnessed in an image of a fighter jet flying over the publication's one panoramic view of woodland, with a solitary sheep in the middle ground below (Figure 11.5). This is in marked contrast to evidence of the other major growth area – water-sports and tourism – following the 'multiple-use' strategy as developed at Grizedale and registered here in photographs of windsurf lessons, or young children in their 'Kielder Water' T-shirts.[50]

The re-appraisal of the documentary tradition in photography from the later 1970s coincided with much wider analysis of cultural representations of landscape, and recognition that landscape as an aesthetic category is implicitly related to structures of power and authority. While John Kippin's Kielder residency was less concerned with pure landscape per se, his images from here would critique

[47] Leona Jayne Skelton, 'The uncomfortable path from forestry to tourism in Kielder, Northumberland: A socially dichotomous village?', *Oral History* (2014), 85.

[48] Falstone coal mine, near Kielder village, closed in 1991. In 1985 it was employing four people.

[49] *John Kippin, The Forest: Kielder, Northumberland*, ed. Craig Atkinson (Southport, Café Royal Books, 2017).

[50] Northumbrian Water Authority with the Forestry Commission had begun to focus on recreational activities from c. 1977.

Figure 11.4 John Kippin, 'Untitled' from 'The Forest', 1985. © John Kippin.
Courtesy of Laura Noble Gallery, London

Figure 11.5 John Kippin, 'Untitled' from 'The Forest', 1985. © John Kippin.
Courtesy of Laura Noble Gallery, London

Figure 11.6 John Kippin, 'Untitled' from 'The Forest', 1985. © John Kippin. Courtesy of Laura Noble Gallery, London

its aesthetic and ideological construction, the conventions of the picturesque, and so on, and signal a longer-term investigation of both the post-pastoral and post-industrial landscape. Through periods of political change, large-scale social and economic collapse and strategies for re-development, traces are still apparent of past traditions and ways of being, despite conscious efforts to conceal that past by public bodies and private businesses heavily invested in forging new directions such as commercial redevelopment, the cultivation of tourism, the commodification of heritage, and, equally, of nature.

The cover of the 2017 Kielder photobook is one of that text's few unpeopled images. In this case a view of a tyre-marked forest road stretching off into the mist with, in the immediate foreground on a churned-up verge, what looks like a discarded oil drum, but with the word POISON crudely painted on the top (Figure 11.6). That one image presages what will be a particular future direction for Kippin; the juxtaposition of, for example, a pastoral image with an overlaid text which works to disrupt the expected associations of the image itself, underlining the social, economic, and environmental issues that counter any assumptions about nature and the countryside as innocent and uncomplicated.

Rural arts and rural development

John Kippin recalled that at the end of his residency and just as the Forestry Commission was beginning to sell off the housing, he suggested to Northern Arts that they buy the house the artists had been allocated at Kielder as a permanent study centre to house photographic facilities and form an archive of the material relating to the history and development of the area and its community. That suggestion was noted in the *Aspects* Side Gallery exhibition review where Barden spoke of the need to make work done at Kielder more accessible to people there, both in terms of a record of the residencies and in encouraging others to participate in taking photographs. Such a move would have helped address much wider, general criticism of artist residency and community arts' schemes in which the value and benefit of mutual interaction was so often lost once the funding came to an end and the artist simply moved on to the next opportunity. The concern, as Barden noted, was to address the longer-term benefits of having a resident photographer for a 'rather isolated community who feel detached from decision-making processes generally'.[51]

Northern Arts did not take up the proposal, as their lack of funds was increasingly an issue. The same year as the Side exhibition, the association produced a policy review document, 'Changing landscape', to inform its strategy for the following 10 years. This responded to continued decline in its income from funders and recognition that the northern region was at that point one of the 12 poorest regions of the European Economic Community. From the mid-1980s local government funds in particular were geared to the urgency of urban economic development; but rural regeneration was equally pressing. By the end of that decade it was recorded by the Rural Development Commission (RDC) that 10 million people, one-fifth of the population, lived and worked in rural areas in England.[52] Despite the attractions of rural life, severe problems included those of any disadvantaged urban area: high and rising unemployment, a large number on low incomes and in poor housing, alongside an elderly age structure, dwindling health and medical

---

[51] *Aspects*, 1985.
[52] Rural Development Commission, 'Facts and figures' (1990). The RDC was the government agency tasked to 'create a climate in which rural businesses and communities can prosper'.

services, plus the progressive closure of rural primary schools and inaccessibility to skills and training for younger people.

A commissioned report of 1984 by Ian Watson, former director of Southwest Arts, noted that literature on rural deprivation had already been mushrooming since the late 1970s with titles such as *Rural Poverty, No Homes for Locals, The Decline of Rural Services, Deprivation in Rural Areas*, and *The Myth of the Rural Idyll*.[53] Following in this vein with its *State of the Countryside* publication, the RDC designated 27 Rural Development Areas covering 35 per cent of England across 28 counties. Within these areas from 1977 to the end of the decade some 15,000 agricultural jobs had been lost. Extensive parts of the northern region had been attributed this status and it was neces- sary for Northern Arts, and indeed the Arts Council at large, to address an imbalance in funding between London and the regions and not to privilege urban over rural areas – a problem that of course had already been identified.

The Arts Council itself developed relationships with the Department of Environment, the Development Commission, and the Countryside Commission. They also drew on existing work by the RAAs, to 'collate models of good practice', seek proposals for a national overview, and achieve a broader definition of the arts, focussing on their social and economic impact, their potential for rural job cre- ation, for tourism and so on. Further research such as Watson's was commissioned. His own report mused on the highly partial alliterative connotations of 'the rural': 'romance, retreat, refuge, retirement, rest', and the implication was a popular consciousness of rural life as of a 'Walter Gabriel quaintness, an other-worldliness which, in the white heat of a nuclear monetarist reality, is endlessly charming and attractive but not, at the end of the day, quite responsible'.[54]

Within this growing urgency, a 1985 International Symposium on Rural Arts recommended the arts be seen as one of many aspects of rural life and integrated into any overall policy for rural provision. Proper consideration was required of the relationship between touring and the importation of work and the development of local creativity. Proper consideration was also needed of the specific nature of a rural community, whether it was long-established or first generation, and of those problems created by distance and isolation, and so on.[55] For, in a situation Peter Davies had already noted in Cumbria 10 years previously, in the mid-1980s art services in rural areas still fell 'roughly into the same category as mains gas, only more so: very few rural areas in Britain can claim any at all'.[56] Cultural develop- ment needed to be an integral part of social and economic strategies. Community

---

[53] *Not the Estonian Corn Dollies*, 1984, ERAB/2/162. Watson had been awarded a three-year fellowship by The City University to study arts provision in rural areas with international comparisons.
[54] *Not the Estonian Corn Dollies*.
[55] The symposium at City University was reported upon by Petra Dolby, ACGB's Assistant Regional Director in her 'The arts in the rural areas: The development of a national policy', ERAB GoI.9.
[56] *Not the Estonian Corn Dollies*. Watson went on in relation to the Arts Council, 'it is a matter of record, that in the nearly 40 years since Keynes urged us all to be merry in our own way, not a single structure, policy or strategy has been advanced to enfranchise the roughly 20% of the British population who

arts projects were to be funded and amateur activities supported, an echo here of the photography course first established at Kielder by Murray Johnston. David Pratley's report, noted above, also spoke of the importance of employment opportunities, for example in the creation of rural museums and of arts parks, with Grizedale of course as his exemplar.

As noted earlier, the paper *Think Rural: Act Now* in June 1989 indicated it was time to follow the leads of Northern Arts and Eastern Arts with their rural initiatives, objectives in their regional plans and strategies including the use of artists working in and with rural communities. The nation's peripheries had provided the model for future ways of working. Given the status of Northumberland and Cumbria together as such a large area of rural communities, Northern Arts clearly saw the importance of the northern region as a national model here, and responded in announcing a 'Rural Arts Initiative', a competitive scheme for project proposals with a professional arts element, but demonstrating local involvement, ways to generate continued activity, to be of value to the local community or environment; to break new ground or expand upon existing work.[57] These were all activities that the two Forestry residency projects had developed in different ways through artists being 'embedded' in local communities, sharing skills, responding to local interests, resources and needs, but focusing too on their individual practice. They had been thinking and acting rurally for some time.

From this point a wider shift in regional discourse emerged in an attempt to combine rural arts from an arts perspective and rural development from an employment and development perspective. It is from here the model developed first at Grizedale began to impact on the wider environment at Kielder in terms of artists working in what were primarily leisure and tourism contexts.

Kielder Water and Forest Park

That emphasis on multiple use forestry noted at Grizedale led to the growing prominence of tourism at Kielder as facilities for water sports, cycling, camping, and other outdoor activities proliferated. Alongside tourism, Kielder village residents increasingly worked for Northumbrian Water as much, if not more than, for the Forestry Commission. For Christine McCulloch, here, as with many other landscapes around the world, 'the commercial forest and the recreational reservoir testify to modernity and domination by global capitalism'.[58] In the process,

---

live in rural areas'. Key funding initiatives had been provided instead by private trusts and foundations such as the Calouste Gulbenkian Foundation, the Carnegie United Kingdom Trust, and the Dartington Trustees.

[57] Northern Arts Press Release, NG/File, TWAM.

[58] Christine McCulloch, 'Kielder Water and Forest Park: The city in the country', in Peter Coates, David Moon, and Paul Warde (eds), *Local Places, Global Processes: Histories of Environmental Change in Britain and Beyond* (Oxford, Windgather Press, 2016), p. 6.

Figure 11.7 John Kippin, 'Invisible', 1989. © John Kippin. Courtesy of Laura Noble Gallery, London

evidence of past community and the multiple forms of existence at Kielder have been continually overwritten.

Such, effectively, was John Kippin's perspective back in 1984 in another of the few unpeopled images shown at his Side Gallery exhibition. This was a view of the valve tower on an exceptionally still and misty reservoir, a rather ghostly image with the tower dead centre in the frame. The work speaks to the extraordinary changes to the environment at Kielder, most particularly of course to the lives and livelihoods of those whose farms and homes were submerged as the reservoir was filled. In a later exhibition held at the Laing Art Gallery in Newcastle in 1989, *Futureland*, and as Kippin had extended his practice of laying text over image, the word INVISIBLE appeared across that same view (Figure 11.7). The photograph appeared there as one of a triptych of tourist sites, connecting new tourism with old industries. Caroline Taylor of Projects UK made the point in the accompanying catalogue to the exhibition that the seemingly idyllic Kielder Water image belies the fact that it was designed for economic use as a reservoir for industrial Teesside, by then in decline; that much of the water is 'deep and completely dead to life' and the central image of the valve tower 'reminiscent of a floating mausoleum'.[59]

That comment underlines a broader concern for what the photographer understood as the exploitation and distortion of heritage. Indeed in the Foreword to *Futureland*, the Laing's Senior Exhibition officer, Mike Collier, spoke of the challenge posed to the gallery in general with its responsibility for the presentation of 'our' collective history. This was especially the case in the 'current boom in the heritage industry which tends to focus on what some people have called a nostalgic "sugar coated past" ', John Kippin's own term, in fact. In a wider context his practice here corresponds to much later observations by writer Jason Orton and photographer Ken Worpole in their study of the landscape of Essex, where the rural landscape as marked by reservoirs, water towers, pumping stations, and electrification schemes has not been significantly 'absorbed into the aesthetic representation of rural life and landscape'. As they note, however, a growing number of photographers are seeking a new aesthetic with which to capture the 'palimpsest of past lives and changing landscapes' and 'the means by which we register absence as playing a shaping role in how we experience the modern world and the modern landscape'.[60]

From 1994 the Forestry Commission and Northumbrian Water, without Northern Arts involvement, began directly commissioning public art for the immediate environs of the reservoir, with the existence of the sculpture trail at Grizedale clearly a model. Albeit with some significant works commissioned in the early period in particular, Kielder sculptures tended to emphasise spectacular or immersive experiences for their own sake, as remained the case in later years in sited structures that were often the result of collaboration between design and architectural practices. In a situation not without some irony given the north's industrial past, such an association between technology and manufacturing is here located within the spheres of leisure, heritage, and tourism, and in relation to consumption rather than production.[61] Encountered by passing tourists, cyclists, and other visitors, what these more recent commissioned sculptures and structures lack, ultimately, is a sense of the extraordinary impact of 20th-century processes of modernisation on the continuously shifting and complex lives of local rural communities. The nature of that impact was clearly registered through the commitment to embedded community interaction and engagement of pioneering rural residency programmes, alongside the innovative structures of support for artists that Northern Arts was able to develop throughout this period.

[59] Caroline Taylor, in *Futureland: John Kippin and Chris Wainwright*, catalogue of an exhibition (Newcastle, Tyne and Wear Museums, 1989), n.p.
[60] Jason Orton and Ken Worpole, *The New English Landscape* (London, Field Station, 2013), pp. 28–29.
[61] On a related note here see Ysanne Holt, 'A hut on Holy Island: Reframing northern landscape', *Visual Studies*, 28:3 (2013), 224.

12

What Happens When Rural Modernity
Ceases to be Modern?

BEN ANDERSON AND MATTHEW KELLY

IF WE ARE to avoid further catastrophic climate change over the next century, the global industrial economy will undergo a transition as fundamental to rural landscapes as the developments that brought about the 'great acceleration' after 1945. This chapter considers Chatterley Whitfield colliery and Fawley power station, two 'new landscapes' that have already undergone this transition. Defined by coal and oil respectively, both are now emblematic of a dirty, polluting history, yet only recently represented a scientific and engineering modernity produced for and by a prosperous, forward-facing workforce. With extraordinary rapidity, the infrastructure and 'new lives' that made these 'new landscapes' has already moved from modern future to backwards past, its destruction serving to confirm, rather than refute, the march of modern progress.

The demolition of chimneys and cooling towers can be a dramatic spectacle, attracting crowds and media attention to a moment of creative destruction that seemingly marks the supersession of one envirotechnical energy regime by another. By obliterating the old, high explosives create a new landscape, rendering high-modernist development into a concrete-laid waste open to a fresh cycle of renewal. New lives are made possible as new landscapes become possible. Notwithstanding the affective power of the spectacle, the apparent caesura it opens up should not obscure the deep connections people have with existing infrastructure-made landscapes – and, indeed, the ghost presence of this infrastructure following demo-lition.[1] This chapter is therefore informed by what Alice Mah has termed 'ruin-ation', the process that begins well before redundancy notices and plant closures and endures long after them. As Mah shows, infrastructure does not cease to be meaning-making with its closure, it is not constituted of 'static objects', but has

---

[1] See Steven High and David W. Lewis, *Corporate Wasteland: The Landscape and Memory of Deindustrialization* (London, Cornell University Press, 2007), pp. 23–40.

Proceedings of the British Academy, **256**, 258–280, © The British Academy 2023.

different and changing relationships with the communities of which it remains a part.[2] This chapter approaches Mah's concept from two directions. In the first of our two case studies, we follow Mah in our community-focused examination of the ruination of a Staffordshire colliery, to understand how closed and derelict sites of post-war optimism become the focus for a changing and dynamic heritage. In the second we examine the lifecycle of an oil-fuelled power station in southern England and emplace the dual ruinations that saw the power station commissioned in the early 1960s, as part of the social compact that produced rural modernity, and then decommissioned in the early 2010s in response to environmental regulations. Without denying the profound dislocation or the social and economic hardship wrought by the loss of jobs, livelihoods, and communities when facilities close, we argue that closure can be contextualised historically as part of a post-war project of state-led modernity that established a logic of fossil fuel path-dependency from which sites and people only escape with difficulty.

This chapter also takes the extensive literature on 'deindustrialisation' into a new landscape. While the industrial closures of the last half-century have been driven by a global capitalism unleashed on workforces by decisions made predominantly by Western politicians and powerful financial institutions, to the next round of closure we must add to this group that part of the environmental lobby that has chosen to harness, rather than challenge capitalism to meet necessary zero-carbon objectives.[3] The global export of coal and steel production, for example, is rightly attributed to the rise of neoliberalism or market capitalism and had nothing to do with environmentalism, but the impetus behind the current drive to zero carbon, particularly in energy production, clearly is environmentalist, bringing a new dynamic to 'deindustrialisation' and posing just as many social and economic challenges.[4] The essential task set by 'zero carbon' cannot be gainsaid, and many communities will benefit from ending extraction in fragile ecosystems, the human costs of this transition – as well as those of opening up new extractive industries to support the promised zero-carbon future – are rarely acknowledged by advocates of environmental solutions that retain the modern interest in 'progress' that was also at the heart of the post-war state.

Our two case-studies demonstrate how the intersections of pasts, memories, presents, and futures are entangled in difficult-to-resolve cases of decommissioning.

---

[2] Alice Mah, *Industrial Ruination, Community, and Place: Landscapes and Legacies of Urban Decline* (London, University of Toronto Press, 2012), p. 3. See also Ann Laura Stoler (ed.), *Imperial Debris: On Ruins and Ruination* (London, Duke University Press, 2013); Sherry Lee Linkon, *The Half-Life of Deindustrialization: Working-Class Writing about Economic Restructuring* (Ann Arbor, University of Michigan Press, 2018), pp. 1–7; Jefferson Cowie and Joseph Heathcott (eds), *Beyond the Ruins: The Meanings of Deindustrialization* (London, Cornell University Press, 2003), pp. 1–2.

[3] For a useful discussion, see Peter Newell and Dustin Mulvaney, 'The political economy of the "just transition"', *The Geographical Journal*, 179:2 (2013), 132–140.

[4] Though in a slightly different context, the same link is made in Ewan Gibbs, 'Scotland's faltering green industrial revolution', *The Political Quarterly*, 92:1 (2021), 57–65.

Chatterley Whitfield colliery, near Stoke-on-Trent, allows an examination of how far coal mining should be understood within the same post-war compact as 'rural modernity' – indeed, as a core part of it. The section argues that, following closure, the industrial architecture and institutions of post-war modernity supported the site's unique mining museum, and continued to inform what decisions could and could not be made about the site. Its subsequent physical abandonment, however, has allowed not just a reintroduction of nature to the site, but of competing narrations of its heritage as well. Here, the decision to allow a site to step outside of the never-ending logic of the 'modern' has allowed communities to tell their own, competing stories.

At Fawley power station on the right bank of Southampton Water, the story mirrors that of Chatterley Whitfield. Here, what was once heralded as the UK's most efficient power station rapidly transformed into its most polluting, but its subsequent narrative betrays the logics of the modern in which such sites are caught. The closure and demolition of Fawley heralded not a return to agriculture, nor an investiture in the New Forest National Park – the site would not be stripped of its rural modernity. Instead, the demolished presence of post-war modernity dictated that the space must be made modern for the 21st century – here, by the private construction of a 'new town', complete with digital infrastructure and appropriate claims of environmental sustainability.

Chatterley Whitfield

The place of a colliery in this volume might seem odd alongside the power stations, motorways, and pylons of the late 20th century, but coal was central to post-war rural modernism nonetheless. While nationalisation has been explained as a project of social justice and managed decline, it also stood alongside planning in the British state's Labour-driven vision of an industrial social democracy.[5] Until the late 1960s, coal-fired power stations dominated UK electricity production, contributing a third of power in 1960, and supplied largely by British coal.[6] It is all too easy to see as inevitable the subsequent replacement of coal by oil and gas, steadily decreasing coal output and employment after 1957. Certainly, this was not the future of coal imagined at the outset of nationalisation in 1947, or in the 1950 *Plan for Coal*, when the central problem was meeting demand in an era of full employment.[7] Even the 1956 revision of the *Plan* predicted optimistically that 'the

---

[5] Jim Tomlinson, 'A "failed experiment"? Public ownership and the narratives of post-war Britain', *Labour History Review*, 73:2 (2008), 228–243. See also Ewan Gibbs, *Coal Country: The Meaning and Memory of Deindustrialisation in Postwar Scotland* (London, University of London Press, 2021), pp. 21–41.

[6] Martin Chick, *Electricity and Energy Policy in Britain, France and the United States since 1945* (Cheltenham, Edward Elgar, 2007), p. 7.

[7] *Plan for Coal: The National Coal Board's Proposals* (London, National Coal Board, 1950), pp. 1, 20–24.

problems of overproduction in the coal industry can scarcely arise', and demanded yet higher production targets.[8] The industry also appeared secure in the concentration of electricity production in 'Megawatt Valley' along the Trent and a belt of coalfields from North Staffordshire to South Yorkshire, slated for expansion by the National Coal Board (NCB), and the fulcrum for Britain's new 'supergrid'.[9] Industrial leaders and planners alike understood the coal industry as inherent to post-war infrastructure projects, and as such, a permanent fixture within the social contract of the newly expanded 'industrial modernity' promised by Fairbrother, something that the NCB's magazine left no doubt about to its employees.[10]

Chatterley Whitfield, a colliery that made much of its status as the UK's first 'million tonner', emerged as central to this imagination of modern coal mining for at least the first decade or so of the NCB, boasting 'week-by-week development plans' until 1967 and a target of two million tons.[11] Yet once contraction in the coal industry began in the late 1950s, the colliery went rapidly from showcase to problem: 'modernisation' now meant not investment, but closure.[12] Nationally, Harold Wilson's government's *Fuel Policy* of 1967 formalised a shift to oil, gas, and nuclear power in the state imagination of the future.[13] Regionally, the colliery no longer fitted either. Its infrastructure was ageing, and it was far from both the West Coast main line, and the planned route for the A500 'D' road. The NCB's response was the 'superpit'; closure and contraction would be offset by giganticism and centralisation projects whose architecture, as well as name, recalled the pylons and power stations of the supergrid. Chatterley Whitfield's complex mélange of buildings in styles from late-Victorian warehouse to Art Deco and Ruhr-style heapstead (Figure 12.1), and an underground of abandoned or collapsed shafts and worked-out seams, meant that serious investment went elsewhere. Output and employment at the site declined 70 per cent by the early 1970s, and the site closed shortly after an underground connection to the Wolstanton superpit.[14]

Both Chatterley Whitfield's rise and fall as a premier Staffordshire pit were accompanied by the languages of modernity. The promise of expansion and centralisation in 1950 was predicated on the assumption of closures at smaller pits and a focus on the more 'productive', 'efficient', and 'modern' coalfields.[15] At those pits

---

[8] *Investing in Coal: Progress and Prospects under the Plan for Coal* (London, National Coal Board, 1956), p. 11.

[9] *Plan for Coal*, p. 6; John Sheail, 'Power to the people: Power stations and the National Grid', in Paul Brassley, Jeremy Burchardt, and Karen Sayer (eds), *Transforming the Countryside: The Electrification of Rural Britain* (London, Routledge, 2017), pp. 38–50 (41).

[10] For example, 'Progress through coal', *North Staffordshire Chamber of Commerce Journal*, 8 (1951), 2–4; *Coal: National Coal Board Magazine* ran regular features on collieries, miners and their families, but also contributions that discussed the benefits of the new society, and miners' place within it.

[11] Lambton Burn, 'Down Hesketh Pit', *Coal*, 11 (1947), 15–18.

[12] See Gibbs, *Coal Country*, pp. 31–36.

[13] Gibbs, *Coal Country*, p. 33.

[14] CW(D)108, in CWMMDA/J T Worgan's Archive Scans/Chat Whit output stats.

[15] *Plan for Coal*, p. 3.

Figure 12.1 Winstanley headgear and Chatterley Whitfield's chimney from the country park. © Kelcey Swain, licensed for reuse under Creative Commons CC BY-SA 2.0, creativecommons.org/licenses/by-sa/2.0

that stayed open, mechanisation, and, at Chatterley Whitfield, the NCB's first computer, helped to provide a modern aesthetic that justified such decisions even as it decreased employment.[16] The miner too looked different. Gone were the whippet, flat cap, axe, and pick imagined by F. L. J. Vodrey in 1977: 'he could no longer be heard clattering down the street, his footwear now were boots, with steel toe-protectors in the toes, and hard hat to protect his head, and with a clip on the front to hold his head lamp, and a belt to carry the battery'.[17] The miners, he continued, now arrived in normal clothes, and changed at the colliery; they rode trains underground, and returned clean – something that benefited women in the community as much as the men. The state, providing pit-head equipment in place of personal tools, created a miner to suit its new image – even if these changes can be traced to

[16] CW(D)107, in CWMMDA/J T Worgan's Archive Scans/Chat Whit Iron Jack IBM Computer.
[17] F. L. J. Vodrey, 'Chatterley Whitfield: History & achievements' (c. 1977), CWMMDA/JTWORGAN'S ARCHIVE SCANS, pp. 2–6. See also Transcript of interview with Bill Brookes, David Souden, *Report for the Oral History Project within Chatterley Whitfield Regeneration Project Conservation Plan* (London, Chatterley Whitfield Regeneration Project, 2000), p. 87, available at CWMMDA/CW LIBRARY docs, books etc/Chatterley Whitfield Oral History Project Report, D. Souden 2000.

an earlier period.[18] The late 20th-century version was clean, safe, expert, and professional, a set of values that surely operated in addition to, rather than replacing, the emphasis on collective physical prowess and masculine bodies found in much other research.[19] As well as the pit itself, the pit-head baths at Chatterley Whitfield provided a space in which that combination might be played out: miners scrubbed each other's bodies, and sang communal hymns in what remained a stronghold for Methodism.[20] The post-war miner was also increasingly diverse. Chatterley Whitfield's growth in the immediate post-war era meant that its workforce included 'migrant' communities from much of Europe's South and East.[21] Many were 'Displaced Persons': Polish servicemen who remained in Britain, or refugees from camps across Central Europe through the 'European Voluntary Workers' Scheme'. Later, the British state supplemented these workers with more explicit schemes of labour recruitment such as the 'Westward Ho!' programme targeting Eastern Europeans.[22] These new communities preceded and set a pattern of movement for the later Windrush migration period, and were similarly instrumental to the post-war settlement. While British citizens arriving from the Caribbean found themselves in mining after encountering colour bars elsewhere, migrant workers from Europe remained formally 'aliens', and could be directed and coerced into understaffed sectors.[23] The 'Balt Cygnets' scheme brought thousands of Baltic-state women to work in hospitals and the new National Health Service, and established a pattern for the targets of Westward Ho!, who arrived to tackle a post-war labour shortage in Britain's heavy industries and agriculture. While by the time the *Empire Windrush* arrived, Chatterley Whitfield was contracting, many black miners worked

---

[18] The art-deco Pit-Head Baths of 1938 for example, were a result of the Miners' Welfare Committee first established in 1926. See 'A history of Chatterley Whitfield Colliery' (2013) CWMMDA/J T Worgan's Archive Scans/A History of Chat Whit, p. 10.

[19] Arthur McIvor and Ronald Johnson, *Miner's Lung: A History of Dust Disease in British Coal Mining* (London, Routledge, 2007), pp. 259–269.

[20] See for example, Stephanie Ward, 'Miners' bodies and masculine identity in Britain, c. 1900–1950', *Cultural and Social History*, 18:3 (2021), 443–462. Souden, *Oral History Report*, pp. 49–51.

[21] Brookes Transcript, p. 3; 'migrant' is problematic in this case, as many were more properly refugees, and continued to see themselves as temporary exiles even as the British states redefined them as 'workers'. See Diana Kay and Robert Miles, 'Refugees or migrant workers? The case of the European volunteer workers in Britain (1946–1951)', *Journal of Refugee Studies*, 1:3/4 (1988), 214–236 and Linda McDowell, *Hard Labour: The Forgotten Voices of Latvian Migrant Volunteer Workers* (London, UCL, 2005), pp. 87–120.

[22] Stephen Catterall and Keith Gildart, 'Outsiders: Trade union responses to Polish and Italian coal miners in two British coalfields, 1945–54', in Stefan Berger, Andy Croll, and Norman Laporte (eds), *Towards a Comparative History of Coalfield Societies* (Abingdon, Routledge, 2015 [2005]), pp. 164–176.

[23] Kay and Miles, 'Refugees or migrant workers?'; *Caribbean Voices: Memories of Stoke-on-Trent and North Staffordshire's Caribbean Community*, directed by Ray Johnson (Staffordshire Film Archive, 2011), 19:51. The 'hostels' in which each group successively lived on first arriving in an area were first built to accommodate 'Bevin Boys'. See, for example, CWMMDA/CW DOCS SCANS/Richard Alfred Lucas (Lucke) ex-miner CW.

in British collieries, including at Chatterley Whitfield and its close neighbours in North Staffordshire.[24]

These groups routinely feature in miners' memories of working in the pit, and continue to be members of social circles amongst North Staffordshire miners and heritage activists.[25] If the animosity to 'foreign' miners found by other researchers ever emerged, moreover, it is yet to feature in recorded memories of the colliery, though there are isolated examples of inter-migrant conflict, and references to Caribbean migrants are rare.[26] It would be wrong to regard the pit bottom, where racial epithets were used readily, as a multicultural haven, but it is clear that like many pits, Chatterley Whitfield fostered significant intercultural respect and exchange.[27]

Little of this was apparent in the Mining Museum which opened after the colliery fully closed in 1977, though members of the European cohorts worked as guides and volunteers. Indeed, at first glance, Chatterley Whitfield Mining Museum offered a narrow view of mining. Yet despite the popularity of the impressive drive gear in the Hesketh Building, iconic headgear (Figure 12.2) and the pit ponies, the museum was not so much an exhibition of objects, as of skills, masculinities, and hard labour. Guided tours included active demonstrations of pit-bottom mainten-ance or undercutting coal faces by hand, all led by an enthusiastic and highly skilled group of ex-miner volunteers:[28]

> They became volunteers for what was one of the best aspects of the museum … the ex-miners … guides. They were one of the prize things: Once people paid their money the whole of their visit was in the hands of ex-miners, the volunteer guides, and that was a star turn.[29]

An emphasis on skill was intrinsic to the decision to use a part of underground workings as the core exhibition space – a decision which meant planning had to be agreed with the NCB, and the museum space effectively treated as an active coal mine. Moving visitors around the underground exhibition in its first, 700ft-deep guise required a safety process integrated into the experience itself. Visitors donned miners' helmets and lamps from the lamp store, read regulations that were both exhibit and warning, and descended in an impressively cramped cage. Led by Brian

[24] Souden, *Oral History Report*, p. 50. McDowell, *Hard Labour*, p. 105. The Black Miners Museum Project, https://blackcoalminers.com [accessed 23 January 2023]. See *Caribbean Voices*, 19:51, 37:20, 39:40.
[25] David Bell, *Memories of the Staffordshire Coalfields* (Newbury, Countryside Books, 2010), p. 119.
[26] Catterall and Gildart, 'Outsiders'.
[27] Souden, *Oral History Report*, p. 50; 'Smallthorne Miners' Hostel', www.smallthorne-history.org.uk/smallthorne-miners-hostel/ [accessed 17 May 2022].
[28] Jim Worgan, 'The decline and fall of Chatterley Whitfield Mining Museum: A personal reflection by Jim Worgan', CWMMDA/J T Worgan's Archive Scans/Decline and Fall of Chat Whit Museum JTW 2001; Ph 1988 348–349 CWMMDA/CW Photo Archive.
[29] Transcript of interview with Brian Burton, CWMMDA/CW LIBRARY docs, books etc/Chatterley Whitfield Oral History Project Report, D. Souden 2000/Transcripts of Interviews/Brian Burton, p. 3.

Figure 12.2 Institute headgear at Chatterley Whitfield. © Kelcey Swain, licensed for reuse under Creative Commons CC BY-SA 2.0, creativecommons.org/licenses/by-sa/2.0

Burton, a small group of men re-engineered the pit bottom of the Winstanley shaft (see Figure 12.1) for ventilation and a new roughly circular route for the tour. Other than this, they left the roads and much of the equipment in place; they could hardly have done otherwise, since much of it was embedded in, and (in the case of roof supports in varying degrees of collapse) intrinsic to the space itself.[30] The result was a walk around what to any non-expert would have been a profoundly mysterious and confusing array of equipment, if it were not for the guides.[31]

The last two decades have seen a reassessment of the meaning inherent to the skills 'lost' with deindustrialisation, and especially to the largely male ex-employees of heavy industries such as mining.[32] For Arthur McIvor, the sudden loss of work entailed a loss of those identities, and a long-term legacy of physical and mental illness that needs to be set alongside the other harms of heavy industry

---

[30] Brian Burton transcript, p. 4. Burton considered only about 10 per cent of the pit bottom to have been 'artificially created' for the museum.

[31] See Ph 1988 348–349.

[32] While the pits continued to be an exclusively male preserve after the 1842 Mines Act banned women and children, 'pit brow girls' remained a core part of a surface workforce picking and cleaning coal well into the 20th century. At Chatterley Whitfield, women continued to work in administration – and especially the running of a computer in the years around 1960 – catering, and in the on-site coal analysis laboratory. The underground tour also had one – lone – female guide.

on the body.[33] The emphasis on skill and expertise, and the physical demonstration of these skills – including not just mining, but, for example, knowledge of safety procedures – can be understood against this research.[34] This is true not only for the tour guides, but for much of the staff of a museum that would not have been possible without the application of coal-mining expertise, knowledge, and understanding. Volunteers drafted designs and plans for the museum using skills developed while proposing coal-mine extensions, and the site employed engineers and a mine manager in addition to standard museum staff. When the closure of North Staffordshire's 'superpit' at Wolstanton forced the first 'underground experience' to close, the planning and design for the 'New Mine' followed the same pattern, using the same people.[35] So too the activities of the Chatterley Whitfield Friends continue to place an emphasis on mechanical skill; their Memorial Garden is part tribute to those who died on the site, and part tribute to the skills of mining, demonstrated in outdoors exhibits that include a working cart-run through wooden roof supports.[36]

At the outset, the promoters of Chatterley Whitfield Mining Museum could be optimistic that their venture had a long-term future, but it relied on a public sector ecosystem which recognised the mutual benefits of supporting a cultural and social infrastructure. In this sense, the museum was a continuity with the closed colliery in another way – it served as a cultural and social hub, supported by the mining industry, just as the NCB and its affiliated organisations sponsored a social and sporting infrastructure. According to Brian Burton, the effective founder of the museum, support came from not just the NCB, but also new museums at Ironbridge or Gladstone Pottery.[37] While long-term direct financial support came from Stoke City Council, the museum also benefited from renting offices to the NCB and a branch of Manpower Services Commission (MSC), a public agency which ran the Youth Opportunities Programme in the 1970s, and which also supplied labour at no extra charge. The museum could use haulage transport for free, and the close inter-relationships of the British state also meant that it housed an 'Energy Hall' sponsored by the Midland Electricity Board. These mutually supporting elements of the late 20th-century British state gradually untangled during late 1980s Thatcherism, in the aftermath of the miners' strike, during which the museum was targeted by picketers.[38] The effective privatisation of youth training provision meant

---

[33] Arthur McIvor, 'Deindustrialization embodied: Work, health, and disability in the United Kingdom since the mid-twentieth century', in Steven High, Lachlan Mackinnon, and Andrew Perchard (eds), *The Deindustrialized World: Confronting Ruination in Postindustrial Places* (Vancouver, University of British Columbia Press, 2017), pp. 25–45 at 27–31.

[34] Worgan, 'Decline and fall', p. 22.

[35] Brian Burton transcript, p. 4.

[36] https://chatterleywhitfieldfriends.org.uk/remembrance-garden/ [accessed 19 January 2023].

[37] Brian Burton transcript, p. 2.

[38] Brian Burton transcript, p. 4.

the local replacement of MSC by a private provider, Laing Employment Training Organisation. While the new provider maintained a relationship with the museum and remained on site, declining supervision of on-site trainees in a period of increasing theft harmed what appears to have been a constructive relationship. The museum appeared to benefit from the closure of another mining museum at Lound Hall in Nottingham in 1990, and was briefly custodian of the vast 'British Coal Collection'.[39] Triumph here was itself symptomatic of British Coal's own hollowing out – shortly after the announcement, British Coal announced its total withdrawal from the Chatterley Whitfield site, starving of resources the same organisation it had only recently awarded its most extensive material archive.[40] Increasingly, the museum began resorting to independent fundraising and seeking private invest-ment, but its chairman, and most significant benefactor, Ron Southern, announced his retirement as Stoke City Council Leader.[41] Within a few years, council funding to the museum had been cut by two-thirds, even as the same corporation stepped in to save a local pottery museum, and rejected funding from nearby Newcastle-under-Lyme.[42] While the exact cause of this sudden abandonment remains unclear, the future of the museum was in question once the public-sector ecosystem in which it emerged began to collapse. That same process also spread beyond the colliery into surrounding communities, where the social and leisure infrastructure once provided by the post-war state and NCB has gradually disappeared.

While the visible heritage of coal disappeared from the skyline of Stoke-on-Trent, its toxic legacies remained – a heritage of deindustrialisation, nationalisa-tion, and the post-war settlement between state, worker, and landscape. Coal dust was embedded in the lungs and bodies of its workers, sulphates from colliery, pottery, and iron waste underlay the houses many continued to live in.[43] As myriad studies of coal legacies, and much of the literature on deindustrialisation demonstrates, this continuing ruination of people, environments, landscapes, and communities pervade the memories of such sites, and thus of the collapse of a post-war compact.[44] For those interviewed in 2000, dust recalled ineffectual water spray treatments, and a state resistant to compensation claims, irrespective of the well-advertised efforts of the nationalised industry to protect its workforce.[45] The legacies of mining on local landscapes are also both one of the post-war

[39] The NCB became 'British Coal' in 1987.

[40] See Worgan, 'Decline and fall', pp. 4–14.

[41] Worgan, 'Decline and fall', p. 16.

[42] Worgan, 'Decline and fall', p. 17.

[43] The 'Red Ash' problem, particularly prevalent in North Staffordshire, results from using sulphate-rich industrial waste beneath concrete flooring. Though not toxic to humans, it causes structural damage to homes such as bowed floors and undermined walls. See Ian Longworth, *Sulfate Damage to Concrete Floors on Sulfate-bearing Hardcore: Identification and Remediation* (Department for Communities and Local Government, 2008).

[44] For example, McIvor, 'Deindustrialization embodied'; McIvor and Johnston, *Miners' Lung*.

[45] Souden, *Oral History Report*, pp. 87–89.

modernist state and of a voracious extractive industry. Much of the dark and geometric shapes of spoil heaps and railway cuttings preceded the Second World
War, but the new state compact also transformed these sites into a new landscape
typified by sports and leisure facilities and derelict 'brownfields'. Of the 600
acres of derelict land designated for clearance in North Staffordshire and Stoke-
on-Trent in 1963, for example, 85 per cent (and 17 out of 24 schemes) were to
provide sites for leisure, sports, or to improve 'amenity' in the area.[46] While these
legacies continue to produce both harm and benefits in communities such as those
connected to Chatterley Whitfield, we need to understand them not as legacies of
a declining 19th-century industry, but rather as one of the early human costs of
the 'Great Acceleration'.

The colliery at Chatterley Whitfield, however, got a reprieve. As it became
clear the museum would close, its last manager arranged for much of the site to
be designated an ancient monument, while its spoil heap and railway successfully
transitioned to a well-used local nature reserve with minimal heritage provision.[47]
The new status has, almost certainly, saved the colliery buildings from demolition, but it has also left them in a position of long-term heritage stasis and physical
decay, as well as, more positively, natural 'rewilding'. The dangerous condition
of most of the site means that it largely sits behind a security fence, with even
limited access restricted to guided tours and heritage professionals. It has also been
a target of repeated ambitious, expensive, and largely failed regeneration proposals
from politicians, local authorities, and heritage bodies – though these also helped
to establish the Chatterley Whitfield Friends group itself.[48] In general, schemes
have relied on refitting the site for a 21st-century modern, typically interpreted as
a leisure, arts and retail park powered by on-site renewable energy – particularly
wind, solar, and geothermal heat-pumps.

A challenge for such schemes is to offer an appropriately 'modern' future whilst
retaining the creative heritage that is a core part of its story, and continues on the site

[46] Hansard HC Deb, 15 March 1963, vol. 673, cc208–11W.

[47] James Hutchinson to J. W. Worgan, 7 December 1993 in Worgan, 'Decline and fall', p. 29;
'£14 million awarded to Chatterley Whitfield', CWMMDA/CW Library docs, books etc/Chatterley
Whitfield, £14 million Award.

[48] For example, AEA Technology, 'Chatterley Whitfield – a centre for renewable energy [report for
English Heritage]' (2001), in CWMMDA/CW Library docs, books etc/Chatterley Whitfield – A Centre
for Renewable Energy; Llewelyn Davies, 'Chatterley Whitfield action plan: Final report', CWMMDA/
CW Library docs, books etc/Chatterley Whitfield Regeneration Plan, Llewelyn Davies (2001);
ERM, 'Economic appraisal of redeveloping the former Chatterley Whitfield coalfield site in North
Staffordshire', CWMMDA/CW Library docs, books etc/Chatterley Whitfield, Economic Appraisal of
Redevelopment (2004); 'Chatterley Whitfield preparation and programme for developer involvement –
cabinet agenda planning session, City of Stoke-on-Trent', CWMMDA/CW Library docs, books etc/
Chatterley Whitfield, Preparation & Programme for Developer Involvement; 'Chatterley Whitfield July
2003', CWMMDA/CW Library Docs, books etc/Chatterley Whitfield, Brief History and Regeneration
Project (2003).

even in its current state.[49] As the memorial garden, guided tours, and heritage centre run by volunteers at Chatterley Whitfield suggests, where sites cease to be one modern but do not become another, they can provide opportunities for community agency and heritage production outside of the logic of capitalism. They also provide sites on which the meanings of that heritage is contested across generations, class, and institutions. While the Friends represent a continuing community of work, largely led by men with personal or family connections to North Staffordshire mining, local young people are now less likely to have family connections to the colliery. Their engagement with the site as a rite of passage nevertheless continues a liminal role for the transition to adulthood attested to in Chatterley Whitfield's previous guises as both productive colliery and museum, yet threaten the Friends' access to the site, as well as the respect which miners' families sometimes feel the site requires.[50] As the last complete colliery in North Staffordshire, and with a still-present, unique museum exhibition lying just underground, Chatterley Whitfield has also been a target for the largely middle-class 'Urban Explorers' so beloved of avant-garde academics.[51] A more-than-human presence of foxes, barn owls, and other birds of prey recall an environment long lost to the colliery, yet now protected by it, and integral to the diversity of the Whitfield Valley nature reserve.[52] These different versions of Chatterley Whitfield compete for space within the confines of the site. So far at least, proposed schemes for redevelopment leave little room for dynamism or change in how different communities interpret or construct the past.[53]

Understanding how to interpret and conceptualise a changing and dynamic heritage has become a preoccupation of researchers concerned with the future of memories of deindustrialisation.[54] As the physical infrastructure of 20th-century carbon culture is (too slowly) replaced by a new landscape of renewable infrastructure, and communities of labour dwindle through death and mobility, memories of industry are creatively remade for a new context, prompting one study to question

[49] See Mah, *Industrial Ruination*, pp. 175–194.

[50] Notes on 'Decommissioning the twentieth century workshop: Presences', online, 15 March 2021, Decommissioning the Twentieth Century, Keele Data Repository.

[51] For example, Bradley L. Garrett, 'Urban exploration as heritage placemaking', in Hilary Orange (ed.), *Reanimating Industrial Spaces: Conducting Memory Work in Post-Industrial Societies* (London, Routledge, 2015), pp. 72–91; Tim Edensor, *Industrial Ruins: Space, Aesthetics and Materiality* (Oxford, Berg, 2005). For a critique, see High and Lewis, *Corporate Wasteland*, pp. 46–63. See, for example, Chatterley Whitfield Colliery, Staffordshire, www.bcd-urbex.com/chatterley-whitfield-colliery/ [accessed 25 January 2023].

[52] 'Presences'.

[53] See Tim Strangleman, 'Deindustrialisation and the historical sociological imagination: Making sense of work and industrial change', *Sociology*, 51:2 (2017), 466–482 at 471–472.

[54] Orange, *Reanimating Industrial Spaces*; Ewan Gibbs, Susan Henderson, and Victoria Bianchi, 'Intergenerational learning and place-making in a deindustrialized locality: "Tracks of the past" in Lanarkshire, Scotland', *International Labor and Working-Class History* (2022), 1–24 at 3.

the 'half-life' metaphor of continual, gradual, and inevitable dissipation. Chatterley Whitfield suggests that similar criticisms might be levelled at 'ruination', defined by Laura Ann Stoler as 'an *act* perpetrated, a *condition* to which one is subject, and a *cause* of loss'.[55] Chatterley Whitfield continues to represent the ruination of deindustrialisation for the same communities who experience it, but *as a* ruin it *does not* ruin; rather it has become a site in which different groups can narrate and make sense of their loss precisely because it is no longer modern.

Emplacing Fawley

Interwar maps of the west bank of Southampton Water inscribe a rural landscape with Cadland Park and Cadland House as its centrepiece. The house and park were part of the Cadland Estate, acquired by the Drummond family in 1772, comprising several thousand acres on the south-east corner of land where Southampton Water meets The Solent, much of which remains with the family today. By the 1970s, similar mapping enterprises described a peri-urban, industrial landscape dominated by modern industrial infrastructure and extensive urbanisation. This rapid transformation was catalysed in 1947 with the strategic decision by the Ministry of Power to make a compulsory purchase order for a large stretch of land alongside Southampton Water, which included approximately a third of the Cadland Estate. Cadland House, including parkland landscaped by Capability Brown, and 40 estate cottages, were demolished; intertidal mudflats were reclaimed. A substantial extension to the existing Esso oil refinery followed, opened by Prime Minister Attlee in 1951 and active today. This represented the first stage in the development of a major industrial complex, that included Marchwood Power Station (1955) and the development of industries that either rely on refinery product – International Synthetic Rubber (1958), Monsanto Chemicals (1958), Union Carbide (1960), and the Hythe Gasworks (1964) – or supported it – Air Products (1961). The development culminated at its southern end with the completion of the oil-fuelled Fawley power station in 1969.[56]

A puff piece published in *The Times* in February 1956 extolled the regeneration of the region. Preservationists might have been alarmed by these developments, the Council for the Preservation of Rural England (CPRE) saying that 'once the "effective natural barrier" of Southampton Water was crossed, the whole area of the New Forest would be endangered', but regional boosters regarded the Esso refinery as the 'outstanding post-war development' in an area undergoing a period of rapid regeneration. Southampton had been heavily bombed during the war but now mixed

---

[55] Ann Laura Stoler, 'Introduction: "The rot remains": From ruins to ruination', in Ann Laura Stoler (ed.), *Imperial Debris: On Ruins and Ruination* (London, Duke University Press, 2013), p. 11. Emphasis in original.

[56] R. H. Lester, 'Industrial development around the Esso Refinery, Fawley', *Geography*, 58:2 (April 1973), 154–159.

'modernity with ruins', renewing its claim to be the 'Gateway to Britain'. Its new university, chartered in 1952, promised to bring further engineering expertise to a city already associated with pioneering aeronautics, but it was the rural west bank of Southampton Water that had 'comparable advantages' unmatched elsewhere in southern England.[57]

If we're looking to emplace the history of the 'great acceleration', as manifest in the increased energy demands that determined the new lives of post-war Britain and the growth of the petrochemical industry, the west bank of Southampton Water provides a prime location. In this new industrial complex was manifest the rapid development of the carbon economy and its transformation of rural places, instantiating the public–private but statist underpinnings of the new landscapes created by modern energy infrastructure. Emblematic not just of the new post-war optimism but also the centrality of private interests to the delivery of public goods was the advertisement taken out by Esso celebrating the opening of the Central Electricity Generating Board's Marchwood Power Station in 1957. Esso would supply the oil.[58] Once Fawley was commissioned, *The Times* regularly carried news of the numerous private contracts, and the employment they generated, that its construction made possible.[59]

But just as Fawley can be emplaced in terms of social democracy and the mixed economy, so the lifecycle of the power station was determined, first, by post-1979 market liberalism, and second, by commitments to decarbonise energy generation. The privatisation of electricity generation in 1990 transferred the power station from public into private ownership, while the European Union Large Combustion Plant Directive (1988/2010) ensured the power station was shut down in March 2013. What, in the 1970s, was promoted as the UK's most *efficient* power station, fired up when there were shortfalls in the grid, was later condemned as its most *polluting*. That shift in optic, in how the power station was evaluated, provides another way of explaining the historical shifts that have determined the use of the site.

Once Fawley was condemned, it became a declining asset, ripe for redevelopment. Notwithstanding its iconic chimney, used as a navigation aid by sailors in the Solent and providing orientation for local communities, and circular control room, a favourite for Hollywood location scouts, attempts to have the power station listed failed, enabling its purchase in 2015 by a private consortium (Figure 12.3). In 2020, the planning authorities approved a fiercely ambitious masterplan to transform the site into a new business and residential complex, a new town according to the promoters. Fawley Waterside is as potentially transformative as the high modernist, statist developments of the 1950s, 1960s, and 1970s. The founder and chief executive of Fawley Waterside is Aldred Drummond, owner of the Cadland Estate and property

[57] *The Times*, 11 February 1956.
[58] *The Times*, 5 June 1957.
[59] Reports in *The Times* include 14 September 1962, 20 September 1962, 19 April 1963, 9 July 1963, 26 July 1963, 15 October 1963, 3 January 1964, 8 January 1964, 11 February 1964, and 13 March 1964.

Figure 12.3 Fawley power station. © Geni, licensed for reuse under Creative Commons
CC BY-SA 4.0, https://creativecommons.org/licenses/by-sa/4.0, via Wikimedia Commons

developer or, as he puts it, a specialist in 'building communities'. Drummond was
apparently determined to regain ownership of the former lands of the family estate,
and he exemplifies how old wealth has been able to capitalise on the opportunities
provided by market liberalism. Fawley Waterside emplaces financialisation, global
capital flows, and the accelerated accumulation of wealth in private hands.

That there are clear differences between the transformation of the site in the
1950s and 1960s, a public–private initiative purportedly in the interest of the
national community, and the transformation currently in prospect, largely for
the benefit of private interests, should not obscure how profoundly environmentally disruptive were post-war interventions. Post-war governments empowered
themselves to act in ways that led to the transformation of rural environments.
Specifically, the planning process that led to the decision to build the Fawley
power station provides an illuminating example of how the development of energy
infrastructure was managed in the south of England where fuel supplies – coal –
could not be extracted locally.

*

In the 1950s, officials considering how to meet the growing demand for electricity in the south of England placed the question of fuel supply at the centre
of their discussions. Coal provided the standard answer, and with the wartime
shortages overcome, the coal industry was increasingly dependent on the Central
Electricity Generating Board (CEGB)'s readiness to build new coal-fired power

stations. But to adopt coal either entailed transporting it long distances or building power stations elsewhere, along with expensive and controversial pylons to carry the electricity south.[60] Locating new power stations in the Midlands might please the National Union of Miners but as Katrina Navickas's chapter in this volume demonstrates, the CEGB was right to fear that the spoliation of local environments for the benefit of distant communities could rouse local opposition, particularly if threatening to enliven perceptions of the north/south divide and place local or regional socio-economic needs in conflict with an emergent sense of environmental justice.[61] The opposition roused by the proposal that one of a string of coal-fired power stations on the River Trent should be at Holme Pierrepont, close to Nottingham and inside the city's Green Belt, evinced how even in a county heavily dependent on the coal industry questions of amenity, and especially public health, limited the CEGB's options.[62]

The brave new world of nuclear power offered an alternative solution, and in the late 1950s the coastal villages of Earnley, south-west of Chichester, and Hamstead, on north-west side of the Isle of Wight, came under consideration. Earnley was rejected on technical grounds, though public anxiety about situating a nuclear power station in a densely populated area exercised the local authorities. Belatedly, the ecological value of the site was acknowledged 'as one of the last remaining wild bits of the Sussex coast', the site's prior use by the RAF having apparently obscured its 'scientific' value.[63] By contrast, the National Parks Commission, supported by the Nature Conservancy, and much public opinion, objected to the use of Hamstead on amenity grounds.[64] The CEGB gamely contended that landscaping might minimise the impact of a power station at Hamstead, which as Ian Waites explains was deployed to such striking effect at West Burton, but it eventually conceded that the 'psychological' effect of a nuclear power station on the Isle of Wight could not be overcome.[65]

Pressure from Sir Christopher Hinton, chair of the CEGB, injected some urgency into the search for an alternative site. It has been suggested that the nuclear proposals were a strategic ploy intended to soften the opposition to Fawley; in any case, it seems nuclear was never a serious option for a power station on Southampton Water. The site was initially considered for a coal-fired power station,

[60] Roy Gregory, *The Price of Amenity: Five Studies in Conservation and Government* (London, Macmillan, 1971), p. 92.

[61] See Ed Atkins, 'Building a dam, constructing a nation: The "drowning" of Capel Celyn', *Journal of Historical Sociology*, 31 (2018), 455–468.

[62] Roy Gregory tells the story, reflecting on the eventual decision to locate the station at Ratcliffe-on-Soar on the outer edge of the Nottingham Green Belt. See Gregory, *The Price of Amenity*, pp. 89–132.

[63] Rural District Council of Chichester to CEGB, 10 April 1959; Note by E. B. Worthington (NC?) on Earnley, 19 March 1959 (FT 3/533).

[64] NPC to C. F. C. Bower (NC), 31 July 1959; M. J. Woodman to N. F. Haylock (Society for the Protection of the Solent Area), 10 April 1959 (FT 3/533).

[65] 'Proposed sites for nuclear power stations on the south coast', 14 December 1960 (FT 3/533).

which might seem surprising given the presence of the Esso oil refinery and the oil-fired power station at Marchwood, but pressure from the NCB and the National Union of Miners, recalling vulnerabilities to oil supply during the war, fomented concern about fuel security. The case for coal soon looked threadbare. To increase the region's dependence on distant coal supplies would lead to higher transport costs, including the costs of a jetty into deep water for the delivery of coal by barge, and higher bills for consumers.[66] Fear of future oil import taxes were met with the claim that proximity to the refinery promised efficiency, though little evidence suggests fuel security concerns ever posed a serious threat to the plan. These arguments were immediately salient, but they also reflected a larger shift in UK energy policy that tended to favour alternatives to coal and were part of the managed decline of the industry.[67]

More challenging to the proposers was concern about the station's local environmental impact. These objections broadly took two interrelated forms. First, fear of the effect of atmospheric and chemical pollution on local and regional ecologies and, second, a more general concern that the extension of the industrial complex further south would encroach on relatively unspoilt country, signalling a general openness by the planning authorities to the further industrialisation of the Hampshire coastline. Voices looking to halt further industrial encroachment called for the new power station to be located north-west of the refinery and close to Marchwood. However, a 2,000KW power station located on the River Test would require either eight cooling towers and a 500-acre site or a seven-mile-long discharge pipe to Stanswood Bay at a cost of £10 million. At Fawley, only a 130-acre site was required because a system of culverts would channel waste waters into the strong tidal currents that animated Southampton Water.[68]

Objections were inevitable and followed the pattern established by the many local public inquiries of the period. Cowes Urban District Council, Winchester Rural District Council, and the CPRE lodged formal objections; Fareham Urban District Council and New Forest Rural District Council made 'precautionary' objections; and among the small number of objections made by members of the public were those of Maldwin Drummond of the Manor of Cadland and his tenants. These latter objections were part of a coordinated effort. Drummond was already aggrieved by the failure to fulfil undertakings related to the dredging of Southampton Water, a condition of earlier developments: contractors had not met their commitment to tackle drainage problems inflicted on Cadland tenancies by the dumping of silt on marshland that preceded industrial developments. Now Drummond registered his objection to the proposal on the grounds that it would intensify apparent problems already associated

[66] 'Proposed sites for nuclear power stations on the south coast'; G. S. Campbell to *Southern Evening Echo*, 21 August 1961 (POWE 14/1316); *The Times*, 25 March 1961.

[67] Gibbs, *Coal Country*, p. 4.

[68] M. V. Bartlett, CEGB, to L. F. Saw, HLG, 25 July 1961 (POWE 14/1315); Senior Engineering Inspector to Richard Wood, Minister of Power, 18 May 1962, pp. 4, 6 (POWE 14/1316).

with the industrialisation of the area. Some objections were specific to the new development. Costly improvements to Ower House would be undermined if fine views over Southampton Water were obscured, and Drummond feared the requisition of estate land for improved roads and the siting of pylons needed to carry the 400KW cables that would transmit the newly-generated electricity from the power station. Some reasons were more general. Drummond's land agent wrote about the likely 'disturbance to rural life, particularly shooting on the estate': increased population density would lead to traffic congestion, the greater incidence of trespass, and fire risk to woodland.[69] Drummond's tenants primarily objected on agricultural grounds, though one lamented the loss of his view of Southampton Water: he did 'not wish to lose this amenity'.[70] Nice try. Amenity, of course, was usually understood in social rather than private terms. The sensibilities of an individual tenant farmer or homeowner was unlikely disturb the sleep of a planning inspector.

Such objections had the potential to develop into a fully-fledged planning dispute if Hampshire County Council, the planning authority, withheld its consent and thereby required the minister to order a local public inquiry. The council, however, accepted the need for new power stations and was principally concerned that one of the two locations south of the refinery under consideration would take the Southampton Water industrial zone not just into the Green Belt agreed in 1958 but also into the area centred on Calshott spit that was central to the council's leisure strategy. The council was already in negotiations with the Crown Estate Commissioners for the long-term lease of the spit, a Second World War legacy holding of the RAF. Faced with the prospect of a formal objection by council, the CEGB turned its attention to the more northern of the two sites, a combination of reclaimed land and saltings.[71] The council now kept the possibility of a formal objection in reserve as it sought assurances that the Ministry of Housing and Local Government would support its case for taking possession of Calshott, tantamount to guaranteeing the lease transfer. Although the CEGB was riled that their plans depended on a quite separate political process, significant planning decisions often involved a string of ministries and related land-use questions. In February 1962, the council got its assurance and promptly announced it would not object to the plans. The objecting district councils and the Cadland Estate and tenants swiftly followed suit, one tenant writing that 'if Cadland Settled Estates withdraw their objection I will withdraw mine'.[72] The National Parks Commission and the CPRE adopted a pragmatic position, passively informing the ministry that it would not, respectively, offer comment or seek a local inquiry.[73] Somewhat comically, Lord Huntingdon, spokesperson for the Solent Protection Society, commented that if 'the

[69] R. Bacon to Ministry of Power, 21 September 1961 (POWE 14/1316).
[70] To Ministry of Power, 19 September 1961 (POWE 14/1316).
[71] *The Times*, 21 March 1961, 25 March 1961, 29 April 1961, 30 May 1961.
[72] Albert Smith to the Ministry of Power, 22 and 24 March 1962 (POWE 14/1316).
[73] H. F. Donglay (NPC) to Ministry of Power, 15 March 1962; Herbert Griffin (CPRE) to Ministry of Power, 29 March 1962 (POWE 14/1316).

design and layout of this station is of the highest standard it could provide a striking and effective termination to the sprawling industrialisation of the Fawley area'.[74] Doubtless he was relieved that the decision effectively shelved the Hamstead proposals, but this seems a little disingenuous.

Only the Hampshire Field Club and Archaeological Society held out. As a gesture of goodwill, the Minister of Power ordered a hearing be held at Jubilee Hall in Fawley to allow the Field Club's case to be heard and answered by an engineering inspector. There was no prospect this process would change the decision. Familiar arguments were rehearsed about why Marchwood was unsuitable and why the great height of the chimney (650 feet), only the third of its kind, was necessary. To the Field Club's fear that thermal down draughts caused by large stretches of cool water would submerge the New Forest in a sulphur cloud, the inspector explained that such was the height of the chimney, by the time the discharged sulphur dioxide came back down to earth it would have been sufficiently widely dispersed and diluted to be harmless. In any case, the oil to be supplied by the Esso refinery, a mix from Libya and the Middle East, would be relatively low in sulphur (3 per cent). The Field Club was also assured of the CEGB's respect for the Green Belt. Should further capacity be required, the power station would only be extended north, towards the refinery.[75] The Field Club was rightly unconvinced by these environmental assurances and refused to withdraw its objection, but due diligence complete, it came as no surprise when the minister gave his consent in June.[76]

In 1972, Roy Gregory observed: 'What with National Parks, Areas of Outstanding Natural Beauty, Areas of Great Landscape Value, Green Belts, Nature Reserves, and Sites of Special Scientific Interest, it was becoming increasingly difficult to find sites that did not provoke opposition from one amenity interest or another.'[77] In contrast to the numerous planning disputes that punctuated the development of rural modernity in post-war Britain, the Fawley process was largely unaffected by the new designation archipelago. Instead, the construction period attracted much favourable press coverage. *The Times* was particularly taken by Fawley as a symbol of technological advance and celebrated the new scale of rural modernity; its stories often read like a glorified press release. Automation at Fawley would rely on the 'largest and most comprehensive power station control system in Europe, probably in the world', the 100ft diameter butterfly valve was the biggest used in any power station, and the planned tunnel under Southampton Water connecting the power station to the city would be two miles long. Photographs of the construction site, particularly the famous control room, featured on several occasions in the newspaper's 'Picture Gallery' and to illustrate other stories, while the newspaper

[74] *The Times*, 18 August 1961.

[75] These details are drawn from the Engineering Inspector's 18-page typed report to the Minister of Power, 18 May 1962 (POWE 14/1316).

[76] R. I. P. Jowitt to A. C. Campbell, Ministry of Power, 4 July 1962 (POWE 14/1316).

[77] Gregory, *The Price of Amenity*, p. 91.

sold advertising space close to these stories to companies keen to boast of their involvement in the project like Mitchell Construction and English Electric.[78] In due course, plans for a still larger oil-fuelled power station at Killingholme near Immingham in Lincolnshire, the latest addition to Megawatt Valley, saw the press turn its attention away from Fawley.[79]

As one of a new generation of oil-fired power stations completed on the eve of the oil crisis in 1973, Fawley's use was significantly inhibited by surging oil prices. Its highest annual output was recorded during the miners' strike in 1985, when it was one of 22 oil- and gas-fired power stations tasked with meeting peak demand when coal stocks began to fail. Inevitably, this politicised the site, though the National Union of Mineworkers' attempt to 'picket' the pipeline from the oil refinery to power station failed to bring out unionised Esso workers on the grounds that the oil would pass a picket line, while the threat that crude tankers would dock without tugs ensured the tug crews of Southampton Water stayed in line.[80] Thus, from the moment Fawley power station was commissioned in the 1960s through to the 1980s, the site can be used to emplace the managed decline and ultimate destruction of the UK coal industry, but this should not be attributed prematurely to the environmental agenda. The decision to run down the UK coal industry, which depended on state subsidies, was mainly driven by marketisation and the global trade in commodities. In the late 1980s, the prospect of a coal-fired power station at Fawley was revived by a Conservative government determined to take advantage of cheap imported coal. Plans for Fawley 'B', 'bigger than St. Paul's cathedral', included a coal importing terminal and the promise of an annual landing capacity that would cover the five million tonnes of coal needed for Fawley 'B' and the three million tonnes to be rail-freighted to Didcot power station in Oxfordshire. Plans were derailed not by concerns about air and marine pollution but by the government's plans to privatise the industry. It could not guarantee that the new distribution companies would buy from Fawley 'B'.[81]

*

The Fawley Waterside scheme was approved in a very different context to that faced by the CEGB in either the early 1960s or the late 1980s. For example, the designation of the New Forest National Park in 2005, part of New Labour's revival of the National Park agenda, helped strengthen the hand of the objectors and there can be little doubt that planning processes had become more complex. Environmental requirements were more stringent, requiring inputs from a wide range of statutory and non-statutory bodies, but as had been the case in the early 1960s, the plans had

---

[78] *The Times*, 7 January 1965, 19 March 1965, 5 April 1965, 1 May 1965, 28 May 1965, 30 October 1965, 13 December 1965, 21 June 1966, 29 June 1966, 25 July 1966, 23 May 1967, 24 September 1968, 28 November 1969, and 20 April 1970.

[79] *The Times*, 30 July 1970.

[80] Frank Ledger and Howard Sallis, *Crisis Management in the Power Industry: An Inside Story* (London, Routledge, 1995, 2018), 125–127, 197, 234.

[81] *The Times*, 28 November 1987, 8 December 1987, 6 April 1988, and 28 October 1988.

a following wind thanks to their alignment with government priorities, though this time it was housing rather than energy policy.

Some objectors fastened onto Tom Tiddler's Ground, a piece of rough grazing inside the site of the original power station *and* the National Park, slated with redevelopment as part of the scheme, but the objections of local authorities were mainly concerned with traffic congestion in and around the A326. Sixty years on from the power station planning process, local concerns were surprisingly similar. What effect would an increase in population pressure – dog-walkers were of particular concern – and traffic congestion have on the agri-habitats of the National Park? Like all early 21st-century housing projects, the reception of the Fawley Waterside masterplan was shadowed by the spectre of inadequate infrastructure. There was some irony in opponents like the Friends of the New Forest, a long-established 'amenity society' in the classic mould, making arguments against the plans of Drummond *fils* that echoed positions once taken by Drummond *pere*, but ultimately this was to no avail. The New Forest National Park Authority approved the planning application, accepting that the loss of Tom Tiddler's Ground, never more than a diversion, would be offset by the significant biodiversity gains promised by the new development.[82]

Beginning in 2019, Fawley power station was demolished piece by piece, each stage in the process orchestrated as a media event that culminated in the detonation of the iconic chimney early on the morning of 31 October 2021. At the time of writing, the control room is intact, though in September 2022 on-site demolition workers told me that it was soon to go. For now, electricity bought from France, carried by cables under the Channel and Southampton Water, feeds the Fawley transformer station, whence it travels the cables strung from the famous pylons that prance across the New Forest. Soon, little trace of the power station will remain, though the power station's subterranean structures, among its most significant engineering achievements, will become the basis of car parks, foundations, and other utilitarian structures.

During the demolition process, the site was used by a Danish firm for painting and storing turbine blades (Figure 12.4). The environmentalist might take satisfaction in this 21st-century use of a site associated with 20th-century energy production, but in the age of anthropogenic climate change, it is illusory to imagine that demolition can erase the material effects of the power station or that those effects can be offset by the environmentally sustainable aspects of the Fawley Waterside masterplan. The lifecycle of Fawley power station, an intrusion onto a southern English rural pastoral, can be used to emplace the transition from post-war social democracy to early 21st-century neoliberalism; to centre the carbon deposits

---

[82] See www.newforestnpa.gov.uk/documents/planning-committee/extraordinary-planning-meeting-28-7-2020/ [accessed 23 February 2022], especially 'Report Item 1 – 19/00365/OUT-Land Adjacent to Fawley Power Station'.

Figure 12.4 Wind turbine blades with Fawley power station control room in the background, August 2022. © Matthew Kelly

formed over millennia the power station so inefficiently burned also emplaces deep time, scrolling forward as well as back.

Conclusion

In her discussion of 'imagining change' in deindustrialised sites, Mah questions the 'one-size-fits-all' logic of redevelopment, which assumes a 'context of economic growth', a 'model of arts- and property-led regeneration', and that the 'best ultimate future' is a post-industrial knowledge economy.[83] Chatterley Whitfield and Fawley offer complementary narratives of how sites that were once modern become caught in a logic that renders them vulnerable to the imposition of that 'best ultimate future'. Chatterley Whitfield's escape from this is only partial and continues to be seen as temporary – at least on the part of those proposing schemes for its redevelopment. At Fawley, meanwhile, the ghost of the power station continues to define the land as ripe for modernity, even after the demolition of the iconic chimney. Though the station had stood on the site for just two generations, that was enough to ensure the continued co-option of this land as a space for legitimate development,

---

[83] Mah, *Industrial Ruination*, p. 177.

in the guise of a sustainable and technological 'new town'. Processes of closure, and the long-term 'ruination' of communities that they cause may well outlast the present circumstances of either site. Nevertheless, when rural modernity ceases to be modern, its sites are not simply recovered by those landscapes in which they were placed with such care in the mid-20th century, and nor do they automatically transform into heritage. The logics and path-dependencies established during the post-war era instead mean that these landscapes are often placed in permanent requisition of the modern.

13

The New 'New Landscapes': A Personal View

TIM O'RIORDAN

As a geographer by training and by inclination, I have always loved landscapes. Many people would say the same. More difficult is how to define a landscape. Most of us think we know a landscape when we see one, especially when encountered as a fine vista that appears to possess an aesthetic coherence or integrity. For me, to think about landscape – or a landscape – is to think about how people and place interact over time at a scale which awards stability of meaning and reliability of expression. When a landscape is managed successfully culture and nature are mutually constitutive: landscape is the unit for effective ecosystems functioning and for geographical belonging. With their enduring notion of the *pays*, the French captured this spirit.

Nan Fairbrother's book was part of my upbringing and my revelation. I took from it a fundamental principle. Sensitive design and robust planning procedures could mitigate the alienating effect that new infrastructure or new agricultural methods might otherwise have on familiar landscapes. Change need not undermine our connectedness to our environment, it might even renew it. Over the course of my career, I've seen both the negative and positive effects of planning regimes and regulatory processes. When I began my research career in the 1960s, I focused on the arable landscapes of East Lothian between Edinburgh and Haddington, around my alter ego home of North Berwick. I was amazed that the burns in the region ran dry every summer, even damp summers. This was because the unregulated and unpriced spray irrigation of the famous Lothian potatoes sucked the wetlands dry. Today potatoes still adorn the red soils of the sandstone regoliths, but the burns flow year round and the freshwater biota flourish. The farmers pay their way, just a little more, and there is a regulatory body, the Scottish Environmental Protection Agency. This is part of the Environment Scotland web, which acts as the custodian of Scotland's landscapes.[1]

---

[1] See www.environment.gov.scot [accessed 24 October 2022].

Proceedings of the British Academy, **256**, 281–289, © The British Academy 2023.

In exciting ways, Fairbrother's holistic vision enabled us to see what was happening to the landscape. By making rapid change legible, she helped bring 'the new' into focus as an object of research and of policy. If the planning could be got right, newly built structures and new forms of land use would produce new landscapes that would change in commendable ways how we identify with the land. Our challenges are no less pressing, but as we reconsider our relationship with the planet, and how to reconcile our immense needs to the exhausted ecologies that sustain our very lives, I am now convinced of the need to shift to sustainable localism. In 1976, I first wrote about ecocentrism as a challenge to the technocentric solutions to environmental problems that politicians and the general public found so reassuring.[2] Technocentrism provides us cover, it's our salvation, the excuse to live the same lives but by different means. It will not save humanity. Embracing ecocentrism is the vital precursor to sustainable localism. For me, this is the endgame of a long process, among whose beginnings was my first encounter with Fairbrother.

*

The 12 chapters which compose this volume are based on the concepts introduced by Nan Fairbrother in the early 1970s in her seminal book of the same title. All the contributions presented here are thoughtful and very varied in their message and analyses. Most cover the mid-20th century and especially the period between 1930 and 1970. This is seen as the period embracing the 'new' which so energised Fairbrother. The chapters examine how shifts in technology, infrastructure, and in rural living influence the processes of coping with rural adjustment and the thoughtful treatment of heritage.

The unique contribution of Fairbrother lay in her eye for the effect of changing architecture in the setting of the rural scene. Her roving vision was not confined to the built structure. She saw newness in the layout of settlements, fields, crops, and the small but often iconic features of copses, trackways, the paddocks of horsiculture, and the glint of metallic additions to posts and road signs. Newness was different but exciting. Newness can also be annoying and despairing, for newness challenges the senses with daring as much as of nostalgia.

All of this was 50 years ago. In recent times the character of the countryside as well as the quality and feelings of rural living have altered enormously. And planning has broadly failed. Despite the high profile of Colin Buchanan's report 'Traffic in Towns' (1963), which to sought safeguard the market town from the ravages of the throughput vehicle, and the noble efforts of Arthur Skeffington's 'Report on Community Participation in Planning' (1969) to bring the values of residents and visitors into planning processes, planning has become embroiled in legal and procedural technicalities, where the commanding sweep of the new is choked and disassembled. Today, planning has lost its creative soul and its always fragile attention to democracy. Newness is not designed as Fairbrother would want.

---

[2] Tim O'Riordan, *Environmentalism* (London, Pion, 1976).

Instead, developers package up the 'new', the 'modern', and the 'contemporary' as marketable commodity all the while promoting their interests by making donations to the ruling political parties.[3]

Planning guidelines over affordability and low carbon energy efficiencies are there to be negotiated away along with casual, almost dismissive, attention to strategic landscape wildlife/amenity safeguards and local or neighbourhood plans.

In Fairbrother's time planning was still a reasonably reliable protection for the great swathes of landscape in the form of national parks and other protected amenity and wildlife designations. The Green Belt, always a battleground in the heady days of settlement separation, held its corner for the most part. And beautifying the new with natural camouflage softened the sharp contours of commercial buildings, theme parks, power stations, and utility corridors.

Subsequently planning as an act of rural desirability fell away and the new became exposed, ill-fitting, and at times glaringly prominent. Important exceptions, such as the Angel of the North (1998), Antony Gormley's dramatic sculpture that welcomes motorists on the A1 to the Tyneside conurbation, and the development of the 19th-century Snape Maltings at Aldeburgh into an extensive arts and performance complex, were all the more valued for their rarity. But in the main, the new became the plaything of the commercial developers and the visiting public became habituated to nature-depleted new landscapes.

Of particular significance during this post-1970 period is the devastation caused to species and to habitats as a result of favourably financed agricultural technologies and overall intensification of production. Across several books, Marion Shoard decried the lack of planning protection over the removal of much-loved hedgerows, grasslands, heathlands, saltmarshes, and ponds.[4] She was a resilient campaigner, vilified by obdurate farming interests, but even she could not prevent the loss of prized landscape features which bestowed beauty, identity, and wildlife havens in every pocket of the rural (and indeed the urban) landscapes. Only now, thanks to modern ecological monitoring and the penetrating deployment of the satellite and the drone, do we know that close to half of all farmland species have disappeared in the past 35 years. This loss constitutes a colossal indictment of the new in agriculture. We're only starting to grasp the political, cultural, and psychological significance of this loss to those who have only known ecologically depleted environments. There is no going back; only a partial retreat.[5]

---

[3] Alex Runswick, 'A plan for action: Progress on reducing corruption risks in local government planning decisions in England?', 18 February 2021, www.transparency.org.uk/planning-application-developm ent-corruption-risk-liverpool-city-london-east-devon [accessed 24 October 2022].

[4] Marion Shoard, *The Theft of the Countryside* (London, Temple Smith, 1980) and *This Land is Our Land* (London, Paladin, 1987).

[5] Food and Agriculture Organization of the United Nations, 'The ethics of sustainable agricultural intensification', esp. section on 'Agricultural intensification' (Rome, 2004), www.fao.org/3/j0902e/ j0902e00.htm#Contents [accessed 24 October 2022].

Another alteration is the massive increase in leisure enjoyment in the country-side and by the seashore. This has transformed both road and rail congestion patterns and encouraged the mass movement of huge concentrations of people, both second home owners and day visitors. And this in turn has altered the pattern of home prices and ownership, and hence the demographic composition of the rural estate. Here newness lies in the renovation and extension of existing housing, often for the purpose of letting to holidaymakers, newbuilds out of sympathy with existing architectural styles, and new shops, cafes, and restaurants, all symptomatic of gen-trifying and commercialising pressures. Newness here can be very crass, but much enjoyed. Its gloss may yet be tarnished by deep recession and real commitment to carbon free transport.

In post-pandemic years another mighty shift has been to home-based working and to new suburban locations for family homes and second homes, along with change in the landscapes of energy supply.[6]

The inner-city renaissance of the late 20th century is giving way to a new pattern of settlement that favours the suburban town with its leafy streets and greater access to greenery, private gardens, parks, and the accessible countryside. Newness will come in many guises, from refurbishment without commitment to historic building patterns and materials, to dinky boxes in pastiche local building fabric, to a stealth shift to self-build. And all the time these boxes are water and energy wasting and carbon creating. Their naïve owners will pay a heavy price in the forthcoming low carbon transition. Nobody is telling them so, but as mortgage payments will rise, so too will the costs of non-carbon thermal comfort. The coming preponderance of heatwaves will add to the burdens of unprepared housing, as cooling becomes an expensive priority.

The drama of creating new nature

It is worth repeating that in the lifetime of over half the present population, nearly half of all countryside plant and insect and bird species have been eliminated.[7]

We don't know how many fungi and micro-organisms have suffered the same fate. In some places, iconic species like the skylark, long a symbol of the beauty of the British countryside, have all but disappeared. Few now hear the sweet sounds offered in the chapter by Kristin Bluemel quoting the 'in between' places of John Johnson:

[6] Anshu Siripurapu, 'The economic effects of working from home', Council on Foreign Relations, 16 July 2020, www.cfr.org/in-brief/economic-effects-working-home [accessed 24 October 2022].
[7] State of Nature Report 2019 can be widely accessed online, where it is hosted by numerous websites. https://nbn.org.uk/stateofnature2019/reports/ [accessed 25 January 2023].

> Birds singing – larks soaring and carolling – grand clouds sailing along the blue sky –
> in the distance seen through trees the green hills bathed in the sunlight – everything at
> peace – no sound but that of the wind through the trees and the birds singing.

To dismiss this as nostalgia is callous indeed. These are living creatures, with whom we co-existed for millennia, both creating and sharing habitat. In Fairbrother's age, which saw a great burst of ecological concern and campaigning, the landscape was already degraded by agricultural intensification. But we should be under no illusions about what has happened in the intervening decades. Despite all the campaigns launched, the societies and associations joined, the government measures taken, and the voluntary work done, large swathes of the UK countryside are now largely birdless and bugless. The decline has been inexorable.

None of this has happened by chance. To a significant degree, the physical state of rural Britain is the product of legislation, and that legislation is the product of much politicking. Local, national, and international campaigning has ensured successive governments adopt environmental policies, but every environmental advance has been met by fierce, well-resourced lobbying representing agricultural, industrial, and commercial interests, often backed by financialised capital. Despite these pressures, in the early 21st century it seemed that the urgency of the climate and biodiversity crises meant that the priorities of the environmental lobby had begun to influence government attitudes and the broader political discourse. Much was in flux, and the shape of a new environmental settlement was far from clear. But by the late 2010s it became possible to imagine that the new landscapes needed by the new lives of the 21st century might become possible.

When the long-gestated Defra 25-year plan was published in 2018 much hope was invested in how Brexit enabled the substitution of production-based agricultural subsidies with nature-friendly agriculture support as the predominant form of state funding for agriculture.[8]

Under existing schemes, nature investments are made on a farm-by-farm basis, making it hard to secure the health of a block of heathland or a riffling stream when neighbouring landowners had different commercial and land use objectives. New Environmental Land Management Schemes or ELMS would not only become the principal source of financial support for farmers but they would also incentivise neighbouring landowners to cooperate across whole landscapes, connecting and integrating ecological processes into new nature panoramas. This connectedness was a legal breakthrough.[9]

---

[8] 'A green future: Our 25-year plan to improve the environment', www.gov.uk/government/publications/25-year-environment-plan [accessed 24 October 2022].

[9] 'Environmental land management schemes: Overview', 15 March 2021, www.gov.uk/government/publications/environmental-land-management-schemes-overview/environmental-land-management-scheme-overview [accessed 24 October 2022].

Furthermore, the Defra plan called for all land use developments which affected existing biota to ensure that on completion there could be a net gain in overall bio-diversity rating. Private enterprises could meet this requirement by funding the creation of new parish-based pockets of nature-rich land with accompanying trails for exercise and for energising mental health uplift. In places where there was too much nitrate and phosphate in the waterways (the killers of river courses) no new development was to be permitted until the overall nutrient pollution was stable and eventually declining. This has stopped all manner of housing in nitrate sensitive areas especially around chalk streams and National Parks.[10]

Something of a change in mood and expectation was evident in October 2022. The environmental lobby was already in a febrile mood owing to uncertainty provoked by the government's post-Brexit plans for new Investment Zones, likely to be subject to weaker environmental regulation. Amid the political chaos caused by the change in prime minister from Boris Johnson to Liz Truss, the government placed both ELMS and other schemes under review. This provoked a furious response from a range of environmental charities, including the National Trust and the RSPB. The hashtag *#natureunderattack* lit up social media in October 2022.[11]

Other issues loomed large. Land drainage in a climate changed world is a target for intense flash flooding. Wherever the culverts and adjacent soils are unable to take the extreme rainfall intensities in the new climate age, muddy spillovers occur. Unexpected inundation of a living room takes months to dry out and years for peace of mind to return.[12] The way to deal with this is to redesign local drainage, particularly for new development, so the trees and regenerated soils take the brunt of downpours. Market capitalist logics suggest nature-based solutions like these should be funded by the private sector combining property developers and insurers.

The transition away from electricity generation based on the burning of fossil fuels has grave land use implications. Proposed onshore windfarm and solar farm complexes are often fought by local residents. But they are both popular among the public as a whole and are a quarter of the price of their offshore renewable counterparts.[13]

One way in which governments can shore up faltering support among some rural voters is by further restricting the available farmland for solar farms on the basis that food production is paramount. Placing a severe limit on the distribution

[10] 'Nutrient neutrality and the planning system', Planning Advisory Service of the Local Government Association, n.d., www.local.gov.uk/pas/topics/environment/nutrient-neutrality-nn-and-planning-system [accessed 24 October 2022]

[11] For an example of the National Trust's work with the RSPB and WWF UK to mobilise its membership on nature conservation issues, see 'Have you say on the nature crisis', www.nationaltrust.org.uk/features/have-your-say-on-the-nature-crisis [accessed 24 March 2022].

[12] 'Mental health costs of flooding and erosion', Environment Agency, 28 October 2021, www.gov.uk/government/publications/mental-health-costs-of-flooding-and-erosion [accessed 24 October 2022].

[13] David Blackman, 'How the government is likely to relax planning rules for onshore wind', *Planning Resource: Independent Intelligence for Planning Professionals*, www.planningresource.co.uk/article/1802069/government-likely-relax-planning-rules-onshore-wind [accessed 24 October 2022].

of solar farms, and the creation of a new landscape for a new age, would pothole the net zero pathway for England.[14]

Perhaps there are tradeoffs to be made. Onshore wind farm companies are required to lay underground cables across kilometres of the countryside. This huge operation interferes with woods, brooks, heaths, and roads, an equivalent to the prominent but disputed overhead power lines that were so controversial in Fairbrother's day. Cabling is a new modernity, but one that comes at a huge cost and with little joy to the affected parishes. But onshore windfarm companies can look for ways to either soften the impact of these developments or compensate for their presence by generating community endowment funding that creates new social opportunities for local communities through active engagement with the cabled landscapes.

Sustainable localism

The early 21st century has seen much turbulence. There is no sign of an imminent becalming. Everything is awry. War, territorial secession, political chaos, economic distress, and loss of nerve are commonplace. As these reflections have shown, the rural estate is no less in a state of flux. One route to the new lives and landscapes so desperately needed lies in the way of sustainable localism.

Climate change, global warming, excessive consumption, waste, nature-devoid neighbourhoods, the COVID-19 pandemic: all are contributing to climate break-down, stressful living conditions, the weakening of the economy, and progressively diminish the opportunity for many to offer wellbeing to their or their neighbours' lives. If not addressed, the outcome is that those left behind will not have the ability to have their basic needs met, many will suffer ill-health or even perish prematurely in suffering and in poverty, yet increasingly few will be noticed.

But there is another way. This is to establish a process of creating local initiatives and economies around where people live, where they have grown up, and where they would like to spend the rest of their peaceful and protected lives. This will be led by communities acting locally. For local action to be effective and persistent, it is necessary to have a trusting relationship between the people and those who act on their behalf. And it is vital that people acting as individuals know they are functioning through the support of their communities.

Sustainable localism is the outcome of joint actions by individuals, households, and communities. One element is the regeneration of natural spaces, for the sake of nature, and for the nurture of healthy minds and healthy bodies. A second is looking out for each other, so the vulnerable are spotted, and no one is left uncared for. A third is living with sufficiency of need drawn mostly from within the locality.

---

[14] 'Solar farms pros and cons: 7 facts we cannot deny', *The Earth Project*, 29 December 2017, https://theearthproject.com/solar-farms-pros-and-cons [accessed 24 October 2022].

All of this is meant to ensure that our next generation is suitably prepared for the changing times to come.

At its heart is wellbeing. This is the combination of self-worth, of personal leadership and responsibility, of trusting everyone to share the same fundamental values, and of hope. Economic security is an important component of wellbeing. But its full purpose is both to help create and to benefit from supportive families, neighbourhoods, and communities. Wellbeing generates a joint belief that shared local commitment will prove the centrepiece of enjoyable living.[15]

How do we get there? Here are some pointers for the new localism. Of course, there needs to be connections with regional, national, and international cooperation. But the essence of sustainable localism is self-reliance and collective belief and determination.

Digital availability

We need to connect everyone to each other. The rapid completion of broadband and the ubiquity of the internet are essential elements to sustainable localism.

Purposeful training

Everyone who needs it should be trained for the expanding digital age. This is particularly the case for those already left behind. There is a need for a variety of training courses and experiences to encourage creative entrepreneurship.

Mentoring and social support

Everyone who requires it should have access to social support in the form of mentoring and care. This extends to keeping a watchful eye on those who are or who might become vulnerable or a danger to themselves or others. This requires support for families and households and a form of welcome mentoring, suitably funded and given meaningful income to those who demonstrate their value.

Community networks of local knowledge

Discovering and identifying help, support, training, and opportunity is vital for community cohesion and local solidarity. Preventable hardship and sadness can be spotted by businesses, by community services, from community organisations, to

[15] 'What is wellbeing, and what matters', *What Works Centre for Wellbeing*, https://measure.whatworkswellbeing.org/wellbeing-explained/ [accessed 24 October 2022].

parishes, to schools, colleges of further education (technical as well as academic), and to universities. Many of those most in need remain presently hidden.

Caring and health provision

Central to this vision is a new emphasis on overcoming inequality, discrimination, vulnerability, ill-health, poverty, joblessness, and childcare. This will require a demanding set of challenging policies and actions. It will involve redistributive income sharing, taxation reform, greater recognition of the role of charities and sensitive solidarity across age, gender, race, sexuality, disablement, and shared outlooks. A start could be locally financed carbon levies feeding sustainability charities.

Localising mobility and economy

Getting rid of atmospheric warming gases demands several fundamental changes of us. We need to reduce movement, expand local living, support local food sourcing, and encourage regenerative agriculture. We need to create, consume, and reuse goods fuelled by local renewable energy technologies. Personal commitment is hugely influenced by neighbourly esteem and common pride. Social esteem breeds carbon-removing action.

Creativity, imagination, and the arts

Sustainable localism must generate creativity, artistic expression, imagination, and social bonding. A sustaining community is an artistic community. This opens the mind, builds confidence, generates all-round health, and stimulates optimism. Imagination is the great purveyor of hope and of innovation.

Spiritual uplift

Sustainable localism connects the new inner worlds of the personal to the expanding outer worlds of the spiritual. We face a century of almost unimaginable suffering for both humans and the functioning of nature. We are facing collective near death experiences. We require a profound sense of the spiritual to spur us into creative and effective change.

All of this might sound fanciful. But we are prosperous enough to share and to care. We should not stand by while our society fragments. Just as the young will not tolerate our avoidable delay to climate safety, so we must avoid a running battle between the old and the young. Sustainable localism provides not just a pathway to the net zero age, but to the healing of our relationship with the natural world.

Index